SOUNDIES
AND THE
CHANGING IMAGE OF
BLACK AMERICANS
ON SCREEN

SOUNDIES
AND THE
CHANGING IMAGE OF
BLACK AMERICANS
ON SCREEN

ONE DIME AT A TIME

—m—

SUSAN DELSON

INDIANA UNIVERSITY PRESS

This book is a publication of

Indiana University Press
Office of Scholarly Publishing
Herman B Wells Library 350
1320 East 10th Street
Bloomington, Indiana 47405 USA

iupress.org

Manufactured in the United States of America
First printing 2021

Cataloging information is available from the Library of Congress.
ISBN 978-0-253-05853-9 (hardback)
ISBN 978-0-253-05854-6 (paperback)
ISBN 978-0-253-05855-3 (ebook)

CONTENTS

PART I

FOLLOW THE MONEY

INTRODUCTION

Turning on a Dime

IN APRIL 2015, A VIDEO titled "102 y/o Dancer Sees Herself on Film for the First Time" was uploaded on YouTube. Shot on cell phones in a Brooklyn nursing home, the seven-minute video shows Alice Barker, a Harlem nightclub dancer of the 1930s and 1940s, watching herself perform in vintage film clips (fig. I.1). Old and young, Barker is entrancing—vivacious in her nursinghome bed, lissome and flirtatious in the film clips, an easy standout among her chorus-line colleagues. The video went viral immediately. By year's end it had racked up close to ten million views and more than eight thousand comments. Five years later, the numbers topped thirty million and sixty thousand, respectively, and continued to rise.

Whether they knew it or not, those millions of viewers had also discovered Soundies.

An obscure film phenomenon of the 1940s, Soundies were three-minute films made to be screened on movie jukeboxes known as Panorams—freestanding, closed-system projection cabinets a little taller than modern refrigerators, which would play a single Soundie at the drop of a dime. The screen was roughly 17 inches high by 22 inches wide—minuscule compared to movie screens or today's TVs, but big enough for a dozen viewers or more. Like music-only jukeboxes, the Panoram's natural habitats were bars, taverns, and cafes—especially around defense-industry plants—and the crowded bus and train stations of a country on the move. They were mostly a wartime phenomenon, totaling roughly 1,880 films, almost all of them produced from 1940 to 1946. Soundies have been called the music videos of their day, but they're more than that. Combining movies and jukebox music—bedrock 1940s pop culture—they emerge

3

Figure I.1. Alice Barker, as seen in the YouTube video "102 y/o Dancer Sees Herself on Film for the First Time." Barker (*right*) appears in the 1943 Soundie *Chatter*. Courtesy Dave Shuff and Mark Cantor Archive.

as a unique form with their own aesthetics and parameters. As a body of work, Soundies offer a rich, largely overlooked chronicle of American popular culture during World War II and just after. Made as feel-good entertainment, they have a surprising knack for revealing what Americans were thinking, especially about topics not talked about openly.

Like race. The war years were a time of intense social upheaval and nation-shaping demographic shifts, as millions of unemployed workers flocked to the newly booming industrial centers of the West Coast, upper Midwest, and beyond. Vast numbers of rural people suddenly found themselves urban, and these mass relocations stoked social change. Throughout the country Black people were determined to take part in the booming wartime economy, and rising Black activism brought the expectation—and in Hollywood, the demand—for changes in the way they were depicted on screen.

At the neighborhood movie palace, those changes took years to happen. But things moved faster in Soundies.

As a body of work, Soundies offer an acutely observed, pop-culture snapshot of racial attitudes during the World War II years. Most of the films feature white performers exclusively and present a world view in which whiteness is an unquestioned baseline. In perhaps three dozen more, persistent racial stereotypes and racist iconography turn up in one form or another. But there's a substantial subset—more than three hundred films—with a radically different perspective.

In these Soundies, Black performers are stars, featured players, and—like Alice Barker—dancers and uncredited extras. They appear as romantic partners, neighbors, colleagues, and friends. They are soldiers, subway conductors, policemen, defense-plant workers—positions that, for Black Americans in the 1940s, were often more readily achieved in Soundies than in real life. Soundies were a significant channel for documenting Black performance on film, bringing it to audiences who might otherwise know it only through records or radio. And they did it on terms that boldly contradicted Hollywood's usual depictions of Black people, in images of success, competence, and style.

In African American cinema history, lost and missing films are a sobering reality, especially from the decades before the 1970s. In this light, Soundies are a remarkably intact archive. At three hundred-plus films, Black-cast Soundies represent roughly 15 percent of the total Soundies output—a significant figure, given that in 1940 the Black population in the United States stood at 9.8 percent. A densely layered history is inscribed in these reels, and many of them register, in a pop-music idiom, the cultural and demographic shifts that marked African American and American wartime life. The breadth of performance that Black-cast Soundies encompass is itself remarkable, particularly with respect to women musicians. Performers include not only stars like Duke Ellington and Count Basie but gospel and blues icon Sister Rosetta Tharpe, the Los Angeles women's jazz combo the Vs, harpist and composer LaVilla Tullos, and singer and trumpeter Valaida Snow (affectionately called the world's second-best trumpeter by Louis Armstrong himself). For some musicians, like pianist Lynn Albritton, these films may be the only surviving record of their performances. There's a sense of discovery in them—watching a teenage Dorothy Dandridge take command of the screen in Cow Cow Boogie, glimpsing the Black metropolis sketched out in Take the 'A' Train, or seeing a Black performer in whiteface portraying, with comic brio, composer Giuseppe Verdi in a swing-time Rigoletto. Without aspiring to anything but light entertainment, many of these Soundies play with, contradict, and otherwise undermine then-prevailing images of Black people on screen.

And in another rarity for that era, they did it for white audiences too. An active "race film" industry made Black-cast features and shorts for movie houses serving Black audiences, but white viewers had limited access to those productions. Stars like Ellington and Basie were broadly famous long before they made Soundies, but for other Black performers Panoram play was a rare opportunity to reach mainstream audiences on film, and in some cases—as with Louis Jordan—to fuel successful crossover careers. Restrictions on manufacturing materials and other wartime constraints choked Soundies' growth as a business, and that created opportunities for Black performers. Every film had to circulate as widely as possible to maximize its earnings. That meant that, for most of Soundies' corporate lifespan, films starring Black performers were routinely included in the weekly multifilm reels that were distributed to Panoram operators around the country. Soundies audiences, Black and white, saw images of sophistication and success playing out in a stream of Black-cast films.

For the most part Soundies were produced independently by a shifting roster of filmmakers, all of whom brought their own ideas and attitudes about race into play. As far as we know, all Soundies producers and directors were men,[1] and most—but not all—were white. Some worked in Hollywood but others worked in New York, at studios in Queens, the Bronx, and in Harlem, where Soundies production was part of a thriving circuit for Black musicians, dancers, and entertainers. That interplay of Black performers, white and Black filmmakers, and audiences of both races was rarely seen in American popular culture of the World War II years.

SLOT-MACHINE MOVIES

Soundies' roots reach back to the 1930s, when the jukebox became an essential part of American popular culture. With the arrival of the 16 mm continuous-loop projector in the late 1930s, a movie jukebox seemed like the inevitable next step. The idea itself had an irresistible aura of cutting-edge technology and, paradoxically, a reassuring familiarity: the new device immediately brought to mind the single-viewer, penny-arcade movie machines of the 1890s and—though it was vehemently denied—the risqué back-room peep shows that followed. But these new movie jukeboxes could easily accommodate a crowd of viewers and, like music-only jukeboxes, a tavern's worth of listeners.

It was, for a moment, the future. Start-up fever ran high, with close to twenty movie-jukebox ventures announced in 1940 and early 1941, and almost thirty firms planning to produce films for the machines.[2] A few Hollywood figures saw movie jukeboxes as a way of augmenting their fortunes: Roaring Twenties crooner Rudy Vallee was a partner and frontman for the Vis-o-Graph Corporation, and veteran producer-director Cecil B. DeMille was a prime mover behind Talkitones.[3] Most of these companies flamed out in a matter of months, Vallee's and DeMille's included, and others never made it past the initial announcement. When the smoke cleared, one survivor dominated the

Figure I.2. Attendees at Soundies promotional events often posed with Panoram machines. The original caption for this 1940 photograph reads: "When Jimmy Roosevelt introduced his new Soundies to New York press folks, Don was on hand and his pal Roy Smeck who had signed to do a Soundies series. On the left are Judge Louis Tepp and an unidentified juke box operator from Newark." The identity of "Don" (*second from right*) is unknown. The guitar, banjo, and ukulele musician Roy Smeck (*far right*), known as the "Wizard of the Strings," did not, in fact, make any Soundies. Courtesy Mark Cantor Archive.

field: the Mills Novelty Company of Chicago, manufacturers of the Panoram movie jukebox and, through a subsidiary company, distributors of the films it played—the jukebox movies called Soundies (fig. I.2).

As a manufacturing concern, Mills Novelty had an unorthodox history that left it uniquely qualified for the new venture. A family-run business established by Herbert S. Mills in 1889, its early specialties were coin-operated arcade amusements, including a coin-operated player piano (a smash hit) and the "Violano Virtuoso," a self-playing violin (cherished by later collectors, but in its day a flop).[4] Other product lines included vending machines, industrial ice-cream freezers, and air-cooling units, but the company's biggest moneymaker was most likely the slot machine. In the early 1900s Mills Novelty was apparently the first (and for a time only) American firm to manufacture them on an industrial scale, and for decades, one-armed bandits were a cornerstone of the business.[5]

After the repeal of Prohibition in 1933, organized crime syndicates shifted their attention to gambling, a boon for suppliers like Mills. But the mob's new investments touched off a prolonged crackdown by federal, state, and local governments, and Mills's slot-machine revenues plummeted. The company turned to the jukebox market, and by the late 1930s Mills Novelty was a top juke manufacturer alongside brands like Wurlitzer, Seeburg, and Rock-Ola.[6]

With the continuous-loop 16 mm projector grabbing industry attention at the 1939 World's Fair in New York, Mills Novelty's leadership—second-generation president Fred Mills and his brothers Ralph, Herb, Hayden, and Gordon—jumped into the new movie-jukebox market.[7] The Panoram movie jukebox was pre-emptively announced to the press in February 1940, several months before the first machine actually rolled off the production line. In breathless prose, the connection to early arcade movie machines was cast as a selling point. "In Mills Panoram Soundies," read the sales booklet for potential Panoram purchasers, "coin machines and the movies, long-separated brothers, unite once more, each giving the other a new vitalization, excitement and appeal!"[8]

It's not beyond reason to suggest that organized crime in Chicago may have had an interest in the new business. Syndicate involvement with jukeboxes and other coin-operated machines—like cigarette machines or pinball games—was widely acknowledged in the entertainment industry, though seldom for attribution. The *Chicago Tribune*, for instance, identified one individual, "an old Capone ally and a slot machine king," as controlling jukeboxes on the city's north side through his vending-machine company.[9] And in a rare industry reference, a 1943 article in *Billboard* blandly announced that Meyer Lansky—a key underworld figure known as "the mob's accountant"—and an associate were the new distributors for Wurlitzer jukeboxes in New York, New Jersey, and Connecticut.[10] Getting Panorams onto the assembly line and Soundies into production would have required substantial capital. Although no confirming documentation has been found (or is likely to be), it is feasible that at least some financial backing came from syndicate sources.[11]

With its manufacturing expertise, Mills Novelty aced its first challenge: a projection system that could be mass produced, deliver a consistently good image, and withstand jukebox-style use without jamming or destroying the film.[12] What would actually appear on the screen was a tougher hurdle. Soundies were not the only movie-jukebox films produced in that frenzied start-up moment, but Mills Novelty was the only venture advanced enough to need films in serious quantity. To produce a steady flow of three-minute movies that viewers would pay to see again and again, the Mills Novelty Company needed Hollywood.

Hollywood had other ideas. The studios saw jukebox movies as an upstart, down-market phenomenon and—though they were reluctant to admit it publicly—a threat. Radio was already siphoning off an alarming percentage of movie audiences, who stayed home in droves to listen to their favorite programs: one cash-giveaway show had reportedly decimated Tuesday night movie attendance nationwide.[13] As the studios saw it, putting three-minute films into bars and taverns would not only pull more paying customers out of theaters but devalue the viewing experience altogether. And a team of Midwestern jukebox manufacturers had little chance of passing as suave Hollywood insiders. All told, Hollywood responded accordingly. When Mills Novelty approached Warner Bros. with a proposal to excerpt some of its 1930s musical short films for Soundies, the studio declined.[14] Inquiries to other studios about working with contract players were also rebuffed.

Snubbed by the industry, Mills Novelty turned to another outlier: James "Jimmy" Roosevelt, President Franklin Delano Roosevelt's oldest son. In 1938, James Roosevelt had launched himself, not entirely successfully, as a movie executive working with producer Samuel Goldwyn (the "G" in MGM). Along with the pre-emptive Panoram announcement, in February 1940 Mills Novelty declared that Roosevelt's company, Globe Productions, would produce all Soundies.

As a publicity ploy it was wildly successful. Roosevelt was a media magnet, and the autumn 1940 roll-out for "Jimmy Roosevelt's Soundies" racked up impressive coverage in newspapers, magazines, and industry publications. But as a plan for turning out more than four hundred films a year, it skirted disaster. Even at three minutes apiece, eight films a week were more than one small company could handle, especially after Roosevelt was abruptly hustled into the military after the big Soundies rollout—1940 was an election year, and the anti-FDR faction had gleefully seized on Jimmy's involvement with "slot-machine movies" and Mills Novelty's links to organized gambling.[15] For political purposes, a quick commission in the Marine Corps Reserve was an essential career move.

Even while Roosevelt was still producing, a few small companies in Los Angeles were quietly filling the gaps in his weekly output. Throughout Soundies' history, Mills-owned and -affiliated companies like RCM Productions in Hollywood and Minoco Productions in New York—both started soon after

Roosevelt's departure—were the backbone of Soundies filmmaking. They were supplemented by a shifting lineup of independents in Los Angeles and New York—by one count, more than forty-five companies at one time or another. All of them functioned as suppliers to the Soundies Distributing Corporation of America (referred to in this book as the Soundies Corporation), the Chicago-based subsidiary of Mills Novelty that bought, packaged, and distributed the films.

Decentralized, with loosely affiliated and independent producers, this set-up was the opposite of the Hollywood studios' tightly controlled production system, and it had a key role in shaping Soundies aesthetics. Individual makers had substantial latitude in choosing talent and material for their films, and they brought a range of sensibilities to bear on what was, until its final days, an evolving entertainment form. It took months for even a fast-tracked studio film to move from initial script to final cut; produced on a weekly basis, Soundies could be far more nimble in responding to popular demand. This flexibility was an important factor in the evolving depiction of Black people in Soundies.

As the first Panorams came on the market in late 1940, Mills Novelty executives confidently predicted that thirty thousand machines would be in place and running, coast to coast, within a year.[16] It was an ambitious figure but not unrealistic—less than a tenth of the estimated number of music jukeboxes then in operation nationwide. According to one source, Panorams cost roughly twice as much as music jukeboxes, but the return was worth it. Where a music-only jukebox might take in $10 worth of coins per week, a Panoram could pull in as much as $50 to $110. In New England, where no other brand of movie jukebox was distributed, the weekly take might hit $150 to $200. Advance orders on Panorams reportedly reached $3 million.[17]

But to succeed, the business needed a large pool of machines in operation. The cost of producing a three-minute film was the same whether it played on three thousand Panorams or thirty thousand, and profitability hung on the number of machines and the reel rentals they generated. In this, the war was a mixed blessing. If the defense-industry boom created thousands of potential Panoram locations, it also made the materials for their manufacture increasingly unavailable. In spring 1941, several months before the United States entered the war, President Roosevelt declared a state of emergency that severely limited nondefense access to aluminum, steel, rubber, and other manufacturing materials. Once war was declared, even that limited access ended. Days after the attack on Pearl Harbor in December 1941, the federal Office of Production Management (OPM) ordered a 75 percent cut in jukebox production—Panorams included—effective February 1, 1942. OPM's successor, the War

Production Board, then barred production completely as of May 1. There was no getting around government restrictions, although Mills Novelty did try, prompting one Chicago newspaper to sardonically inquire, "Are Juke Boxes Arms?"[18]

Despite the limited number of Panorams in operation, Soundies had a significant cultural presence. Theoretically the machines could be plugged in anywhere, and they did sometimes turn up in odd spots. Over the course of the war Panorams made documented appearances—usually for patriotic purposes—at department stores, military air shows, and Chicago's city hall.[19] Other sightings included the Alaska bush and, after the war, Guatemala.[20] Even with a relatively small network of Panorams, there was clearly an audience: in June 1944, the Office of War Information began using Panoram Soundies as a propaganda channel, producing a handful of short films—all with white performers—to be included in the weekly reels as bonus Soundies that screened free of charge.[21]

With their hybrid lineage of movies and pop music, Soundies might borrow and riff on Hollywood film language, but at the corner tavern they were treated like jukebox tunes—played repeatedly and, in the best cases, enthusiastically. With one crucial difference: unlike music-only jukeboxes, which offered a choice of tunes, Panorams were set up to play whatever film came next on the reel, no choice involved. Conscientious Panoram operators noted which films their clientele preferred, and Soundies executives kept a close watch on those tallies. Although informal, the feedback loop between audiences, Panoram operators, and Soundies executives was tight and responsive.

With revenue built dime by dime, it had to be. Not that ten cents was insignificant: in 2021 currency, a 1940 dime equals almost two dollars. Tossing a few into the Panoram would have been a gesture of goodwill—an investment in collective entertainment akin to buying a round of beers. At a time when a cup of coffee (or a tune on a music-only jukebox) cost a nickel, at ten cents a play Soundies were, minute for minute, "the highest-priced cinema entertainment, the equivalent of a single feature bill [movie] necessitating an expenditure of $3.25," wrote the *New York Times*. "On such a basis a customer would have paid $7.30"—roughly $135 today—"to see 'Gone with the Wind,' a realization that must fill David O. Selznick with envy."[22]

A DIFFERENT MARKET

A significant amount of documentation on Soundies production has survived, but information about their distribution, audiences, and reception by viewers is less readily available. This book brings to light a previously undiscovered

source with particular relevance for Black-cast Soundies and their audiences—
a product of the New York State legal system.

In 1944, L.O.L. Productions, Inc., an independent Soundies producer,
brought suit against the Soundies Corporation, the Mills Novelty subsidiary
that distributed the films. At issue was the Soundies Corporation's cancellation
of L.O.L.'s contract on the basis of poor production values—an assessment that
any number of L.O.L. Soundies will confirm—as well as problems with state
censorship boards and, significantly, L.O.L.'s continuing use of white actors in
blackface over the Soundies Corporation's strenuous objections. The case went
to the New York Supreme Court. The trial transcript—which this book will
revisit and cite throughout—runs hundreds of pages, and the testimonies of
Soundies Corporation executives and their plaintiffs contain revealing insights
into the business and its day-to-day workings.

Passages from the transcript give a sense of the films' distribution, geographic reach, and possible audiences. According to testimony by Soundies
Corporation vice president and general manager George P. Ulcigan, Panoram
machines were located in "48 states including Hawaii and Alaska" (which at
that point were not states but US territories).[23] Of these, he said, the Soundies
Corporation saw the bulk of its activity—"somewhere between sixty and seventy per cent of our business"—in the states with active censorship boards:
Maryland, Virginia, Kansas, and "the most populous states," Ohio, Pennsylvania, and New York.[24]

Even assuming some exaggeration on Ulcigan's part—he was, after all,
trying to win a lawsuit—the concentration of business in these states raises
the possibility that Black viewers were a larger percentage of Soundies audiences than they might have been if the Panoram circuit had been more broadly
national. In 1940, Ohio, Pennsylvania, and New York were home to six cities
with populations of three hundred thousand or more, most with Black populations ranging from 9 to 13 percent.[25] The one exception, New York City, had
a lower percentage of 6.1, but in a metropolis of more than seven million, that
meant a Black population of 458,444—slightly greater than the entire population of Cincinnati. In Maryland and Virginia, two other states that Ulcigan
named, Baltimore in 1940 had a population that was 19.3 percent Black; in
Norfolk, that figure was 31.8 percent. In Wichita, Kansas—the only city in that
state with more than three hundred thousand people in 1940—the population
was 11.3 percent Black.

In his testimony, Soundies Corporation production and promotion manager
William Forest Crouch asserted that the films were a largely urban phenomenon catering to a working-class audience. Under questioning, he stated that

the majority of Panorams were sited in "big cities . . . mostly in the outlying parts," areas where new factories and defense plants were often located. Asked whether the films attracted "a farmer audience who attend taverns," Crouch replied, "No, that is not a large part of our audience."[26] In a letter to L.O.L. producer Arthur Leonard submitted as evidence in the lawsuit, Crouch described the typical Soundies viewer as "mostly male of an average age of about forty years who frequent taverns, not [the more upscale] cocktail lounges . . . a mill worker on the swing shift who wants something light and gay while he downs a few beers."[27]

If Soundies distribution was in fact centered on the states that Ulcigan named, it's unlikely that all those beer drinkers were white. The same for all Panoram operators, as African American newspapers noted. In covering the 1940 Hollywood rollout of Panoram Soundies, the *Pittsburgh Courier* wrote that "as far as Negroes are concerned, they are welcome to obtain these machines," and in 1943, an entertainment column in the *Chicago Defender* reported that the "newest juke box king is Jimmy Allison, whose main business is handling those 'Soundies' machines."[28] In 1942, when a Panoram operator in Norfolk posted advance word of upcoming Soundies with Cab Calloway and other Black stars, "the crowds almost jammed traffic on the streets trying to get in to patronize the machines," the trade paper *Billboard* reported.[29]

If, as the geographical data suggest, Black viewers were a significant sector of the Soundies market, their responses may have had a crucial role in shaping the portrayal of Black Americans on Panoram screens (fig. I.3). For Soundies, profitability demanded a steady stream of dimes, and company executives were quick to identify the films and filmmakers—like L.O.L. Productions—that failed to resonate with their audiences. In a letter submitted in the court case, Crouch warned Arthur Leonard that one of L.O.L.'s Soundies was "bound to bring us a storm of protest from our Negro locations, where they look upon your use of white people in blackface make-up as ridicule to the Negro race."[30] White actors in blackface were still common in 1940s entertainment, and Crouch's position flew against prevailing norms. "Don't you know that Amos and Andy have made pictures in blackface even though they were white?" the L.O.L. attorney asked Crouch. "And Eddie Cantor has also made blackface pictures? . . . And those pictures were very popular, were they not?" To which Crouch replied, "With the white people, yes." "But that wasn't good enough for Soundies?" the attorney pressed. "No sir," Crouch responded, "because we have a different market."[31]

That said, it's unlikely, in fact nearly impossible, that Black Americans were the only audiences for Black-cast Soundies. The economics of the business

Figure I.3. Nat "King" Cole, seen on a Panoram in the 1945 Soundie *Frim Fram Sauce.* Library of Congress, Motion Picture, Broadcasting and Recorded Sound Division.

dictated otherwise, especially after the halt of Panoram production in 1942. White viewership of Black-cast Soundies was anecdotally confirmed in a 1945 profile of Crouch published in the *New York Amsterdam News,* which wrote that he "became interested in all-Negro subjects three years ago, when he noticed an increased demand for such pictures coming from juke-box locations in white communities throughout the country."[32] Between them, Black and white audiences eager for Black-cast Soundies were a market segment that the company could not ignore.

MARKET-DRIVEN CHANGE

As an entertainment form, Soundies offer a different take on the World War II years—a street-level version fueled by music and popular culture, which reinforces wartime social norms on one hand while undermining them on the other. As an offspring of Hollywood movies and popular music, Soundies were susceptible to the worst of both—pop music's reliance on stereotyping as a cultural shorthand, and the film industry's stubborn reluctance to rethink its caricatures. But in Soundies, the pop-culture DNA of music and movies often combined in less predictable ways, giving individual films an unexpected currency, intensity, and occasional streak of dreamlike surrealism. In these instances, the fantasies and anxieties of a nation at war are clearly if inadvertently exposed. Race is part of this collective stream of consciousness and emerges in eloquent ways.

More than seventy-five years have passed since the end of World War II—long enough for the realities of lived experience and personal memory to give way to collective mythmaking. Over time, the conflicts and contradictions of that era have been folded into a simpler story line—a "greatest generation" narrative of patriotism and national unity that obscures a more complex history. A close reading of these films cannot help but complicate that narrative. With Soundies, contradictions, inconsistencies, and messy open-endedness seem to come with the territory. Individual Soundies aren't always progressive about race, and Soundies as a whole reflect the jagged course of wartime race relations. But something else also unfolds, in parallel, in the great majority of Black-cast films. Seen as a coherent body of work, many of these films take on the character of an ad hoc cultural incubator, a space for exploring different images of Black Americans on screen. As a marginal entertainment form with a seat-of-the-pants business style, Soundies made (and broke) their own rules, and that spirit of invention characterized the Black-cast films, their many different makers, and their performers. Substantive issues were rarely thrashed out on Panoram screens, but traces of the era's Black activism are visible in film after film.

Historians have cast the war years as part of the "long Civil Rights Movement" extending from the 1930s to the 1970s.[33] It is interesting to approach the films from this perspective, and to consider how they might have contributed to a climate of possibility and change. For Black performers, Soundies were a relatively unmediated channel for connecting with Black audiences through film. They were also a rare entry point for Black performers, music, and culture into the visual mainstream.

That visibility, in turn, had an impact on the films. Over Soundies' brief lifespan their portrayal of Black people shifted profoundly, if not consistently, with Hollywood-style stereotypes giving way to images that were increasingly in sync with wartime and postwar realities. The most successful were often the product of creative exchanges with performers who, in their work with Soundies producers and directors, became what film historian Donald Bogle calls "nondirectorial auteurs"—collaborators who actively shaped the style, look, and impact of their films.[34] "The privilege of 'eccentric' sites of invention," writes art historian John Rajchman, "is precisely the freedom to draw from many sources, experiment with many ideas at once, out of order, mixing them together in new ways."[35] Although Rajchman writes on another topic, it's hard to imagine a better description of the cultural dynamics at play in Soundies, particularly the Black-cast films.

This is not to deny the existence of racist Soundies, or the Hollywood-style racism that surfaces in some of the Black-cast films. World War II made the United States acutely aware of itself as a multiracial and multiethnic nation, and that realization brought both social change and its vehement denial. Both are reflected in Soundies, in significantly different proportions. The overwhelming number of films with and about Black Americans reflect the active interest of performers and makers in reshaping the image of Black people on screen.

Black-cast Soundies are little known and have yet to be fully considered as a body of work. But they are vital to our understanding of mid-twentieth-century America and the cultural landscape of the World War II years. In pursuing commercial success the films became an informal arena for negotiating how Black performers and characters were presented on screen, and the densely layered histories they contain demand close examination. *Soundies and the Changing Image of Black Americans on Screen* is among the first books to focus exclusively on Black-cast Soundies, but I am confident it will not be the last.

The first three chapters of the book introduce Soundies and situate them in their commercial, aesthetic, and cultural contexts. Chapter 1 considers how the films fit in with—and depart from—other media and entertainment forms of their day, including mainstream Hollywood movies, race films, radio, and the music industry. Chapter 2 goes further into the Mills Novelty Company's rocky commercial path with Soundies, exploring the ongoing interplay between Soundies business and aesthetics, and how commercial constraints created opportunities for Black performers. Chapter 3 turns to the major Soundies producers and directors, introducing the makers who were largely responsible for Black-cast Soundies—among them the prolific white producer-director William Forest Crouch, pioneering Black producer William D. Alexander, and Black football great turned entertainment impresario Frederick Douglass "Fritz" Pollard. In closing, this chapter recounts the Soundies Corporation's steps and missteps in distributing Black-cast Soundies as a segregated product—the M films—in an increasingly fragmented market, and what it says about the racial climate of that time.

Organized thematically, the next five chapters immerse us in the films themselves and the imagined world that they create. Chapters in this section consider the films' depiction of Black American participation in World War II; their vision of urban spaces as sites for creativity, adaptation, and exchange; and the reframing of a rural, largely southern past in light of an urban present. Two chapters explore the re-envisioning of Black women, heterosexual relationships, and gender roles—including a close look at the films of Dorothy Dandridge—in a visual language that freely borrows from Hollywood movie-musical romance. Chapter 9 turns to instrumental groups and the Soundies that straightforwardly document their performances, spotlighting a number of exceptional musicians rarely seen elsewhere. Chapter 10 considers the representation of racial integration in Soundies as that concept gained momentum in the 1940s. The closing chapter looks at the Soundies Corporation's final days, the Harlem-focused film scene that briefly flourished in its wake, and Soundies' transition to television, the home-movie market, and the digital era. With an eye to facilitating future research, the book's appendixes include the films I've identified as Black-cast Soundies; performers and their films; and producers and directors and their films.

One goal of the book is to discredit the notion, implicit in some writing about Soundies, that the films are essentially alike, with little to distinguish one maker's work from the next. In fact, the opposite is true. The array of styles, degrees of competence, and range of racial assumptions in the films clearly point to individual makers with distinct sensibilities. *Soundies and the Changing Image of Black Americans on Screen* is, among other things, a portrait of significant Black-cast Soundies makers and their work. To that end, in each chapter the first mention of a Soundie title is followed by the last names of its producer(s) and director(s), and the year the film was copyrighted. (If the same maker produced and directed, his name is repeated.) Throughout the book, *Black* is capitalized when referring to race, including quotations from primary and secondary sources.

With historian and archivist Mark Cantor, I've also attempted to identify uncredited performers, like Alice Barker, whose films are discussed at length. This is a fundamental step toward re-establishing not only their legacies but the entertainment history encompassed in these films. It's especially true for the uncredited women actors who give the films such verve. Whether filling out a background crowd, smiling to the camera, or pairing off with male stars, they're a defining factor in the films' stylish savoir faire, and in Soundies as a space for envisioning Black women on screen.

Readers who haven't seen many Soundies might want to consult the book's appendixes and search out a few online. It can be surprisingly difficult to pivot from the printed page to the screen and back again, so to make it easier, I've gathered as many of the Soundies discussed in this book as possible for viewing online. (For details, see my website, susandelson.com.) As you go through the book, I encourage you to look at any of the films that catch your eye. The book can be read from start to finish without watching a single Soundie, but viewing at least a few adds enormously to the experience. Conceived for a distracted audience, composed for the reduced dimensions of the Panoram, with a running time geared to on-the-fly viewing, Soundies have made themselves at home in the digital sphere. As much as I hope *Soundies and the Changing Image of Black Americans on Screen* will contribute to the conversation about these Soundies, reading about them can't beat watching the films themselves. They are too interesting, too valuable, and altogether too entertaining not to experience for yourself—beer optional, no dimes required.

1

—ᴍᴜ—

CIRCA 1940

Race and the Pop-Culture Landscape

THE FIRST BLACK-CAST SOUNDIE, DOROTHY Dandridge's *Swing for Your Supper* (Coslow-Berne, 1941), debuted in spring 1941. By that autumn, Black performers were appearing regularly in the weekly Panoram reels. To get a sense of what those films might have meant for audiences of the time, and how much of a departure from mainstream thinking some of them were, it's useful to take a broader look at race and popular culture in the 1940s—particularly pop culture's prime movers, the movie and music industries.

Let's start with *Gone with the Wind.*

In December 1939, the movie opened with a three-day gala in Atlanta, followed by star-heavy premieres in New York and Los Angeles. The 1936 novel that inspired the film had already sold more than a million copies—in the midst of the Depression, at an extravagant three dollars apiece—and picked up a Pulitzer Prize and National Book Award for its author, Margaret Mitchell. But runaway best-seller status was merely a prelude to the fever that *Gone with the Wind* ignited on screen. At a time when even top movies had premiere runs of only one week, two at most, before moving to neighborhood theaters and then disappearing, *Gone with the Wind* was in continuous distribution, at premium prices, from December 1939 through April 1941. By then it had sold some forty-five million tickets—the entire US population at the time being slightly more than 130 million.[1] The imminent prospect of war did little to loosen the film's grip on the nation's imagination. *Gone with the Wind* went on to another three thousand movie-house bookings in general release before being rereleased almost immediately in March 1942.[2] Its years-long run made *Gone with the Wind* a constant cultural presence in the early phases of World War II.

For Black Americans, the film was a problematic mix of progress and throwback. Capping a string of 1930s movies set in southern plantations—from *Dixiana* (1930) to *The Littlest Rebel* (1936) and *Jezebel* (1938), among others—*Gone with the Wind* was seen, on one level, as an advance in Hollywood's portrayal of Black characters, particularly in the figure of "Mammy." Film historian Miriam J. Petty has pointed out that for Black actors in the 1930s, "a speaking role with any significant screen time, or a character who could boast any depth or dimensionality, was an exceptional, phenomenal occurrence."[3] The role of Mammy fit that description, especially as actor Hattie McDaniel interpreted it. The *Pittsburgh Courier, New York Amsterdam News, Chicago Defender,* and other Black newspapers lauded McDaniel's performance and celebrated her Oscar win for Best Supporting Actress, a historic first for a Black performer. But praise for McDaniel was frequently coupled with a repudiation of the Mammy character and the white supremacist, proslavery world view that the movie advanced so stirringly. In a 1940 column titled "*Gone with the Wind* Is More Dangerous Than *Birth of a Nation*," Black newspaper critic Melvin B. Tolson applauded the actor but strenuously rejected her role and the film's positioning as a definitive history of the South and the Civil War.[4] McDaniel's affecting performance, he argued, was essential to the movie's success as white supremacist propaganda. Today the film's stereotypes and romanticized vision of the antebellum South are glaringly obvious—to the point that in June 2020, amid the outpouring of protests over the police killing of George Floyd and other Black Americans, the streaming service HBO Max temporarily pulled the movie from its roster.[5] At the time, though, the contortions of American racial politics meant that the movie could be hailed as a milestone for Black actors in Hollywood and Black characters on screen, even as it was denounced as racist mythmaking—and even as it fueled, across mainstream America, a powerful, culturally pervasive nostalgia for the "Old South" and all that went with it.

That nostalgia should not be underestimated. More than a hundred years after it emerged as an entertainment form, the minstrel show was still circuiting through American culture—including Hollywood, where stars like Judy Garland and Bing Crosby were "blacking up" for minstrel-style production numbers in *Babes on Broadway* (1941), *Holiday Inn* (1942), *Dixie* (1943), and other hits.[6] Musical "specialty numbers" with Black performers were routinely cut from film prints sent to theaters in the South. Hollywood experiments with Black-cast productions—from early sound movies like *Hearts in Dixie* (1929) and the short film *Yamekraw* (1930) to the later star-studded *Cabin in the Sky* (1943)—often involved plot lines that brought their main characters right back to where they'd started, usually a farm in the Deep South.

Swayed by the supposed box office clout of southern movie audiences, Hollywood resisted demands for change. Citing the industry's "morbid fear" of having their pictures cut or banned by southern censors, historians Clayton R. Koppes and Gregory D. Black note that the studios "willingly molded their Black characters to the tastes of the most racist part of the country."[7] With active markets in Maryland and Virginia, Soundies were not immune to this sort of pressure. But the South wielded formidable clout in other spheres as well. A powerful southern congressional bloc strongly influenced the handling of race relations throughout the Roosevelt years, from the New Deal through World War II, and the interests of this group repeatedly overrode attempts to improve the status of Black Americans.[8]

A CHANGING REALITY

With World War II, Hollywood's usual depiction of Black people ran headlong into the official wartime rhetoric of America as a bastion of democracy and equality. The 1930s had seen an increase in the number of Black performers in Hollywood films but little change in their presentation, and the Office of War Information (OWI)—the federal agency in charge of war-related propaganda—was sharply critical of the studios' wartime output.[9] An OWI analysis of Hollywood movies released in late 1942 and early 1943 concluded that "in general, Negroes are presented as basically different from other people, as taking no relevant part in the life of the nation, as offering nothing contributing nothing, expecting nothing." Of the few films that African Americans did appear in, the report said, more than three-quarters depicted them as "clearly inferior."[10]

The NAACP and other organizations pressured the industry to change. Even before the war, the Negro Actors Guild of America—established in 1937 by performers Fredi Washington, Paul Robeson, and Ethel Waters, composer W. C. Handy, and others—had been working to secure less stereotyped roles, and more of them, for Black actors. In 1940, soon after McDaniel's Oscar win, NAACP executive secretary Walter White made the first of several trips to Hollywood in pursuit of the same goal. The campaign was supported by the National Negro Congress, led by actor Clarence Muse, as well as the National Negro Publishers Association, the Greater New York Committee for Better Negro Films, and other organizations.[11] White met repeatedly with studio heads and industry influencers, but he ignored and antagonized Hollywood's Black acting community—including performers like McDaniel, whose stardom had been achieved in circumscribed and subservient roles—at times seeming to blame actors themselves for the limited parts available to them.[12]

The success of earlier Hollywood Black-cast movies like *Hallelujah* (1929) and *The Green Pastures* (1936) had shown that cosmopolitan audiences had an interest in Black performers, characters, and themes.[13] With these viewers in mind, or perhaps in response to OWI pressure, in 1943 two major studios released Black-cast musical features. Unlike the films of the 1930s, both MGM's *Cabin in the Sky* and Twentieth Century–Fox's *Stormy Weather* present Black Americans as part of a growing urban population. But *Cabin in the Sky* relies on a narrative theme common to the earlier films, in which the city—or anything modern—symbolizes evil, and a timeless, rural "antebellum idyll" symbolizes goodness. *Stormy Weather* departs from this precedent, explicitly focusing on Black migration between the World Wars and presenting the city as a place of creativity and engagement.[14]

In an era that saw patriotic unity as a national imperative, the racial separatism of Hollywood's Black-cast musicals was not embraced by either the OWI or the NAACP, and wartime production of these films effectively ended with *Stormy Weather*. Instead, the studios made a few dramatic features—usually with wartime settings—that included one Black actor in an often ethnically diverse cast, as in *Bataan* and *Crash Dive* (both 1943). But these films were rarities. Between 1941 and 1945, the major Hollywood studios released 1,522 features; of these, only a dozen or so address racial issues in any context.[15] Beyond those films, wartime mainstream movies continued to present Black actors in prewar stereotypical roles—if at all.[16] Pressured to rethink their depictions, Hollywood studios frequently responded by writing Black roles out of their movies entirely.[17] LA's show business community was hard hit: according to one source, membership in the Black actors' union fell during the war years by some 50 percent.[18] Hollywood had turned away from Black-cast movies, there were fewer roles for Black actors in white-cast films, and many of those roles were out of step with a changing reality. Under the circumstances, audiences looking for Black performers on screen might logically seek them elsewhere.

OTHER VOICES, OTHER SCREENS

Race films were one long-standing option. The silent-film era had seen the development of an independent Black film industry in the 1910s and 1920s, led by pioneers like William Foster of the Foster Photoplay Company and Oscar Micheaux of the Micheaux Book and Motion Picture Company.

The history of race-film production and exhibition suggests a strong foundation of Black spectatorship that Soundies were able to tap into. Historians Jacqueline Stewart and Cara Caddoo have each explored how the films and their screenings shaped concepts of identity, community, and modernity among Black Americans in the first decades of the Great Migration.[19] Stewart's *Migrating to the Movies* includes a map of "The Stroll," the entertainment district in Chicago's South Side "Black Belt," during the years 1906–1920: along with eighteen theaters, the map shows four film companies.[20] New York, Los Angeles, and Philadelphia were also centers for Black film production in the silent era.

The coming of sound film in the late 1920s shattered the industry, largely due to the increased costs of production and converting theaters to sound projection. The 1929 stock-market crash was another blow. Even before sound, race-film companies were often undercapitalized, surviving film to film and sometimes folding after a single production. With the advent of sound films, Hollywood suddenly saw Black performers—more specifically, Black voices—as ideally suited to the new medium. This touched off a flurry of Black-cast Hollywood moviemaking that, though largely over by 1931, brought African American performers to the studios' attention. As a result, Black actors appeared with greater frequency in Hollywood films of the 1930s, both in musical short films and—in limited, stereotyped roles—in features. In the 1940s those roles would diminish dramatically, but the late 1930s saw race-film producers actively competing with major studios for performers and viewers. To meet Hollywood head-on, they turned to the industry's bread-and-butter genres: musicals, comedies, Westerns, and gangster movies.

Paula Massood writes in detail about these films—particularly Black-cast gangster movies starring Ralph Cooper and Westerns starring singer Herb Jeffries—and her observations point to some interesting parallels between the race films of the late 1930s and the Black-cast Soundies that began appearing three or four years later.[21] As with much of the race-film industry, most of the personnel involved with Black-cast Soundies production were white. But like Cooper, Jeffries, and other race-film stars, Black performers in Soundies—from top names to uncredited bit players—often had strong input in shaping their own presentation on screen. As in films like Cooper's *Dark Manhattan* (1937), most Black-cast Soundies present performers as city dwellers in contemporary settings—blending "the urban with the urbane," as Massood puts it, through markers like fashion and music.[22] In both Black-cast Soundies and late 1930s race films, Harlem is an idealized locale—shorthand for a modern, urban Black population and the implicit possibilities for change that the city holds. That aura extends to the four Westerns that Jeffries made from 1937 to 1939. Three have "Harlem" in their titles, immediately linking the films' Western settings with a contemporary Black sensibility.[23] In Soundies, that dynamic (and the Western locale) is most closely paralleled in Dorothy Dandridge's *Cow Cow*

Boogie (Coslow-Berne, 1942), with its saloon setting and lyrics about a "swing half-breed" with a "Harlem touch." As part of a weekly eight-film Soundies reel, *Cow Cow Boogie* reached a broad mix of market sectors. Unlike most race films, Jeffries' Westerns did too, cross-promoted to non-Black audiences beyond the race-film circuit.

Black-cast Soundies and race films share a similar approach to performers and their music. Frequently set in city night clubs and cabarets, the musical numbers showcase big bands and smaller combos, chorus lines, and solo dancers. In these films, Harlem clubs and cafes serve a sophisticated, exclusively Black clientele who are part of a complex urban milieu. Race-film stars like Jeffries, Edna Mae Harris, Theresa Harris, and Francine Everett later appeared in Soundies—sometimes as stars, sometimes as uncredited extras. His Western-movie career behind him, Jeffries appeared as a vocalist with Duke Ellington and His Orchestra in *Flamingo* (Coslow-Berne, 1942). Edna Mae Harris, who played opposite heavyweight champ Joe Louis in the race film *Spirit of Youth* (1938), made four Soundies copyrighted in 1942. Theresa Harris, who starred with Ralph Cooper in *Bargain with Bullets* (1937), turned in a witty comic performance in *The Outskirts of Town* (Coslow-Berne, 1942).

The crossover wasn't limited to performers. The Cabin Kids' Soundie *Swanee Smiles* (Hammons-Kane, 1943) was clipped from the 1937 short *Rhythm Saves the Day*, and two of bandleader Lucky Millinder's 1942 Soundies were clipped from the 1939 race film *Paradise in Harlem*. Released in 1944—after her starring roles in *Cabin in the Sky* and *Stormy Weather*—Lena Horne's three Soundies were taken from the 1941 short *Boogie Woogie Dream*.

For all the similarities, Soundies also differed from late 1930s Black-cast genre movies in certain respects—in part because, coming a few years after those films, Soundies were able to expand upon them and the Black urban modernity they represented. That modernity, and Harlem as a specific milieu, were more of a given in Soundies—to the point that they could be evoked with a simple painted backdrop, as in *Pigmeat Throws the Bull* (Crouch-Crouch, 1945) and *Get It Off Your Mind* (Crouch-Crouch, 1946). Too, the fact that Soundies were not part of longer movies—and shown in informal settings rather than theaters—meant that audiences could enjoy the performances simply as performances, freed from the plot lines and character arcs that full-length movies demanded. Instead, Soundies showed people enjoying themselves, often in venues like the ones in which viewers watched the films (fig. 1.1).

How long the race-film industry lasted and how far it reached are a matter of some debate. According to Massood, Black theater ownership plummeted from approximately two hundred in 1925 to seven in 1942, and race-film production

Figure 1.1. In a café, Nat "King" Cole duets with his filmed self on the Panoram (fig. I.3, p. 14) in the 1945 Soundie *Frim Fram Sauce*. The other members of his trio are seated at the counter behind him. Library of Congress, Motion Picture, Broadcasting and Recorded Sound Division.

all but ceased by 1945.[24] But a 1946 article in the *Chicago Defender* heralded an upswing in race-film production in New York and put the number of movie houses serving Black audiences—though not necessarily Black-owned—at six hundred nationwide.[25] The volume of race-film production unquestionably fell by the war's end, particularly on the West Coast. But as the *Defender* article suggests, it continued for a few more years in New York, with two pivotal Soundies makers—Black producer William D. Alexander and white producer-director William Forest Crouch—active in race-film production into the late 1940s.

MACHINES FOR MUSIC

As a film form Soundies were rooted in music, and they were as much a part of the music industry as the movie industry, if not more so. In this, jukeboxes were the inspiration and the model. After the repeal of Prohibition in 1933, bars, taverns, and cocktail lounges sprang up nationwide. The explosion of neighborhood drinking spots transformed jukeboxes from a minor industry into a pop-culture phenomenon that brought the recording industry along with it. "Already about 350,000 Juke-boxes are scattered through the United States," one writer reported in late 1940, "and more are being installed every day. Together they chew up 44 per cent of the American production of popular records, and nothing speeds a performer to national fame so swiftly as the Juke or Electrical Phonograph Record coin machine." Jukes had been a rare high-growth business during the Depression, and the writer projected 1940 industry grosses of $150 million or more (almost $2.8 billion in 2021 dollars). The jukebox, he concluded, "is all-American, as native as the hot-dog."[26]

On a more modest scale, so were Soundies and the Panorams that played them. The films were so integral to the music industry, in fact, that from early 1941 to early 1946, the weekly Soundies reels had their own review column in *Billboard*. A regular feature of the Amusement Machines section, these Movie Machine Reviews offered capsule assessments, from a commercial perspective, of entire reels (called programs) and each film in them. "Locations that go for vocal numbers should really like this Soundie," *Billboard* wrote of Program 1047 in January 1942. "Five of the eight subjects feature solo vocalists, while a duo, trio and quartet respectively contribute the other three. Plenty of variety in the subjects." The quartet in question was the Black vocal group the Deep River Boys—who, *Billboard* wrote, "give out in a strictly jumpy number called *Toot That Trumpet!*, which will click with swing fans but does not display the talents of this quartet to best advantage. Plenty of boogie-woogie dancing in this."[27] Many *Billboard* reviews of Soundies with Black performers specifically reference their race—using terms like "sepia," "dusky," and "copper-colored," as well as "Negro"—but others, like this one, do not. The references are random enough to suggest no official editorial policy on racial identification—leaving it, perhaps, to individual writers.

Film historian Arthur Knight has written about Black actors in 1930s Hollywood, like Hattie McDaniel, who in his estimation neither achieved true star status nor maintained a vital connection to Black audiences.[28] But that connection was fundamental for performers in Black-cast Soundies. They were primarily musicians and vocalists, not actors, and their music-industry circuit routinely included live shows, record releases, jukebox play, and often radio. Audience connection was essential to their work. Film appearances, in either Hollywood or race movies, were relatively rare. And there was little chance of bankrolling a movie-star lifestyle with Soundies work. Most performers were booked for one, two, or at most three production sessions, sometimes years apart, each lasting a few days at most. Top names aside, the pay was often union scale or less, especially as the company's finances foundered. Instead, Soundies were a means of promoting and maximizing performers' main sources of revenue and recognition: live performances, record releases, and jukebox and radio play.

Radio had seen spectacular growth in the 1930s. By 1940, less than one in ten urban households was without one, and Americans considered radio listening one of their favorite pastimes.[29] Black music and musicians had been crucial to commercial radio's growth and popularity, but by the 1940s they were being edged out of national broadcasts by white swing bands. Like sound-film production, broadcast radio was a capital-intensive business. According to one historian, "African Americans could not buy their way onto the national airwaves [through radio-network ownership] or influence their content through their power either as performers or as consumers."[30] Even in the 1930s, this absence had been obliquely noted: Black sponsorship of an imagined Black-cast radio program is the premise behind *The Black Network*, a 1936 Warner Bros. short starring Nina Mae McKinney, its title a riff on NBC's Red and Blue Networks.

In 1939, the performing rights and licensing organization Broadcast Music, Inc. (BMI) was founded to challenge the older, more restrictive American Society of Composers, Authors, and Publishers (ASCAP). BMI quickly zeroed in on music that the more highbrow ASCAP did not represent—country, folk, Latin, and, significantly, the music of Black composers and performers. The leverage that BMI offered in turn sparked the rise of independent radio stations and recording labels—particularly during the American Federation of Musicians' strike of 1942–44—that exerted a strong market presence during the war and more emphatically after.[31] In 1942, *Billboard* inaugurated its "Harlem Hit Parade," which compiled the week's top sellers at several Harlem record stores.[32] In a nod to the rising popularity of Black music, three years later *Billboard* replaced the Harlem chart with "Most Played Juke Box Race Records," based on "reports received from leading juke box operators thruout the nation."[33] By 1949, the "Race Records" list had morphed into a standalone Rhythm & Blues Records section, with individual charts for best-selling retail records, most-played juke box records, and advance releases.[34]

One influential radio program of the 1940s bears comparison with Black-cast Soundies and their creative milieu. Debuting in late 1942, *Jubilee* was produced by the Armed Forces Radio Service (AFRS) specifically for servicemen and -women. The program occupies an interesting spot in the 1940s audio-cultural landscape. Not broadcast to civilian audiences, it was out of the home-front eye but, given the size of its military audience, not exactly out of sight. In its early years, *Jubilee* featured Black performers exclusively, but was deliberately not promoted as a "Negro" show. Broadcast to everyone in the military, it was simply presented as the latest in "jump and jive." Almost immediately, *Jubilee* became one of the AFRS's most popular programs. Performers were not paid, but there were significant promotional advantages to appearing on the show, especially in its first two years: as a military broadcast, *Jubilee* was exempt from the nationwide recording ban imposed by the musicians' strike of 1942–44, which, as we'll see, had a devastating effect on Soundies.

Jubilee closely paralleled Black-cast Soundies in its approach to presenting Black music and musicians, its racially mixed audience, and the creative leeway it offered performers. In the relatively constrained sphere of radio, writes one historian, *Jubilee* was notable for having "more of an exchange between directors and performers, with more opportunities for improvisation and nuance"—a description that applies to many Black-cast Soundies.[35] Performers overlapped as well. Duke Ellington, Nat "King" Cole, Louis Jordan, Ida James, Savannah Churchill, Maurice Rocco, Ivie Anderson, and many others appeared in Soundies and on *Jubilee*. Like Soundies, *Jubilee* gave Black entertainers access to a significant white audience.

But only Soundies offered visibility. Throughout the late 1930s and 1940s, record sales, jukebox play, and radio—*Jubilee* included—brought Black performers and music into the audio mainstream. In visual media, access was harder to come by. In this, Soundies had a dual function: as a relatively unmediated platform for Black entertainers looking to connect with Black audiences through film, and as a point of entry for Black culture, music, and performers into the visual mainstream (fig. 1.2).

This visibility mattered. Critic Gary Giddins writes that "the point at which indigenous American music becomes pop culture is the point where white performers learn to mimic Black ones," and the swing era harbored more than one example of the process. Giddins notes that "Many of [Benny] Goodman's biggest hits were virtual duplications of records that Fletcher Henderson and Chick Webb had recorded months, even years, before."[36] In presenting Black musicians on screen, Soundies pushed in the opposite direction, visibly identifying African American performers with their own creative production. Most of the time, that is. In Soundies as in Hollywood, music tracks were recorded separately, usually before the visuals, and in a few instances—particularly when dusting off an unused older recording—Soundies producers were blithely pragmatic about grabbing whoever was on hand to mime (or "sideline") another

Figure 1.2 (*this page and following*). a. Johnny Taylor (*at piano*) and "Hot Cha" (*center*) with uncredited actors in *Good-Nite All* (1943); b. June Richmond and Roy Milton and His Orchestra in *Hey, Lawdy Mama* (1944); c. the Delta Rhythm Boys and uncredited women performers in *Take the 'A' Train* (1941). Courtesy Mark Cantor Archive.

group's soundtrack performance. Even with these occasional disconnects, an overwhelming number of Soundies with Black performers document the musicians heard on their soundtracks, and this visual record is one of Soundies' most significant contributions to American entertainment history. But their contribution extends beyond the performers themselves. As film historian Ellen C. Scott writes, "Soundies realistically rendered the places of Black communal pleasure rarely seen on screen," with musicians, dancers, and spectators caught up in moments of pure enjoyment. For Black and white viewers alike, "Soundies crossed a Hollywood-established color line that barred such open, free-acting Black pleasure."[37]

THE CASE FOR CREATIVE PROGRAMMING

The fact that Panorams could play only the next Soundie on the reel—no choice involved—was a serious limitation, and it called for creative programming.

Figure 1.2b.

The weekly general-release reels included a mix of titles intended to appeal to the broadest possible audience—or more accurately, the broadest amalgam of niche audiences. The typical eight-film reel was a cultural grab bag, with a mix that might include "hillbilly" and Latin music, an Irish ballad, a Black-cast Soundie, and an Eastern European polka, along with the usual big-band tunes—and the Latin-boogies, jitterbug-polkas, and other hybrids that are among Soundies' most intriguing musical legacies.

Although Panoram operators could order custom reels of their own Soundie selections, most used the general-release reels, and this was crucial for the Black-cast films' exposure. From mid-1941 to early 1946, most of the weekly reels included at least one Soundie starring Black performers, and occasionally two. Performers generally made between two and four films in a Soundies session, guaranteeing at least two appearances on Panoram screens. Along with star performers, most Black-cast Soundies include uncredited extras—dapper men and women who fill the living rooms, cafés, nightclubs, and streetscapes of these films, and dancers who bring those spaces to life.

Alice Barker was one of those dancers. Her work reflects the extent to which Soundies were part of the Black show-business circuit, especially in New York.

Figure 1.2c.

To date, she's been identified in seven Soundies, and likely did more. Performing in pick-up ensembles hired for a day or two of filming, she's never credited
by name—only as an anonymous member of the Sepia Steppers, Ebonettes,
Ze Zulettes, or whatever the scratch troupe happened to be called that day.
In those years she was actually a member of the Zanzibeauts—the chorus
line at Café Zanzibar, a midtown Manhattan nightclub that catered to racially
mixed audiences. Barker is a polished chorus-line presence in Soundies like
Toot That Trumpet (Crouch-Crouch, 1943), and no less professional in the
stereotype-riddled *Jive Comes to the Jungle* (Barry-Waller, 1942) and *Jungle
Jamboree* (Crouch-Crouch, 1943). She's arguably at her most beguiling when
she's not dancing at all, as one of the extras in *Legs Ain't No Good* (Barry/
Waller-Graham, 1942). Seated at an open-air lunch counter with war posters
behind her, she cheerfully flashes a smile and some leg on behalf of home-front
patriotism (fig. 7.3, p. 145).[38]

   In Soundies, fleeting moments like these often packed an outsized cultural
punch. The 1940s brought distinct challenges and opportunities for Black
Americans, including a collective grappling with doubts about the war and,
paradoxically, a bitter struggle for the right to serve their country in combat.

America during World War II was not so much a melting pot as a pressure cooker, erupting in racial violence that swept the country in 1943 and continued to simmer long after. In this context, Soundies' informal role as a space for rethinking images of Black people on screen takes on added significance. Undeclared, ad hoc, and improvisational, this work often took place at the margins of this already marginal entertainment form—in unspoken glances and gestures, insouciant walks, photographs informally added to living-room walls, and performers like Barker meeting the camera on their own terms. Against the jagged course of wartime race relations, a current of activism, expectation, and progress runs through many of these films.

2

—ᴧᴧ—

RISKY BUSINESS

FOR ALL THE CULTURAL IMPACT that Soundies might have had, they were first and foremost a business. As a commercial proposition, Panoram Soundies began with a jukebox-industry model grafted onto a distinctly un-Hollywood-like production system. It was an audacious venture, for sure, but it could also be described as miscalculated, ill-prepared, and eventually coming apart at the seams.

That trajectory is, at its heart, a story of Soundies aesthetics and how they were shaped by Soundies as a business. There is a consistent, dynamic inter-play of commerce and creativity at work in these films and an escalating tension between economic imperatives and inventive production. How Soundies became a space for envisioning Black people on screen is a story in which the marketplace figures prominently: Soundies didn't become a ground for cultural experimentation in spite of being a commercial enterprise but *because* of it. How the business was structured and how it responded to unanticipated crises were crucial in shaping the creative space in which Black-cast Soundies were made and presented. Ironically and unexpectedly, commercial constraints ended up sparking experimentation rather than limiting it.

The stark reality is that Soundies were a barely profitable business. Mills Novelty was forced to halt Panoram production in 1942, only a few months after the US entered into World War II. A year later, Soundies Corporation president Gordon Mills estimated the number of machines in commercial operation at forty-five hundred, with fifteen hundred of these run by another Mills subsidiary, the Soundies Operating Company. An additional fifteen hundred, he wrote, had been placed in schools and defense plants "for educational purposes."[1] Two years later, the total was put at three thousand or fewer.[2] It was a modest network at best, and a fraction of the thirty thousand envisioned at the Panoram's 1940 debut. The company was stuck. To keep the business running, it had to turn out a constant flow of Soundies for an exhibition circuit that might not break even, let alone turn a profit.

Under those circumstances every dime mattered, and crowd-pleasing films with strong repeat-viewing appeal were essential. More than forty-five independent and Mills-affiliated companies produced Soundies at one point or another, virtually all of them in New York or Los Angeles. The Soundies Corporation packaged this output into the eight-film reels that were the lifeblood of the business, releasing a new reel each week to Panoram operators who installed them in their machines. It was an intense schedule for both the company and its producer-suppliers, and budget and time constraints could weigh heavily against the need for high-quality, crowd-pleasing films.

L.O.L. Productions, Inc. was one of those independent suppliers, and its contentious relationship with the Soundies Corporation is an illuminating entry point into Soundies as a business. By and large, L.O.L.'s films were not hits with Panoram audiences, and in May 1943, the Soundies Corporation canceled the company's contract. With thirty-two films remaining on the agreement, L.O.L. sued for breach of contract. In December 1944, the case was heard in the Appellate Division of the New York Supreme Court, with the Honorable Bernard L. Shientag presiding.

ORDER IN THE COURT

The trial and its transcript are a deeply revealing intersection of Soundies' aesthetics and commerce. Key figures testifying in the case include Arthur Leonard, vice president in charge of production at L.O.L.; George P. Ulcigan, vice president and general manager of the Soundies Corporation; and William Forest Crouch.[3] Crouch, originally the Soundies Corporation's production and promotion manager, later moved into production himself, turning out a prodigious number of Soundies, including a majority of the Black-cast films. Like all of the Soundies Corporation leadership, Ulcigan and Crouch were white—Leonard too. Compared to Crouch, Leonard had a stronger production resume: he'd worked at Warner Bros. as an assistant casting director in the short films division, and in the late 1930s he directed and coproduced three race films, including two starring Nina Mae McKinney.[4] As Soundies production geared up in New York in early 1941, Leonard became a principal in Cinemasters, an independent producer-supplier that was almost immediately replaced by the Soundies Corporation affiliate Minoco. In December 1942, Leonard and two backers formed another independent company, L.O.L. Productions. For all practical purposes, the Soundies Corporation was L.O.L.'s only client.[5]

Crouch's background was largely in promotion and marketing, as a studio publicist, an editor on film-industry publications, and similar positions. Coming to the Soundies Corporation in 1941, his duties included assembling the weekly reels—selecting the films and determining the order in which they appeared. At the trial, Ulcigan stated that the company relied on Crouch's judgment "almost entirely" for the quality of the films in the weekly programs.[6]

As a production executive, Crouch had repeatedly complained about Leonard's shoddy production values and the high incidence of censorship of L.O.L.'s Soundies, which effectively removed the films from some of their biggest markets. For his part, Leonard was galled to come under fire by someone with so little background in actual film production. "I had more experience," he told the court. "Mr. Crouch had never made a picture before. . . . There were jealousies that were existing, sir, definite jealousies."[7] But there were more fundamental differences too, including a profound disagreement over the depiction of Black people on screen.

At stake in the lawsuit were the damages claimed by L.O.L. as a result of the canceled contract, variously figured at $13,880 and $14,885.[8] Even at the lower figure, it was a substantial amount for both struggling businesses—more than $200,000 in 2021 dollars. Between them, Crouch and Ulcigan drew a vivid picture of Soundies Corporation operations and the problems with L.O.L.

Shortly after joining the company, Crouch testified, he made an extensive tour of Panoram locations on the East Coast and in the Midwest, speaking informally with Panoram operators, venue owners, and Soundies viewers. "I have talked to the man that comes in and puts in the dime, and asked him what he thought of it," Crouch said. "I investigated to find out what people like, what they don't like, the people who put the money in our machines."[9] Under his initiative, the company conducted polls "where every location sent in cards telling the reaction to the programs. That ran on a weekly basis." When the opposing lawyer pointed out that the inability to select a specific Soundie made it difficult to tell which films were popular, Crouch countered: "That is right. But after a picture has been played, the location owner or the patron can comment as to whether or not he liked it, and it is those comments that the patrons make, or when a patron comes in and asks for a number similar to the one perhaps he saw a week or two before, or something like that. It is through that medium that we determine which numbers are the most popular and which are not."[10]

Along with poor production quality and censorship, Crouch's issues with L.O.L. centered on the depiction of Black people in L.O.L.'s Soundies, which included minstrel-show settings and white actors in blackface. The lawsuit had been triggered by the Soundies Corporation's rejection of three L.O.L. Soundies—including one blackface film, *Plenty of King*—and the subsequent cancellation of L.O.L.'s contract.[11] In *Plenty of King*, Crouch told the court, Leonard had "used a white man blacked up with an all-Negro cast, and we had considerable repercussions on that," including angry feedback from the film's Black performers.[12] This aspect of the dispute suggests that Black audiences may have been a significant segment of the Soundies market.

A STRIKE AND AN OUT

The trial transcript also sketches the parameters of the Panoram network and the basic distribution system for releasing Soundies. According to Ulcigan, Panorams were installed by their owner-operators "in restaurants, public places, bus terminals, railroad stations and the like, wherever large crowds of people congregated, or wherever people of the transient character frequented."[13] He put the national number of Panoram owner-operators at approximately four hundred—each of whom, as Crouch noted in his testimony, might run from five to fifty machines.[14] As for the films, Ulcigan said, "we have released a new program of eight subjects every week since January of 1941," adding that "our so-called release date is on Monday of each week."[15] To meet that need, he told the court, required a minimum of 416 films per year. It's an impressive figure, and Ulcigan undoubtedly used it for dramatic effect—throughout its lifespan the Soundies Corporation never once achieved it, relying on rereleases and clips from other films to make up the shortfalls. Asked about a backlog of films to cover programming emergencies, Ulcigan admitted somewhat wistfully that "it is always the objective of the company to have that," but they had achieved it only "at various intervals."[16]

There were good reasons for that. When RCM, the Mills-affiliated West Coast production house, began regular Soundies production in late 1940, expectations and budgets were high. Louis Armstrong and his orchestra, for instance, were paid at least $2,500 for their Soundies—the equivalent, in 2021 dollars, of a little over $46,500, a substantial amount for a few days' work.[17] By the time the L.O.L. case reached the New York Supreme Court in late 1944, the situation had changed dramatically. Not only had wartime regulations cut off Panoram production in spring 1942, freezing the number of commercially operating machines at an almost unworkably low figure, but that summer, the

American Federation of Musicians went on strike nationwide. This meant that union musicians—including virtually every member of a professional band or combo—were prohibited from making recordings of any kind for the US market. The recording ban affected most of the entertainment industry, with Hollywood movies being the one major exception (Armed Forces Radio Service programs like *Jubilee* being another), and it is widely seen as hastening the end of the big-band era. For the Soundies Corporation, the strike was crippling.

Announced in June, a few weeks before it went into effect on July 31, the strike left Soundies producers scrambling to secure new music tracks for visuals to be filmed later. With lucrative recording royalties at stake, the union was ready for a tough fight. For the Soundies Corporation the strike lasted more than a year (and for some record companies, more than two years).[18] Soundies producers quickly ran through their stockpiled soundtracks and were forced to devise other strategies for filling the weekly reels. Like the record companies, they turned to performers exempt from the ban, such as a capella vocalists, foreign and nonunion musicians, and musicians whose instruments (harmonicas, for instance) didn't qualify them for union membership. They brought in dancers, comedians, animal acts, and most likely a few union musicians willing to anonymously bootleg their performances. The Soundies Corporation began rereleasing large numbers of older Soundies, and musical numbers were clipped from old features and shorts, including race films like *Paradise in Harlem* (1939). Previously recorded tracks were purchased from music agencies, and inventories of former competitors were bought, revamped, and rereleased.

Despite these efforts, revenues fell. Turning films out quickly had always been a priority, but with no new Panorams going into operation and few top musicians available for filming, Soundies now had to be made cheaply too. Money jumped into the driver's seat and stayed there for the rest of the Soundies Corporation's lifespan.

L.O.L. Productions was incorporated in December 1942, in the midst of the strike, and its first contract with the Soundies Corporation went into effect in January 1943. According to Ulcigan, there was a special appeal in working with the new company: L.O.L. partner Samuel Oliphant had assured Ulcigan that even with the strike in place, L.O.L. could deliver desperately needed big-band Soundies. "Mr. Oliphant said that he was a very close friend of Mr. Padway, counsel for the AF of M [American Federation of Musicians, the striking union] and that he would have no difficulty making pictures for us with bands," Ulcigan testified. Asked if he expected L.O.L. to violate the strike, Ulcigan responded: "I don't know what he would do or how he would do it but that is what he said he would do."[19] A listing of L.O.L.-produced Soundies, included

in the transcript as part of "Defendant's Exhibit P," identifies the forty films—
eight per month—made for the Soundies Corporation between January and
May 1943. Not one is a big-band film. Four star African American or Caribbean
performers; one features a Black performer in an otherwise white cast; and four
(including the one that the Soundies Corporation rejected outright) feature
white performers in blackface.[20]

Each film on the L.O.L. list was billed to the Soundies Corporation at
$1,250—a price that included everything from music licensing to sets, cos-
tumes, and editing—with each monthly bloc of eight generating $10,000 in
revenue for L.O.L. According to a 1944 *Billboard* article, the network of three
thousand Panorams in commercial operation earned an average of $6.50 per
machine in weekly reel rentals.[21] If that figure is accurate, the total revenue
that each eight-film reel generated for the Soundies Corporation might be less
than $20,000—an amount that would have had to cover not only payment to
producers like L.O.L., but lab work, film prints, and distribution costs, plus
any profits. According to Leonard's somewhat vague testimony, the average
amount spent on talent for L.O.L. Soundies was $322 or $200 per film[22]—not a
substantial amount in either case—and the actual figure may have been significantly lower. "In looking over the lineup, I do not see one act that should have
cost more than $150.00 at the most," Crouch wrote in a confidential appraisal of
L.O.L.'s first eighteen films, submitted as evidence in the trial. "There are lots
of what we call $25.00 acts, so the talent cost in these pictures is considerably
below average."[23] It was one reason he found L.O.L.'s Soundies so exasperating.

KEEPING THE BARTENDER HAPPY

Crouch analyzed L.O.L.'s output in detail, and his critique amounts to a crash
course in Soundies as a new entertainment form. "The first thing to bear in mind
in a Soundie production is how does it sound?" he told the court. "If you see
something on the screen which you dislike, you can turn your head and not look
at it, but you can't turn the sound off." It wasn't always customers who objected.
"In taverns, the bartender hears these soundtracks over and over," Crouch said.
"He has the picture running constantly some nights when the place is very busy,
and if there are certain sounds in there that are distracting, he will pull the plug
on the machine," cutting off revenue entirely.[24] For the same reason, dialogue-
heavy films, including comedians' monologues, were a problem. One of the
L.O.L. films that the Soundies Corporation rejected outright was a routine by
white comedian Henny Youngman. Even Dewey "Pigmeat" Markham, a popular comedian on the Black revue circuit, made only one Soundie.

Soundtrack quality was another issue. "On arriving at the office here this morning I found that our laboratory coordinator, who is in charge of inspection of all prints going out to operators, was greatly perturbed over the poor soundtrack of the [white-cast] subject *Hit 'Em Hard and Hit 'Em Again*" (Oliphant/Leonard-Leonard, 1943), Crouch wrote to Leonard in May 1943. "I was much chagrined to admit that we had to take this subject the way it was."[25] In a brief courtroom appearance, Virgil Bowers, the Soundies Corporation's film technician, offered his own assessment of *Hit 'Em Hard and Hit 'Em Again*: "I thought it stunk," he said, asking: "May I comment on that, sir?" "No," Judge Shientag responded, "I think you have made enough of a comment."[26]

L.O.L.'s Soundies "have been ground out like sausages," Crouch wrote in his confidential memo, filmed "at the rate of no less than four a day and no extra time is taken in set building or preparation of properties, etc." Conceding that "a set does not make a Soundie [and] all the production value in the world will not make the picture good," he insisted that while "the main thing is getting good performers, the next thing is to present them properly so as to get the most out of what they do."[27]

Three of the four Black-cast Soundies that L.O.L. produced were among the eighteen films that Crouch critiqued in his memo. He singled out *Quarry Road* and *Willie Willie* (both Oliphant/Leonard-Leonard, 1943), starring Trinidadian performers Sam Manning and Belle Rosette (aka Beryl McBurnie), as having more "production value" than most L.O.L. Soundies (fig. 2.1).[28] "These numbers have a fair amount of extras," he wrote, "and although most of them are Negro performers who can be hired at a minimum cost, the numbers nevertheless give a semblance of production."[29] The lack of extras in most L.O.L. Soundies "cuts down considerably the entertainment value the picture has," he continued, "because a number of nice-looking girls, etc. often add a great deal to the picture and the cut-away shots to them often give you a change of pace and make a picture more complete."[30] In critiquing the third Black-cast film, *Rug Cutters' Holiday*, Crouch again noted the lack of cutaway shots and the unimaginative camera work: "All of the action takes place in the center of the room here, and the camera is moved in and out to pick it up as best it can. The set is very simple and there is nobody of importance in the cast."[31]

For extras, bit actors, and "nobody of importance," the pay level in Soundies was generally not high. But Crouch's comment about "Negro performers at minimal cost" is rare evidence—in the court transcript or other documents—that Black performers may have been paid less than white performers. As the company's finances worsened and the Soundies Corporation struggled to meet the demand for new releases, the availability of affordable Black

Figure 2.1. Sam Manning and Belle Rosette in the L.O.L.–produced Soundie
Willie, Willie (1943). Courtesy Mark Cantor Archive.

talent—including performers not in the striking musicians' union—may have
been a consideration in the large number of Black-cast films that the Soundies
Corporation distributed and that Crouch and other makers produced.

But it was not the only factor, and presumably not the primary one. As the
company discovered with the L.O.L. Soundies, even the most cheaply produced
films were money-losers if they didn't pull in their share of dimes. "Our program
#1114, which contained four L.O.L. subjects, hit an all time low for the amount of
business done," Crouch told Leonard in May 1943. "This was due, many operators report, to the extremely poor quality of the L.O.L. pictures in the program.
Our exchange manager reports that we suffered a loss of revenue on this program
of approximately $2,500.00 and that we have on hand a large supply of prints of
this program which have been uncalled for."[32] Poor quality may not have been
the only factor: the L.O.L. films on the program included *Ask Dad* (Oliphant/
Leonard-Leonard, 1943), which had white actors in blackface in a minstrel-show
setting. By contrast, the demand for Black-cast Soundies was strong enough
to warrant production, starting in 1943, of additional films beyond the weekly
reels—the only category of Soundies to receive this extra treatment.

Despite extensive testimony by Crouch and Ulcigan, the jury in the court case unanimously found in favor of L.O.L. The prosecution had argued that the Soundies Corporation had canceled L.O.L.'s contract not because of poor quality or other issues but to use that money to purchase sixty-four films from another company, which had been produced before the musicians' strike and included several big-band numbers. The jury apparently found the argument credible. Or perhaps, as Soundies Corporation attorneys argued, jurors' sympathies lay with Leonard as "an enlisted man of the United States Navy, who was then serving his country in connection with the production of confidential films."[33] Reaching a verdict in little more than an hour, the jury awarded L.O.L. Productions a total of $8,000, minus $465 for music licensing fees that the Soundies Corporation had covered on L.O.L.'s behalf.[34] It was a setback the Soundies Corporation could hardly afford.

MORALITY IN PENNSYLVANIA—AND NEW YORK AND VIRGINIA

Even before the 1944 verdict, censorship had come to play an increasingly important role in the Soundies economy, further entangling commercial and aesthetic considerations. Off-color lyrics were a perennial hazard for jukebox play, but films drew far more attention from censors. With every Soundie expected to at least cover its own costs, films that were censored out of high-traffic markets meant significant losses. Risqué lyrics were almost certain to raise red flags for the films, and both Crouch and Ulcigan testified that L.O.L. routinely failed to submit song lyrics for review before filming.[35] According to Ulcigan, more than a quarter of the Soundies that L.O.L. produced between January and April 1943—nine films out of thirty-two—encountered censorship problems in one or more states, with five banned outright and four others requiring deletions. This percentage, he asserted, was twice as high as that of any other Soundies producer.[36] The court transcript mentions only two of the nine censored L.O.L. films and neither is a Black-cast Soundie. *Pepepeto* (Oliphant/Leonard-Leonard, 1943) apparently included a shot in which a dancer's costume slipped, triggering a ruling of indecent exposure by censors in Virginia. New York State censors judged the other film, *Stand Up for Your Rights* (Oliphant/Leonard-Leonard, 1943), as "indecent—would tend to corrupt morals."[37]

A letter to L.O.L. from Soundies Corporation treasurer R. P. McNamara gives a detailed glimpse into the formula that the company used for determining losses from censorship, and an additional indication of audience demographics. "The enclosed list [unfortunately not included in the court transcript] shows that .0142 percent of our national volume goes into the State of Virginia, and therefore, when your picture 'Pepepeto' was eliminated by the censor board in Virginia, .0142 percent of the cost of the negative was lost to us, or $17.75," McNamara wrote. "Inasmuch as we were unable to exhibit this picture in that state, we feel that a credit amount of $17.75 is due to our company from your company for this particular picture in the State of Virginia."

Despite the reported popularity of Black-cast Soundies in Norfolk, the .0142 percent figure suggests that Virginia was not a Soundies hot spot. But other states with active censorship boards, such as Ohio, Pennsylvania, and New York—where *Stand Up for Your Rights* was banned—clearly were. As McNamara wrote, "The enclosed list shows a total loss to us based on the above formula of $539.04, and of course, does not include our loss resulting from the purchase of positive prints, which we were ultimately unable to use, nor have we asked you for credit to reimburse us for the many other charges such as re-recording, shipping, censorship fees, etc., to which we would ordinarily be entitled."[38] Under the formula that McNamara applied, excluding Virginia, censorship of L.O.L. films had cost the Soundies Corporation more than $500 in losses, most of it presumably in the high-traffic states that Ulcigan had named: New York, Ohio, and Pennsylvania.

Film historian Ellen C. Scott has conducted detailed research in the censorship of Black-cast Soundies. Based on a review of censorship records for Maryland, New York, Ohio, Pennsylvania, and Virginia, she found that these states were more likely to censor Black-cast Soundies than white-cast ones. L.O.L.'s nine censored Soundies shrink in significance against Scott's totals: some 175 Soundies (out of approximately 1,880) were censored in one form or another, and of these 58—roughly a third of the total—feature Black performers. This is a high number, considering that only 325 or so Soundies in total feature Black performers. Scott found that in some states the percentage of censored Black-cast Soundies was much higher—more than half the Soundies censored in Ohio, for instance. Certain performers were censored frequently, including Louis Jordan and Vanita Smythe (six apiece), Dorothy Dandridge and Mable Lee (five apiece), and three each for Lucky Millinder and Noble Sissle.[39]

Clearly, from a censorship perspective, there were commercial risks in producing films with Black performers. The fact that the Soundies Corporation continued to produce them is one more indication that the audiences for these films were a valuable market segment. It also suggests that the gains from producing the films would have offset the problems posed by their censorship in some states.

Too, Soundies had a flexibility in dealing with state censorship systems that Hollywood studios, bound by federal censorship, did not. On paper, the Soundies Corporation took censorship seriously. "Before any Soundies film is released to operators it is first sent out to censorship boards in Ohio, New York, Pennsylvania, Virginia, Maryland, Kansas, Chicago and Kansas City—all the boards there are," *Billboard* wrote in 1944. "If these boards demand any changes they are made before [the] film is released to operators, but should the film fail to pass any of the boards it is then scrapped."[40] In reality, things played out differently. Censored films were routinely included in the weekly reels and listed in the Soundies catalog, along with a fine-print, front-of-book disclaimer.[41] Several Louis Jordan Soundies, for example, were censored in at least one of the states Scott investigated, yet they were not only included in the weekly reels but compiled into two separate medleys rereleased in later reels. While it's possible that deletions were made to accommodate censors' rulings, there are no obvious cuts in the versions of these films that appear online.

It's likely that the Soundies Corporation developed a range of strategies for evading censorship and its enforcement. For one thing, the sheer volume of Soundies releases could be overwhelming. Based on its full case load—Soundies included—the Maryland censorship board, for one, required an emergency budget to keep functioning.[42] "The vast number of films submitted by the Soundie concern, indeed, made for so much paperwork that it is difficult to trust existing data," Scott writes.[43] Given the avalanche of submissions—and the fact that censorship inspectors didn't always check screening locations other than movie theaters—in all probability the Soundies Corporation could slip films past censors with relative ease. Even in states that censored fewer films, repeated submission of the same films could jam the docket: according to Scott, the Dorothy Dandridge Soundie *Yes, Indeed!* (Coslow-Murphy, 1941) was submitted to the New York board no fewer than forty-two times. While approval was pending, the film may well have completed its Panoram run.

Long after the Soundies Corporation settled with the musicians' union in late 1943, budget continued to drive production. Nothing but thousands more Panorams in commercial operation could have changed that. Filmmaking was hamstrung in the critical ways described earlier, but for Black performers the constraints opened opportunities that might not have emerged under other circumstances.

With rehearsal and shooting time cut to a minimum, Soundies producers increasingly counted on performers to furnish material for filming, usually from their own live acts. Bare-bones storylines and minimal directorial input often encouraged actors to improvise, enabling many to sidestep stereotypes in favor of more authentic portrayals. With pressure to make the most of already standing sets, nightclubs and city living rooms became default backdrops in many Black-cast films, further nudging on-screen demographics toward the urban. And if, as Crouch's comment in the trial transcript suggests, Black performers were paid less, that situation—though hardly an advantage—might have encouraged producers to make more Black-cast Soundies.

Editorially, the budget pinch often translated into longer takes, simpler cutting, and in many cases less mediation (or interference) in the documentation of performances, especially in Crouch's lightning-fast productions. In some instances the footage itself ended up in more than one film. Two Skeets Tolbert Soundies, *Blitzkrieg Bombardier* and *'Tis You, Babe* (both Crouch-Crouch, 1945) open with the same wide shot of the musicians performing above a modernistic circular bar. Pianist Pat Flowers's screen presence in *Coalmine Boogie* is faked using shots from one of his previous Soundies, *Dixie Rhythm* (Crouch-Crouch, 1945), and his presence on the soundtrack is also a matter of some debate.[44]

Songs in the public domain, available without licensing fees, were given inventive updates. In *Rocco Blues* (Crouch-Crouch, 1943), Maurice Rocco does a boogie piano version of the traditional Irish tune "Molly Malone," and Pat Flowers puts a similar spin on "Oh, Susannah" and "Loch Lomond" in *Dixie Rhythm* and *Scotch Boogie* (both Crouch-Crouch, 1945). In *Swanee Swing* (Crouch-Crouch, 1944), harpist LaVilla Tullos does the same for Stephen Foster's "Old Folks at Home."

According to Crouch's testimony, the companies making Soundies had considerable creative autonomy. Production houses like L.O.L. not only chose the songs and talent for their films but determined the cinematic treatments, settings, and story lines. Soundies Corporation executives reviewed the proposed film lineups and song lyrics, and in extreme cases—as with *Plenty of King*—might reject a finished film.[45] But as long as producers turned in acceptable work on deadline, the creative decision-making was largely in their hands. This was critical to the development of Black-cast Soundies. On the most basic level, it meant that filmmakers who were interested in working with Black talent could do so, and it gave the filmmakers leeway to experiment with how Black performers were presented on screen.

LEANING TOWARD TELEVISION

Despite modest budgets and speedball schedules, Soundies producers understood that, theoretically at least, they weren't just condensing and recycling standard Hollywood fare but making something new. "The Soundie, unlike the regular movie, has to get itself over with the public inside of three minutes, instead of an hour or two," declared the sales booklet for prospective Panoram operators. "It is very much different, too, from the fifteen-minute movie short which you have seen in your theatre. All movies, heretofore, were created with the intention of being seen only once by the same persons . . . Soundies must be so good, so rich in fast and concentrated action and meaning, that the same persons may want to see the very same film fifty or more times!"[46]

What "so good, so rich" actually looked like on celluloid was left to individual filmmakers to figure out. Shot in 35 mm but released in 16 mm, Soundies were created, first and foremost, for the Panoram.[47] Even so, it took months of trial and error to discover what really worked on the small screen or, more to the point, what didn't. One early misfire, *Grand Pianos and Gals* (Feher-unknown, 1941), was a white-cast, Hollywood musical–style extravaganza that demonstrated all too clearly its minimal budget and the ant-like effect of too many performers crowded into the small-scale Panoram frame.

Beyond those limitations, the viewing situation itself called for a fresh approach. Instead of the black box of a movie theater, Soundies were usually viewed in conditions that anticipated television: small-screen, nonimmersive, with life (and beer) going on in the background. In response, Soundies developed a visual aesthetic that also anticipated television. A year after the regular release of Soundies reels began in early 1941, Minoco head Jack Barry described the new approach in *Billboard*. "We have had to tailor our productions with the fact in mind that customers don't give the screen the prolonged concentration they give the theater screen: therefore certain types of intricate treatment are out," he wrote. "Elaborate settings for long shots and intricate routines are just as much out of place as they would be in the intimate night club, where the accent must be on intimate delivery. That's why we've leaned heavily to featuring personalities who have the friendly, intimate, 'be yourself' style of delivery."[48]

The visual language that grew out of this approach also emphasized intimacy and immediacy. Close-ups and medium shots predominate in Soundies, catching performers' faces and their hands during musical solos. With the exception of dancers and women striking pinup poses, full-body shots are relatively rare. Again foreshadowing television, Soundies deliberately undercut the "fourth wall" of classical Hollywood cinema—the illusion of a self-contained cinematic universe, separate from the audience. In many cases, performers in close-up speak directly to viewers or exchange knowing looks with them through the camera. It's an informality that takes its cue from live performance—the juke joint, the café, the nightclub—rather than the movie screen.

And while this informal approach isn't the only style to emerge in Soundies—big-band numbers, for example, can have an entirely different look and feel—it shows many Black performers to great advantage. Though their individual styles couldn't be more different, pianists Fats Waller, Nat "King" Cole, and Phil Moore share an ability to connect with viewers in relaxed, easygoing rapport (fig. 2.2). Cab Calloway's expressive mugging to the camera in films like *The Skunk Song* (Barry/Waller-Snody, 1942) and Maxine Sullivan's spoken thanks to the audience at the start of *Some of These Days* (Barry/Waller-Primi, 1942) underscore Black performers' contributions to this evolving presentation mode and its "friendly, intimate, 'be yourself' style of delivery."

This approach parallels a performance style that emerged in early television, which placed a similar premium on informality and direct address. The nascent television industry, underway by the late 1930s, was seriously sidetracked by the war.[49] That was something of a lifesaver for Soundies, which in those years saw little competition for its small-screen entertainment niche.[50] With respect to television, Soundies may have functioned as something of a performance laboratory, where entertainers accustomed to live presentation could hone their screen personas and their skill in playing to the camera in the intimate style that Soundies favored.[51] That approach transitioned well to television, and Soundies stars Nat "King" Cole and Bob Howard are among the Black performers who hosted musical-variety shows on broadcast television in the 1940s and 1950s.[52] But even as Soundies paralleled television in some important respects, they diverged in others. Film theorist Amy Herzog has written of Soundies' ability to evoke a "strange amalgam of intimacy and longing in a public setting,"[53] more akin to jukebox play than television viewing. She also cites the films' affinity for an "affective excess that makes the stereotype resonate differently" and transforms the usual cultural clichés into "springboard[s] for new associations."[54] These characteristics emerge in several Black-cast Soundies, from the poignant over-interpretation of song lyrics that Herzog describes in *Paper Doll* (Coslow-Berne, 1942) to the casual subversion of Hollywood-musical conventions in *Shoeshiners and Headliners* (Feher-unknown, 1941).

When commercial broadcasting resumed in earnest in 1946, bars and taverns were among the first venues to install TV sets.[55] With its continuous programming, television brought a qualitative change to the barroom environment, converting patrons into audiences with little control over their viewing or listening experiences. But commercial television's wartime slowdown had given Panoram Soundies the space to define, on its own terms, what moving-image entertainment looked like outside the movie theater. Black-cast Soundies figured significantly in this cinematic landscape, in a way that set Soundies apart

Figure 2.2. Connecting with viewers (*from top*): Fats Waller in *Ain't Misbehavin'* (1941); Nat "King" Cole in *Got a Penny, Benny* (1946); Phil Moore in *The Chair Song* (1946). Courtesy Mark Cantor Archive.

from Hollywood and suggested a direction that postwar television might—and to some extent did—follow.

From the Soundies Corporation's industrial beginnings through the spectacularly bumpy ride that followed, the commercial constraints that defined Soundies as a business also shaped it aesthetically. Ironically, those economic challenges created not only opportunities for Black performers but a cultural space for rethinking the depiction of Black people on screen. Manufacturing limitations and other economic exigencies meant that Soundies had to be produced cheaply; razor-thin profit margins encouraged the use of less expensive talent; and the need to fill eight slots per week gave producers broad latitude in their choice and presentation of performers. Individual Soundies filmmakers brought a range of styles and sensibilities to their work with Black talent, and each of them left a distinct imprint on Black-cast Soundies as a whole. The overlapping career paths of these makers—particularly the first and the most prolific among them—piece together a more intimate history of Black-cast Soundies production, and a more granular perspective on racial attitudes in 1940s America and the dynamics of change.

3

STARTING IN HOLLYWOOD,
HEADING TO HARLEM

AS WILLIAM FOREST CROUCH STATED in his L.O.L. court testimony, Soundies filmmakers had considerable creative power over their productions, including the choice of talent. Pinched budgets and a relentless weekly schedule made this autonomy a virtual necessity. Close to thirty producers and directors worked on Black-cast Soundies at one point or another, including several who were instrumental in shaping the business—producers who, in addition to making their own films, supervised other filmmakers and production companies on behalf of the Soundies Corporation. Each of them had a distinct approach to depicting Black people on screen, and a strong impact on the films they supervised.

Their history is studded with contradictions. Cosmopolitan filmmakers sometimes produced films with racist themes and imagery, and progressive work was done by makers whose other films were objectionable and worse. Chronology doesn't always figure into it either: some of the most forward-looking Soundies were made early on, and racist imagery recurs late in the game. On the whole, New York City was more progressive in its production than Los Angeles, but racist stereotypes turn up in a few New York–made films, and some classic Soundies—like Duke Ellington's *Jam Session* (Coslow-Berne, 1942)—were made in LA. Other factors included performers' involvement in the creative decision-making, and how closely a finished film aligned with their sensibilities. In this, *Jam Session* and the other Ellington Soundies are a useful case in point. They also introduce the earliest figure in Black-cast Soundies production, Sam Coslow.

49

Coslow became production head for the Soundies Corporation in late 1940 after James Roosevelt's abrupt exit as hands-on producer. A few months later he began producing Black-cast Soundies. A long-time Tin Pan Alley tunesmith, Coslow had spent more than a decade as a contract songwriter for Paramount before branching into producing with the low-end comedy feature *Dreaming Out Loud* (1940). He had also taken up some of the production slack when Roosevelt's Globe Productions fell behind, making Soundies through his own companies, Cameo Films and Century Productions. For Coslow, Soundies offered an unconventional but appealing leap up the producing ladder. He became a partner in RCM—the production company that succeeded Globe as the Soundies Corporation's main West Coast supplier—and the nominal head of Soundies production on both coasts. Coslow personally produced dozens of films and supervised dozens more. He readily exploited his industry connections on Soundies' behalf: the *Los Angeles Times*, for instance, is dotted with quick items about his hires at RCM and the Soundies they were producing.

A prolific songwriter, Coslow was comfortable with pop-culture clichés and stereotypes, including blackface. Under his leadership Black-cast Soundie production had a stumbling start. The first, *Swing for Your Supper* (Coslow-Berne, 1941), was produced by Coslow's own company, Cameo Films. It was copyrighted in April 1941, soon after RCM began regular film production in January. The first RCM-produced Black-cast films didn't appear until that November and December. Produced by Coslow, they were directed by Dudley Murphy, and in one case by Murphy and Josef Berne.

An inventive, independent-minded filmmaker who'd been active since the silent era, Murphy had his own difficult relationship with Hollywood, swerving in and out of the studios without scoring the hit that would have cinched his status in the industry. From his earliest silent-era shorts, Murphy had used music to structure his films, a strategy that culminated in *Ballet mécanique* (1924), the avant-garde classic that he made with artists Man Ray and Fernand Léger. A sophisticate with cosmopolitan tastes, Murphy admired Black performers, preferred New York to Los Angeles, and enjoyed Harlem nightlife. He was the director and prime mover behind Bessie Smith's only film, *St. Louis Blues*, and Duke Ellington's sound-film debut (opposite a luminous Fredi Washington) in *Black and Tan* (both 1929). Murphy was the driving force in bringing *The Emperor Jones* (1933) to the screen, putting his career on the line to direct Paul Robeson in what was arguably his strongest movie role. The film was a critical success but stumbled at the box office: in 1933, making a Black actor—even one of Robeson's stature and magnetism—the sole star of a Hollywood movie was a high-stakes gamble. Murphy's industry fortunes never recovered, and his Soundies stint was one of the last stops in his film career.[1] He didn't last long at RCM, but of the ten Soundies he directed, five starred or featured Black performers, initiating a period of more regular Black-cast production at RCM.

Overall, a small fraction of the Black-cast Soundies were produced in Los Angeles—approximately seventy, little more than one-fifth the total—and Coslow figured prominently in that output. Close to half of the West Coast Black-cast Soundies were copyrighted during his tenure, from 1940 to 1942, and of those, Coslow himself produced or executive-produced all but two. On these films and others, his most frequent collaborator was director Josef Berne.

The Russian-born Berne (né Bernstein) was no Hollywood insider. Working on the fringes of the industry, his pre-Soundies projects included the lyrical art-house short *Dawn to Dawn* (1933) and a Yiddish-language feature, *Mirele Efros* (1938).[2] His only studio film, done for MGM, was the short *Gypsy Night* (1935), an early experiment with three-strip Technicolor.[3] Very little in Berne's background suggests the dexterity he brought to Soundies or his adroit pivots from one musical genre to another. Berne directed roughly 290 Soundies, making him second only to Crouch in productivity and easily beating Crouch in years spent as a Soundies maker.[4] Berne's output included more than forty-five Black-cast titles—not only Duke Ellington's but several with Dandridge, June Richmond, and the Counts and the Countess, among others. Crouch, like Coslow, valued Berne's versatility and finesse, and in 1945 he had Berne direct several Soundies in New York, including four by the vocal trio Day, Dawn, and Dusk.[5] But the bulk of Berne's directing was done in Los Angeles, most of it with Coslow as producer.

In the early days of Soundies expectations were high, and Coslow booked some of the top names in the business, including the Mills Brothers and Louis Armstrong, whose signing was hailed with a brief item in the *Los Angeles Times*.[6] Coslow immediately recognized Dandridge's star potential, producing seven sessions' worth of Soundies with her in 1941 and 1942. But the Black-cast films made under his supervision veer wildly from modern, sophisticated depictions to tone-deaf stereotypes. Coslow and Berne might cast Dandridge as a vivacious co-ed type in *Swing for Your Supper*, then jam her into a barely-there "native" outfit for the stereotype-laden *Jungle Jig* (Coslow-Berne, 1941)—and again the next year in *Congo Clambake* (Coslow-Berne, 1942). On the other hand, the two were also responsible for the exquisitely off-kilter *Paper Doll* (Coslow-Berne, 1942) and the Ellington Soundies. Coslow had worked with Ellington at Paramount in 1934, and the Soundies they made together are among Coslow's most progressive. This is in large part due to Ellington, whose five films—including two adapted from his 1941 musical revue, *Jump for Joy*—exemplify the power of performers' creative involvement in their Soundies.[7]

Despite his production experience Coslow was above all a song writer, and his films underscore a basic rule of Soundies construction: the song comes first. Ellington numbers aside, Coslow's choice of material at times reflected Hollywood's thinking about Black people—there's not much to do with a song like "Jungle Jig" other than choose not to use it. To some degree Coslow's song picks also reflected the contingencies, economic and otherwise, that influenced Soundies production and gave it such an improvised air: the sometimes prohibitive costs of music licensing, the need to maximize the use of already constructed sets, and Coslow's film- and music-industry connections, among other factors.

Too, the films that Coslow supervised were made in 1941 and 1942, before and just after the United States entered the war. At that point the era's social and economic shifts were only beginning to make themselves felt, and wartime Black activism had not yet achieved its full impact. Los Angeles was a factor too. Despite being the world's moviemaking capital and the center of a vibrant art and literary scene, in the early 1940s LA was not particularly cosmopolitan in its thinking about race relations. Its Black population in 1940 was a demographic sliver: not quite sixty-four thousand, or 4.2 percent, in a city of roughly 1.5 million.[8] As the war continued, the booming aircraft industry substantially increased the city's non-white population, but Los Angeles remained, as historian Carey McWilliams put it, "a bad town for Negroes."[9]

Given their own sensibilities, their connections to major studios, and the movie industry's covertly watchful eye, Coslow and his RCM colleagues weren't the likeliest filmmakers to question the prevailing depiction of Black people on screen. Many of them, Coslow included, eventually returned to the studios, and a few went on to careers in television. But by mid-1941, a change in production was already underway. Months before RCM debuted its first Black-cast Soundie in late fall 1941, the locus of production for the Black-cast films had already moved to New York.

SHIFTING THE FRAME

Expanding Soundies' production capacity in New York had an enormous impact on the Black-cast films. Between the city's nightclubs and theaters and the East Coast's big-band touring circuit, New York Soundies makers had a large pool of talent to work with. There were more major cities in the Northeast, upper Midwest, and eastern seaboard states, with arguably more audiences interested in Black performers—a supposition supported by Ulcigan's testimony in the L.O.L. court case. From New York to Pittsburgh to Chicago, a network of Black newspapers reported on Soundies performers and productions. Even *Billboard*, the music-industry bible, was published in Cincinnati. More East Coast Soundies producers were inclined to work with Black performers, and they brought a distinctly non-Hollywood sensibility to their presentation of Black people on screen.

Even so, production of Black-cast Soundies in New York got off to a slow start. The independent start-up Cinemasters, briefly engaged as the Soundies Corporation's New York production house, made no films featuring African American talent. Within weeks of its January 1941 start date, Cinemasters was out and Minoco Productions, the newly created Mills Novelty affiliate, took over as the principal East Coast Soundies producer. That summer, John F. "Jack" Barry was announced as Minoco's new president.

Barry was a veteran studio executive with more than fifteen years at Paramount's office in New York, and his Soundies team brought a cosmopolitan perspective to Minoco's production slate. Barry had been with the company from its first recording session in February 1941, but it wasn't until he took over that Minoco began producing films with Black performers. Within weeks, the company copyrighted the Charioteers' *Swing for Sale* (Barry/Waller-Snody, 1941), quickly followed by three more films by the group. October 1941 saw six Black-cast Soundies copyrighted, with another eight appearing in November. This burst roughly coincided with Crouch's first months as a production and promotion executive with the Soundies Corporation. He might have encouraged it, but the initiative was most likely Barry's—the copyright date on *Swing for Sale* is August 11, roughly a month after Barry took charge at Minoco and a month before Crouch came on board in Chicago.

Minoco's talent roster reflects the company's interest in working with Black entertainers. Cab Calloway and Count Basie made multiple Soundies with Minoco, as did Fats Waller, Lucky Millinder, and, as Millinder's vocalist, Sister Rosetta Tharpe (fig. 3.1). In a January 1942 *Billboard* article, Barry described a Minoco poll of Panoram operators and customers to pick the top fifty bandleaders to feature in that year's Soundies.[10] Calloway, Waller, Basie, and Millinder made the list, along with Les Hite—who, though mainly based in Los Angeles, made his four Soundies in New York with Minoco.

Like Coslow at RCM, Barry had a hand in most of Minoco's Black-cast Soundies. More than Coslow or Crouch, Barry understood Soundies as a distinct form with its own visual and performance aesthetics, much of which anticipated early television. In an era when the biggest movie palaces seated two thousand or more, Barry made a direct connection between the Panoram's more intimate viewing arrangement—"the fact that the movie audience is within 25 feet of the

Figure 3.1. Two from Minoco (*from top*): Sister Rosetta Tharpe and bandleader Lucky Millinder in *Four or Five Times*; Fats Waller and Vivian Brown in *Ain't Misbehavin'* (both 1941). Library of Congress, Motion Picture, Broadcasting and Recorded Sound Division (*top*); courtesy Mark Cantor Archive (*bottom*).

screen at all times"—and the need for a warmer, more informal performance style that acknowledged and included the viewer.[11]

Barry frequently served as executive producer on Minoco Soundies, working with Fred Waller (no relation to Fats). A producer and inventor who at one time ran the special-effects department at Paramount, Fred Waller had also directed musical shorts there in the 1930s and had worked with Calloway and Ellington—including directing Ellington's 1935 short, *Symphony in Black: A Rhapsody of Negro Life*.[12] Waller's ease with cinematic effects is evident in the cross-fades and other optical treatments used throughout that film. In Soundies, Fats Waller's relaxed, raucously ad lib performances, polished set pieces like Calloway's *Blues in the Night* (Barry/Waller-Snody, 1941), and the comic romance *Hark! Hark! The Lark* (Waller-Snody, 1941) reflect Fred Waller's expertise and low-key style. As producers, Barry and Waller worked with a circle of directors that included Warren Murray, John Primi, and Robert Snody, who directed more than twenty Black-cast films for Minoco.

Though rural scenes aren't unheard of, Minoco's urban sensibility is immediately apparent in its Soundies, communicated through everything from settings—nightclubs, street corners, tenement back yards—to performance styles. As with RCM, there are serious missteps. Minoco was the only Soundies producer to routinely open each film with its own live-action company credit, and racist stereotypes turn up in some of the openings and occasionally in the films themselves. For the most part, though, under Barry's leadership Minoco pushed Black-cast Soundies in another direction, tilting the on-screen demographics toward a sophisticated urbanity. Coming early in Soundies' history, the Minoco films were essential in portraying Black-cast heterosexual romance, in moving Soundies away from the classic Hollywood performance style and encouraging performers' direct engagement with the audience in the "be yourself" approach that Barry championed.

ON-THE-JOB TRAINING

For Black-cast Soundies, Crouch was the key figure in the Soundies Corporation lineup, from his stint in the corporate hierarchy (1941 through 1943) to his years as a producer and director (1942 to early 1947). As the company's production and promotion manager, he had the crucial task of programming the weekly reels that played in most Panoram locations. When the federal government halted wartime manufacture of Panoram machines in spring 1942, followed by the musicians' strike that summer, the Soundies Corporation temporarily shut down production in Los Angeles and New York. Coslow, Berne, and RCM production manager Ben Hersh relocated to Chicago in summer 1942, but their time there was brief and produced few films. By autumn, all three were back in LA.[13] At that point Crouch expanded into filmmaking himself. "Because of the current record ban," read a note in a February 1943 issue of *Billboard*, "most of the Soundies are no longer made by Sam Coslow, of RCM, and Jack Barry, of Minoco." Instead, said *Billboard*, they were produced "by Soundies itself, under the direction of William C. [*sic*] Crouch, its publicity head."[14]

Even for Crouch, producing in Chicago apparently held little appeal. Days after the February announcement, *Billboard* reported that "Crouch is now in his third week in New York producing shorts," observing that "so far the most successful . . . were those of Louis Jordan and his band."[15] Once he started filming in New York, Crouch never again produced a Soundie in Chicago, though he continued to work there in an executive capacity, splitting his time between Chicago and New York through 1943.[16] He then turned to producing and directing Soundies full time. An old studio at 2826 Decatur Avenue in the Bronx—built in 1907 by Thomas Edison to house his film company—became his production headquarters until Soundies folded in early 1947.

While Crouch was producing under the Soundies label, he was also making Soundies through his own company, WFC Productions, also based at the Bronx studio. In autumn 1943, after the Soundies Corporation settled with the musicians' union, Crouch set up Filmcraft, a successor to WFC Productions, which produced the bulk of the Black-cast Soundies. After months of dwindling involvement, in January 1944 Jack Barry left Minoco and the company dissolved.

For Black-cast Soundies, Crouch's shift from corporate management to full-time production was the most significant realignment to come out of the economic reversals of 1942. The transition took several months, but almost immediately he became the de facto producer for Black-cast films. On the West Coast, RCM's new production head, Ben Hersh, turned out a scant thirty-six of them between 1943 and 1946, roughly a fifth of Crouch's output in that time. Admittedly, numbers don't tell the full story, and production values on the West Coast films usually beat Crouch's conveyor-belt aesthetics by a wide margin. Even so, Crouch's output ensured a steady supply of Soundies starring Black performers.

But his segue into New York production meant that Crouch was no longer working directly with Soundies Corporation executives in Chicago and, at some point, no longer programming the weekly reels. As we'll see, that change brought its own complications for the distribution of Black-cast Soundies.

As a filmmaker, Crouch differed from his fellow production heads in a few significant respects. For one, he had virtually no Hollywood production

Figure 3.2. William Forest Crouch on location at an amusement park in New Orleans, filming the Soundie *They Go Wild (Simply Wild Over Me)* (1945) with white bandleader Lawrence Welk and His Orchestra. Courtesy Bruce Lawton & The Malkames Collection. Film frame scan generated by Helge Bernhardt.

experience—a fact that the aggrieved L.O.L. producer-director Arthur Leonard was quick to point out in his court testimony.[17] With Soundies production Crouch more or less learned on the job, and it shows. Many of his films lack the polish that came naturally to Coslow and his West Coast colleagues. But Crouch was a master of the assembly-line Soundie, cranking them out at an impressive rate, and in this, the lack of professional training was arguably a plus. His technical standards were notably lower than his colleagues', particularly in matters of sound and picture sync. Some of his films have a streak of gleeful anarchy, particularly in the use of optical effects, notably absent from the more polished productions. Nor was his output limited to Black-cast Soundies. By the time production ended in late 1946, Crouch had produced and/or directed more than 550 films, Black-cast Soundies included—almost 30 percent of the entire Soundies Corporation catalog, created over roughly three years (fig. 3.2).

But Black-cast films were clearly a focus. Crouch produced, executive-produced, and/or directed 169, more than half the total. "Bill Crouch has very set ideas on the Negro's place in the entertainment field," as a 1945 profile in the *New York Amsterdam News* stated. "He feels that the real history of the Negro has yet to be told on the screen and is right now planning to do what he can to get it there. . . . Crouch's tolerance and fair-mindedness have earned for him wide respect."[18]

At the same time, his sensibility was undeniably raunchy. Under Crouch's direction, the usual cheesecake leg-and-torso shots often became crotch shots, especially when high kicks were involved (though rarely, it should be said, in the Black-cast films, probably due to censorship concerns). What most emphatically distinguished Crouch from his production-head colleagues was his interest in bringing Black talent into play behind the scenes as well as before the camera. On his watch, Black-cast Soundies production became increasingly anchored in the Harlem entertainment community, thanks in large part to the involvement of two men: Fritz Pollard and William D. Alexander.

A TASTE FOR MOVIEMAKING

In casting, rehearsing, filming, and possibly distribution, one of Crouch's most consistent collaborators was Frederick Douglass "Fritz" Pollard. A legendary All-America college halfback and, in the 1920s, the first Black head coach in the NFL, Pollard was a well-connected figure in the New York sports and entertainment communities. He was a close friend of Paul Robeson in their college football years, and in 1933 was Robeson's assistant during the filming of *The Emperor Jones* at the former Paramount Studio in Astoria, Queens. The experience gave Pollard a taste for moviemaking. In 1938 he attempted to set up a film company, Negro Productions Ltd., with white production manager John Doran, who had run the Astoria studio.[19] But financial backing was a problem, and by the early 1940s Pollard was associated with Black theatrical producer and choreographer Leonard Harper in Sun Tan Studio, an audition and rehearsal space on 125th Street in Harlem.[20] Harper died suddenly in early 1943, and coverage of his funeral made the front page of the *Amsterdam News* (greatly overshadowed by news of a brutal lynching in Georgia). A delegation of musicians and composers, including Andy Kirk, J. C. Johnson, and W. C. Handy, reportedly asked Pollard to continue with Sun Tan Studio, and Pollard agreed.[21] The *New York Amsterdam News* story on Harper's funeral closed with the announcement that at Sun Tan, choreographer and revue stager Llewelyn Crawford, "apt pupil of Leonard Harper, would carry on as usual."[22]

With Pollard as its director, Sun Tan Studio quickly became a pivotal part of Crouch's production system, and the *New York Amsterdam News* began covering Soundies in earnest. Noting Crouch's intention "to form a complete album of current Negro talent" in Soundies, an August 1943 article reported that "through Mr. Crouch, the Sun Tan Studios, 217 W. 125th Street, has charge of the casting."[23] Pollard acted as a talent scout for the films, and Sun Tan Studio functioned as an off-site casting office, audition hall, and rehearsal space. Noting that songwriters Andy Razaf ("Ain't Misbehavin'," "We Are Americans Too") and Porter Granger ("Tain't Nobody's Business If I Do") were on staff at the studio, the article concluded that "any incipient talent may readily be developed there."[24] With Sun Tan as its preproduction staging area, filming at Soundies' Bronx facility could continue without interruption, a necessity given the manic production schedule. Crouch's connections undoubtedly extended beyond Pollard and Sun Tan—managers at various nightclubs, for instance, may have supplied dancers for some films—but the Black press continued to link Sun Tan and Soundies. "Fritz Pollard is major domo of Harlem's part in the Soundies now," the *Chicago Defender* wrote in 1944, and Soundies like *The Pollard Jump* and *Sun Tan Strut* (both Crouch-Crouch, 1946) reflect the close connection between his operations and the Soundies organization.[25] Pollard himself appears as the pianist in both films.[26]

According to biographer John M. Carroll, Pollard's involvement with Soundies may have extended further. In August 1942, Carroll writes, Pollard joined the Soundies Corporation as its New York regional manager, overseeing Panorams in "saloons, pool halls, hotels, and restaurants in both Black and white neighborhoods of New York."[27] There is scant corroboration on this point—even the *New York Amsterdam News* didn't frame the relationship in those terms—but it is possible. As the Soundies Corporation's New York manager, Pollard would have been a one-man feedback loop between production and distribution, doing what Crouch had done on his early fact-finding tours: meeting Panoram operators and location owners, working to place more machines in venues, gathering responses to films and performers, and gauging their popularity with various clientele. That information would have been quickly put to use at Sun Tan Studio and the Bronx production facility. Pollard may have had a financial interest in the Soundies enterprise, too, at least for a time: years later, he implied that he and other Black stakeholders had been forcibly bought out, though the details were vague.[28] In any case, the working relationship between Pollard and Crouch continued to the end of Soundies' active production period and beyond.

While Pollard and Sun Tan Studio were central to Crouch's filmmaking machine, the secret of his prodigious output may have been his production manager, John Doran. Doran was a well-known figure in the East Coast film world, having run or worked at several New York facilities in the 1930s. He'd been Pollard's partner in his 1938 film company start-up, and it's conceivable that Pollard introduced him to Crouch. Or they might have met through L.O.L. Productions, where Doran had sometimes served as production manager. Doran took over at Soundies' Bronx studio in late 1942 or early 1943, running it, perhaps literally, at a killer pace—the "rotund, jovial" Doran died suddenly in October 1946, at age 63, earning him one of the rare obituaries for whites in the *New York Amsterdam News*.[29] Describing him as "a moving spirit in the campaign to get better roles and conditions for Negroes on the screen," the *News* observed that, through his work with Crouch and Soundies, "Doran lived to see what he wanted—Negro performers getting the breaks in the movies, before he passed."[30] Others on Crouch's team were also vital to his prodigious output: cinematographer Don Malkames, for instance, shot most of Crouch's Black-cast Soundies, as well as race-film shorts and features for other New York producers.

Several titles made in and after 1943 underscore how tightly Soundies production was networked into the 1940s Harlem entertainment community. Soon after Pollard took over at Sun Tan, the studio's choreographer, Llewelyn Crawford, appeared in and likely staged the dance routines for *Backstage Blues* (Crouch-Crouch, 1943)—one of three Soundies that Lynn Albritton made in 1943. An accomplished but relatively little-known Harlem boogie pianist, Albritton had been the accompanist at Leonard Harper's funeral. Other entertainers were also active at Sun Tan and in Soundies. A *New York Amsterdam News* item from August 1943 announced that Crawford and dancer-choreographer "Shim Sham" Sam were ready to assist new talent at Sun Tan, and a photo caption later that year noted that the "dance stylist and teacher" known as "Shim Sham Shimmy" was "making pictures for the Soundies."[31] Choreographers weren't the only talent in demand. The August article also singled out "songs by colored composers" used by Crouch in his Soundies, mentioning five tunes by title and alluding to more.[32]

Several of the songs were attributed to Dan Burley, a well-known Harlem figure and a core staff member at the *Amsterdam News*. At one time or another he filled the roles of entertainment editor, city editor, and sports editor, and he had a regular nightlife column, "Dan Burley's Back Door Stuff," which frequently included Soundies news. Burley was also a musician and songwriter. As a pianist, he recorded with Leonard Feather, Lionel Hampton, and others, as well as with his own group. Burley is the credited songwriter, soundtrack pianist, and probably the music director for five 1946 Soundies starring Vanita Smythe.

In one, *Low, Short and Squatty* (Crouch-Crouch, 1946), he also appears as her accompanist. As a Harlem personality his involvement may have boosted the films' popularity, particularly in New York and East Coast Panoram locations.

A SAVVY REVAMP

Black-cast Soundies production faltered after the war. At that point, Black producer William D. Alexander assumed an influential role in their creation, albeit at arm's length from the Soundies system.

Alexander is an intriguing figure in 1940s documentary film and in the presentation of Black people on screen. During the war he worked for the Office of War Information, producing propaganda films for Black audiences. With two partners—Black producer Claude Barnett and white producer Emanuel M. Glucksman—in 1942 he started a company, All-American News Inc., to produce newsreels for Black movie-house audiences.[33] The company produced newsreels through 1945 and possibly later. According to film historian Spencer Moon, Alexander coproduced more than forty newsreels, and film historian and archivist Pearl Bowser put All-American's total output, produced under Alexander's supervision, at 250.[34] The audience reach was impressive: by one account, All American's weekly newsreels were seen in 365 of an estimated 450 movie theaters serving Black audiences.[35]

Two clips from these newsreels apparently found their way into Soundies. The 1946 Soundies catalog lists them as *All American News #1* and *All American News #2*, but their contents are unknown. While prints of some All-American Newsreels are held by collectors and archives (including the Library of Congress, which has posted more than thirty of them online), no prints of the Soundies excerpted from them are known to exist.[36] There are no copyright or release dates for these two Soundies, but judging by their catalog numbers, they were most likely released between January and September 1943. Although All-American was established to make newsreels, the company also produced shorts and features starring Black entertainers, including *Romance on the Beat*, a 1945 featurette starring Soundies vocalist Ida James. None of the All-American music films were used as source material for Soundies.

By 1945 Alexander may have already left All-American for his own company, Associated Film Producers of Negro Motion Pictures, Inc. In 1946 he made a series of films starring Black musicians, and several were excerpted for Soundies. Six Soundies came from the short film *Rhythm in a Riff*, starring crooner Billy Eckstine, and three were taken from a film on the International Sweethearts of Rhythm, an all-woman big band (figs. 3.3 and 10.3, p. 201).[37] Three more were

Figure 3.3. William D. Alexander with bandleader Anna Mae Winburn of the International Sweethearts of Rhythm. Collection of the Smithsonian National Museum of African American History and Culture, Gift of Pearl Bowser.

excerpted from *Lucky Millinder and His Orchestra,* and another four were taken from *Love in Syncopation,* a short film featuring Henri Woode and his band.

Alexander is the sole Black producer on the Soundies roster, and his business relationship with the Soundies Corporation appears to have been a savvy revamp of the usual arrangement between the company and its producer-suppliers. Though he solicited feedback from Soundies executives, Alexander apparently produced his projects without advance payment or support from the Soundies Corporation.[38] He then clipped musical numbers from his films and packaged them as individual Soundies, which he sold to the Soundies Corporation. (The opening credit for the Soundie *Jump Children,* for instance, identifies it as "An Alexander Production.") It was a smart arrangement, particularly in light of Soundies' worsening postwar finances. Members of Crouch's production team, including cinematographer Don Malkames, worked with Alexander on his productions, ensuring a smooth transition from the full-length film to excerpted Soundies. According to Alexander's assistant, Harryette Miller Barton—one of the few Black women in film production at the time—Soundies and the shorts they were taken from "helped to pay the rent and salaries" for the company, being "quick, easy to set up, and requir[ing] little or no costuming."[39] Soundies distribution also extended the films' reach to audiences beyond the race-film theaters where the full-length versions would have played. At the same time, Alexander's filmmaking was a real advantage for Soundies at a point when high-quality production was badly needed. His sixteen Soundies represent more than a quarter of the Black-cast titles copyrighted in 1946. They bring a distinctive style to the postwar Soundies output, emphatically foregrounding the music, the bands, and their musicianship.

The acquisition of Alexander's Soundies was negotiated by Soundies Corporation vice president George Ulcigan (who, in a name change, was then known as George Allen). It was most likely Ulcigan/Allen who programmed the weekly reels after Crouch moved into production. His input, and that of regional operators and other home-office executives in Chicago, had significant consequences for Soundies distribution. Even while Crouch was presumably still involved, the handling of Black-cast Soundies started to shift in ways that complicate our understanding of the films and their audiences.

MORE FILMS, FEWER SCREENS: THE M FILM CONUNDRUM

As we've seen, very little in Soundies' history runs in a straight line, and the distribution of the Black-cast films is a stellar case in point. It throws into high relief the racial climate of the era and the cultural environment in which Black-cast Soundies were produced and presented.

Three Soundies catalogs published between 1941 and 1946 offer a basic outline of events. After *Swing for Your Supper* was copyrighted on May 5, 1941, Black-cast Soundies steadily gained ground in the weekly lineups. A Soundie with Black performers appeared in one reel per month in June, July, and August; in September, three of the weekly reels included Black-cast films.[40] Then, starting in October 1941 and continuing into 1945, nearly every weekly reel included at least one Black-cast Soundie. Several reels, notably the late 1941 releases, had two.

It's reasonable to assume that this jump in production was at least partly market driven, and that the reels with two Black-cast films were popular among urban audiences, especially in core markets in the Northeast. But they inspired furious pushback elsewhere. In a January 1942 letter to Minoco head Jack Barry, Ulcigan praised the Black-cast films that Minoco was producing but noted that "in view of the expressions received from [Panoram] operators during the past two months"—when seven out of nine weekly reels included two Black-cast films apiece—"it is definitely concluded to be advisable" to curtail their placement. Most operators were fine with one Black-cast Soundie per week, Ulcigan wrote, but there were a few who, "because of racial prejudice," felt that "they should be limited even more drastically" to one every two weeks. Ulcigan himself considered that extreme—"undue criticism and objection" was the phrase he used—and he attributed it to "the fact that during the past 13 weeks a series of programs were released which, of necessity, contained two such subjects and as high as three."[41]

Placement of Black-cast Soundies remained a hot-button issue through early 1942. "During the last two days we have had three complaints regarding the number of colored subjects in our recent releases," an interoffice memo noted a few days after Ulcigan's letter was sent in mid-January. "All of the operators like at least one colored subject," it continued, but *at least one* didn't mean more than one was okay: "They say that the customers complain when there are two colored subjects in any release."[42]

By mid-February 1942, a maximum of one Black-cast film per reel was the rule and remained so into 1945. But the issue continued to simmer. In March 1942, a letter to the main office in Chicago quoted a district sales manager in Atlanta. "I find that most of our operators are cutting Negro pictures out of the reel and trying to get along the best they can on the shorter reel," the Atlanta manager wrote. "This is one of the hardest things I have to overcome." His tone was apologetic and dire. "I am sorry to have to mention it, but the prejudice in the South is so deep set," he wrote. "You cannot change this prejudice with a hundred million dollars. It will surely wreck us unless we can do something about it."[43]

Already struggling with a too-small network of questionable profitability, the company now faced another potentially ruinous dilemma: the furious objection, by one segment of the market, to films that were moneymaking hits with another. From the documentation in hand, it's hard to discern the scale of the pushback by white Panoram operators and audiences or—other than the Atlanta manager's comments—its geographic extent. But the pressure apparently continued, and the Soundies Corporation was forced to respond. At the same time, the company could not jeopardize its success with the audiences that enjoyed and supported Black-cast films. For a corporate leadership with solid business sense and the ability to make tough decisions, balancing these competing interests would have been a challenge. For the Soundies Corporation—which possessed neither of those qualities in abundance—it was nearly impossible, and the solutions they came up with grew increasingly byzantine.

We can assume that pressure from white Panoram operators continued beyond early 1942, since the first system-wide change was not made until more than a year later. Beginning with Program 1122, copyrighted June 21, 1943, Black-cast films were, with very few exceptions, slotted as the eighth film— usually the final spot on the weekly reel. Occasionally a white-cast film might occupy that position, but after this date, Black-cast films did not appear in any other spot on the weekly reel. The letter quoting the Atlanta sales manager suggests one likely rationale: if Panoram operators were taking it upon themselves to cut Black-cast films from the reels—or if, by that point, regional Soundies distributors were doing it for them—then moving the films to the end of the reels would have made the process easier, with less potential for jamming the machines playing them.

Another change occurred in March 1944. In the Soundies catalog, the Black-cast film listings began to be tagged with a "(C)" after the title (presumably for "colored"). Applied somewhat haphazardly, the (C) designation—like the eighth-slot rule—continued until February 1946. At that point, the Black-cast films vanished entirely from the weekly reels until early 1947.

Before their abrupt disappearance, Black-cast Soundies had been part of virtually every weekly reel. Of the 147 reels released between January 1942 and January 1945, only 12—less than 10 percent—did not include at least one Black-cast Soundie, and the last of these omissions occurred early on, in April 1943.[44] Even the Panoram operators who'd objected most strenuously to two Black-cast films per week had wanted to decrease their frequency, not eliminate them completely.

But the films' near-continuous inclusion in the weekly reels isn't the only factor pointing to Black-cast Soundies' popularity or their importance as a revenue stream. Some time after the eighth-slot positioning came into play, probably in autumn 1943, the Soundies Corporation began releasing individual Black-cast Soundies separate from—and in addition to—the Black-cast films in the weekly reels.

Known as M films, these limited-distribution Soundies were available to Panoram operators by special order. Before 1946, M films were not listed in the Soundies catalog, and operators most likely found out about them through single-sheet notices and catalog inserts. Distribution of M films was inconsistent at first but became more regular in early 1945. An internal Soundies Corporation memo from February 1945 stated that in accordance with the company's "New Victory Plan"—essentially a cost-cutting campaign of rereleasing previous titles—"we will now release a new colored 'Limited Distribution' subject each month," starting with Skeets Tolbert's *Blitzkrieg Bombardier* (Crouch-Crouch, 1945).[45]

A year later, when Black-cast Soundies were dropped from the general-distribution reels, the release of M films was stepped up to compensate. Ten M films were copyrighted in 1945, but there were more than fifty in 1946—roughly the number that would have appeared in the general-release reels that year.

The M films' exclusion from the Soundies catalog ended with its final edition. Published in 1946 as the business was sliding into its death spiral, this catalog was a notable contrast to its predecessors. A hand-typed, makeshift affair riddled with errors, it listed Soundies alphabetically by title, not by weekly reels, with only a numerical code to indicate the program in which a film originally appeared. War-related Soundies were pulled from the main listings into a separate category labeled "Patriotic and Dated." Crucially, for the first time the catalog separated Black-cast Soundies—including the M films—from other titles in a "Negro Alphabetical Index."

The following year brought a final distribution twist: in February 1947, Black-cast Soundies were brought back into the general-release reels, a few weeks before the ultimate collapse in March.

It's a convoluted history and in some ways a confounding one. Until 1946, the M films were extra productions beyond the Black-cast films included in the weekly reels—a means of increasing the number of Black-cast films in circulation. Notably, Black-cast films were the only Soundie category to receive this treatment. At the same time, the M films' separate distribution system, and their exclusion from the Soundies catalogs before 1946, effectively rendered them invisible to Panoram operators who weren't interested in them—and by extension to their audiences. When the Black-cast films were dropped from the general-release reels in 1946, not only the M films but all Soundies starring Black performers would have vanished for mainstream audiences, returning only in the last few reels of 1947.

This was the M film paradox: increased production but narrower distribution, or more films on fewer screens. It points to a market that, beyond multiple overlapping segments, may have bifurcated in one significant respect: audiences that actively sought out, enjoyed, or tolerated Soundies starring Black performers, and those that did not.

It is possible to read the entire chain of decisions regarding Black-cast film distribution as responses to one of these audiences or the other. Locking the films into the final spot on the reel, adding the (C) designation, and splitting off the Negro Alphabetical Index may have made the films more visible to

Panoram operators who were looking for them or, conversely, those looking to avoid them. Similarly, the 1946 decision to drop Black-cast Soundies from the general-release reels may be read as an attempt by the Soundies Corporation to retain a market segment that rejected the films. Or it could be interpreted, more provocatively, as something of a protective maneuver—particularly if Crouch were involved—to remove mainstream tastes as a factor in the films' concept and production.

If this were the case, it's logical to think that a tighter, more focused audience would have increased the M films' use as a space for progressive depictions of Black people. One of the earliest M films persuasively supports this idea: *We Are Americans Too* (Crouch-Crouch, 1943) interprets the Andy Razaf–Eubie Blake–Charles L. Cooke song as an expression of Black patriotism and a demand that Black Americans' contributions be recognized. But the M films as a whole don't support the hypothesis. With few exceptions they're light entertainment and prime examples of straightforward performance documentation. As might be expected, Crouch produced most of the M films, and his preference for plain documentation meshed with the Soundies Corporation's ever-tightening economics. So did the strategy of excerpting performances from existing films: most of William D. Alexander's Soundies, clipped from his musical shorts, were released in 1946 as M films. As previously noted, censorship was a concern for the Soundies Corporation, and Black-cast films were frequent targets. With simpler strategies at its disposal, it's unlikely that evading censorship was the Soundies Corporation's primary rationale for isolating the M films from general distribution, but it may have been a factor.

In the 1946 Soundies catalog, an introductory note about the Negro Alphabetical Index stated that "All Negro subjects have been grouped to facilitate use by operators dealing in Negro material only."[46] Whether the audiences for Black-cast films wanted *only* those films is a matter of speculation, but the films clearly had a market. Its existence is indicated not only by the data discussed in this book's introduction but by the number of Black-cast Soundies that were produced. Between 1943 and 1946, not quite one hundred M films were copyrighted and released in twenty-nine separate series, in addition to approximately 145 Black-cast films included in the weekly reels during the same period. Together these figures represent close to 75 percent of all Black-cast Soundies produced in the company's lifetime, and a significant investment for a struggling business.

What remains in question is the audience that did not want to see these films. Its existence is underscored by the complaints of white Panoram operators in early 1942, and by later measures taken by the Soundies Corporation to isolate the M films and then all Black-cast films from general Soundies markets. But the size and geographic spread of this audience remain a subject of speculation, and it's not unreasonable to think that its impact may have been larger than its demographics. More than one historian has questioned the "myth of the southern box office" and the outsized influence, relative to actual revenue, that the region wielded in Hollywood.[47] Soundies' corporate decision-makers may have been susceptible to this way of thinking, even if the complaints were coming from a vociferous minority. Although it's nearly impossible to ascertain at this point, it would be interesting to know if the company did in fact ship reels with Black-cast Soundies clipped out—and if so, how often, where, and to how many operators. Documentation about M film distribution has yet to emerge, but the films' continued production suggests that they were moneymakers in one way or the other. The likeliest scenario is that they were added, by special order, to standard eight-film reels—at least until 1946, when Black-cast films were dropped from the weekly reels. At that point, it's conceivable that in some markets, one or more white-cast films may have been clipped out and M films added. But without documentation, conjecture about possible custom reels remains just that.

If Soundies audiences did divide along these lines, they would have mirrored a shift underway in the culture itself—particularly in 1943, when the first changes to Black-cast Soundie distribution were made. As the war began, populations long immobilized by the Depression streamed into defense-industry hubs around the country and into the massively expanding armed forces. On both fronts racial and ethnic conflict quickly became a fact of wartime life, and in 1943 these tensions exploded. More than 240 confrontations, from workplace "hate strikes" to full-blown riots, took place that year in close to fifty US cities and towns.[48] In June, a front-page headline in one prominent Black newspaper, the *Pittsburgh Courier*, put it succinctly: "Race Riots Sweep Nation."[49] A united, patriotically committed citizenry remained a national necessity—more so as the war ground on—but as cities large and small became flashpoints for conflict and the country grew increasingly polarized, the concept of national unity was stretched to the breaking point.

Given their position in the pop-culture marketplace, Soundies may have been caught up in these tensions more than either the movie or jukebox industries. Unlike Hollywood movies, Soundies showcased Black performers on a regular basis, in casual viewing situations that encouraged audiences to respond vocally to what they saw on screen. (Too, the blood-alcohol level of movie-house patrons usually didn't rise as they watched a double bill.) Jukeboxes stood in virtually every bar and tavern, but juke customers could select the tunes they wanted to hear, while Panoram viewers were obliged to watch what-ever came next. More than twice as many Black-cast Soundies were released as general-distribution films than as M films—some 225 versus not quite 100—and many Soundies that depicted Black people in terms of city life, romance, patriotism, and success were included in the widely distributed weekly reels. That visibility may have carried a strong element of intent on the part of produ-cers like Crouch and Barry, but the immediate, overriding motivation would have been the unrelenting pressure to fill eight slots per week—Soundies with racist stereotypes ended up on those reels too. The last Soundie to reach the public was an M film: Crouch's cobbled-together *Coalmine Boogie*, released as 29M2 on March 10, 1947.

It's difficult to reconcile the increased production of M films with the increasingly limited distribution of Black-cast Soundies in general. But that conundrum may reflect most clearly the state of American race relations in the 1940s—the sense of incipient change and its vehement denial, the images of competence and sophistication inhabiting a filmic universe still studded with blackface and racist caricature. If the war years were a pivot point in the "long Civil Rights Movement," Soundies chronicled the shift in pop-culture terms and contributed to it. With their comments, reactions, and above all their dimes, the audiences who supported Black-cast Soundies gave clear feedback on what they wanted to see in the films and what they were willing to repeatedly pay for. Shoestring production values and lesser talents took their toll on Soun-dies viewership across the board, and with the war's end commercial television resumed its march. Even so, audiences interested in Black performers remained a broadly underserved market, and the fact that M films were released until the end affirms these viewers as an active market segment. Amid a national climate of racial friction and animosity, Black-cast Soundies continued to be produced in significant numbers and presented to audiences who supported this work.

In the cultural arena of these films, audience is the crucial element: the juncture at which Soundies as a business empowered Soundies as a space for reimagining the presentation of Black people on screen. That juncture brings us to the films themselves: the Soundies that those audiences would have watched on their neighborhood Panoram screens.

PART II

FOLLOW THE MUSIC

4

GOING TO WAR

DESTINED LARGELY FOR TAVERNS AND other leisure-time locales, Soundies were by nature escapist entertainment, and most of the films reflect it. But
World War II was an ever-present reality, and dozens of films in the Soundies
catalog reference it in one way or another. Some support the troops and boost
home-front morale, sell war bonds, or exhort defense workers to stay on the job.
Others take a more entertainment-minded approach, with comic treatments of
military life, wistful ballads about the girl back home, raunchy numbers about
servicemen on leave, and Hitler-bashing sing-alongs.

Almost all of them are white-cast films. For a fact of life so inescapable, the
war makes a surprisingly minor appearance in Black-cast Soundies.

The first Black performer to reference the war is Louis Armstrong, who
serves up a quick sight gag along with his classic tune in *I'll Be Glad When You're
Dead You Rascal You* (Coslow-Berne, 1942). Making sly use of the song's bale-
ful lyrics, late in the film Armstrong aims his smiling ire—usually directed at
a romantic rival—toward a photo spread of Hitler, Mussolini, and Hirohito,
obligingly held up to the camera by pianist Luis Russell (fig. 4.1). *Billboard*
approved. "This one lacks in interest," read the film's capsule review, "until a
newspaper picture of the Axis leaders is flashed while Armstrong emphasizes
the title."[1] In the version later released for television and home-movie use (and
in some videos online), the wartime reference is eliminated. Russell is shown
holding up the newspaper but the shot of the photo, its topicality long gone, is
replaced by a cutaway to the band's drummer.

Figure 4.1. Louis Armstrong scrutinizes Axis leaders in the newspaper as orchestra members look on in *I'll Be Glad When You're Dead You Rascal You* (1942). Courtesy Mark Cantor Archive.

I'll Be Glad was released in July 1942, more than six months after the bombing of Pearl Harbor—a considerable lag, given that twenty-five or more white-cast patriotic Soundies had been released in that time. Even more notable, *I'll Be Glad* is one of only a dozen or so war-related and patriotic Soundies to feature Black performers—less than a tenth of the white-cast Soundies produced on those themes.

Reasons for this scarcity touch on the dynamics of the Soundies marketplace, on 1940s race relations, and the war's impact on the ongoing project of Black advancement. But the films' significance is greater than their numbers might suggest. With them, Soundies acknowledged and made visible Black Americans' contributions to the war effort as the war was going on—a time when those contributions were barely registering in the broader culture, and racial tensions around the country were exploding into conflict. As the war progressed, the handful of Black-cast, war-related Soundies charted an evolution of their own, moving from jokey stereotypes to depictions of wartime life from a Black American perspective.

ON ONE END, A MINSTREL SHOW

The second Black-cast Soundie on a war-related topic was released roughly two months after Armstrong's. *I've Got a Little List* (Coslow/Moulton-Moulton, 1942) is a wartime spin on the tune of the same title from the comic Gilbert and Sullivan operetta *The Mikado*.[2] Comedian Billy Mitchell stars as an admonishing "Lord High Slapper-Downer"—his title spelled out in an arc over his head—reading from a list of those who, per the Gilbert and Sullivan lyrics, "never would be missed." Dressed in white gloves, top hat, and a diplomat's sash and medals, Mitchell stands behind an open book, quill in hand, against a cartoonish sky-and-clouds backdrop. He's flanked by a pair of female scribes who echo his pronouncements from throne-like chairs. (Dorothy Dandridge's sister, Vivian Dandridge, is at frame left.) Mitchell's list is wide ranging, including not only Hitler, Mussolini, and Hirohito, but men who don't enlist, leaving the war for others to fight; war profiteers; speeders with no regard for rubber rationing; and isolationists. Brandishing a gigantic straight razor, he declares (paraphrasing Charles Dickens): "In fact, it would be good riddance to bad garbage."[3]

The film's emphatic list-making stands in sharp contrast to the equivocal situation that the war presented to Black Americans, called on to defend democracy abroad while forcibly denied its benefits at home. As the war began, racial discrimination in America was pervasive, deep, and showed few signs of changing despite the idealized rhetoric of patriotic unity. As the country started rearming and the first peacetime draft in US history got underway in 1940, Black people looking to enlist—which they did by the thousands—met with widespread rejection. The military did not want them.[4] At the time, only forty-seven hundred of the nearly half a million men in the regular army— roughly one percent—were Black. There were no Black servicemen in the Marine Corps, Tank Corps, Signal Corps, or Army Air Corps.[5] In the Navy, Blacks could serve only as messmen: "seagoing bell hops, chambermaids and dishwashers," as one group of sailors bitterly described themselves, only to be dismissed from the service for speaking out.[6] Black people were beaten by soldiers at recruitment offices, barred from officers' training and specialist schools, and routinely segregated from their white counterparts.[7] Blood donated by Black servicemen was not used for white servicemen.[8]

Things were no better on the emerging home front. As factories retooled for defense production and new plants were hastily constructed, manufacturers refused to hire Black workers. "You will find an almost universal prejudice against Negroes—and in the West Coast plants against Jews," *Fortune* magazine reported.[9] The NAACP magazine *The Crisis* put it in more graphic terms. The cover of its July 1940 issue carried a photo of planes on an assembly line stamped FOR WHITES ONLY. "Warplanes—Negro Americans may not build them, repair them, or fly them," the caption read, "but they must help pay for them."[10]

Faced with these realities and the bitter memory of Black Americans' treatment after their unstinting support for World War I, the community's attitudes reflected what historian Richard M. Dalfiume, writing in the late 1960s, calls "a built-in cynicism."[11] An undercurrent of pro-Axis sentiment was sufficiently widespread, he writes, "for the Negro press to make rather frequent mention of it."[12] In a survey of Black Americans, the federal Office of Facts and Figures found that while respondents overwhelmingly abhorred Adolf Hitler and the Nazis, close to 50 percent believed they would fare at least as well, if not better, under Japanese rule because "the Japanese are also colored and, therefore, would not discriminate."[13] For Black people turned away from recruiting offices in 1940 and 1941, Billy Mitchell's comic slap at men who didn't enlist was a cruel joke, but his jab at isolationists may have held a grain of truth.

Job discrimination became a wedge issue. In early 1941, labor leader A. Phillip Randolph announced plans for a July 1 march on Washington by African Americans to demand an end to exclusionary hiring practices. Confronted with the prospect of twenty-five thousand or more demonstrators massing on the Mall, in late June President Roosevelt signed into law Executive Order 8802. The order specified nondiscriminatory employment in companies with government contracts and established the Fair Employment Practices Commission to enforce it. When that had little impact on defense-industry hiring practices, in February 1942 the *Pittsburgh Courier* launched a national Double V campaign, linking the Allies' battle for global democracy with Black Americans' fight for democracy at home. The *Chicago Defender* soon joined with a similar Dual V campaign.

The double-victory movement became a defining aspect of wartime Black American culture, with Double V dances, baseball games, flag-raising ceremonies, and other events held around the country. Women adopted hairstyles and clothing with double Vs worked into their design. Within six months, the *Courier*'s campaign had recruited some two hundred thousand members, many of them actively pressuring their legislators and lobbying local industries for nondiscriminatory hiring. The government slowly exerted its economic clout, channeling lucrative contracts to companies in compliance with federal labor policies, and as the war continued many Black Americans saw their standards of living rise. Enlistment and the draft brought increased numbers into the military, in more branches, though still in segregated noncombat units. Without abandoning the double-victory campaign, the Black press broadened its coverage to reflect African Americans' increasing participation in the war. In mid-1942—a few weeks before the release of Armstrong's *I'll Be Glad*—a photo caption in the *Pittsburgh Courier* summed up the change: "Okay, Uncle Sam, we're ready!"[14] By the time *I've Got a Little List* debuted on Panorams that fall, more than a quarter million Black people were serving in the armed forces, and Mitchell's admonishment about enlisting was no longer such a bitter joke.[15]

The newspaper sight gag in *I'll Be Glad* meshes easily with Armstrong's on-camera persona, but the trappings of *I've Got a Little List*—Mitchell's "Lord High Slapper-Downer" title, his costume, and that razor—are a throwback to a minstrel-show sensibility. In a manner of speaking, so is *The Mikado*. Shortly after it debuted in London in 1885, a minstrel version, the *Black Mikado*, appeared in the United States, running for hundreds of performances in 1885 and 1886.[16] In 1939, two competing Black-cast *Mikado*s premiered on Broadway: *The Swing Mikado*—produced by the federal Works Progress Administration (WPA)—and the more up-tempo *Hot Mikado*, produced by future movie mogul Mike Todd and starring dancer Bill "Bojangles" Robinson.[17] *I've Got a Little List* may have coincided with a patriotic upswing among Black Americans, but its minstrel-show overtones sprang from an entirely different tradition. Made with Sam Coslow's active involvement, *I'll Be Glad* and *I've Got a Little List* were among the few war-related Black-cast Soundies made in Los Angeles. After that, most were produced and directed by William Forest Crouch in New York. Working with an East Coast talent pool, Crouch and his team began putting a different spin on Black Americans and the war.

ON SCREEN, IN UNIFORM

Crouch produced the majority of Black-cast Soundies and turned out the bulk of the war-related ones as well. By inclination, patriotic morale boosters were not his specialty—documenting Black talent and cranking out cheesecake were more like it—but he made his share. The first one with Black performers did not appear until mid-1943, some ten months after *I've Got a Little List*, but the shift in perspective is notable. *I Gotta Go to Camp to See My Man* (Crouch-Crouch, 1943) features Edna Mae Harris, a popular star on the race-film and Black stage-show circuits, singing as she packs for a visit to her serviceman beau. Like most Soundies, it was expected to appeal to a broad audience. Noting that Harris "voices the longing of many a girl today," the film's catalog description declares that "she gives this timely tune a sincere and colorful interpretation that is bound to be popular."[18] *Billboard* thought so too: "Good voice for this type of song," it noted in its mini-review. "As an added attraction, one of her roommates does a short dancing routine."[19]

I Gotta Go to Camp is the first Soundie to reference Black people in the military, but *When Johnny Comes Marching Home* (Crouch-Crouch, 1943) is the first to show and celebrate Black servicemen on screen. It's the last in a set of three Soundies, copyrighted in August and September 1943, starring the Four Ginger Snaps. The group includes three women singers (Leona Virginia Hemingway, Ethel E. Harper, and Ruth Christian) and one man (Charles Ford) who sometimes joins on the vocals and otherwise accompanies the women on piano. The Ginger Snaps scat and swing with ease, and by the mid-1940s they were enjoying considerable success with nightclub appearances, record releases on RCA Victor, and at least one magazine advertising campaign (for Royal Crown Cola).[20] Their popularity earned them a coveted spot on a wartime V-Disc (records distributed free of charge to overseas servicemen), sharing the A side with the top-of-the-charts Andrews Sisters.[21] The group's wide-ranging exposure underscores Soundies' place in a broader music-industry circuit that included live appearances, record releases, and in this case, a print advertising campaign. "With voices in fine blend," *Billboard* wrote in 1943, "Ginger Snaps are devoted to the smooth rhythm and smartly tailored harmonies."[22]

Set as a parade to welcome returning servicemen, *When Johnny* updates a popular Civil War tune (an interesting twist in itself). It opens with a wide shot of women in street clothes, waving small flags in time to an a capella vocal riff on a military drum roll. Dressed as an Army officer, Ford enters the frame at the head of a small group of servicemen—Navy seaman, Marine, and Army soldier—who march arm in arm with women friends. The camera tracks to find the three women Ginger Snaps, then cuts to a close-up of Ford in his officer's hat, turning to the camera and smiling broadly. As he stands among the vocalists, they fuss over him fondly (fig. 4.2). Updated lyrics and side comments reflect pride and affection: "He'll wear a medal for bravery," "Don't he look good in that?" *Billboard* responded with enthusiasm. "The Four Ginger Snaps sing the old favorite . . . with considerable wham," the reviewer wrote, perhaps deliberately mentioning another of the group's hit tunes ("Wham") before singling out one minor-key chorus as "especially effective."[23] Coming near the end of the song, that chorus adds a touch of gospel to the patriotic fervor ("Shouting hallelujah to the skies / When Johnny comes marching home"). The film fades out on the lead vocalist and Ford in a romantic clinch—a standard closing shot since the silent era, but in Hollywood one that rarely featured Black performers.

Figure 4.2. The Four Ginger Snaps in *When Johnny Comes Marching Home* (1943). Courtesy Mark Cantor Archive.

When Johnny was released in late September 1943. The armistice was still nearly two years away, and its jubilant parade reflects a fatigued nation's wishful thinking. It also speaks to the growing number of Black people in the military. At the end of 1943, the percentage of Black enlisted men in the Army stood at 9.25, an almost 50 percent jump over the 6.32 percent in December 1941, and close to the 9.8 percent of Black people in the overall population in 1940.[24] That increase had not come easily. In September 1943, the date *When Johnny* was copyrighted, 60.6 percent of all Black registrants reporting to military induction stations were rejected. In all of 1943, the average rejection rate for Black registrants was 53 percent; for whites, it was a considerably lower 33.2 percent.[25] Once in the service, Black inductees faced segregation and broad discrimination. Racial conflict and rioting took place at virtually every southern army base, and many in the North and abroad.[26]

Despite the ongoing discrimination and conflict, *When Johnny* reflects an expectation that, as Dalfiume puts it, "great changes favorable to the Negro would result from the war and things would never be the same again."[27] It was not the only Soundie to address this point. A month later, Crouch and his team wrapped up work on *We Are Americans Too.*

A MUSICAL MANIFESTO

When Johnny Comes Marching Home and *We Are Americans Too* were released at a watershed moment in wartime race relations. The summer of 1943 had seen major riots across the country. In June, more than one thousand whites—mostly sailors and soldiers—tore through Los Angeles, attacking Black Americans and Mexican Americans in what became known as the "Zoot Suit Riots."[28] In Detroit some two weeks later, tensions over the wartime housing shortage touched off racial battles that left thirty-four people dead, more than seven hundred injured, and the loss of more than one hundred million labor hours of wartime production. In August, rioting in New York led to five deaths and five hundred injuries. White hate-strikes against the hiring of Black workers were staged in Maryland, Michigan, New York, and Ohio. When Philadelphia hired eight African Americans as trolley motormen, a walkout by white workers halted the city's transportation system for a week.[29]

In the fluctuating crowd of Soundies filmmakers, it's unlikely that any producer but Crouch would have chosen, at that moment, to interpret a Civil War tune as a contemporary Black-cast Soundie or to follow it with *We Are Americans Too.* Written in 1940 for the revue *Tan Manhattan*, the song "We Are Americans Too" was composed by Eubie Blake and Charles L. Cooke, with lyrics by Andy Razaf. A songwriter since the 1910s, Razaf frequently collaborated with Fats Waller, turning out classics like "Honeysuckle Rose," "Ain't Misbehavin'," and "The Joint Is Jumpin'" (all made into Soundies starring Waller). Razaf was part of the Soundies orbit through his association with Fritz Pollard and Sun Tan Studio, the rehearsal space that served as Soundies' informal Harlem headquarters. During the war, Razaf wrote or cowrote more than a dozen patriotic songs, with titles like "War Bond Man," "That's Why I Buy Bonds," and "Goin' on an Errand for Uncle Sam." He also cowrote the theme song for the *Pittsburgh Courier*'s Double V campaign, "A Yankee Doodle Tan," paying tribute to Black servicemen with lyrics that proclaim, "His color doesn't run." More than a decade earlier, Razaf had cowritten (with Waller and Harry Brooks) the radically race-conscious song "(What Did I Do to Be So) Black and Blue."

Razaf's original lyrics for "We Are Americans Too" were a scalding indictment of white racism. Fearing the song would sink *Tan Manhattan* before it opened, Blake, the show's producer Irving C. Mills, and Razaf's wife Jean prevailed on him to moderate the message. In its final form, "We Are Americans

Too" became a wartime testament to African American patriotism: "Black America's ultimate patriotic call to arms, a truly exasperating irony, given the lyricist's original intentions," writes Razaf's biographer.[30] Razaf himself performed the song at countless war bond drives. In late 1941, two weeks after the attack on Pearl Harbor, "We Are Americans Too" was included in an episode of *Freedom's People*—a 1941–42 NBC Radio series on African American history and culture—focusing on Black people in the armed services.[31]

The Soundie *We Are Americans Too* stars the Chanticleers, a male quartet with a mellow, close-harmony sound. The group made six Soundies in 1943, all produced and directed by Crouch. Most of them feature easygoing, romantic tunes delivered in nightclub and living-room settings, like *Lovin' Up a Solid Breeze* and *If You Treat Me to a Hug*. These films are straightforward performance documentations, but *We Are Americans Too* takes a different approach. In patriotic Soundies, Crouch often relied on documentary film to add a touch of real-life urgency, leaning heavily on the military and defense-industry footage that the federal government routinely released to the media. Using a standardized approach, he whipped out a string of white-cast morale-boosting Soundies like *Farmers of the U.S.A.* (Crouch-Crouch, 1944) and *Don't Be an Absentee* (Crouch-Crouch, 1943)—which, according to the Soundies catalog, included "actual scenes of our invasion of Sicily."[32] *We Are Americans Too* is the only one of Crouch's morale-booster Soundies to focus on Black Americans, and the film description sent to the Library of Congress reflects a determination to portray them in a different light.

> Regarding WE ARE AMERICANS TOO, Soundies No. 1043-1-54, all of the players are colored. The picture opens with a medium close shot of a male quartet, known as The Chanticleers. All are wearing uniforms of various branches of the armed forces. As they sing, there are stock shots of a parade of World War I soldiers, a large troop ship moving away from shore, and several battle scenes. These are followed by scenes of colored people working in a laboratory, one photographed as a welder, two colored men in a prize fight ring and at a track meet. The Chanticleers are photographed again as they end their song.[33]

As with *When Johnny Comes Marching Home*, the fact that the singers appear in uniform makes a statement in itself. More obliquely, so does the footage of a Black welder: in May 1943, a few months before the film was copyrighted, twenty thousand white workers at a shipyard in Mobile, Alabama, rioted when a dozen Black men were promoted to a previously all-white welding crew, and National Guard intervention was required to quell the escalating violence.[34] *We*

Are Americans Too is a stirring expression of patriotism and support for the war, but it also carries a second emphatic message: Black people's contributions and rights must be recognized. "By the record we've made and the part that we've played / We are Americans too," Razaf's lyrics begin. "By the pick and the plow and the sweat of our brow / We are Americans too." If making *We Are Americans Too* was a bold move in that tumultuous, racially violent year, its distribution was pragmatic. Reflecting the strategy discussed in chapter 3, *We Are Americans Too* was released as an M film, which meant that its distribution was limited to Panoram operators who actively sought out films with Black performers.

SCATTING FOR WAR BONDS

In parallel with military-themed Soundies, a handful of 1943 Black-cast films dealt with home-front issues. Roughly a month after Edna Mae Harris packed her bag in *I Gotta Go to Camp to See My Man*, and a month before *When Johnny Comes Marching Home* hit Panoram screens, the Four Ginger Snaps made their Soundies debut with *Keep Smiling* (Crouch-Crouch, 1943). Set in the lobby of a busy movie theater, with patriotic posters covering the walls, the film is an unabashed plug for war bonds—the US government-issued securities that enabled private citizens to support the war while earning a solid return on their investment.[35] A theater lobby was the ideal setting for this pitch. War bonds were regularly sold at movie houses, often earning free admission for purchasers.[36] In this respect, the film may have succeeded brilliantly, but there are some jarring aspects that are worth a closer look.

Billboard described the song "Keep Smilin', Keep Laughin', Be Happy" as "one of those righteous jump tunes based on a simple and solid riff," and it's full of home-front cheer.[37] But in their performance, the Ginger Snaps start out deliberately stone-faced and unsmiling. They stay that way for much of the film, thawing just a little near the end. That might have been Crouch's directorial idea, or it may have come from the singers themselves. In either case it's evocatively dissonant with the tune's revised lyrics, which not only urge listeners to buy war bonds and war stamps but to "Slap the Japs," "Slap the Nipponese," and "Get the Führer" (fig. 4.3). A mention of Mussolini prompts a quick, puff-cheeked imitation of the Italian dictator by one of the women, but "Slap the Japs" has her repeatedly pulling a toothy, cross-eyed caricature of Japanese people in general. Racist references to Japanese were a staple of wartime propaganda, and *Keep Smiling* isn't the only Soundie to include one.[38] But it's a surprisingly crude gesture, especially from these singers, with their polished delivery and deliberately sober demeanor.

Figure 4.3. The Four Ginger Snaps sing "Get the Führer" in *Keep Smiling* (1943).
Library of Congress, Motion Picture, Broadcasting and Recorded Sound Division.

The Ginger Snaps' final Soundie, *Wham* (Crouch-Crouch, 1943), has nothing
to do with the war. It's a straight-up swing number that has the women letting
loose with the body language, with Ford on piano and a well-rehearsed chorus
line filling the frame on the instrumental break. Beyond their own Soundies,
the Ginger Snaps point to an intriguing phenomenon: the comparative rarity of
hit-making Black female close-harmony vocal groups in the 1940s. The wartime
music scene was otherwise full of female groups, most of them billed as sister
acts—not just white acts like the Andrews Sisters, the Four King Sisters, and
the Dinning Sisters, but the Kim Loo Sisters (widely known as the Chinese
Andrews Sisters) and the Cuban American De Castro Sisters, among others.
There are at least a dozen well-known close-harmony groups of Black men,
too, from the Mills Brothers to the Charioteers, the Chanticleers, and Day,
Dawn, and Dusk. Some twenty years later, "girl groups" like the Supremes
would power their way through the pop charts. But when Ford sits down at the
piano and Christian, Harper, and Hemingway take over the vocals, the Four
Ginger Snaps become, for a few moments, one of the rare Black female close-
harmony groups of the war years.[39]

If Soundies made a point of picturing Black people in the military, fewer of them depicted Black defense workers. Several white-cast Soundies are set in factories or take defense work as their theme—*Swing Shift Swing* (Coslow-Berne, 1942), *Navy Yard* (Crouch-Crouch, 1943), *On Time* (Barry-Curran, 1943), and *Stop That Dancing Up There* (Hersh-Berne, 1944), to name a few. Among the Black-cast films, though, only the Chanticleers' *Ain't My Sugar Sweet* (Crouch-Crouch, 1943) makes so much as a passing reference to war work: the singers are dressed in factory uniforms, but the film is set in a café. The brief documentary shots of a welder and laboratory workers in *We Are Americans Too* are the only explicit indication of Black people's participation in defense and war-related work.

Two additional films may have touched on this aspect of Black Americans' wartime experience. In 1946, music-driven short films by producer William D. Alexander furnished the material for sixteen Soundies, but three years earlier his All-American Newsreels supplied the footage for two others. Made by Alexander in partnership with Black producer Claude Barnett and white producer Emanuel M. Glucksman under the aegis of the Office of War Information (OWI), All-American Newsreels presented topics of interest to the African American community, including Black people's participation in the war effort.

The newsreels were not without controversy. The NAACP's Walter White, among others, argued that exclusively Black newsreels diminished the coverage of Black servicemen in mainstream newsreels. Too, All-American Newsreels were sponsored by Milton Starr, a white southerner who owned a chain of movie houses in Black neighborhoods and served as a $1-per-year advisor on African American matters for the OWI. Starr reportedly charged Black movie theaters more for All-American Newsreels than for other newsreel services.[40] Despite these issues, the newsreels are a valuable record covering a broad mix of topics: a Black Coast Guard unit undergoing training, Roosevelt's valet speaking about his travels with the president, and entertainers Butter Beans and Susie doing a quick vaudeville gag, for example. To what extent the two Soundies clipped from the All-American Newsreels reflect the Black community's wartime participation—rather than vaudeville entertainers like Butter Beans and Susie—remains a question, as no prints of these Soundies have been located.

I'll Be Glad When You're Dead and *I've Got a Little List*—the two war-related Black-cast Soundies of 1942—took a humorous approach to the war, but the films made in 1943 were marked by a certain gravitas, particularly *When Johnny Comes Marching Home* and *We Are Americans Too*. With home-front race relations hitting a violent low, the circumstances that conceivably prompted Crouch to make *We Are Americans Too* may have also persuaded the Soundies

Corporation to keep the film out of general release. In its assertive depiction of Black people's contributions to the war effort, unmitigated by cheesecake shots or a romantic clinch at the fade-out, *We Are Americans Too* is something of a manifesto: an affirmation, in pop-culture terms, of Black Americans' participation in the war and expectations in return.

On this point it may be productive to compare *We Are Americans Too*—and by extension, Soundies as a market-driven commercial product—with *The Negro Soldier*, a forty-three-minute film produced by the US War Department in 1944. Acclaimed as a groundbreaking contribution to the national conversation about race, *The Negro Soldier* was originally shown to Black military recruits, then shown to all military recruits, and finally to the general public. The film had a strong emotional impact. But as a federal project it was subject to review by Congress and its influential southern bloc, and *The Negro Soldier* had to walk a careful line about the racial status quo and possibilities for change.[41] *We Are Americans Too* occupied a different market niche. As a Soundie dependent on viewers for revenue, it was answerable to its audiences rather than to the government. Marketed as an M film, it reached viewers who were interested in seeing Black people on screen. As three-minute entertainment it wasn't expected to tackle tough issues, but Razaf's lyrics made a powerful point. Where *The Negro Soldier* was obliged to skirt issues of racial injustice, in addressing the preferences of its viewers *We Are Americans Too* could—and arguably had to—take a more assertive stance.

We Are Americans Too marks another turning point in the character of the Black-cast war-themed Soundies. In the films that followed, patriotism and support for the war were a given, a prima facie assumption borne out by the increasing numbers of Black people in the military. After *We Are Americans Too*, wartime Black-cast Soundies pivoted toward the films' fundamental strengths—music, entertainment, and a contemporary urban focus—as participation in the war effort expanded.

GI JIVE

As the war continued, the number of Black people in the armed forces increased dramatically. In December 1941, there had been 96,686 Black enlisted men in the US Army and 462 officers. By March 1944, those figures stood at 663,164 and 4,690 respectively, a more than sixfold increase in enlisted men and tenfold increase in officers.[42] Other services saw similar leaps. By the war's end there were 165,000 Black people in the Navy, and the total entering the Marine Corps jumped from zero to 20,000.[43] With few exceptions the military remained rigidly segregated and most Black troops continued to serve in labor and sup-port units, but there were a few hard-won advancements. The Tuskegee-trained 99th Fighter Squadron began flying in spring 1943, promptly earning a Distin-guished Unit Citation for operations over Sicily. A second Tuskegee unit, the 332nd Fighter Group, went into service in February 1944.[44] At the end of that year, Black support troops, volunteering for active combat in the face of massive infantry losses, played a crucial role in winning the Battle of the Bulge.

The production of war-related Black-cast Soundies kept pace with this deeper involvement. More Black-cast Soundies addressing the war were pro-duced in 1944 than in any other year, and a greater number featured performers in uniform. Instead of the clumsy propaganda of *Keep Smiling*, the patriotic pride of *When Johnny Comes Marching Home*, or the moral imperative of *We Are Americans Too*, several later films have a playful, ironic touch, an unstated sense of control, and at times a teasing sexual undertone. In short, they are cool.

In his landmark 1973 essay "An Aesthetic of the Cool," historian Robert Farris Thompson traces the concept to its spiritual dimension in West Afri-can cultures. Calling it a "metaphor of moral aesthetic accomplishment," he describes *cool* as the "ability to be nonchalant at the right moment," adding that "it is particularly admirable to do difficult tasks with an air of ease and silent disdain."[45] For Thompson and others, a sense of deliberate restraint was also part of the definition: "silent yet knowing," as Amiri Baraka put it.[46]

Many of these characteristics are expressed in war-related Black-cast Soun-dies of 1944. Interestingly, the first to reflect this sensibility, *Shoo Shoo Baby* (Hersh-Berne, 1944), does not feature Black performers. Only the songwriter, Phil Moore, is African American, but he suffuses the tune—and by extension, the film—with cool to spare.[47] Written in 1943, "Shoo Shoo Baby" is a sailor's farewell to his girl. It opens on a sentimental note, setting up a teasing contrast to the insouciant lyrics that follow: "Bye bye bye baby / Your papa's off to the seven seas." With death shadowing many servicemen's departures, "Shoo Shoo Baby" was, as one music historian put it, "arguably the hippest musical goodbye of the war."[48]

Moore made several Soundies with his combo, the Phil Moore Four, in 1945, but "Shoo Shoo Baby" wasn't one of them. It wasn't one of Ida James's Soundies, either, even though she was so closely identified with the song that she became known as the "Shoo Shoo Baby" and the "Shoo Shoo Girl." Released in early 1944, at the height of the song's popularity, the Soundie *Shoo Shoo Baby* starred white vocalist Carolyn Gray and guitar wizard Les Paul and his combo. Set in a cocktail lounge, it's a straightforward performance film that wisely favors shots of the musicians' playing, especially Paul's.

By 1944 it was clear that the Allies were winning the war, and the song picked up on the nation's surging confidence. Even with Paul's guitar, musically speaking *Shoo Shoo Baby* doesn't beat Ida James's interpretation (recorded on film but not on disc), or the hit versions by the Andrews Sisters and white vocalist Ella Mae Morse.[49] But the Soundie easily catches the relaxed confidence of Moore's tune and lyrics, and their ability, in Thompson's words, "to be nonchalant at the right moment."

In their war-related Soundies, Louis Jordan and his combo take that confident, teasing undertone to another level. If ever a performer were made for Soundies, it was Jordan. His persona—witty, risqué, carnivalesque—was perfectly aligned with the Soundies sensibility, and his smart musicianship kept the hits coming. Jordan was one of the era's few crossover stars: between 1944 and 1949, nineteen of his singles made the mainstream pop charts, nine of them hitting the top ten. Despite the bid for wider audiences, writes music historian David Andrew Ake, "Jordan's sound and subject matter remained deeply rooted in African American forms and styles." His small combo was a musically agile, less expensive alternative to the much larger big bands, with a compact, hard-swinging rhythm section producing what Ake calls "a lighter and more flexible texture," rather than the dense, multihorn arrangements of the big bands.[50]

More than most performers, Jordan and his manager Berle Adams understood Soundies' potential as a marketing tool and shrewdly exploited them to that end.[51] Soundies boosted Jordan's popularity, especially as he began reaching wider audiences. With Crouch as director or producer-director, Jordan made fourteen Soundies. Each of them pulled dimes into Panorams at a gratifying clip and—released just ahead of bandstand tours or new records—marketed Jordan as no other medium could. Jordan on screen is a relaxed, slyly humorous presence. His ease with Crouch and his crew is evident, and they went on to make other films together. Jordan's last four Soundies, in fact, are excerpted from the 1945 Crouch-directed short film *Caldonia*.[52] In addition to their debut Panoram runs, a number of Jordan Soundies were packaged into two solo medley reels for custom distribution—a distinction no other Soundies performer could claim.[53]

Although Jordan began making Soundies in 1942, all four of his films that reference the war were made in 1944. This parallels a shift in his music that began in late 1943, when he recorded "Ration Blues," a tune that he cowrote.[54] Jordan used humorous references to the war as a canny strategy for reaching mainstream audiences, and "Ration Blues" became his first crossover hit. He followed in March 1944 with the Johnny Mercer tune "GI Jive," and that broke even bigger. Jordan's version went head-to-head with one by Mercer himself.

The competing discs turned the song into what music historian John Bush Jones calls a "maxi-hit of epic proportions among both civilians and servicemen," percolating through the pop-music charts for close to a year.[55]

Released within weeks of each other in spring 1944, Jordan's Soundie versions, GI Jive and Ration Blues (both Crouch-Crouch, 1944) capitalized on the continuing popularity of both songs. Debuting first, GI Jive is a performance film set in a café. With its good-natured grousing about Army life, the song all but requires performers to appear in uniform, and Jordan and his musicians oblige (apparently all as sergeants). Musicians turn up in military uniform in several white-cast Soundies, but they're rare in films with Black performers. It's a smart strategy for GI Jive, visually reinforcing Jordan's connection to the tune and to virtually every Soundies viewer in uniform. It makes a broader point too: although by 1944 the number of Black people in the military had risen dramatically, the visibility of Black servicemen in mainstream culture was almost nonexistent, even in the news media.[56]

With five men on camera in military uniform (six, counting a quick cutaway shot of an enlisted man in the audience), GI Jive stakes a visual claim for Black Americans' participation in the war. There's a similar dynamic at play in the soundtrack, which, more than the visuals, imbues the film with Jordan's personal cool. His version subtly emphasizes lines in the lyrics that speak most directly to the experience of enlisted men—including the ever-present obligation to salute—and Black enlisted men in particular, serving in a segregated military and routinely commanded by white officers.

Jordan takes a more straightforwardly humorous approach in Ration Blues, burnishing the tongue-in-cheek complaints with playful sexual innuendo. By 1944, rationing was a fact of home-front life, with government regulations restricting everything from shoes to gasoline. For Jordan this was fertile ground for double entendres, and his enjoyment is evident in the sly references to sugar, meat, and gas.[57] Like GI Jive, Ration Blues is a bandstand film, set against a backdrop of oversized ration booklets, with the musicians in civilian clothes. The other Jordan Soundies that reference the war are echoes of these two. Picking up on Ration Blues, in If You Can't Smile and Say Yes (Crouch-Crouch, 1944), Jordan alludes to wartime shortages in a line about men being even harder to find than nylons. In the instrumental Jordan Jive (Crouch-Crouch, 1944), the reference is entirely visual. The Soundies catalog entry describes Jordan as "that juke box idol of the swing fans" playing "a hot saxophone," but the setting has the musicians again in uniform, in a café packed with Black servicemen and their dates.[58]

A few other Black-cast Soundies casually allude to the war or home-front shortages in their lyrics, including Who's Been Eating My Porridge?

(Hersh-Berne, 1944), Phil Moore's *I Want a Little Doggie* (Crouch-Crouch, 1945), and *Blitzkrieg Bombardier* (Crouch-Crouch, 1944), notable for its raunchy double entendres. Beyond the Jordan films, though, one more war-related Soundie of 1944 stands out: *Hey! Tojo, Count Yo' Men* (Crouch-Crouch, 1944).[59]

Despite the faux-dialect *yo'* in the lyrics, the song is an upbeat tribute to Black American troops in the Pacific, framed as a slap at Japanese prime minister Hideki Tōjō. The Pacific war was hard-fought with steep losses, especially in early defeats at Bataan and Corregidor. For much of the war African American units in the Pacific provided security and support, including artillery fire, for white combat troops, at times coming under fire themselves. (According to one historian, more Black soldiers in service and labor units experienced combat than those in actual combat units.[60]) In March 1944, soldiers of the First Battalion, Twenty-Fourth Infantry, were among the first Black American troops to officially engage in active combat, joining in the defense of Bougainville, an island in the northern Solomons.[61] *Hey! Tojo* was copyrighted a few weeks later.

The song's lyrics celebrate Black soldiers in active combat, portraying a nonchalant grace under fire. "They had rhythm when they'd load their gun / Then they'd point it at the Rising Sun," pianist Bob Howard sings. Playing to an informal gathering of Black soldiers, he closes *Hey! Tojo* with a Fats Waller-esque ad lib that echoes the casual racism of *Keep Smiling.* "Tōjō! Hirohito! All you Japs with the slanty eyes! Take inventory and count your men," he says. "Ha ha! You ain't so smart. Evacuate yourself!"[62]

Hey! Tojo was the last Black-cast Soundie to depict servicemen on screen. Roughly a year later, the vocal-and-piano duo Johnny and George appeared in one final war-related Soundie, *Write That Letter Tonight* (Crouch-Crouch, 1945). By that point both the topic and its treatment seemed tired. A nudge to a truly war-weary home front, the film is set against a backdrop of oversized envelopes—not unlike the ration books in *Ration Blues*—with a line of young women adding visual interest to what is, in essence, an old-fashioned music-hall performance. With the country already looking ahead to life after armistice, *Write That Letter Tonight* went into M-film circulation in June 1945, a month after Germany's surrender and two months ahead of Japan's defeat in August.

REDEFINING UNITY

The Black-cast Soundies that touch on the war and home front are only a sliver of the hundreds that feature Black performers, but their impact exceeded their numbers. Black people's participation in the war effort had been virtually excluded from the broader cultural narrative; these Soundies made a point of inserting it into the national conversation in pop-culture terms. With the exception of *We Are Americans Too, Blitzkrieg Bombardier,* and *Write That Letter Tonight,* all Black-cast Soundies referencing the war were distributed in the weekly general-release reels. Several of the films feature men in military uniform, visually underscoring Black Americans' participation in the war. In others, the military is a tacit reference—the absent boyfriend in *I Gotta Go to Camp to See My Man,* or the support-our-troops urgings of *Write That Letter Tonight.* If early Black-cast Hollywood films sought to contain their characters in a timeless "antebellum idyll," war-themed Black-cast Soundies did the opposite, visibly inserting Black Americans into contemporary history as part of the nation's most vital undertaking.

Beyond basic visibility, a number of films speak to popular perceptions of Black people and the war, especially ones made in 1943 and 1944: the heroism implicit in *When Johnny Comes Marching Home;* the assertive, deeply patriotic stance of *We Are Americans Too;* the unspoken patriotism underpinning *GI Jive;* and the combat cool of *Hey! Tojo, Count Yo' Men.* Unlike the early Soundie *I've Got a Little List,* with its minstrel-show framing, later Soundies portray Black involvement in the war in a solidly contemporary light.

It's no coincidence that Crouch produced the films most indicative of this shift. These Soundies address and reinterpret African American involvement with the war, and Crouch's hand is evident in the choice of material like "We Are Americans Too" and "Hey! Tojo, Count Yo' Men." His films start on familiar ground with the light entertainment of *I Gotta Go to Camp,* stumble with the crude propaganda of *Keep Smiling,* and regain momentum with the infectious patriotism of *When Johnny Comes Marching Home. We Are Americans Too* makes a more overtly political declaration, followed by a turn toward cool in the war-related Soundies starring Louis Jordan. The Jordan Soundies continue to make the Black American war effort visible on screen, buttressed by the explicit tribute of *Hey! Tojo* and followed, in the war's final months, by a return to light entertainment with *Write That Letter Tonight.*

These films suggest a certain willingness to push the cultural envelope, along with a pragmatic flexibility about strategies: if, in insisting that Black Americans' rights and contributions be recognized, *We Are Americans Too* was too emphatic for general consumption, Louis Jordan in uniform was not. But even with Crouch's Soundies, envelope-pushing went only so far. The pressure of wartime patriotism was intense, and in that light, what the films do not address is as revealing as what they do. Other than the decision to film *We Are Americans Too,* there is no allusion to the racial tensions that so frequently exploded during the war years. Nor is there any mention of the Double Victory campaigns in the Black community, and—aside from the isolationists in *I've Got a Little List* or the dancers in *Sugar Hill Masquerade*, discussed in chapter 6—nothing that so much as hints at Black Americans' ambivalence about the war. The brief documentary shots in *We Are Americans Too* are the only depictions of Black people at work in war-related industries. Only one other Soundie portrays them as factory workers—and even then, not in the factory. (Black women defense workers make no appearance at all.[63]) The war years were rife with home-front problems, from crisis-level housing shortages to juvenile delinquency, and white terrorism continued to inflict a horrifying toll in the South and elsewhere. But in Black-cast Soundies, home-front challenges are reduced to rationing—portrayed as a humorous inconvenience—and the imperative to buy war bonds. Cloaked in humor and innuendo, these films are still pointedly patriotic.

None of this is surprising. The most interesting thing isn't that contentious social themes turned up so rarely in Soundies, but that they turned up at all. Much of the popular media avoided or made light of the era's most challenging social issues, and the fact that these topics appear in Soundies suggests the interest that Crouch, his production team, the performers, and perhaps the Soundies Corporation's home office may have had in bringing them into the public eye. As it was, Crouch and his colleagues were obliged to deal with a difficult and somewhat competing set of demands: to make films about the war and home front that aligned, at least to some degree, with a Black perspective, that appealed to mainstream audiences, and were entertaining enough to trigger the volume of repeat play needed to turn a profit. Perhaps more than any other Soundies, the handful of Black-cast, war-related films illustrate how Soundies operated within a tightly circumscribed cultural arena. The fact that so few were made reflects the challenges involved in making them; that only three were withheld from general distribution suggests their popularity and their importance for Soundies as a wartime venture. Beyond the Soundies arena, the films may be seen as part of a broader turn, led largely by popular music, toward imbuing the war and the very concept of patriotism with a Black American sensibility. Combining on-screen visibility with a positive take on Black people's engagement with the war, these films suggested that the definition of American wartime unity could be questioned, reimagined, and made more inclusive.

5

ENCOUNTER AND IMPROVISATION

Reimagining the City

THE MUSIC STARTS OVER A black screen, a few seconds before the first image appears. Abruptly, Duke Ellington and His Orchestra slam into the opening bars of "Cottontail." As the music continues, the film opens with a wide shot of the Orpheum theater in Los Angeles, its three-sided marquee blazing with light. That's followed by a quick close-up on a poster of Ellington and his band. Then we're with them on stage, with Ellington at the piano introducing Ben Webster as he begins his horn solo.

It's a standard start to a big-band Soundie, but less than a minute later we're outside again. A quick fade from a microphone to a loudspeaker brings us to the sidewalk beneath the theater marquee. There, under the doorman's approving eye, Whitey's Lindy Hoppers claim the space for an electrifying jitterbug performance. The film cuts back to Ellington and his band every so often and ends—like all of his Soundies—with a close-up of Ellington himself. But in *Hot Chocolate ("Cottontail")* (Coslow-Berne, 1942), the real action is on the street.

The cultural map of Black-cast Soundies begins with city streets. Many films are set on corners and avenues, building stoops and fire escapes. Others take place in public spaces—parks, movie theaters, lunch counters, night clubs. Still others unfold in modern urban living rooms. In imagining this terrain, Black-cast Soundies are early exemplars of what Paula Massood calls "Black city cinema," a filmic approach that rejects Hollywood's rural, ahistorical version of African American life in favor of a vibrant urban modernity.[1] As a commercial entertainment form, Soundies were shaped not only by filmmakers and performers but by audiences and their feedback. In pursuit of viewers Soundies became, almost by default, a site for exploring the era's evolving notions of urbanity, hybridity, and the depiction of Black people on screen.

—w—

In 1940 the US population was largely rural and small-town, with most Americans living in municipalities of twenty-five thousand or fewer.[2] The war upended that profile, funneling unemployed workers into densely crowded defense-industry hubs. African Americans were a significant part of this wave. Between 1940 and 1945, half a million—an estimated 17 percent of the Black population in the South—moved to other parts of the country; by 1950, that number was 1.5 million.[3] Since the 1910s, the Great Migration had seen millions of African Americans flee the region for Chicago, New York, Pittsburgh, and other northern centers, and those cities continued to draw Black people in large numbers.[4] But the war also sparked a dramatic increase in migration to the West Coast. As home to roughly half the nation's aircraft and shipbuilding industries, California was a top destination, attracting 338,000 Black newcomers during the war years.[5] In San Francisco alone, between 1940 and 1945, the African American population soared from roughly 4,850 to 32,000, a slightly less than sevenfold increase. Across the bay, Oakland also saw an impressive jump, and the Black population of Los Angeles grew at least four times faster than the city's population overall.[6] Farther up the coast, industrial hubs in Oregon and Washington saw large influxes. In Washington, DC, a record number of Black people held wartime federal government positions—by one estimate, an increase of 400 percent.[7] During the 1940s, Black Americans became, for the first time, a predominantly urban population. Outside of the South, more than 90 percent lived in cities.[8]

Black people weren't the only ones on the move. Some 2.6 million whites, largely from outer southern states like West Virginia, Tennessee, and Texas, left the region during those years. Los Angeles and Detroit drew not quite a million between them.[9] More than three million southerners, Black and white, exited the region from 1940 through 1945, virtually all of them heading for industrial centers elsewhere.

Panorams thrived in the bars, taverns, and cafes where newcomers congregated. These gathering places were a wartime necessity, prompted by dislocation and homesickness, round-the-clock factory schedules—three eight-hour shifts a day, often with overtime—coupled with abysmal housing and acute shortages of consumer goods. The great irony of the wartime home front was that with prosperity finally returning, there were no goods to buy—no automobiles, refrigerators, or radios—and for a mobile, badly housed labor force, often nowhere to put them. In cities packed beyond capacity, newcomers slept in their cars or in "hot beds" rented in eight-hour shifts. Alarm clocks were in such short supply that some workers brought them to the job each day for fear they'd otherwise be stolen.[10]

Instead of things to buy there was entertainment of every description, tailored to a workforce in perpetual need of relaxation. In military barracks and home-front factories, life was lived communally and publicly, and during off hours it was more of the same—on dance floors, in all-night movie theaters with their "swing-shift matinees" (for workers coming off the job at midnight or 8 a.m.), and in the bars, taverns, and cafes that served as communal living rooms. In those shared aural spaces, music offered a way of dealing with difference, finding common ground, and reinforcing a sense of identity among transplanted newcomers.

In Soundies, this played out as a multicultural smorgasbord, with Eastern European polkas, Irish jigs, Hawaiian hulas, and other ethnic specialties spliced into virtually every general-release reel. On the whole, these films affirmed distinct cultural identities within an Americanized framework—conjuring Hollywood-style versions of distant homelands, giving traditional music an up-tempo swing, and making exotic cultures reassuringly familiar. Even in Americanized form, that diversity was rare on wartime screens. As music historian Kristin A. McGee points out, "in their willingness to present a multiethnic, cosmopolitan, and pluralist coalition of music, dance, comedy, and drama during World War II America," Soundies were, for their time, "revolutionary."[11]

Black-cast Soundies were an essential part of this mix. But with few exceptions, their point of view differed significantly from white ethnic films with their polkas and jigs. Instead of looking back with Americanized nostalgia, as ethnic Soundies often did, most Black-cast films focused decisively on the present. For many Black Americans the war years were a time of change and expanded possibilities, and the majority of Black-cast Soundies reflect this.

Writing about this decade, historian Guthrie P. Ramsey Jr. casts 1940s America through a prism of "Afro-modernism," which he defines as "a loose system of thought ... connected to the new urbanity of African American communities, the heady momentum of sociopolitical progress during the first half of the twentieth century, and the changing sense of what constituted African American culture (and even American culture generally speaking)."[12] Ramsey frames Afro-modernism as a post–World War II phenomenon, but the dynamics he describes were already in play during the war years, and his concept speaks productively to what is ahead-of-the-curve about Black-cast Soundies:

African Americans portrayed as sophisticated city dwellers who are not only at ease with modernity but active in shaping it. New forms of media often lend themselves to the construction of "imagined selves and imagined worlds," as anthropologist Arjun Appadurai has noted, especially in the context of large-scale migrations.[13] Soundies were a new entertainment form targeting a highly mobile, rapidly urbanizing viewership, and it's interesting to consider the Black-cast Soundies as a vehicle for this work of collective imagination.

Between military service and the defense industry, the war threw enormous numbers of disparate people into tense, overcrowded proximity. Under the circumstances there was little choice but to get acquainted, culturally if not personally. "These new cultural exchanges produced a variety of musics that were popular among urban Blacks and whites," Ramsey writes, and Soundies were a channel for their visual interpretation and diffusion.[14] Fueled by their music, the films construct a vision of the city that is capacious, creative, playful, and fluid, and markedly more progressive than the actual environments that many newcomers found waiting for them. With their open-ended interpretation of the metropolis, Black-cast Soundies modeled, in pop-culture terms, what it meant to be urban at midcentury: a modern take on city life exemplified by Black Americans. Across the Panoram Soundies circuit, the films functioned as an informal primer for all urban newcomers, not so much in what the city actually was but what it could be: a place where viewers, regardless of their point of origin, might feel at home. At the same time, Black-cast Soundies became a space for reframing the rural past in light of an urban present, and for indexing the adaptation to city life through the markers of style, language, and swing.

A PIANO ON THE SIDEWALK

In film after film, urban settings invite easy, playful encounters. In *Ain't She Pretty* (Crouch-Crouch, 1944), the Three Peppers sing the praises of a woman walking by to mail a letter. In *Legs Ain't No Good* (Barry/Waller-Graham, 1942), Edna Mae Harris and "Slim" Thomas dance past an open-air lunch counter with its leggy lineup of female customers. In other films, the street is a more expansive gathering place—the spot for a neighborhood dance party in *Sugar Hill Masquerade* (Barry/Waller-Graham, 1942) and *Block Party Revels* (Crouch-Crouch, 1943), or for welcoming returning servicemen in *When Johnny Comes Marching Home* (Crouch-Crouch, 1943). The communal space extends to rooftops, backyards, and fire escapes, as in Duke Ellington's *I Got It Bad and That Ain't Good* (Coslow-Berne, 1942), the gossip-scolding *Babbling Bess* (Crouch-Crouch, 1943), and the opera send-up *Rigoletto Blues* (Barry/Waller-Snody,

1941). In this imagined city, any pretext for putting a piano on the sidewalk—a moving job or even an eviction, as in *Dispossessed Blues* (Crouch-Crouch, 1943)—is an opportunity to celebrate the richness of the street as a place of encounter and improvisation (fig. 5.1).[15] In Soundies like these, Scott writes, "with no white people present, Black people overtake public space and overwrite its rules."[16]

That dynamic is evident in *Backstage Blues* (Crouch-Crouch, 1943), in which dancers take obvious pleasure in performing for each other, and *Steak and Potatoes* (Hersh-Gould, 1944), starring Mabel Scott as a server in a busy café, dishing out down-to-earth reflections on romance along with the title entrée. *Tuxedo Junction* (Crouch-Graham, 1942; fig. 11.1) has Edna Mae Harris and her friends dancing through a train station populated entirely by Black people, and the bustling lobby in *Keep Smiling* (Crouch-Crouch, 1943) is filled with Black moviegoers and theater staff. Although there is some question as to how many Panorams were actually sited in high-end nightclubs, upscale clubs with Black clientele are the settings for many Soundies, including *Lovin' Up a Solid Breeze* (Crouch-Crouch, 1943), *We're Stepping Out Tonight* (Crouch-Weiss, 1945), *Jumpin' Jack from Hackensack* (Crouch-Crouch, 1943), and *Drink Hearty* (Crouch-Crouch, 1946).[17]

References to Harlem turn up frequently. Other cities had thriving centers of Black culture and community, including Chicago's Bronzeville, the U Street corridor in Washington, DC, Central Avenue in Los Angeles, and Birmingham's Tuxedo Junction. But Harlem is the only one to appear regularly by name in titles, settings, and lyrics—a shorthand for Black urbanity, creativity, and style that Soundies audiences would have readily understood. The reality was arguably less glittering: the Depression left many residents struggling, the uprising known as the Harlem Riot of 1935 had destroyed lives and property, and a second upheaval in 1943 would accelerate the neighborhood's physical decline.[18] But the nightlife scene remained vital—smaller and tighter, with fewer white visitors—and the Harlem that emerges in these Soundies affirms a dynamic Black modernity. It was, as fashion historian Monica L. Miller describes it, "a theatrical, spectacular place," where "Black people manifested self-regard, explored and redefined the relationship of race, gender, and sex through their elegant, sophisticated, and playfully fine self-representation."[19] Though shot in Los Angeles, Ellington's *Jam Session* (Coslow-Berne, 1942) opens with a sign reading "Harlem Cats Eatery," effectively setting the scene for the after-hours session that follows. When the singers in *Jack, You're Playing the Game* (Barry/Waller-Snody, 1941) need a style makeover, they head to a Harlem clothing store. *Pigmeat Throws the Bull* (Crouch-Crouch, 1945) and *Get It Off Your Mind*

Figure 5.1. A piano on the sidewalk (*from top*): Dancers in *Dispossessed Blues* (1943), with pianist Lynn Albritton at left; Leonard "Lennie" Bluett dances in the foreground as Meade "Lux" Lewis plays in *Boogie Woogie* (1944); Lynn Albritton at the piano in *Block Party Revels* (1943). Courtesy Mark Cantor Archive (*top, bottom*); Library of Congress, Motion Picture, Broadcasting and Recorded Sound Division (*center*).

(Crouch-Crouch, 1946) use nearly identical painted backdrops of 145th Street and Lenox Avenue, and a quick shot of the actual street signs appears in *Take the 'A' Train* (Barry-Waller/Snody, 1941) as those words are sung on the soundtrack. The title of *Sugar Hill Masquerade* references a Harlem locale, and half a dozen Soundies have "Harlem" in their titles. Many more mention it in their songs.

Even without explicit reference, the population of this imagined metropolis embodies Harlem's verve and sophistication. With few exceptions, the performers in these Soundies portray cosmopolitan urbanites—contemporary, stylish, self-assured—and the camera takes pains to present them that way. In *Boogie Woogie* (Gould-Gould, 1943), pianist Meade "Lux" Lewis, in the guise of a worker for the Boogie Woogie Moving Company, sits at a baby grand temporarily left on the sidewalk. But his performance isn't necessarily what the camera is interested in. Drawn by the music, a stylish crowd breaks into a succession of quick solo dances. As they gather around the piano, the camera pans slowly across their faces in a series of admiring close-ups. Though they're uncredited bit players, each performer presents her- or himself with ease, meeting the camera's gaze with none of the self-consciousness seen in many Soundies background players. The pan begins on comedian Dudley Dickerson, who clowns for the camera, then shifts to Avanelle Harris, Dickerson's uncredited costar in two other Soundies.[20] Next up is Leonard "Lennie" Bluett, in a tailored suit and fedora, laughing with pleasure.[21] Pretty women are the usual fodder for Soundies close-ups, but the camera lingers appreciatively on Bluett before moving to a two-shot of the women at frame right. In *Hot Chocolate ("Cottontail")*, the young dancers get similar treatment. The close-up pan across the performers' faces is faster, and the dancers don't meet the camera with the same deliberate intent, but the takeaway is much the same: poised, stylish city dwellers at home in the metropolis.

The high-voltage jitterbugging in *Hot Chocolate ("Cottontail")* foregrounds the role of dance in defining this cinematic city (fig. 5.2). The dancers are members of Whitey's Lindy Hoppers, the premier jitterbug troupe of the 1930s and 1940s. (The jitterbug was first known as the Lindy hop, in honor of Charles Lindbergh's solo transatlantic flight in 1927.) Organized and managed by Herbert "Whitey" White, the group originated at the Savoy Ballroom—the most competitive dance floor in Harlem—and went on to Hollywood, where they appeared in the Marx Brothers' *A Day at the Races* (1937), *Hellzapoppin'* (1941), and other movies. The dancers in *Hot Chocolate ("Cottontail")* include Frankie Manning, whose innovative "air step" choreography reshaped the Lindy hop, and his partner Ann Johnson—the last couple to solo—along with William Downes and Frances "Mickey" Jones, Albert Minns and Willa Mae Ricker, and

Figure 5.2a–d (*this page and following*). In *Hot Chocolate* ("*Cottontail*") (1941), Whitey's Lindy Hoppers take over the space outside the Orpheum Theater as inside, Duke Ellington and His Orchestra provide the music. Library of Congress, Motion Picture, Broadcasting and Recorded Sound Division [or] Courtesy Mark Cantor Archive.

Figure 5.2c and 5.2d.

Billy Ricker and Norma Miller.[22] Other members of the troupe appear in *Sugar Hill Masquerade*, where they similarly claim city space for their own enjoyment.

In *Block Party Revels* and *Dispossessed Blues*, the Six Knobs and Four Knobs, respectively, join the Harlem Cuties dance troupe in making use of streets and sidewalks as performance spaces. The Harlem Cuties are also part of the crowd in *Backstage Blues*, which—though set in a rehearsal studio rather than a city street—has a similar air of camaraderie. Powered by Lynn Albritton's boogie piano, a succession of performers take part in a music-and-movement jam session, ending with a joyful dance by two women (fig. 5.3). The film's male soloist, identified as "Lou Ellen," is Llewellyn Crawford, the choreographer-in-residence at Fritz Pollard's Sun Tan Studio in Harlem, the main audition and rehearsal center for Black-cast Soundies in New York. In other films, dancers grab the spotlight with high-powered performances in nightclub, bandstand, and living-room settings, notably the Three Chefs in *Breakfast in Rhythm* (L. Weiss/A. Weiss-Bricker, 1943), the Swing Maniacs in Louis Jordan's *Jordan Jive* and *Jumpin' at the Jubilee* (both Crouch-Crouch, 1944), and *Good-Nite All* (Oliphant/Leonard-Leonard, 1943). Films like these underscore Soundies' affinity for showcasing Black dance as artistry and, in standout moments, sheer pleasure.[23]

Shortly before starting his Soundies work in fall 1941, Duke Ellington completed a twelve-week run of *Jump for Joy*, the Black-cast musical revue that had opened at the Mayan Theater in Los Angeles that July. With numbers like "Uncle Tom's Cabin Is a Drive-In Now" and "Passport to Georgia," the show was, as Ellington later described it, "an attempt to correct the race situation in the USA through a form of theatrical propaganda."[24] Two of his five Soundies were adapted from *Jump for Joy*, and the show's influence is evident in his others, including *Hot Chocolate ("Cottontail")*, particularly in the amount of screen time devoted to dance.[25] Taken from *Jump for Joy*, *Bli-Blip* (Coslow-Berne, 1942) features some of the sharpest duo dancing in the entire Soundies catalog. And *Flamingo* (Coslow-Berne, 1942) gives much of its screen time to Janet Collins and Talley Beatty, two dancers who performed with Katherine Dunham. A pioneer in bringing Black dance traditions into contemporary choreography, Dunham appears with her troupe in a non-Ellington Soundie, *Cuban Episode* (Coslow-Berne, 1942).

THE REQUISITE COOL

For wartime migrants accommodating themselves to city life, personal appearance was one of the most visible markers of progress along that curve. In those years, as historian Eric Lott writes, "the requisite cool" of the urbane city dweller

Figure 5.3. From *Backstage Blues* (Crouch-Crouch, 1943). Courtesy Mark Cantor Archive.

was "unattainable unless negotiated through style."[26] In a comment on late twentieth-century culture that could easily apply to the 1940s home front, cultural theorist Stuart Hall observes: "Within the Black repertoire, *style*—which mainstream cultural critics often believe to be the mere husk, the wrapping, the sugar coating on the pill—has become *itself* the subject of what is going on."[27]

Style pervades many Black-cast Soundies: Dandridge's glamorous turns in *Easy Street* (Coslow-Murphy, 1941) and *Yes, Indeed!* (Coslow-Murphy/ Berne, 1941), the sharply tailored men's suits in *Rug Cutters Holiday* (Oliphant-Leonard, 1943), and Cab Calloway's debonair ensembles in Soundies like *The Skunk Song* and *Blues in the Night* (both Barry/Waller-Snody, 1942), among others. The West Coast Soundie *Emily Brown* (Williams-Gould, 1943) scores style points with a theatrical version of city chic, notably in the costumes worn by costar Chinky Grimes. As the object of singer Bob Parrish's affections, Grimes makes her entrance in a stylish leopard-print ensemble, then encores in a sleek, bias-cut wedding gown.

The Delta Rhythm Boys' *Jack, You're Playing the Game* is a virtual playbook for acquiring city cool. The film opens with two of the singers in suits having their shoes shined by the other two. The dapper men instruct their more humbly dressed colleagues in the elements of style, starting with zoot-suit tailoring: a "Harlem design" with a long coat "pegged so fine." They advise the men to acquire girlfriends with steady jobs who can "keep you out of hock," along with an apartment on Sugar Hill and a new car gotten through easy credit. Summing up the essentials—new clothes, stylish apartment, big car, "and the dame," they sing: "Maneuver that jive, and Jack, you're playing the game." The hepsters depart and the shoeshiners look with dismay at their own apparel. The next shot has them beating each other through the door of "Harlem Credit Clothing." Instantly transformed into avatars of urban cool, they join the others for the closing lines of the song, paired off with four stylish women.

The Delta Rhythm Boys (Traverse Crawford, Otho "Lee" Gaines, Clinton Holland, and Harry Lewis) made nine Soundies, five in 1941 and four in 1945. Most are buoyant celebrations of city life, including *Jack, You're Playing the Game*. Made in late 1941, it's the first Black-cast Soundie to explicitly address personal style as a marker of urban cool. The tune was written by the singers and their pianist, Rene DeKnight. In cataloging the elements of city style, the song and the film capture a moment of national anticipation just before the Pearl Harbor attack: defense industries were gearing up, the country was not yet at war, and prosperity was in sight. Though it would be sharply curtailed during the war, at that moment the consumer-credit industry was thriving—in 1940, installment loans totaled more than $5.5 million nationwide (over $100 million in 2021 dollars), with car loans representing more than $2 million of that figure.[28] The shoeshiners' sartorial makeover is the visual centerpiece of the film, but the lyrics (and the sign for "Harlem Credit Clothing") suggest the role that credit might have played in acquiring urban cool. "The idea of the togged-out man avoiding work and seeking pleasure was familiar to anyone who read Black newspapers," historian Kathy Peiss writes about the film.[29] She also points out a sign near the shoeshine stand reading "Peace." In 1941, many in the Black community were ambivalent, if not cynical, about the war, and the film may have touched on that isolationist sentiment—or, she writes, it may have linked antiwar sentiment to the irresponsibility attributed, in some quarters, to zoot suiters.

That perceived irresponsibility was inseparable from the style itself. With its long, double-breasted jacket and wide, high-waisted trousers, a complete zoot suit consumed yards of fabric. An extravagance in peacetime, once war was declared and clothing restrictions were imposed, the suits came to be seen, in many instances, as provocatively unpatriotic. In some cases they triggered mob violence against those who wore them, as with the Los Angeles "Zoot Suit Riots" of 1943. Even so, they were the height of home-front cool for young Americans, particularly young Black and Latinx men.

Black performers in Soundies appear less frequently in work clothes. In a dozen or more largely white-cast Soundies, Black actors appear in nonverbal walk-ons as waiters, porters, janitors, and maids—jobs of the prewar status quo. But a small number of Black-cast Soundies push the workplace theme into more contemporary territory. Starring the Chanticleers as factory workers relaxing after their shift, *Ain't My Sugar Sweet* (Crouch-Crouch, 1943) is one of the few wartime Soundies to give visibility to Black defense workers. The same for *We Are Americans Too* (Crouch-Crouch, 1943), with its documentary footage of a Black welder and Black laboratory technician. In other films, the normalcy of workplace depictions is a message itself. The cop on the beat singing about his sweetheart in *Emily Brown*, the wise-cracking waitress in *Steak and Potatoes*, and the subway conductor in the Delta Rhythm Boys' *Take the 'A' Train* (Barry/Waller-Snody, 1941) reflect a city not only populated by Black Americans but fashioned and sustained by them as well.

A HEPSTER'S DICTIONARY

As entertainment destined for factory-worker taverns, defense-plant break rooms, bus and train stations, and other public spots, Soundies didn't have the luxury of catering to a single audience. Commercial viability depended on a wide revenue stream, and the wartime mix of languages and constantly evolving slang made speaking in multiple registers essential. That included viewers who easily caught the films' alternative meanings as well as those who were oblivious to them.

As one of the few cinematic platforms open to African American performers during the war years, Black-cast Soundies were both a channel for Black performers looking to address Black audiences and a vital diffusion point for Black popular culture—interpreted by Black performers—into the broader visual culture. The dynamics of that dual role could get convoluted. In *Brother Bill* (Crouch-Crouch, 1945), for example, the Jubalaires perform a comic song by Louis Armstrong about a hunting expedition in Maine. Things go wrong when the bear being tracked "turns white" and starts chasing the hunter. Taking off across a field, he runs so fast that "they couldn't catch me in an automobile." The lyrics might have held little significance for white audiences, but most Black viewers would have understood why running was called for. The song's narrator reverses the usual escape route: instead of heading north for safety, he's "Alabama bound." The film's visuals complicate the reading. Standing before a dramatic fieldstone fireplace in a rustic-modern hunting lodge, the singers wear Sherlock Holmes-style deerstalker hats and boldly patterned hunting jackets, including one covered with dollar signs. At variance with the lyrics, which have the narrator dropping his gun and running for his life, all four singers hold hunting rifles as they sing—a rare instance at that point, as Scott notes, of Black men not in military uniform carrying firearms on screen.[30]

The war years were an inventive time for American slang, sparked by the intense mixing of diverse populations. Black slang was fundamental to this proliferating vocabulary, and it quickly diffused through pop-culture pathways, including music.[31] Songs aimed at mainstream audiences were sometimes overtly instructional: "We the cats shall hep ya," Cab Calloway sings in the Soundie of that name, and bass player Dallas Bartley and his band take a similar approach in *All Ruzzitt Buzzitt* (Crouch-Crouch, 1945), with vocalist/trumpet player Bill Martin introducing the "hep talk" of the day. Despite the tutorials—including Calloway's book, *Hepster's Dictionary*, first published in the late 1930s—impenetrability was part of slang's appeal, especially for younger audiences.[32] The barrage of sartorial hep talk in *A Zoot Suit* (Coslow-Berne, 1942), for instance, is a shibboleth of cool, all but unintelligible to outsiders.

The Delta Rhythm Boys' *Give Me Some Skin* (makers unknown, 1946) further instructs viewers in cultural etiquette. "Shaking hands is all taboo when you come to Harlem town," they sing. Copyrighted in 1946 after the war ended and Soundies had begun their final slide, *Give Me Some Skin* is something of a mystery, its producer, director, and production date unknown. Its unidentified female performer is a background player in the Delta Rhythm Boys' 1941

Soundies *Rigoletto Blues* and *Take the 'A' Train*, but that might be pure coincidence. It's possible that the film was not made as a Soundie at all.[33]

Despite (or perhaps due to) those circumstances, *Give Me Some Skin* is among the most cinematically experimental Soundies, marshalling style, language, camera work and sensibility into an oddly effective whole. As the film opens, the singers are heard jive-talking over a musical intro by pianist Rene DeKnight, then seen in a classic Soundies setup: in tuxes, arrayed along a grand piano, their figures casting deep, sharply silhouetted shadows behind them. Dizzying swish tilts link quick shots of outstretched hands and a stylishly dressed woman and man, visually introducing the theme of "giving skin." Additional swish-tilts, pans, and diagonally framed close-ups of hands slapping create a visual flow that quickly extends to the singers, as if picking up the energy of the adjacent footage. The camera starts framing them on the diagonal too, shot from one angle and then the other (fig. 5.4). The men gradually add hand gestures to their performance, loosening the tuxedoed formality, while cutaway shots literally interpret—or comically overinterpret—lyrics spoken on the soundtrack.

By the time *Give Me Some Skin* was copyrighted, several of its visual strategies—the sharply silhouetted shadows, low camera angles, and extreme diagonal shots (known as "Dutch angles")—had become familiar clichés for depicting the interior life of Black characters on screen. "The required Negro motif," was how African American critic John Louis Clarke had described it in 1932.[34] Film historian Ryan Jay Friedman traces this visual approach from its appearance in *Black and Tan*, the 1929 Duke Ellington–Fredi Washington short by Soundies director Dudley Murphy, through films like *Yamekraw* (1930), Murphy's *The Emperor Jones* (1933), and beyond. "Murphy conceived of African American culture in thoroughly symbolic ways: as simultaneously primitive and modern but always exotic and spectacular," he writes.[35] Rummaging through this visual toolkit, *Give Me Some Skin* puts the "required Negro motif" and its clichés to more self-aware use, turning them into a light-handed, at times sublimely silly form of expressive play.

If the visuals for *Give Me Some Skin* are experimental, almost expressionistic, the music couldn't be more sedate. There's a constant expectation that the tune will jump into swing tempo, but it maintains the same easy pace throughout, as if to provide a stable base for the adventurous camerawork. As the song nears its end, the lyrics mention "my pal, my gal, my friend," prompting bass Lee Gaines to intone to the camera, "and you *are* my friend." His finger-pointing address to the viewer—along with a midsong verse spoken to the camera, and the singers offering their hands to the camera for a slap—emphasizes the intimacy of the presentation and the film's willingness to undermine the usual separation of performer and audience.

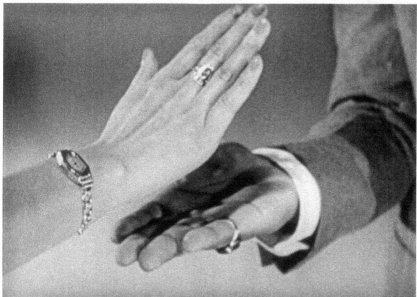

Figure 5.4a–d (*this page and following*). The Delta Rhythm Boys and an uncredited woman performer in *Give Me Some Skin* (1946). Courtesy Mark Cantor Archive.

Figure 5.4c and 5.4d.

As an interesting counterpoint, an online search for *Give Me Some Skin* is likely to also turn up "Gimme Some Skin, My Friend," a different tune performed by the Andrews Sisters in the 1941 Abbott & Costello movie *In the Navy*. Released some five years before *Give Me Some Skin* was copyrighted, the number is crisply choreographed, shot, and edited, with an up-tempo flair that throws the rough-edged, experimental style of *Give Me Some Skin* into high relief. There's no reaching out to the audience here—as in most Hollywood films, the viewer is firmly positioned outside the action and remains there. But there's a more crucial point of comparison between the two numbers: who commands the narrative and in what voice. It's one thing for the Delta Rhythm Boys to speak authoritatively about Harlem etiquette and an entirely different matter when the Andrews Sisters do it. Appearing well ahead of *Give Me Some Skin*, "Gimme Some Skin, My Friend" candidly appropriates Black culture for white consumption. At the same time, it recognizes Harlem as an emblem of yearned-for cool among whites. Lott has written at length about "the dialectical flickering of racial insult and racial envy" that characterized the nineteenth-century minstrel show and its white audiences, and an undercurrent of that envy flows through "Gimme Some Skin, My Friend," starting with its opening line about shaking hands "like they do it in Harlem."[36]

That envy is notably mined in one white-cast Soundie in particular. Performed by the vocal trio the Dinning Sisters, *Clancy* (Crouch-Crouch, 1945) is the tale of a Harlem-obsessed white policeman who manages to get himself transferred uptown. There, thanks to a Lenox Avenue mentor, he achieves the coveted cool: "And when he struts down the street, people repeat / Brother, how'd that Irish copper get that boogie beat?"

SKEWERED BY SWING

In the late 1930s and early 1940s, swing was more than a musical style. It was a change agent that pervaded the culture at large—a generational rebellion that was essential for shaking off Depression-era doldrums and catalyzing the unity needed to fight the war. Swing signaled greater cultural inclusiveness, a willingness to scrap social rigidities, and a streak of carnivalesque humor. Historian Joel Dinerstein characterizes swing as a collective coming to terms with the industrialization and mechanization of twentieth-century life, powered almost entirely by Black creative energy. "Through contact with Euro-American musicians and cultural elites, as well as with Black workers and the urban soundscape," he writes, "African American artists integrated the speed, drive, precision, and rhythmic flow of factory work and modern cities into a nationally (and internationally) unifying cultural form: big-band swing."[37]

For Dinerstein, big bands, tap dancing, and the Lindy hop—all of which figure prominently in Soundies—were "public models of humanized machine aesthetics" and prime examples of swing culture.[38]

As a musical style, swing emerged from the 1920s and 1930s jazz bands of Fletcher Henderson, Duke Ellington, and other Black bandleaders. Predictably, swing gained its broadest popularity through white interpreters—or, as Kevin Young points out, quoting Amiri Baraka, "when it moved from verb to noun," becoming "a commercial popular music in cheap imitation of a kind of Afro-American music" that bebop would later reject.[39] Despite its commercialization, swing's influence extended beyond music, particularly during the war, and its buoyant rhythms quickly became a vehicle for energizing, updating, and poking fun at the culture at large.

With their affinity for carnivalesque play, Soundies were ever alert to swing's antic potential. Like other popular entertainment, Soundies took a lowbrow glee in skewering highbrow culture, and swing was a natural ally in the cause. The Delta Rhythm Boys' *Rigoletto Blues* is done in swing time, and classical music gets the swing treatment in white-cast films like *Swing It, Mr. Schubert* (Coslow-Berne, 1942) and *William Tell Overture* (Crouch-Crouch, 1944). Other Soundies use swing as a marker of modernity, with old people, aristocrats, and other unlikely types becoming enthusiastic converts, usually through dance. In the white-cast *Kerry Dance* (Barry/Waller-Owen Murphy, 1942), disapproving oldsters are taught to swing an Irish jig, and a coonskin-capped, jitterbugging grandpappy scorches the dance floor in *The Covered Wagon Rolled Right Along* (Barry/Waller-Murray, 1941). "Yippee!" he yells. "I'm a jivin' wildcat!"

Although swing-powered rejuvenation is not a major theme in Black-cast Soundies, it makes an occasional appearance. In *Never Too Old to Swing* (Crouch-Crouch, 1945), guitarist Tiny Grimes sings about his "mom and pop" who "do the boogie woogie by the clock." His jitterbugging parents are left offscreen, but the older generation gets a visible workout in *Dance Your Old Age Away* (Crouch-Crouch, 1944). Interpreting his own tune, songwriter-arranger Tosh Hammed appears as a grizzled old-timer, accompanied by six chorus-line dancers in various stages of aged decrepitude. The women's swing-triggered rejuvenation is miraculous but Hammed tops them all, with a performance that includes a full somersault pitched from a standing start.

Swing's potential to subvert cultural norms comes into focus in a second Soundie riffing on the opera *Rigoletto*. Where *Rigoletto Blues* features the Delta Rhythm Boys, *Rigoletto* (Crouch-Berne, 1945) stars the vocal group Day, Dawn, and Dusk (Robert Caver, Ed Coleman, and Augustus "Gus" Simons). Caver and Simons reportedly met in the 1920s as members of the acclaimed Hall Johnson

Choir, with Coleman joining them a few years later.[40] As a nightclub and theater act, Day, Dawn, and Dusk had a flair for musical comedy, performing in Europe as well as the United States. Known for a sophisticated cosmopolitanism, they were as comfortable recording the Yiddish standard "Mein Shtetela Belz" (My Little Town Belz) as "Basin Street Blues" (both released in 1946).

The Soundie *Rigoletto* opens on a proscenium stage, with Caver at the piano and Simons standing nearby, both in hepcat streetwear. Launching into a swing-and-scat riff, they're halted midnote by Coleman as composer Giuseppe Verdi (fig. 5.5). Dressed in a nineteenth-century frock coat, Coleman's Verdi appears in a white-haired wig and a thick layer of light-colored greasepaint—one of the few, perhaps only, instances of a Black performer of that era appearing on screen in what could be called whiteface. "Please don't swing my masterpiece," he solemnly implores the hepcats. To which Simons retorts, "We hate to tantalize you / But we mean to modernize you," and "We want to syncopate it / Even though we know you hate it." The musical tug of war continues in a complex vocal arrangement: "You know you're wrong / To swing my song," Verdi complains, to which Simons archly replies, "Oh, it's dreary! / Your weary little melody / That's why we swing it / The way it ought to be." At last the composer is won over and the three agree to "Rigolet-*to* it, hi-de-hi-de-*ho* it," closing on a sustained high note.

Rigoletto easily demonstrates swing's capacity for carnivalesque disruption. Race is denied as a boundary in portraying cultural figures. The film skewers high culture while also laying claim to it, musically and culturally, as common heritage and material for invention and reinterpretation—a site for both resistance and play. *Rigoletto* is also terrific fun, puncturing not only high culture and outraged classical composers but the hepsters bent on bringing them into the modern era.

The film also makes it clear that as a subversive tactic, swing goes only so far, and only in the right hands. When they filmed it in 1945, "Rigoletto" was already a popular part of Day, Dawn, and Dusk's repertoire, and a recording released the following year credited it as "A Day, Dawn, and Dusk Original Based on Verdi."[41] Whatever subversive streak the film possesses is attributable almost entirely to the performers, not Soundies producers or other intermediaries. Day, Dawn, and Dusk made a total of four Soundies: *Fare Thee Well* (Crouch-Berne, 1945) is a straightforward gospel performance reminiscent of the Hall Johnson Choir and its repertoire, but the other three have a witty sophistication that speaks in multiple registers, obliquely jabbing at race and gender while playfully claiming and shredding one cultural icon after another. *Rigoletto* and the gender-tweaking *Faust* (Crouch-Berne, 1945) unfold on a proscenium stage, but the other two—*Fare Thee Well* and *Sleep Kentucky Babe* (Crouch-Berne, 1945)—take place, tellingly, in a city apartment.

Figure 5.5. "Please don't swing my masterpiece": Day, Dawn, and Dusk (*from left in top photo,* Robert Caver, Augustus "Gus" Simons, and Ed Coleman) in *Rigoletto* (1945). Courtesy Mark Cantor Archive.

THE IMPROVISATIONAL LIVING ROOM

In Black-cast Soundies, living rooms are prime real estate. More than the street or nightclub, the well-furnished living room signifies mastery of city life: not only enjoying the metropolis as a place to find interesting, like-minded people, but having the comfortable private space in which to enjoy them. Given the woefully inadequate housing that many workers had to contend with, and the rioting that wartime housing issues sparked, the notion of a comfortable living room was itself somewhat aspirational. But it had an essential place in the collective imagination as a space of camaraderie, recreation, and shared privacy.

The Panoram's small screen size and casual viewing conditions meant that the most successful Soundies were often the most intimate, in both performance style and the use of cinematic space. As a setting, the living room is well suited to those criteria. Performances in these spaces are among the most informal in the entire Soundies catalog, underscoring Black Soundies performers' contributions to an evolving on-camera style that blossomed in the early years of television. Generally, the stars are shown singing and playing music for friends, as the Delta Rhythm Boys do in *Dry Bones* (Crouch-Berne, 1945), or Hilda Rogers does in *I Can't Give You Anything But Love* (Crouch-Crouch, 1944). The rooms are comfortably furnished, sometimes with grand pianos. In a few notable instances, the decor personalizes the performer's on-screen identity. In *Legs Ain't No Good*, for instance, the hallway table in Edna Mae Harris's apartment holds a framed silhouette of a Black man, which Harris touches briefly but tenderly on her way out. (There's also an Art Deco–style silhouette of a woman, done in white, which she ignores.) In the set used for Day, Dawn, and Dusk's *Fare Thee Well* and *Sleep Kentucky Babe*, the effect is more informal, with unframed, glossy photos of Black women shown as subtle additions to the standard living-room artworks. While the camera doesn't pick out the photos, sharp-eyed viewers certainly would, especially with repeat viewings. Similarly, although the photos behind the band in June Richmond's *47th Street Jive* (Hersh-Berne, 1944) are not immediately identifiable, they depict Black performers and meaningfully personalize an extremely spare setting. In films like these, the extra set-dressing may have been supplied by the performers rather than Soundies' production staff, and these touches suggest a willingness on producers' part to work with performers in defining the films' creative space.

Through camera angles, pans, and wide shots, Soundies living rooms are often made to appear more spacious than they are, particularly in the area allotted to performance. That space is often quite tight, effectively concentrating the action and permitting much of the camera work to be done in the close-ups and two-shots that played best on the Panoram. In *Rug Cutters Holiday*, an impressive stream of performers—jitterbugging couples; dance teams Freddie and Flo (Fernando Robinson and Florence Brown), Slap and Happy, Snap and Snappy; and an uncredited solo performer—pull off their acrobatic moves in a remarkably small area, without breaking the informal living-room atmosphere. The leisurely pan that opens the Delta Rhythm Boys' *Just A-Sittin' and A-Rockin'* (Crouch-Berne, 1945) makes the most of the film set. It starts on a group clustered around a piano, slowly travels left to a larger group on the sofa, and comes to rest farther left, on the group that includes Lee Gaines as he sings. As the performance continues, the camera frequently cuts to medium shots of the various groups and occasionally to wide shots that include most of the actors, playing the visual pleasure of seeing the full crowd against closer shots of the individual groups.

Good-Nite All (Oliphant/Leonard-Leonard, 1943) merges a relaxed performance style with a smart use of filmic space (fig. 1.2a, p. 29). It was directed by Arthur Leonard of L.O.L. Productions, the company whose blackface Soundies were a crucial part of the New York Supreme Court case discussed elsewhere in the book. Nothing of that controversy is evident in *Good-Nite All*. According to Leonard's testimony, the film was a last-minute addition to his production slate. "I had the talent available," he told the court, and a "hot swing tune that had been especially written for an act like this."[42] He'd requested and received an immediate go-ahead from Crouch, at that time the Soundies Corporation's production manager. "As long as I had the time to shoot it," Leonard testified, "I told him that I would like to do it that day."[43]

The last-minute scheduling of *Good-Nite All* put the film largely in the hands of the performers, whose easy rapport suggests a troupe that had already been working together. In fact, that might have been the case: Leonard's courtroom transcript indicates that the women, and possibly all the background actors, were performers from the Ubangi Club, a nightclub in Midtown Manhattan.[44] The storyline involves a group of partygoers who decide to sneak out en masse while their less-than-charming host is in the kitchen, preparing what will surely be a disappointing meal. Anchoring the action at the piano, Johnny Taylor and an uncredited female performer (identified in the Soundies catalog as "Hot-Cha")[45] outline the protocol for fleeing the scene: "When you pour and the bottle is empty / And your host says you've all had plenty / The easy way out is politely shout / Good-nite all." Taylor and his partner hold the screen with a bantering chemistry, reinforced by the lively responses of two uncredited performers at the other end of the piano. The camera defines the space economically, staying on a tight two-shot of Taylor and Hot-Cha before pulling back to a wide shot that reveals the full room. Hot-Cha is the first to claim the performance space in front of the piano, moving in to sing to the crowd. Before long, the compact area is filled with one, two, and then three couples jumping in for a quick dance, ending with the furtive mass exit and, a moment later, the comic consternation of the host.

In other instances, the warmth of the living-room setting is put to added use. Some Black-cast Soundies deliberately juxtapose stereotypical characters against the urbane sophisticates that usually fill the films. In these Soundies, Scott argues, stereotypes benchmark Black progress in contemporary life.[46] The Delta Rhythm Boys' *Dry Bones* is a prime example. As the singers perform for fashionable friends in a comfortable living room, a building janitor in overalls stops in to listen for a while. He leaves to turn out the hallway lights, where he's apparently scared witless by a dancer dressed as a skeleton. Enacting what by then was a standard racial pantomime of eye-popping fear, the janitor returns to the living room, speechlessly attempting to convey what he's seen. Two of the singers look down the hall and, seeing nothing, laughingly wave him off before returning to finish the performance for their friends.

With their overwhelmingly metropolitan settings and cosmopolitan characters, Black-cast Soundies brought the screen image of Black Americans into sync with the emerging wartime reality. That in itself is no small achievement. Historian Henry Louis Gates Jr. has chronicled the ongoing effort by African Americans in the twentieth century to counter the caricatures and distorted representations of Black people that pervaded American culture in the Jim Crow era and beyond. Gates frames it as a "war of imagery" between the stereotyped figure of the "Old Negro" and the "increasingly urban and urbane, modern, educated, cultured" figure of the "New Negro."[47] His description of that cosmopolitan new figure applies to many characters and performers in Black-cast Soundies. As usual, commerce has a bearing on this. Beyond budget exigencies and other factors, the sheer number of films with urban settings suggests that these were Soundies that viewers wanted to see, and to see repeatedly. Under the combined influence of audiences, performers, and makers, Black-cast Soundies became a space for collectively envisioning what a modern American city and its inhabitants might be like, and more significantly, what they might become.

And to a certain extent, where they came from. A small but significant number of films explore the rural past that many viewers had in common, tilting it toward a modern urban present. Using the languages of style, pop song, and film, these Soundies draw explicit connections between the vitality of Black urban life and its rural—and specifically southern—roots, leveraging a shared past in service of an imagined future.

6

—~~~—

RURAL REVERB

ONCE THE WARTIME ECONOMY WAS in full swing, relocation to a distant city often took no more than a few weeks, including the job hunt. The shift to an urban consciousness was a longer process, involving not only an evolving relationship to the city but a reimagining of what had been left behind. If cafés, bars, and taverns were places to hear the music of different cultures, they were also spaces for recalling home through music.

Historian Guthrie P. Ramsey Jr. posits an ongoing exchange during the war years between the industrial urbanism of cities in the North and West and the "southernisms" that a continual flow of Black migrants from the South brought with them.[1] This dynamic enriched the popular music of the era, and it extended to Soundies as well. While most Black-cast Soundies are set in cities, there are a few that take rural life as their subject or setting—though not to recall it with nostalgia. Instead, these films imbue a rural past with the verve, sophistication, and at times the politics of a modern urban sensibility. Connecting Black urban life with its country roots, these Soundies propose a unity of experience that flatly contradicts the good-bad, country-city binaries of many Black-cast Hollywood films, embracing the robust, ongoing exchange that Ramsey describes.

One early example is *I Dreamt I Dwelt in Harlem* (Barry-Snody, 1941), a Minoco production shot in New York. With a title that riffs on high culture— the nineteenth-century operatic aria "I Dreamt I Dwelt in Marble Halls"—both song and film locate Harlem as the epicenter of Black life, especially in its music, nightclubs, and glamour. The film opens with the Delta Rhythm Boys as farm-hands lounging in a country shack, singing of Harlem as the place to "dream

116

about." A filmic effect flips the scene to a city nightclub, where the singers, now in tuxedoes, are part of the stylish crowd taking in a chorus-line floor show (fig. 6.1). The lyrics pick up some city slang too: "I dreamt I had a pad in Harlem / You dig me?" After a quick spin on the dance floor, the film sends the singers back to their rural setting, but home is not the same. Drifting off to sleep, they vow to return to Harlem before settling down "to dream some more."

Like many Black-cast Hollywood musicals of the 1930s and 1940s, *I Dreamt I Dwelt in Harlem* has a circular plot line that leaves its characters back where they started. But instead of the ahistorical timelessness and good-bad binaries of movies like *Hallelujah* and *Cabin in the Sky*, *I Dreamt I Dwelt in Harlem* sketches a more deliberate relationship between rural and urban, with a dynamic flow that enriches them both. In the film's universe, Harlem is so accessible that the characters can will themselves there. For them, the city—and Harlem specifically—is not an emblem of evil but literally the place of their dreams, and the song's closing lines emphasize that connection and their intention to return there.

A more lighthearted urban-rural interplay—with the accent on rural—is part of the Minoco-produced Soundie *The Darktown Strutters' Ball* (Barry/Waller-Murray, 1941), starring the Charioteers. Although the film is set at a country barn dance, with the singers in overalls and straw hats, the women they're paired with are stylish enough for any city avenue—a version of "back home" re-envisioned with urban flair (fig. 7.1, p. 132).[2] In the Deep River Boys' *Booglie Wooglie Piggy* (Barry/Waller-Snody, 1941), a slapstick comedy about a piglet run amok at a country picnic, the urban aspect is even more subtle: instead of a farm-bred pragmatism toward escaped livestock, the women respond like city sophisticates catching sight of a mouse, playfully lifting their skirts in fright (and, this being a Soundie, showing some leg while they're at it).

Some songs, though, were impervious to updating. Stephen Foster's "Oh, Susannah" is one of most enduring tunes in the American songbook, but its lyrics about a freed slave loyally returning to his master reflect its 1800s minstrel-show origins. Shot in the same barn-dance set as *The Darktown Strutters' Ball*, the Charioteers' *Oh, Susannah* (Barry/Waller-Murray, 1941) includes the same uncredited women performers, gamely swinging along to a traditional version of the tune. In this case, though, the gloss of sophistication they provide cannot offset the lyrics, and the film emerges as more an antebellum throwback than a modern update.

When performers were in command of the material, however, the dynamic could be more forward-looking in both music and pop-culture terms. The rural-to-urban transition was central to Louis Jordan's musical identity, and

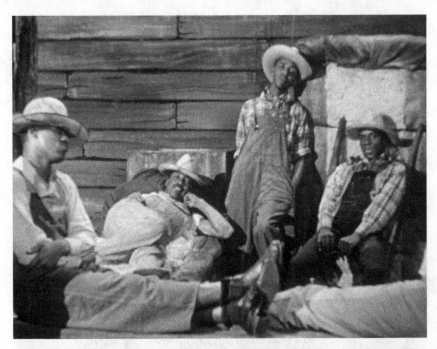

Figure 6.1. Rural and urban: The Delta Rhythm Boys in *I Dreamt I Dwelt in Harlem* (1941). Courtesy Mark Cantor Archive.

no Soundies performer was more adept at mining it for Top Ten hits. Rooted in the blues and call-and-response gospel, Jordan's "jump" style brought flexibility and wit to down-home music forms and themes. As one music historian has noted, even though the titles of many Jordan tunes ("Saturday Night Fish Fry," "Ain't Nobody Here but Us Chickens") suggest rural life, their subjects are in fact city scenes.[3]

In Soundies, Jordan's playful spin on tradition is most evident in *Old Man Mose* (Crouch-Graham, 1942). The film opens with Jordan on the bandstand, sprinting through the song—even with a joking call-and-response, his performance clocks in at little more than a minute. Then a slightly rearranged set presents Jordan at a center pulpit, with young women at either side and the musicians behind them. Wearing a pair of flamboyantly fake eyeglasses, he launches into a sermon in the character of "Eat Moe Jordan," reprised from the Soundie *Five Guys Named Moe* (Crouch-Graham, 1942), produced in the same session.

For some Soundies viewers, Jordan at the pulpit might have recalled the comic "hard-shell sermon" routine that Black vaudeville entertainer Amon Davis performed (in blackface) during the ragtime era and reprised years later in Oscar Micheaux's film *The Darktown Revue* (1931).[4] It may have also brought to mind church scenes in *Hallelujah*, *The Emperor Jones*, and other Black-cast Hollywood movies of the 1930s and 1940s. The previous year, Soundies director Dudley Murphy had staged a fervent prayer meeting—with ecstatic worshipers, a quick baptism, and the sharp-shadowed lighting he'd pioneered in *Black and Tan* and *The Emperor Jones*—as the setting for Dorothy Dandridge in *Yes, Indeed!* (Coslow-Murphy/Berne, 1941). *Old Man Mose* pushes that earnest approach into raunchier territory. Jordan's sermon includes some jovial double entendres: "We're going to have a holy rolling meeting this morning at five o'clock down at my church," he declares. "I want *all* you brothers to bring your own sisters to roll with! I'm gonna have mine." The visuals take a similar approach, with cutaway shots of the playfully posing congregation—their arms uplifted, dramatically lit in the "required Negro motif" style that Murphy uses in *Yes, Indeed!*—radiating a humorous self-awareness (fig. 6.2). Close-up shots of the young women show them good-naturedly pretending to be caught up in the spirit. If *Old Man Mose* opts for a joking, slightly distanced take on tradition, the film and Jordan's performance are still rooted in the Black American South. That sensibility is notably absent from an earlier, white-cast Soundie version, *Ol' Man Mose* (Barry-Waller, 1941), starring vocalist Ginger Harmon and jitterbugs Judy and Buddy Allen.

Figure 6.2. The "required Negro motif" and its send-up: *Yes, Indeed!* (1941, *top*) and *Old Man Mose* (1942). Library of Congress, Motion Picture, Broadcasting and Recorded Sound Division (*top*); courtesy Mark Cantor Archive (*bottom*).

As evident from *Oh, Susannah,* when urban-rural interplay was imposed by Soundies filmmakers, the results could be clumsy or worse. The Mills Brothers were the essence of suave sophistication, but only one of their three 1942 Soundies portrays them that way: *Paper Doll* (Coslow-Berne, 1942), which places them, in their usual tuxedoes, in a genteel porch-and-yard setting. The other two films were shot on the same set, but you'd never know it. In *Rockin' Chair* (Coslow-Berne, 1942), the men seem to have wandered into a Ma and Pa Kettle movie.[5] Though the tune is a mellow ballad, the singers are decked out in plaid shirts, overalls, and straw hats—outfits that here read less as farmhand gear than standard-issue "hillbilly" costumes, complete with the obligatory moonshine jug. *Caravan* (Coslow-Berne, 1942) takes a similar approach. Interpreting the classic Duke Ellington–Juan Tizol tune, the film would have been a natural for a nightclub or city living-room setting. Instead, the outdoor set is reconfigured as a farmyard where the singers, still in their hillbilly outfits, rouse a group of short-skirted dancers and their partners with a smooth a capella version of the tune. (The moonshine jug turns up here, too, in an odd visual coda at the close.)

Black Soundies performers weren't the only ones to sometimes find themselves down on the farm, but in Black-cast Soundies the mismatches could take a jaw-dropping turn. Produced in Los Angeles by RCM, *Juke Box Boogie* (Hersh-Gould, 1944) easily belongs in a café, club, or living room setting. Instead, pianist Gene Rodgers and the all-woman combo known as the Vs gamely perform inside a giant, hay-strewn watermelon, literally enveloped by a racist cliché. It's by no means the first appearance of this motif on screen—in the 1935 Vitaphone Pepper Pot short *An All-Colored Vaudeville Show,* for instance, the Five Racketeers and Eunice Wilson perform before a similar backdrop. But in 1944, when the cultural landscape had already begun to shift and racist stereotypes had largely disappeared from Soundies productions, it was a stunning lapse. It underscores the creative independence that, for better or worse, individual filmmakers exercised in Soundies' decentralized production system. It also shows the inconsistency of some Soundies filmmakers in their depiction of Black people. Racist backdrops were a real blind spot for the film's producer, Ben Hersh, and director, Dave Gould, when working as a team. Together they made three more late Soundies—including a second one with Gene Rodgers and the Vs—with racist caricatures as background images.[6] On his own, Gould—an Oscar-winning dance director—also directed the buoyant romance *Emily Brown* (Williams-Gould, 1943) and the street fantasia *Boogie Woogie* (Gould-Gould, 1944), with its admiring close-ups of young urban sophisticates. And Gould and Hersh together were responsible for Mabel Scott's star turn as the straight-talking waitress in *Steak and Potatoes*

(Hersh-Gould, 1944). Individually and as a team, Hersh and Gould's Black-cast Soundies manage to hit progressive and regressive extremes, epitomizing the uneven racial terrain of Soundies as a whole.

In the context of reframing a rural past, one more Hersh-Gould production bears consideration, less for its performances or racial politics than its set and costumes. Like the Mills Brothers' "hillbilly" Soundies, *Yankee Doodle Never Went to Town* (Hersh-Gould, 1944) takes place on a farm, but in this case it's a farm out of *The Cabinet of Dr. Caligari*—an obviously flat rendering of a barn and silo, painted in an angular, expressionist style. A more direct inspiration may have been the 1930 Black-cast short film *Yamekraw*, which was itself influenced by *Dr. Caligari* and featured a flat, painted cabin rendered in a similar style. Mabel Scott stars in *Yankee Doodle Never Went to Town*, but instead of the gingham dress or overalls one might expect in that setting, she wears a tailored satin jumpsuit topped by a satin bomber jacket—glamorous and wartime functional. The expressionist farmyard encores in a later Hersh production, *It's Me, Oh Lord* (Hersh-Berne, 1945), a Black-cast gospel number featuring vocalist John Shadrack Horance backed by Johnnie Moore's 3 Blazers. Horace, like Scott, wears satin—in this case, a gleaming version of farm overalls. Like *Yankee Doodle, It's Me, Oh Lord* presents a sophisticated, artfully skewed vision of life back home for audiences who had already left it behind.

DISSING DIXIE

In a few Black-cast Soundies, the work of reimagining "back home" extends beyond a generic sense of the countryside to the South as a cultural symbol and a distinct strand of American identity. When Soundies began production in 1940, the Civil War had been over for seventy-five years—the same length of time as the end of World War II to 2020. It was still within the lifespans of its oldest survivors and vividly present in the nation's cultural memory. Not surprisingly, the Soundies catalog is dotted with *Gone with the Wind*–infused nostalgia like *Dear Old Southland* (Barry/Waller-Snody, 1941) and *Just a Little Bit South of North Carolina* (Barry-Waller, 1941). But three Soundies stand out for their use of the South as a symbolic space and cultural trope. In these films, performers appear to be originators and active collaborators. The approach is more subtle than overt, and one key reference zooms by in a matter of seconds. Even so, these films figure in the cultural geography of the Black-cast Soundies as a back-home counterpart to the forward-looking vision of the metropolis.

Most of the action in Cab Calloway's *Virginia, Georgia and Caroline* (Barry/Waller-Snody, 1942) takes place on the bandstand, with Calloway conducting the orchestra or singing with the Cabaliers (aka the Palmer Brothers), a quartet of tuxedo-clad vocalists. The song pays admiring tribute to the three women of the title—the "lovely sisters of the South" who "live next door to one another," and whose mother is "dear old Dixie." From the bandstand, a quick edit takes Calloway to a garden setting where he's joined by three women in floral dresses—Vivian Brown, Marion Egbert, and Venna (aka Verna, Vearna) Smith. Calloway sings their praises as they look on, smiling to him and the camera. In the guise of a paean to feminine charm, the song is a fond salute to the region; as a Calloway Soundie, it claims the South on behalf of Black Americans and imbues it with the sophistication of city life.

Released in late November 1942, the jitterbug delight *Sugar Hill Masquerade* takes a different approach, more explicit and yet so fleeting as to be almost subliminal. This is one of the few Soundies to touch, even obliquely, on Black Americans' early ambivalence toward the war. At the same time, it underscores the relationship between Soundies and the music industry, the pervasive influence of wartime patriotism, and how the Soundies system at times functioned to performers' detriment.

The film features what appears to be trumpeter Walter Fuller playing for Whitey's Lindy Hoppers and other performers portraying costumed dancers at an uptown block party. As it opens, Fuller and his combo offer a few quick bars, in military tempo, of old standards that had been pulled into the war effort— "Yankee Doodle," "Dixie," and "Columbia, the Gem of the Ocean"—only to see them shouted down, one after the other, by the young dancers yelling "No, no, no!" The musicians give up and switch to a fast swing number, "After You've Gone," and the crowd breaks into dance. (Alice Barker and her chorus-line compatriots take their turn a little more than a minute in.) As teenage sentiment, the message implied by this opening sequence—"Forget the patriotic stuff, we want to dance"—is perhaps understandable. But in late 1942, when the war was going badly and popular support was an urgent national concern, "Forget the patriotic stuff" was a bold assertion no matter who was making it. And at a time when top Hollywood stars were still appearing on screen in blackface—including Bing Crosby as the white composer of "Dixie"—even a fleeting shot of Black people shouting down the tune was not likely to appear on any screen but a Panoram.[7]

The circumstances behind the making of *Sugar Hill Masquerade* don't diminish the casual audacity of that shot, but they deepen the story. Although Walter Fuller gets star billing in the opening credits, above Whitey's Lindy Hoppers, the camera quickly drops him for the dancers without returning for so much as a cutaway shot. *Sugar Hill Masquerade* was conceived as a dance film, but there's another reason that Fuller disappears so fast: he's not the musician on the soundtrack. That would be Roy Eldridge, star trumpeter in Gene Krupa's band, with Krupa drumming behind him. At a time when few high-profile big bands were racially integrated, Eldridge was the group's sole Black member, and "After You've Gone" was one of their big hits. Shouting down the old tunes was a popular part of the arrangement, with the other band members encouraging Eldridge to drop the square stuff and play some real music. Krupa's group released its hit version in June 1941, several months before the United States entered the war. But their Soundies recording—a new version, done specifically for the film—was made on December 18, 1941, little more than a week after the attack on Pearl Harbor. It could be that the band, its popularity soaring, didn't have time to film the visuals for this tune. But it might also be that, with post–Pearl Harbor emotions running high, shouting down even the squarest patriotic song was suddenly off limits. In any case, the Soundies track for "After You've Gone" remained on the shelf for several months. Meanwhile, Krupa and his band debuted in the Soundies *Let Me Off Uptown* and *Thanks for the Boogie Ride* (both Barry/Waller-Snody, 1942), featuring two other numbers they'd recorded in that December session.

Krupa was one of the hottest names in Soundies, and the thought of leaving one of his tracks in the vault must have been excruciating for Soundies Corporation executives. When the musicians' strike of mid-1942 made new band recordings impossible, the pressure to repurpose existing tracks increased dramatically. The scenario devised for *Sugar Hill Masquerade* was a radical rethink, turning what normally would have been an on-camera showcase for Krupa and his band—similar to *Let Me Off Uptown* and *Thanks for the Boogie Ride*—into a dance film credited to other musicians. It strategically allowed the music to shine, driving the action without drawing undue attention to the musicians on screen. And apparently it worked. "The jitterbugging matches the torrid music," *Billboard* wrote approvingly in its mini-review.[8]

But the film is a striking example of the sometimes feckless way that Soundies operated. Though music was the raison d'être behind the entire enterprise, producers could be remarkably cavalier about grabbing anyone who happened to be on hand and putting them in front of the camera, regardless of who was actually heard on the track. Though cost and availability were probable factors, it's not entirely clear how Walter Fuller and his colleagues came to mime the musical performance in this film. A respected trumpeter who'd soloed with Earl Hines's band in the 1930s, Fuller does not appear in any other Soundies. As a dance film *Sugar Hill Masquerade* is a delight, but in terms of musical history there's a downside, with Fuller misattributed as soloist and a prime Krupa-Eldridge track widely overlooked for decades.[9]

How the film's jitterbugs ended up shouting down "Dixie" adds another twist. On the original Krupa disc, the tunes that the band members shout down are "Yankee Doodle" and "Stars and Stripes Forever." "Dixie" and "Columbia, the Gem of the Ocean" are heard only on the version recorded for Soundies (along with "Yankee Doodle"). The new lineup may have been an attempt to extend this popular part of the arrangement, or perhaps to soften the antipatriotic implications of all those Nos—better to shout down "Columbia, the Gem of the Ocean" than "Stars and Stripes Forever." But it's interesting to consider that, if the *Sugar Hill Masquerade* soundtrack had gotten the same visual treatment as *Let Me Off Uptown* and *Thanks for the Boogie Ride*—with Krupa's band on camera and Eldridge spotlighted—the film would have opened with the novel prospect of Eldridge playing "Dixie," only to have it shouted down by his white bandmates.

The scenario for *Sugar Hill Masquerade* gives the track a completely different reading, especially in the opening sequence. It transposes the action onto young people impatient to dance, shrewdly blunting the antipatriotic implications of saying no to "Yankee Doodle Dandy." Similarly, the masquerade-party premise puts the dancers into outlandish costumes rather than controversial zoot suits. But an edge of resistance still permeates the film, especially the brief opening sequence. It takes roughly ten seconds of screen time for the crowd to reject the patriotic tunes, and the shot of them shouting down "Dixie" barely lasts two (fig. 6.3). Blink and you might miss it, as some viewers undoubtedly did. But others would have caught what the shouting was about. The film's celebration of bodies in motion, Scott writes, "is based on modern Harlem youth's rejection of the Dixie past" and the high-pressure patriotism of the wartime present. For Black audiences, *Sugar Hill Masquerade* would have conveyed "the kinetic kick and zeitgeist of rejecting the South and America's patriotic national culture as forces that would govern their bodies."[10]

The film's opening sequence may have started as an inventive workaround for a problematic soundtrack, but it demonstrates the provocative subtexts—sexual and political—that sometimes slipped into these films. *Sugar Hill Masquerade* was produced by Minoco head Jack Barry and longtime musical-film specialist Fred Waller. Under Barry's leadership, Minoco produced dozens of Soundies with Black performers, including many discussed in this chapter. But *Sugar Hill Masquerade* was the only Minoco Soundie to touch, even obliquely, on issues of patriotism and the war, and certainly the only one to diss "Dixie."

Figure 6.3. Dancers shouting down "Dixie" in *Sugar Hill Masquerade* (1942). Library of Congress, Motion Picture, Broadcasting and Recorded Sound Division.

NO MORE MILK

The gulf between a rapidly solidifying urban sensibility and *Gone with the Wind* nostalgia was explored at greater length in Day, Dawn, and Dusk's *Sleep Kentucky Babe* (Crouch-Berne, 1945). Copyrighted in September 1945, just after the war's end, the film is something of a capstone to the urban relocations that shaped the era so incisively, delivered by a vocal group that embodies the subversive cosmopolitanism of Black-cast Soundies.

With lyrics by Irish American songwriter Richard Henry Buck, "Kentucky Babe (Plantation Lullaby)" debuted in 1896 and quickly became an American standard. Written in pseudo-Black-southern dialect, over the decades it has been performed and recorded by at least a dozen white vocalists. The selection on YouTube alone includes Bing Crosby, Eddy Arnold, Dean Martin, and the Lennon Sisters on the *Lawrence Welk Show*. Set in the same living-room space as Day, Dawn and Dusk's Soundie *Fare Thee Well*, the film opens with Robert Caver at the piano and Ed Coleman standing nearby. As they begin to sing, the camera tilts down from Coleman to Gus Simons, in a suit and a baby bib, tucked into an oversized cradle. They start the tune as a straightforward rendition in luscious three-part harmony, meticulously enunciating the pseudo-dialect of the lyrics. The first indication of rupture comes on the refrain, which starts, "Fly away Kentucky babe, fly away to rest." At that point Simons climbs out of the cradle and the song goes upbeat with the phrase "Fly, fly, fly away," followed by an energetic "Shoo!" In close-up, Simons breaks from the song to proclaim, proto-rap style: "Put on my bibble, shoot me the nipple, rock me in the cradle of the Deep, boy"—likely a reference, in that era, to the Deep South.

Simons makes a terrific baby—alternately sleepy and fussy, pulling at his bonnet, rubbing his eyes and periodically wailing. Coleman as his father tenderly urges, "Baby Dumplins, go to sleep." To which Simons responds, "No, no, Baby Dumplins wants to *eat*." In a close-up he stolidly rejects the usual fare: "Please, Daddy, don't give me no milk!" Exasperated, the others ask in unison: "Well, what *do* you want?" Still fidgeting, baby reels off a menu of 1940s urban diversity: kosher corned beef, Maryland fried chicken, spaghetti, minestrone, watermelon citron, Chinese chop suey, Irish stew, chili beans, and bacon, topped off with a pig foot. "Me too!" the others exclaim, surprised only to find such worldly appetites in one so young. As the song ends, Simons reluctantly settles to sleep against Coleman, and all three sing repeats of "Fly, fly, fly, fly away." With each "Shoo!" they vigorously flap their arms, as if the Kentucky babe and all of its cultural baggage were no more than an annoying pigeon.

In the metropolis of Black-cast Soundies, the likeliest spot for *Sleep Kentucky Babe* is an intersection—between a rural southern past and 1940s present, and between a stereotype and its subversion. The film reflects the wit and sophistication of its performers, with their slyly disruptive attitudes toward norms of race and gender. It also suggests an appetite on the part of at least some Soundies viewers for films that spoke to and represented a more diverse and inclusive culture. As much as any Soundie, *Sleep Kentucky Babe* exemplifies how a new media form like Soundies might lend itself to the collective work of creating "imagined selves and imagined worlds," especially in a time of mass migration.[11] In putting a different vision of the city on screen, and in reframing a rural Black American past and the South itself, Black-cast Soundies acknowledged and contributed to cultural realignments that accelerated with the war and continued long after it ended.

7

~m~

ROMANCE, RELATIONSHIPS, LEGS

FOR SOUNDIES FILMMAKERS IN GENERAL, the female body was a primary preoccupation. This was true for Black-cast Soundies makers too, but from a somewhat different perspective. Black-cast Soundies weren't free of sexualized female display—otherwise known as "cheesecake"— but many of them took a more encompassing approach, portraying women and heterosexual relationships in the everyday contexts of romance, humor, workplace, and community.

Thinking of this as a deliberate goal may be attributing more intention to Soundies filmmakers than they actually had. For them, the bodily display of attractive women was an essential Soundies ingredient, and despite the constraints of censorship, scantily dressed dancers turn up with some frequency in the Black-cast films. But filmmakers weren't the only ones involved in making Soundies, and many performers, from stars to bit players, seized the opportunity to portray characters and relationships in a more authentic light. These films make a persuasive case for Soundies as a space for interpreting Black heterosexuality on screen, using the visual language of movie-musical romance to present flirtations and relationships that seldom appeared in Hollywood studio productions.

Much has been written about American women's mass entry into and ejection from the wartime labor force, a trajectory that saw Black women's participation in industrial work nearly triple—to 18 percent from a prewar 6.6 percent—only to plummet once the war ended.[1] But another phenomenon, less widely discussed, had comparably far-reaching impact: the de facto recruitment of American women's sexuality on behalf of the war effort. This was an appropriation of women's bodies in symbol and reality, a conflation of sex and

128

patriotism not seen in American wartime before or since. Culturally, its focal point was the pinup.

Presenting glamorous young women striking mildly—or in some cases very—suggestive poses, pinups were everywhere during the war years. (A photo of white film star Betty Grable in a bathing suit and high heels, winking over her shoulder, was an iconic World War II pinup, with more than five million copies in circulation.) Historian Despina Kakoudaki writes of the pinup's "near domination of the mainstream visual landscape during World War II" and its appropriation by the military-industrial complex that was then taking shape.[2] Commonly appearing on war posters—and in musicals, cartoons, movies, pop songs, and other media, including women's magazines as well as men's—the pinup was a focus of family-oriented war propaganda and patriotism. Considering the effect of pinup culture on women of the era, historian Marilyn E. Hegarty surveys the emergence of "khaki-wackies," "V girls," and "patriotutes," and concludes that as the country moved closer to war, "female sexuality was in a sense nationalized, and a discourse of obligatory sensual patriotism circulated around American women."[3]

As might be expected, Soundies embraced this phenomenon with enthusiasm. Hundreds of the films transpose the pinup aesthetic to the moving image, adapting it to the Panoram's small screen and casual viewing situations. These films have an undeniable antecedent in peep shows. The camera is frankly appraising, gliding up or down the body to linger on legs, hips, and buttocks. In a wartime culture where ogling images of women could be construed as a patriotic obligation, cheesecake-laden Soundies fit right in.

Those Soundies, by and large, are white-cast. Classic cheesecake shots are relatively rare in Black-cast Soundies. In the cinematic city that the Black-cast films create, romance and relationships take place in social spaces—nightclubs, cafés, living rooms, and the occasional rooftop. In these surroundings, Black women are presented as glamorous, competent, and self-possessed, a combination that—Lena Horne notwithstanding—rarely figured in the mainstream cultural terrain of the time. Paradoxically, as women in white-cast Soundies were objectified as pinups and cheesecake, women in many Black-cast Soundies took up the romantic positioning that Hollywood usually allotted to white women.

Men, too, are depicted differently. Where mainstream movies "neutered Black men," Scott writes, "the Black male pleasure that Hollywood deemed illicit came into relief on the Soundies screen."[4] But Black male pleasure is arguably not the main motivator in these Soundies. Instead, it may be seen as a response from male performers to the active agency of the women who share the film frame with them—women who present themselves not only as desirable sexual objects but dynamic subjects who initiate, respond to, and participate in the action around them.

GRAB THAT GAZE

Despite their anonymity, female background actors were crucial to the films' vision of romance and male-female relationships, especially in Soundies' early years. Uncredited female players are everywhere in the Black-cast films— smiling to the camera, filling the instrumental breaks with quick dance numbers, walking arm-in-arm with male stars and listening appreciatively to their performances. In the majority of these films, women bit players are dynamic and personable, relating to other performers rather than the camera. As noted, it took several months for the Soundies organization to start producing Black-cast films. But once it did, a battalion of chic, self-assured women actors, working primarily in New York, began expanding and enriching the depiction of African American romance on screen.

Like bit players everywhere, background performers in Black-cast Soundies generally appear briefly in nonspeaking roles. Within those limitations, the women in these films have broad capabilities: they insert themselves into the action, respond to their partners and each other, and improvise with flair. (Watch Winnie Johnson, in the uncredited role of girlfriend, welcome singer Jimmy Rushing in Count Basie's Take Me Back, Baby [Barry/Waller-Snody, 1941], then turn on him after finding his little black book—clearly mouthing the word "Shit!" as she reads it.)[5] The camera often lingers on performers' vividly expressive faces as they gaze at their partners or each other. Visual historian Deborah Willis has written about the "participatory self-representation" of Black Americans sitting for photographic portraits in the late nineteenth and twentieth centuries, and this self-defining, collaborating-with-the-camera dynamic is part of these performances as well.[6] The number of Black women appearing in the films is enough to set Soundies apart from Hollywood movies of the time (and most of American film up to that point), but the contributions of even minor female players go beyond simply being in the frame.

In several Soundies made by New York–based Minoco Productions, women bit players are paired with members of close-harmony vocal groups like the Charioteers, the Deep River Boys, and the Delta Rhythm Boys. This casting is less lopsided than it might seem. Though the singers are the stars, they're identified as a group rather than as individuals, with no performer singled out for special treatment. There is a profound visual pleasure in seeing three or four couples fill the frame in a typical movie-musical lineup, with the aura of warmth and affection multiplied across different pairings. In general, male performers in these films are at ease with their partners and respond to them appreciatively. Set in a comfortable living room, the Chanticleers' *If You Treat Me to a Hug* (Crouch-Crouch, 1943) shows two of the singers settled into easy chairs with women (Laverne Keane and Francine Everett) who exchange fond, teasing glances with them. A similar warmth pervades the opening shots of the RCM–produced *Paper Doll* (Coslow-Berne, 1942), which picture three of the four Mills Brothers seated with women—Avanelle Harris, Lucille (Lucy) Battle, and Juanita Moore—in their laps. As Harry Mills solos, Moore shares the frame with him, playing off his performance with attentive glances and relaxed, affectionate body language.

Flirtatious byplay is also central to the Charioteers' *The Darktown Strutters' Ball* (Barry-Snody, 1941). Near the beginning and again in the closing sequence, the film transforms the 1917 tune into a series of intimate moments (fig. 7.1). Seated in a descending diagonal, the women are shown with their partners in a string of quick two-shot vignettes. As her partner sings about wearing a top hat, the first woman (Deanie Gordon) gestures to her own wide-brimmed hat with a teasing expression. As the frame shifts to the next couple, the second woman (Tweedie Mason) responds with an exaggerated glance skyward, then back to her partner. The third (Jackie Lewis) reacts to a line about winning a prize for "being dressed so fine" with a gesture of kidding disbelief and a smile to the camera. As the song nears its close, the fourth woman (Hilda "Hibby" Brown) exchanges a sustained, laughing look with her companion, and the film ends with a wide shot of the four couples in affectionate embraces, gazing out at the camera.

A multicouple lineup is also the payoff in *Hark! Hark! The Lark* (Waller-Snody, 1941), a comic romance that has the Deep River Boys wooing four sisters (Winnie Johnson, Vivian Brown, Hibby Brown, and an unidentified performer), the daughters of an irascible patriarch.[7] The film neatly bridges urban and rural: despite a woodsy setting, the singers wear tailored suits and fedoras, and upstairs at the window, their sweethearts are a stylish crowd. (The grouchy father, unidentified and uncredited, gets a nice bit of slapstick too.) The action plays out against a medley of the old tune "Li'l Liza" and the title song, which is an adaptation of a poem by Shakespeare, set to a Schubert *leider*—a typical Soundies cocktail of high and pop culture with a swing-time twist. As the film closes, the couples pair off at the doorway, then line up in the garden for a slow pan capturing each duo in close-up, followed by a final wide shot of them beaming at the camera.

Figure 7.1. *Clockwise from top left*: Deanie Gordon, Tweedie Mason, Jackie Lewis, and Hilda "Hibby" Brown partner with the Charioteers in *The Darktown Strutters' Ball* (1941); *below*, the film's closing shot. Courtesy Mark Cantor Archive.

The abundant two-shots and close-ups in these Soundies echo the visual language of Hollywood romance but also make sense for the Panoram screen, which handled intimate framing much better than large-scale spectacle. When the camera does pull back to full-body long shots, it frequently reveals figures in confident motion rather than the static poses and isolated legs and hips of cheesecake shots. In the Delta Rhythm Boys' *Take the 'A' Train* (Barry/Waller-Snody, 1941), the vocalists' female companions single themselves out with distinctive, dancing walks, then play to the camera as it slowly pans across their nightclub table. In *Ain't She Pretty* (Crouch-Crouch, 1944) and *Emily Brown* (Williams-Gould, 1943), individual women are praised in song by male performers, who look on admiringly as the women take the spotlight with solo dances.

Narrative structure in these films could be minimal, which left room for improvisation. One performer who scored brilliantly in the improvisational arena was Vivian Brown. A stage performer and Cotton Club dancer, Vivian and her sister Hibby were known in entertainment circles as the Brown Twins. Solo or with Hibby, Vivian makes eye-catching appearances in upward of a dozen Soundies, including *Hark! Hark! The Lark* and *Virginia, Georgia and Caroline* (Barry/Waller-Snody, 1942), *Dear Old Southland* (Waller-Snody, 1941), and *Toot That Trumpet!* (Barry/Waller-Snody, 1941).[8] In *Hark! Hark!*, for example, she has a deft bit of business at the upstairs window, about a minute into the film, in which she eloquently bickers with Hibby over which man each will end up with. Lasting a mere two seconds, it's a vivid example of seizing the moment—any moment—for improvisation.

Vivian Brown appears in all four of Fats Waller's Soundies, in performances ranging from background extra to uncredited featured player. Dancing alongside the man with the outsized "pedal extremities" in *Your Feet's Too Big* (Barry/Waller-Murray, 1941), her screen time is minimal and largely focused on her lower legs. As a jitterbug in a striped T-shirt and neck scarf, she starts out in the background in *The Joint Is Jumpin'* (Waller-Murray, 1941) but grabs the spotlight with a quick hip-shaking entrance as Waller comments, "What is that that just walked in, just look at the way it's twitchin'. Oh, mercy!" In *Honeysuckle Rose* (Waller-Murray, 1941), Brown is the archetypal "girl on the piano," sharing an easy nonverbal camaraderie with Waller, then joining the dancers on the instrumental break before returning to the piano for more byplay with Waller and a strategic show of leg.

Ain't Misbehavin' (Barry/Waller-Murray, 1941) is Brown's quasi-star turn and the only Soundie in which she appears to sing (fig. 3.1, p. 54). In fact, she lip-syncs, or sidelines, a soundtrack recorded by vocalist Myra Johnson, and in the recording Waller calls her by Johnson's name. (Johnson herself appears on camera in *The Joint Is Jumpin'* and three non-Waller Soundies, showing off her own flair for musical comedy in *Let's Get Down to Business* [Crouch-Crouch, 1943]). In *Ain't Misbehavin'*, Brown more than holds her own against Waller's mugging, and their chemistry has a satisfying fizz. When her rivals' high-kicking chorus line distracts his eye ("Sweet essence of pink buttermilk! Look what's goin' on here!"), she jumps down to flirt with the other musicians until Waller calls her back for a turn on the vocals. He weaves his ad-libbed counterpoint through her lines, and they end the film side by side at the piano, smiling to the camera, not quite cheek to cheek.

It's no coincidence that the Fats Waller Soundies and most of the others mentioned here were produced by Jack Barry and/or Fred Waller. Barry was the head of Minoco, the Soundies Corporation's New York production company, and both he and Fred Waller had extensive musical production experience. In Minoco's first year of filming, affectionate romance and active, self-assured women bit players quickly became hallmarks of the company's Black-cast films. The Brown sisters aren't the only ones to turn up regularly: Winnie Johnson, who plays Jimmy Rushing's sweetheart in *Take Me Back, Baby*, is also his dance partner in *Air Mail Special* (Barry/Waller-Snody, 1941) and on camera in two of the Fats Waller Soundies. She's one of the daughters in *Hark! Hark! The Lark*, part of the crowd behind Sister Rosetta Tharpe in *Shout! Sister, Shout!* (Barry-Primi, 1941) and a nightclub patron in *Take the 'A' Train*, and she gleefully pelts the Delta Rhythm Boys with rotten vegetables in their swing-powered *Rigoletto Blues* (Barry/Waller-Snody, 1941).

From the start, Barry and his colleagues saw Soundies as a distinct cinematic form, and they took a briskly experimental attitude toward what might work in a three-minute film playing on a small screen in a noisy bar. The uncredited women players in Minoco's Black-cast Soundies were a big part of the films' appeal, largely because they had the latitude to develop their own approaches to self-presentation on camera, which Barry described as Soundies' "be yourself" performance style.[9] Unlike scripted roles in Hollywood movies and race films, these brief, nonverbal performances rely on movement, gaze, and gesture to create expressive on-screen presences. Individual shots go by quickly, at times almost subliminally, but the effect is cumulative. Coming early in Soundies' development, the Minoco Black-cast romances opened a space for the performance of heterosexual relationships, which evolved over time with the changing roster of Soundies makers, performers, and music.

THE OTHER SIDE OF ROMANCE

The absence of Black female vocal groups in Soundies rules out a reverse of the multicouple pairings that characterize the male-vocal-group films. Black-cast Soundies with female stars usually spotlight one woman rather than a group, and it's more common for male stars to be supported by women bit players than for female stars to receive that treatment from men. This is especially true in the Minoco productions. Active women bit players may be the house style in Minoco's Black-cast Soundies, but women stars generally are not. Only Maxine Sullivan and Sister Rosetta Tharpe achieve that status in the Minoco films, and Tharpe shares the billing with Lucky Millinder and His Orchestra.

Women stars fare better with other Soundies production companies, often with the support of male background players. A mutely admiring suitor (Jess Brooks) shares Dorothy Dandridge's open carriage in the RCM-produced *Easy Street* (Coslow-Murphy, 1941), fading into the background as Dandridge strolls the avenue and then welcoming her as she returns for the closing shots. A dashing young man in top hat and tails, silent but attentive, escorts an evening-gowned June Richmond in Filmcraft's *We're Stepping Out Tonight* (Crouch-Weiss, 1945), and Vanita Smythe serves up cake and double entendres to a wordlessly beaming companion in *Back Door Man* (Crouch-Crouch, 1946). At the self-effacing end of the performance spectrum, a stone-faced cop listens impassively to Smythe's account in *They Raided the Joint* (Crouch-Crouch, 1946)—the opposite of the anonymous actor hovering near Una Mae Carlisle's piano in *I'm a Good, Good Woman* (Crouch-Crouch, 1944), who responds almost too expressively to Carlisle and her music. In Smythe's *Get It Off Your Mind* (Crouch-Crouch, 1946), singer-songwriter Claude DeMetrius takes a role not unlike Winnie Johnson's in *Take Me Back, Baby* or Vivian Brown's in *Ain't Misbehavin'*, turning in a suavely comic, completely silent performance. Unlike the women, though, he gets costar billing.

As the war dragged on, some films took a more down-to-earth approach to sexual relationships. Playing off the anxieties of wartime separations, a few are not just humorous but downright cynical. In two Soundies made in 1942 and 1944, respectively, comedian Dudley Dickerson catches his partner in a clinch with the iceman (making a delivery for the pre-electric ice box, which was literally cooled by chunks of ice). In *The Outskirts of Town* (Coslow-Berne, 1942) Dickerson sings at the table (lip-synching vocals recorded by Louis Jordan), as behind his back, a vivacious (and screen-credited) Theresa Harris frolics with a stream of arrivals, moving from the iceman to the grocery boy, mailman, and milkman. "It may seem funny, honey / As funny as can be," Dickerson sings morosely to the camera, "But if we have any children / I want them all to look like me." In *Low Down Dog* (Gould-Gould, 1944) an uncredited Avanelle Harris nabs even more screen time. Openly contemptuous of Dickerson (here voiced by Joe Turner), she flounces off to the living room to flirt with Meade "Lux" Lewis, who happens to be there playing the film's piano track.[10] With an abrupt costume change, she then phones another beau (Leonard "Lennie" Bluett, also uncredited), who arrives to whisk her away as the song winds down, with Dickerson's character protesting to the last.

In *Low, Short and Squatty* (Crouch-Crouch, 1946), Vanita Smythe—long and lean herself—sings the joys of the pint-sized paramour ("Shorty" Jackson, uncredited) who gazes up at her ecstatically. The same odd-couple pairing turns up in *We're Stepping Out Tonight*, not between star June Richmond and her companion but two dancers at the instrumental break. Soundies were fairly scrupulous about not poking fun at heftier women headliners like Richmond, but masculine fitness was a wartime obsession and male performers didn't always escape unscathed. Jimmy Rushing's aversion to physical activity is the visual punch line in Count Basie's *Air Mail Special*, and Les Hite's gym workout is played for laughs in *Pudgy Boy* (Barry/Waller-Snody, 1942). There, though, the last laugh is Hite's. After lamenting his own lack of sex appeal, he exposes a supposed strongman as a fraud, bending an iron rod that turns out to be rubber. In the closing lines Hite gets the girl, who admonishes him against losing weight. Like the large woman jitterbugging through *I Want a Big Fat Mama* (Barry-Primi, 1941), Hite's "pudgy boy" is presented as a legitimate object of desire.

In one of the few (perhaps only) Black-cast Soundies to show a couple in their bedroom, at least one partner is in no shape to make any moves. In *Sho Had a Wonderful Time* (Crouch-Crouch, 1946), Claude DeMetrius shares star billing with Vanita Smythe but steals the show as a painfully hungover party animal, clutching an ice bag to his head. DeMetrius cowrote the song with Louis Jordan, who had a hit with it the following year as "Sure Had a Wonderful Time."[11] Not much can top the offhand nonchalance of Jordan's delivery, but DeMetrius and Smythe give the tune a warm domestic spin—despite a carefully maintained physical distance—and clearly have fun with the lyrics if not each other (fig. 7.2).

Soundies' varied depictions of heterosexual relationships suggest an interesting parallel with *Jubilee*, the radio program for US servicemen that, in its early years, featured Black performers exclusively. Sexual candor played a large part in *Jubilee*, with men and women commenting on and critiquing relationships. Women *Jubilee* performers in particular—including Soundies stars Ida

Figure 7.2. Claude DeMetrius and Vanita Smythe in *Sho Had a Wonderful Time* (1946). Courtesy Mark Cantor Archive.

James, Ivie Anderson, and Maxine Sullivan, among others—enjoyed a latitude of self-presentation similar to that of women performers in Black-cast Soundies. "As a community of Black entertainers," historian Lauren Rebecca Sklaroff writes, "*Jubilee* provided many Black women with a degree of comfort in exhibiting sexual candor, not solely for the purpose of entertaining white individuals, but as part of their own self-expression."[12] The same may be said of women performers in Black-cast Soundies—not only stars like Dorothy Dandridge, Edna Mae Harris, Mable Lee, and Vanita Smythe but background players like Vivian Brown and Winnie Johnson.

Though largely played for laughs, less flattering portrayals of women could be revealing indicators of masculine anxieties. *Baby Don't Go 'Way from Me* (Crouch-Crouch, 1946) plays out as a comic exercise in female sexual predation, pairing Mable Lee with veteran Hollywood actor Lincoln Perry as his character Stepin Fetchit, "The Laziest Man in the World." Perry was "a near-virtuoso scene stealer," writes Miriam J. Petty, playing a figure who was "the apotheosis of the 1930s chief African American racial stereotype—as well as a blatant parody thereof, for those able and willing to see his performance as such."[13] In *Baby Don't Go 'Way from Me*, Lee's sexuality carries an assertive, almost aggressive edge, while the Stepin Fetchit character—made over as a stylish but still bumbling zoot-suiter—is cast as her hapless victim.

A taut sexual undertone runs through *Is You Is or Is You Ain't My Baby* (Hersh-Berne, 1944), starring the King Cole Trio and vocalist Ida James. Cowritten by Louis Jordan, the song playfully reflects wartime relationship anxieties, but Cole's performance has a sharper edge than the lyrics suggest. He shoots annoyed offscreen glances toward James and attempts to win the viewer's corroboration with an exchange of looks through the camera. (In this he's repeatedly stymied by the film's editor, who cuts away the moment Cole connects with the lens.) As James approaches, Cole turns up his jacket lapel as if warding off a sudden chill. James, for her part, combats his hostility with unctuous charm. She sends sustained, loving looks in his direction but faced with his intransigence, she moves on to guitarist Oscar Moore instead. What should be a light, teasing romance comes off as oddly tense, its strained humor and affection giving perhaps a truer reflection of wartime anxieties than originally intended.

Occasionally the joking about women turns truculent, usually prompted by the song lyrics. Set in an urban backyard, *Babbling Bess* (Crouch-Crouch, 1943) is the barbed depiction of a nonstop gossip—often seen as a wartime security risk—with the Chanticleers disgustedly upbraiding an attractive woman (Francine Everett) who sits yakking with friends. "It's a wonder your tonsils ain't sore," they complain. Taking a more cheerful approach, the refrain in Louis Jordan's *Caldonia* (Adams-Crouch, 1945) is so infectiously catchy that its insult almost slips by: "Caldonia! Caldonia! What makes your big head so hard?" In *Honey Chile* (Adams-Crouch, 1945), he blithely describes his sweetheart as "the ugliest woman you've ever seen." Like Jordan, Phil Moore in *Lazy Lady* (Crouch-Crouch, 1945) is good-natured and upbeat, but his lyrics are a string of put-downs: "She's dumb, she's numb, she's slow as they come." Women were achieving wartime financial clout, and a later line suggests this as a possible source of the antipathy. Noting that the woman in question has no need of a husband—or love, for that matter—he complains: "She wouldn't fall if you gave her a shove."

If *Lazy Lady* is a skein of humorous insults, Moore's *Chair Song* (Crouch-Crouch, 1946) is an extended double entendre about a woman and her "chair." "Look at that bottom," he sings, adding that "she sits down on it, just won't give it away." It is perhaps the only Black-cast Soundie to suggest the wartime sexual pressures on women—a theme that runs through a number of white-cast Soundies, from Jimmie Dodd's *Lackadaisical Lady* (Ratoff-Berne, 1941) to Carolyn Ayres's *On Time* (Barry-Curran, 1943). Vanita Smythe's *Get It Off Your Mind* is one of the rare Black-cast Soundies to push back on this score, and

Myra Johnson does the same—up to a point—in *Let's Get Down to Business* (Crouch-Crouch, 1943).

Though there are clearly a few Black-cast films that express critical attitudes toward women, it's rare for one to show women turning the tables. The closest may be Mable Lee's *Cats Can't Dance* (Crouch-Crouch, 1945)—a nightclub number that has her rejecting otherwise stellar suitors because they're hopeless on the dance floor—or June Richmond telling off her faithless love in *Time Takes Care of Everything* (Crouch-Crouch, 1946). On this point white-cast Soundies are more outspoken. There are several in which women reject men, humorously or not, and at least one in which a female star complains to the camera about a disappointing bedmate (*Stupid Little Cupid*, Roosevelt-LeBorg, 1941). But relatively few Black-cast Soundies criticize either sex, and this in itself suggests one limitation on how far the films would go, and in what direction, in envisioning heterosexual relationships on screen.

MARRIAGE AND OTHER PARTNERSHIPS

Not until the war's final phases do themes like homecoming, marriage, and family start turning up with any frequency in Soundies. Even then they're relatively rare, especially among the Black-cast films. But African American representation of these themes was even rarer in mainstream wartime culture as a whole, and on that basis alone the films merit a quick look.

Walking With My Honey (Crouch-Crouch, 1945), with Cab Calloway and vocalist Dotty Saulter, is perhaps the only Black-cast Soundie to explicitly mention betrothal and honeymooning. Beyond that, only one film presents a wedding on screen. Staged by Oscar-winning dance director Dave Gould, *Emily Brown* (Williams-Gould, 1943) has the look and feel of a number in a Hollywood backstage musical. It opens with Bob Parrish as the cop on a big-city beat, singing about his sweetheart to a chorus line of smartly dressed women dancers. Eventually Emily herself (credited costar Chinky Grimes) makes her entrance, dancing solo and with Parrish, and in a grand finale she returns as his bride. There are perhaps a dozen white-cast Soundies in which weddings figure in the narrative—including one, *The Blushing Bride* (Barry/Waller-Snody, 1942), in which the bride, momentarily left to her own devices, does a smiling striptease. The only Black-cast Soundie to end with wedding bells, *Emily Brown* is joyous rather than joking. Its closing shot has the newlyweds as the moving-image center of a two-dimensional drawing, its radiating sections depicting a bride and groom, a figure pushing a baby carriage, two saxophone players, and other wedding and music motifs—a low-budget approximation of a Hollywood special-effects ending.

Parenthood is another theme explored in only one Black-cast Soundie, but it hints at the shift toward family life that began as the war wound down. In *His Rockin' Horse Ran Away* (Coslow-Berne, 1944), Ida James is a mother singing a humorous, up-tempo account of her young son's house-wrecking playtime. But the staging undercuts the lyrics: instead of the chaos that the song implies, James is exquisitely outfitted in a ruffled blouse and skirt, singing to women guests in a comfortable, notably unwrecked living room. At the instrumental break, the supposed little terror makes an entrance in his pajamas, as well-behaved as a four- or five-year-old can be. James sings the second part of the song to him, embracing him on the sentimental closing lines. Her refined interpretation counters a version that white performer Betty Hutton introduced earlier that year in the movie *And the Angels Sing* (1944). Staged as a nightclub number, Hutton's performance is a YouTube classic, with broad physical comedy that has her galloping across the stage astride a chair, miming the relief of shucking a too-tight girdle and other earthy touches. James's Soundie offers a different vision of family life—a sophisticated woman entertaining guests in an immaculate home, attentively mothering a charming child, with his father present in the lyrics if not on camera. By 1944, it was a vision that many an overworked wartime parent might have wished for.

Beyond marriage and family life, a different dynamic emerges in other Soundies: a sense of partnership that has more to do with the performance than the narrative behind it. *Bli-Blip* (Coslow-Berne, 1942) stars singer-dancers Marie Bryant and Paul White, who originated the number in the Duke Ellington revue *Jump for Joy*.[14] They sing their love and mutual admiration in hepcat slang but rarely share the camera frame, let alone the sort of fond embraces seen in *Paper Doll* or *If You Treat Me to a Hug*. The first half of the film is largely constructed from individual close-ups, switching to a wide frame to capture the duo's razor-sharp dance moves. The energy that crackles between them is more performative than personal. Unlike the romantic Black-cast Soundies, the groundbreaking aspect of a film like *Bli-Blip* lies outside its narrative, in the parity between its two performers. This may be attributable, in part, to *Bli-Blip*'s roots in theater. A similar side-by-side style characterizes the veteran song-and-patter duo Apus and Estrellita (Montrose Morse and Estrellita Bernier), whose two Soundies were likely developed from their stage act. Marital bickering is the meat of their comic routine in *I'm Tired* (Crouch-Crouch, 1944), but the duo's solid performance partnership gives the material its punch.

A different but no less effective set of performance partnerships unfolds in a series of Cab Calloway Soundies made in 1945. Though indisputably the star, he pairs off with women in three spirited performances. As noted, in *Walking with*

My Honey he trades vocals with singer Dotty Saulter, posing arm in arm as a soon-to-wed couple framed by a rose-decked garden arch. In *I Was Here When You Left Me* (Crouch-Crouch, 1945), he's strictly a bandleader, energetically supporting Saulter's turn as solo vocalist. And in *Foo, a Little Ballyhoo* (Crouch-Crouch, 1945), he partners with dancer Rusty Stanford for an electrifying jitterbug. One could make a similar claim for *Good-Nite All* (Leonard-Leonard, 1943, discussed in chap. 5), in which singer-pianist Johnny Taylor joins forces with a female colleague to set the film's urbane, archly humorous tone. But in that film, Taylor is the only one with screen credit; in the Calloway Soundies, the women are not only prominently featured but prominently credited.

In depicting heterosexual relationships, Black-cast Soundies' greatest strengths are arguably the intimacy of their on-screen pairings and the active agency of their women performers. The films discussed in this section go a step further, embedding those relationships in a broader social fabric, in idealized terms that celebrate them as life milestones: joyous betrothal, stylish wedding, serene parenthood. Those depictions are augmented by films that spotlight the creative parity of female-male performance partnerships. In these ways and others, Black-cast Soundies extended and consolidated the depiction of heterosexual relationships on film in the World War II era.

CHEESECAKE AND CENSORSHIP

Despite their coteries of chic, fully clothed, and actively participatory women, there was no way that Black-cast Soundies could avoid cheesecake entirely, or necessarily want to. The aggressively heterosexual wartime culture and unending need for revenue made a certain amount of female display inevitable. It was a pinup-mad era, and with or without a patriotic subtext, the screen time that Soundies lavished on female extras would have been an obvious way to keep the dimes rolling in. As noted earlier, cheesecake is nowhere near as prevalent in Black-cast Soundies as it is in the white-cast films, but there are a few exceptions. Even in Black-cast Soundies, Crouch would occasionally set the camera at crotch level, especially when high kicks were part of the dance routine. And despite Dorothy Dandridge's college-coed image in *Swing for Your Supper*, Coslow and Berne had no compunctions about outfitting her in as little as possible for her two "jungle" Soundies.

The dichotomy in Dandridge's Soundies persona demonstrates the broader ambiguity surrounding images of women in home-front culture, and the conflation of wholesomeness and allure, patriotism and sexuality that define the wartime pinup. For servicemen, connoisseurship in this sphere was a requisite of barracks life: "Every soldier boy has his pride and joy in his beauty cavalcade," proclaims the white-cast Soundie *Pin-ups on Parade* (Crouch-Crouch, 1943). As the number of Black people in the armed forces increased, the demand for Black pinups surged. "The whole thing that made me a star was the war," Lena Horne remarked in a 1990 interview. "Of course the Black guys couldn't put Betty Grable's picture in their footlockers. But they could put mine."[15]

Horne appears in three Soundies copyrighted in 1944 and 1945, but she herself never performed before a Soundies camera. Her films were clipped from a two-reel short made in 1941, before her 1943 Hollywood hits *Cabin in the Sky* and *Stormy Weather*. For Soundies, Dorothy Dandridge was a quintessential pinup figure, and she negotiated that fraught terrain to emerge as one of the Panoram's first stars.

Even in her "jungle" Soundies, Dandridge is never literally depicted as a pinup, holding a static pose as the camera lens moves up or down her body, nor is she reduced to a series of body parts—treatments common for women in white-cast Soundies. She's most often depicted in motion and in character, in close-ups of her face and long shots of her moving figure that present her as whole and utterly individual. That depiction is consistent with Black-cast Soundies' overall style—women background players are shown this way too. But it's also a testament to Dandridge's magnetism as a performer, even in the Soundies intended to show off as much of her body as possible.

There is one aspect of the pinup aesthetic, however, that Dandridge makes her own. While Black women background players turn their active gazes toward male stars and at times each other, Dandridge is unsurpassed in her ability to relate to the viewer. Kakoudaki notes that in a two-dimensional magazine or photo pinup, the figure "usually has a direct eye-line connection to the implied viewer, and this imagined mutual recognition between viewer and model gives the pin-up its characteristic allure and sexual content."[16] In her Soundies, Dandridge displays a seemingly effortless ability to establish this type of connection through the camera, and her close-ups are a moving-image embodiment of that dynamic—a cinematic analog to the paper pinup's intimate glance.

Despite the obvious dime-drawing power of female bodily display, there was a pragmatic reason to downplay it in Black-cast Soundies. Though not subject to federal oversight, the films were actively reviewed by censorship boards in states like New York, Ohio, and Pennsylvania, where significant Soundies audiences were located—and, as George Ulcigan testified, where the Soundies Corporation did most of its business. As noted, Black-cast Soundies drew a disproportionate amount of censorship, totaling almost sixty of the 175 Soundies cited by one board or another.[17] Frequent triggers included risqué lyrics, suggestive dancing, and indecent exposure.

Over time there was a shift toward less bodily exposure in the Black-cast films that isn't seen in Soundies as a whole, suggesting that a perception of Black female sexuality could itself trigger censorship. Dandridge's abbreviated apparel in *Jungle Jig* drew censorship rulings in multiple states, but Mable Lee's feathered outfit in *Chicken Shack Shuffle* (Crouch-Crouch, 1943) had perhaps four times the coverage of Dandridge's plumage, and that film was censored all the same. In *Sho Had a Wonderful Time* and *Does You Do or Does You Don't* (Crouch-Crouch, 1946), the allure of Vanita Smythe's sheer negligee is all but canceled by the armor-like brassiere and panties underneath, but both films drew rulings nonetheless.

The largest number of censored Black-cast Soundies apparently involved Black women dancers performing, solo or in groups, with sexually suggestive movements and costumes as frequently cited reasons. In some cases, light-skinned Black women appearing with darker men may have created, in censors' eyes, the impression of miscegenation—a hot-button issue for censorship in general. When Fredi Washington played opposite Paul Robeson in *The Emperor Jones* (1933), for instance, she'd been required to perform in dark makeup lest her natural skin tone create the impression that she was white.[18] For the most part, women dancers and bit players in Soundies are light-skinned. Given censors' sensitivity to miscegenation and how rarely light-skinned Black women appear in Hollywood films of the 1930s and 1940s, the colorism in Black-cast Soundies is problematic but may also be seen as transgressive—creating a space where, as Scott writes, "the reality of a multi-colored African American population could be perceived."[19] The dancers in Soundies like *Close Shave* (Coslow-Berne, 1942) and *Rhythmania* (Crouch-Crouch, 1943) have a range of skin tones, but in many other films the women are notably light-skinned. New York–produced Soundies in particular were likely to feature dancers from nightclub floor shows, revues, and musical theater, which often cast light-skinned performers. Their prevalence in these films, and the censorship that their presence could provoke, clearly made female display a commercial risk in Black-cast Soundies.

Given the state of Soundies budgets after 1942, it's entirely possible that, along with the dancers, the costumes and choreography were borrowed too. And the costuming could be suggestive: the West Coast–produced *Close Shave* opens with a line of dancers, their backs to the camera, who appear to be wearing nothing but ruffled panties and full-length gloves. Only when they turn is the upper half of the costume visible. For the most part, though, exposure is more cautiously limited to legs and midriff, as in *Jackpot* and *Poppin' the Cork* (both Crouch-Crouch, 1943). In *The Pollard Jump* (Crouch-Crouch, 1946), starring dancer Nicky O'Daniel, Crouch's camera is uncharacteristically frank in its appraisal, suggestively catching the dancers' high kicks and appreciatively tilting up O'Daniel's legs and torso. The camera also lingers appraisingly on Mable Lee and the Ebonettes in *Coalmine Boogie*. Not surprisingly, at least some of these films were censored in one or more states.

In general, though, this sort of suggestive treatment is rare in the Black-cast films, especially for nondancers. In the King Cole Trio's *Frim Fram Sauce* (Crouch-Crouch, 1945), for instance, the camera catches a fashionably dressed woman at the café counter, tilting from a close-up on her face down to her crossed legs. The effect is almost polite: her legs are displayed only to the knee, and the camera doesn't pause, even for a moment, to ogle them.

Only one Black-cast Soundie overtly references wartime pinup culture, and its show of leg is as well-mannered as the display in *Frim Fram Sauce* and even more good-natured. The wink to the viewer is a key feature of the two-dimensional pinup, and it's frequently used by bathing beauties and other cheesecake figures in white-cast Soundies. *Legs Ain't No Good* (Barry/Waller-Graham, 1942) is one of the few Black-cast Soundies to use it as a recurring motif. The film opens with Edna Mae Harris at her bedroom dressing table, adjusting her stocking with a show of leg before winking to the camera as she heads out the door. Once on the street, she joins "Slim" Thomas to perform a short dance and to sideline a soundtrack recorded by white vocalists Peggy Mann and Tommy Taylor, backed by white bandleader Teddy Powell and His Orchestra: "Tain't No Good," a song that had been a big hit for Cab Calloway a few months earlier.[20]

As Harris and Thomas dance down the street, the film cuts to a row of women seated nearby at an outdoor lunch counter. Patriotic war posters, prominently displayed in the background, make the connection between female display and the war effort: as the camera pans left to right, the women present their legs one by one, almost as if for military review. Later, the camera returns to dancer Alice Barker, seated alone at the counter, as she lifts her skirt, extends her leg, and winks to the viewer. The film closes on a shot of Harris, with the camera tilting up her body as she raises her skirt slightly and strikes a bent-leg, pinup-style pose, ending with a close-up on her face as she repeats "Tain't no good" and winks again to the camera (fig. 7.3). The tone is playful and knowing, and both Harris and Barker appear to have fun with the leg-show premise. The lengths of leg they bare are modest by almost any standard, and the camera is interested but polite. Wartime pinup culture may have been inescapable, and the "obligatory sensual patriotism" that Hegarty noted might have been onerous, but those pressures barely register in *Legs Ain't No Good*.

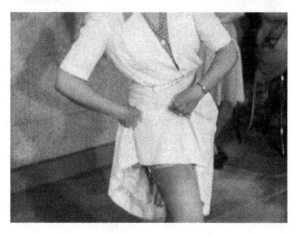

Figure 7.3. *Legs Ain't No Good* (1942): Framed by patriotic posters, Alice Barker winks to the camera as she shows a little leg (*top*); Star Edna Mae Harris ups the ante with a pinup-style wink (*center and bottom*). Courtesy Mark Cantor Archive.

GIVING GENDER A NUDGE

Beneath the cultural obsession with cheesecake was the unspoken assumption of an emphatic, pervasive heterosexuality. As a business and an entertainment form, Soundies were heavily invested in that patriotic sexuality, and an overwhelming number of the films reflect it. But in this, as with other cultural friction points, Soundies' decentralized production system created a space for alternate meanings. While most of the films aggressively reinforce prevailing gender norms, there are some that subtly or blatantly undermine them.

Only a few Black-cast Soundies so much as nudge the era's ironclad assumptions about gender, and all of them feature men. In *Sugar Hill Masquerade* (Barry/Waller-Graham, 1942), dancers at a neighborhood costume party take the spotlight in groups and pairs, in performances that are exuberant and at times playfully, heterosexually suggestive. Then, not quite two minutes in, a tall Lindy-hopper in women's clothing partners with a smaller male dancer to perform an athletic variation on the short-tall comic mismatch. Towering over the other dancers, the Lindy-hopper is a singular performer, and his apparel—a flowered dress with lace collar and cuffs—further sets him apart. He moves with awkward, angular grace, spinning and lifting his partner with ease. The crowd responds appreciatively, smiling and clapping in encouragement, as they do for all dancers taking a turn. Amid the pointedly heterosexual performances of other dancers, the inclusion of a male couple—especially one that features such a striking figure—and the crowd's response exemplify the open-minded outlook toward difference found in many Soundies: not only tolerant but embracing, even joyful.

In other films, the high-culture pretensions of opera—and the eminently lampoonable figure of the operatic soprano—invite broad gender play. The Delta Rhythm Boys' *Rigoletto Blues* (Barry/Waller-Snody, 1941) presents two of the singers in semidrag, with dresses worn over trousers. The singers deal matter-of-factly with their wigs and padded bustlines, playing them for laughs. They occasionally flip their blond curls aside, and as the song winds down, one singer gives his frontage an irritated upward shove. The men's outfits have a haphazard appearance, and though the wigs suggest otherwise, the backyard washday setting implies that their dresses might have been pulled off the laundry line for some spontaneous fun.

Faust (Crouch-Berne, 1945) explores opera's potential for gender play with more gusto. Starring Day, Dawn, and Dusk, the film deliberately evokes high culture, the better to puncture it with swing. Unlike *Rigoletto Blues*, with its city backyard setting, *Faust* unfolds in high culture's own habitat—a proscenium stage with an appropriate backdrop. As the film opens, Ed Coleman sits center

Figure 7.4. Day, Dawn, and Dusk (*from left*, Robert Caver, Augustus "Gus" Simons, and Ed Coleman) in *Faust* (1945). Courtesy Mark Cantor Archive.

frame, wearing long blond braids and a sheer dress over his trousers. With Robert Caver frame left at the piano, Coleman gazes into a hand mirror, trilling happily, adjusting his hair and admiring the brooch perfectly placed at his collar. Augustus "Gus" Simons enters as the Devil, attempting to seduce Coleman into fleeing with him. When Coleman refuses, Simons stabs him dead. A quick optical effect flips the film frame, and Caver and Simons reappear in stylish 1940s streetwear to launch into an energetic version of the tune "Uptown." Coleman returns, minus the braids, wearing an extravagantly ruffled dress over his trousers and a feathered chapeau set at a rakish angle (fig. 7.4). His ensemble is chic, witty, and clearly not snatched off a clothesline. "Whatcha waitin' for, tall skinny mama?" the others sing to him. "Let's dance, hot pants, let's dance," he sings back to the zoot-suited Simons, and they launch into a jitterbug that quickly dissolves into something better suited to a vaudeville stage.

Faust was released in spring 1945, a few years after *Rigoletto Blues* and *Sugar Hill Masquerade*. At that point the war was all but over, and it's conceivable that the intense pressure for heterosexual conformity had started to ebb—or perhaps had begun to assume another form, in the postwar pressure to settle down and start families. In any case, the film's ease and evident pleasure in gender play most likely have more to do with Coleman, Caver, and Simons than with the possible loosening of cultural norms. The latitude that Soundies' production system offered to individual producers and directors applied, to some extent, to performers as well. The Soundies catalog is filled with entertainers who supplied their own material for filming, and media coverage of Day, Dawn, and Dusk indicates that they brought *Faust* to Soundies rather than the other way around. Produced by Crouch, the trio's Soundies were among the few New York titles directed by Josef Berne, the West Coast Soundies stalwart who had been Sam Coslow's go-to director at RCM Productions. *Faust* attests to Crouch and Berne's willingness to give gender norms a playful jab, even as the great majority of their other Soundies stridently affirm them. But whatever envelope-pushing the film achieves is almost entirely attributable to Day, Dawn, and Dusk.

MARKET-DRIVEN ROMANCE?

Many Soundies extend the "Black city cinema" of 1930s Harlem-centered race films and move well beyond the schema of Black-cast Hollywood films, which frequently equated the city, and city women, with evil. Instead, these Soundies populate their streets and living rooms with active, engaged women whose performances reinforce a concept of the city as a space of creative encounter and possibility, erotic and otherwise.

Individual producers and directors left their stamp on these films. Jack Barry's and Fred Waller's shaping of the Minoco Soundies, especially the male-vocal-group romances, is one example. Director Dudley Murphy's portrayal of Dorothy Dandridge as a figure of glamour and sophistication is another. Soundies filmmakers learned and borrowed from each other too. In Los Angeles, Coslow and Berne were responsible for Dandridge's two "jungle" Soundies, but their final film with her, *Paper Doll*, opens with the kind of romantic multicouple pairings developed by Minoco in New York. Individual performers had considerable impact, from the flirtatious byplay of Fats Waller and Vivian Brown to June Richmond's full-figured glamour in *We're Stepping Out Tonight*, and the gender play of Day, Dawn, and Dusk.

But the range of women and heterosexual relationships that Black-cast Soundies depict is so broad that individual performers, producers, and directors may not fully account for it. Perhaps a more encompassing explanation lies in the commercial nature of the Soundies enterprise—and in Soundies audiences. The L.O.L. courtroom testimony outlines the geographic concentration of those audiences and the strategies that Soundies executives used for gauging responses to specific films and performers. That raises questions: If Soundies' depiction of Black women, romance, and relationships was at least partly market-driven, which part of the market drove it? And did those audiences differ from the viewership that Crouch and Ulcigan described? More specifically, is it possible that there were more women in the audiences for Black-cast Soundies? And that this may have had some bearing on how women and relationships were portrayed?

No testimony in the L.O.L. court transcript addresses women as Soundies viewers, or the depiction of relationships and gender on Panoram screens. But anecdotally at least, it's possible to place Black women in the types of venues where Panorams were commonly found. Historian Christine Sismondo points out that wartime labor shortages drove women into nontraditional workplaces beyond the factory floor. "We hear a lot about Rosie the Riveter, but not enough about the lesser-known 'Bessie the Bartender,'" she writes, adding that across the country, women held wartime positions running bars and taverns and even as wine sommeliers.[21] In her study of Black music clubs in Richmond, California—a Bay Area defense-industry hub—Shirley Ann Wilson Moore writes that "North Richmond's blues clubs were relatively free of gender constraints. Not only did Black women participate as patrons and performers in the clubs but a few also could become owners and managers."[22] At least one Black woman interviewed for New York University's "Real Rosie the Riveter Project" recalled the music clubs she visited as a young defense worker.[23] Without definitively linking them to Soundies, the presence of Black women in these settings raises the possibility that, in some cities at least, they may have been a significant part of the audience for Black-cast Soundies, and their feedback may have been influential in shaping the films.

Whether shaped by audiences, performers, makers, or all of the above, the majority of Black-cast Soundies present a version of Black heterosexuality and a perception of Black women that differs profoundly from the broader culture of the time. Opportunities were taken and, intentionally or not, Soundies' cinematic space was bent toward that unspoken end—augmenting, contradicting, and at times subverting mainstream representations of Black women and men on screen. In this, *unspoken* is the key word. Expressed through body language, glance and gesture, costume and setting, these changes were channeled through the margins of this already marginal form, at a remove from written scripts or plot lines and unmentioned in the *Billboard* mini-reviews. Clearly, performers were active participants in this unstated project, and their agency—particularly among women bit players—is evident in film after film. In laying claim to the cinematic conventions of romance, in depicting women as capable, glamorous, and contemporary, and in casting a humorous eye on relationships, mismatches, and gender play, Black-cast Soundies became one of the few wartime cultural arenas for this unspoken but intensely visible work.

In the depiction of Black women and female sexuality, Dorothy Dandridge is a pivotal figure, not only in Soundies but in the culture at large. The ten Soundies she made in 1941 and 1942 were instrumental in shaping Soundies as an entertainment form. Conversely, her Soundies are an overlooked but crucial factor in the development of her screen persona. In a departure from the book's thematic organization, the next chapter considers Dandridge's Soundies in depth, and the role they played in her career. It presents another vital perspective on Black-cast Soundies, their relationship to classic Hollywood film form, and their impact on American culture.

8

—ᴍᴍ—

ONE PERFORMER, TEN SOUNDIES

Another Look at Dorothy Dandridge

ON MAY 5, 1941, THE Soundies Corporation released *Swing for Your Supper* (Coslow-Berne, 1941), making Dorothy Dandridge the first Black performer to star in a Soundie. Over the next year and a half she made nine more, cementing her status as a Panoram breakout star. Sam Coslow, head of West Coast Soundies production from late 1940 through 1942, wrote that Dandridge and white performer Gale Storm "were responsible for more dimes being dropped into our juke boxes than anyone else we had under contract."[1] Today, most of Dandridge's Soundies are online in multiple uploads, drawing hundreds of thousands of views.

Dandridge had been a stage performer nearly all her life. With her sister Vivian (and later a third singer, Etta Jones), she had toured the Black nightclub and revue circuit under the management of her mother's companion, a brutally abusive woman.[2] She was nineteen when her first Soundie was released. The year before, she'd finally left the Dandridge Sisters for a solo career.[3] When *Swing for Your Supper* hit the Panoram, Dandridge had already had a leading role in the race film *Four Shall Die* (1940) and a credited part in the John Wayne movie *Lady from Louisiana* (1941).

Dandridge's Soundies present her in a different light: indisputably the star, often glamorously so. They showcase her singing, dancing, and—this being Soundies—her lithe body and authoritative way with a shoulder shimmy. Soundies' intimate shooting style spotlights Dandridge's remarkable ease as a performer, and her impeccable ability to relate to audiences through the camera. Through her years of performing with the Dandridge Sisters, the Black community nationwide had watched her grow up, and Soundies were an important step in her transition to adult solo performer. Her performances also caught the attention of the movie industry, which surreptitiously eyed Soundies' emerging talent. As young unknowns, later film stars like Doris Day, Cyd Charisse, and Ricardo Montalban made Soundies, but on Panoram screens Dandridge outdrew them all.

Today, most audiences know Dandridge through her starring roles in Otto Preminger's *Carmen Jones* (1954) and *Porgy and Bess* (1959), or from *Introducing Dorothy Dandridge* (1999), the made-for-TV biopic starring Halle Berry. Before her *Carmen Jones* breakthrough, Dandridge's dramatic work had been a patchwork of supporting roles—often brief, nonspeaking, or uncredited, mostly portraying maids or African royalty in jungle settings. But Dandridge was also a musical entertainer, appearing in four Hollywood movies from 1941 to 1945. In accordance with industry practices of the time, her segments were billed as "specialty numbers" that could be clipped out without disrupting the plot. Inserted into otherwise white-cast movies, these performances tap the nondramatic side of Dandridge's screen persona, the entertainer who was such a hit on the Panoram. Disconnected from a broader story line, these big-screen numbers are akin to Soundies, and it's useful to consider them on a continuum with her Panoram performances.

According to biographer Donald Bogle, once Dandridge became a star she never mentioned her Soundies, understandably eager to put the dime movies behind her. But her work in these films demands another, closer look. Dandridge's Soundies helped shape her early career and screen persona. They also reveal, with startling clarity, how Soundies both followed and broke with the mainstream movie industry's thinking about Black people on screen.[4] Folding her Hollywood musical numbers into the discussion enriches the understanding of Dandridge's performance style, and in particular how she adapted the intimacy of Soundies to the considerably larger scope of the commercial-film sound stage. In her ten Soundies, Dandridge created a distinctive screen persona that offers not only a glimpse of the mature performer she became but the performer who, under radically different circumstances, she might have been.

GOSPEL, GLAMOUR, AND LOST IN THE JUNGLE

With *Swing for Your Supper*, Dandridge's Soundies persona immediately cut against the usual stereotypes. The film opens on a hand-made sign for a rent party: "Mr. and Mrs. Jefferson Lincoln Jones / Come in and jive / Admission twenty five" (meaning, in those days, twenty-five cents, not dollars).[5] The next shot catches Dandridge syncopating by an upright piano in the living

Figure 8.1. Dorothy Dandridge (*center*) in *Swing for Your Supper* (1941). From the Soundies Distributing Corporation of America photographs of the Margaret Herrick Library, Academy of Motion Picture Arts and Sciences.

room, where—with Cee Pee Johnson and his combo most likely miming the music—she launches into the song (fig. 8.1).[6] Wearing a form-fitting, short-sleeve sweater, she looks like a demure 1940s college co-ed. In this case the camera is demure too: though it cuts in for a close-up on her face as she sings, it never wanders below the waist. Full-body framing is reserved for the jit-terbugs who take over at the instrumental break, and a quick cutaway shows Dandridge laughing and clapping as she watches their performance. The film ends on a medium shot of her as she wraps up the song, framed by the horn player and pianist.

As so often happens with Soundies, the most telling details are in the back-ground. Since the days of *Shuffle Along*—the 1920s Black-cast Broadway hit by Eubie Blake and Noble Sissle—the Harlem rent party had been a go-to setting for showcasing Black performers. In this case, though, the setting is at odds with the set itself. Despite the sign at the film's opening, the Jones family living room looks comfortably middle-class, and scarcely in need of a quarter-a-head rent party. In a lengthy shot of Cee Pee Johnson with his drums, behind him at frame left is an old-fashioned china hutch displaying decorative plates, and at right, an ornate vase on a pedestal table. The economics of Soundies production called for the frequent re-use of standing sets, and perhaps that's the case here. But it's also feasible that the set was deliberately dressed to highlight Dandridge's refined, all-American appeal. In her sorority-girl outfit and hairstyle, she fits right in.

That aura of genteel respectability is blown to smithereens in Dandridge's next Soundie. Recorded in the same April 1941 soundtrack session as *Swing for Your Supper* and released in June of that year, *Jungle Jig* (Coslow-Berne, 1941) reflects the hold that stereotypes of "darkest Africa" still exerted on the American cultural imagination, and the longstanding conflation of cartoonish African "natives" with Black music.[7] Kevin Young notes that for mainstream audiences, the jungle obsession and *Gone with the Wind* nostalgia were two sides of the same coin: "In venues such as Paris's *La Revue Nègre* and Harlem's Cotton Club," he writes, "the two were, if not directly conflated, then suggestively interchangeable."[8]

Jungle Jig is framed as this sort of floor show, presented at the "Harlem Jungle Club."[9] The sight of Cee Pee Johnson and his band—bare-chested, faces painted, mugging to a soundtrack that was again most likely recorded by others—is dismaying even before Dandridge makes her entrance in a tiny bikini and feathers, simultaneously sexy, wholesome, and impressively above it all. Released about a year later, *Congo Clambake* (Coslow-Berne, 1942) is worse. This is not one of Dandridge's Soundies readily available online, which is just as well. Again featuring Dandridge as a sexy "native"—this time with a soundtrack by white bandleader Stan Kenton and his orchestra—*Congo Clambake* traffics in uninhibited stereotypes and faux ethnography, complete with documentary footage.

The first of Dandridge's Hollywood "specialty numbers" is next in the chronology, appearing in *Sun Valley Serenade* (1941). Although it was most likely shot before her April 1941 Soundies session, the movie was not released until that August, after *Swing for Your Supper* and *Jungle Jig* had had their Panoram runs. *Sun Valley Serenade* is a light romantic comedy showcasing white skating star Sonja Henie, comedian Milton Berle, and Glenn Miller and His Orchestra. One of the numbers the band performs is "Chattanooga Choo Choo." Conceived as a show-stopper, it clocks in at a lengthy eight minutes, starting with a full instrumental version by Miller's orchestra and topped by a round of vocals by band member Tex Beneke and Miller's singing group, the Modernaires.

Together these performances consume the bulk of the screen time, roughly five minutes.

But oh, those last three minutes. The camera glides away from the band to a separate setting—standard technique for numbers likely to be clipped from some prints—to find Dandridge in a black satin dress with rhinestone straps and a fetching little hat, carrying a ruffled parasol. She saunters past dancers Fayard and Harold Nicholas, who snap to attention. The three sing the tune, then execute a stylish tap routine. Dandridge holds her own with the legendary dance duo, accenting her moves with the distinctive body language already seen in *Swing for Your Supper* and *Jungle Jig*. As they finish, she exits into a stage flat representing a train caboose, disappearing with a flirtatious wave. The Nicholas Brothers then deliver one of their classic performances—polished, precise, strenuously athletic—finishing on either side of the caboose doorway. Dandridge reappears to strike a final pose with them, smiling first at Harold Nicholas, then Fayard, and then the camera.

Shot for the big screen, the "Chattanooga" dance sequence uses mostly full-body wide shots, with none of the Soundies-style close-ups meant to establish direct connection with the viewer. Interestingly, when Dandridge dances with the men, the performance space they occupy is almost as compact as in some of her Soundies—an intimacy that subtly contributes to the segment's appeal. At the time it was filmed, Dandridge was romantically involved with Harold Nicholas—the two would marry the following year—and her ease with both men is evident. "Your feet tap, your pulse rises," the *New York Sun* wrote of the trio's performance. "You swing."[10]

Sun Valley Serenade premiered before Dandridge's second Soundies session, in October 1941, with director Dudley Murphy. Though now largely forgotten (except for "Chattanooga Choo Choo"), *Sun Valley Serenade* was a popular hit. It's likely that Murphy and Coslow would have seen it, especially after the reviews lauding Dandridge's work. Her appearance in the film may in part account for her callback for the second Soundies session, and more significantly, for Murphy's vision of her as a chic and sophisticated figure.

Murphy's first Dandridge Soundie, *Yes, Indeed!* (Coslow-Murphy/Berne, 1941), gives her a welcome gloss of glamour in a resonantly African American setting. Written by Black composer-arranger Sy Oliver, "Yes Indeed!" is a gospel-style tune that, by the time Dandridge recorded it, had already been a hit for both Bing Crosby and Tommy Dorsey and His Orchestra. In his version, Crosby and white vocalist Connee Boswell assume jokey, pseudo-Black personas, but Murphy takes the song more or less at face value. He sets the film in a Black church, with Dandridge testifying before the congregation, backed by a male vocal group, the Five Spirits of Rhythm. Although Coslow's usual collaborator, Josef Berne, is credited as co-director, *Yes, Indeed!* bears the stamp of Murphy's cinematic style, and he liberally quotes from his own work. (His 1933 feature, *The Emperor Jones*, for instance, opens with Paul Robeson as a New York–bound Brutus Jones bidding farewell to a similar churchful of worshipers, who see him off with a medley of gospel songs.) With quick shots of a baptism and congregants overcome by the spirit, the cutaways in *Yes, Indeed!* underscore Murphy's interest, as a white filmmaker, in Black life and culture, and his attempts to present them with some degree of authenticity. Dandridge introduces an entirely different aesthetic. Posed near the pulpit in a not-quite-strapless dress, fluffy boa, and high-brimmed Sunday hat, she's the epitome of polished glamour in full performance mode. Vigorously supported by the Five Spirits of Rhythm, her vocals power the film to its upbeat conclusion.

Easy Street (Coslow-Murphy, 1941), the last of Dandridge's films with Murphy, was released in late December 1941, two weeks after the badly off-kilter *Lazybones* (discussed in chap. 10). Here she returns to the glamour of *Yes, Indeed!*, turning up in a shimmering, low-cut dress, another marvelous hat, and a distracting feather boa that she handles with great aplomb. The film itself is more ambiguous, taking its lyrics almost too literally. "Easy Street" is presented as an exaggerated "Hollywood Negro" version of paradise, including a café giving away free gin, a crate of chickens labeled "Help Yourself," and a Black cop who blithely strolls past a sidewalk dice game. Dandridge enters frame left in an open-top, bike-powered carriage, which she shares with an admiring beau (Jess Brooks) and a smiling driver who sprays them from a perfume flask labeled "Love's Dream." Dandridge sings the first few lines, then climbs down to stroll along the street, performing a dance that manages to be both provocative and refined. The carriage comes for her and she ascends, singing the final lyrics as the film closes.

Even more than *Swing for Your Supper*, the setting for *Easy Street* has a story to tell, but the message is open to question. When the film was released in December 1941, many Americans were still reeling from the Depression and the economic recovery was just starting. In this light, the wish fulfillment played out on the film's "Easy Street" may have resonated with a range of Soundies audiences.

Yet this version of paradise is so stereotyped that it undercuts its own premise. At his best Murphy took pains to present Black performers to their advantage, but he was not immune to Hollywood-style thinking. Both aspects are evident in *Easy Street*. The stereotypical background action stands in sharp contrast to Murphy's appreciation of Dandridge as a performer and screen presence, and his interest in showcasing her as a figure of glamour and sophistication.

GOING MAINSTREAM: *TOUT ZOOT*

By the time Dandridge's next Soundie, *A Zoot Suit* (Coslow-Berne, 1942), was released in March 1942, the United States was four months into World War II. The film's song, "A Zoot Suit (For My Sunday Gal)" celebrates a style of dressing favored by young Black and Latinx people and others of the wartime generation, which flaunted cloth rationing and to some degree the patriotism that went with it.

The styling of a zoot was an exercise in personal self-expression and creative one-upmanship. Most zoot suits were individually ordered through tailors and were custom- or "semi-custom" made to the buyer's specifications. By early 1942, when *A Zoot Suit* reached Panoram screens, Black zooters' slang was already filtering through the culture, and white teenagers in small towns were wearing zoot-inspired styles of their own.

As a pop-music hit, "A Zoot Suit (For My Sunday Gal)" contributed substantially to this diffusion. As written, the song opens with a reference to stepping out in Harlem, but that line was omitted from the hit versions by the Andrews Sisters, Bing Crosby, bandleader Kay Kaiser, and other white performers.[11] Instead, the zooter and his "gal" became stand-ins for any young couple. As the war went on, the zoot suit became a polarizing symbol of class, race, and cultural difference, particularly with the "Zoot Suit Riots" in Los Angeles in 1943.[12] But in early 1942, the song was still an exuberant emblem of post-Depression energy and a fresh style accessible to all.

In *A Zoot Suit*, Coslow and Berne finally hit their Soundies stride with Dandridge. The film pairs her with comedian Paul White as a couple eager to impress each other with their new outfits. It's a crisply structured piece of filmmaking, with parallel solo turns followed by a satisfying duet (fig. 8.2). It's also a study in contrasting performance styles—White's broadly gesticulating, eye-popping delivery versus Dandridge's more restrained gestural range, scaled to the intimacy of the camera close-up.

Like *Swing for Your Supper, A Zoot Suit* opens with a sign—in this case for the tailoring business Groove Clothiers. "Our stitches are hep to the jive," the sign reads. "Males & Frails."[13] The next shot cuts to White with his tailor, explaining what he wants in the new suit: reet pleat, drape shape, and stuff cuff, among other details. Then it's Dandridge's turn to deliver her list to the dressmaker: zop top and hip slip on the dress, and a scat hat and zag bag to match. Line by line, their sartorial slang acquires a satisfying density. In White's delivery it retains an edge of inscrutability, but Dandridge punts it squarely into the mainstream. Wearing a modest dress buttoned up to the collar and a ribbon in her

Figure 8.2a–c (*this page and following*). Paul White and Dorothy Dandridge in *A Zoot Suit* (1942). Courtesy Library of Congress, Motion Picture, Broadcasting and Recorded Sound Division.

Figure 8.2c.

hair, she exudes a girl-next-door appeal that's anything but hepster-rebellious, and her self-referential gestures and eye contact with the viewer give the lyrics an intimacy that undercuts their impenetrability. White delivers a few lines to the camera but sings most of them to his tailor, never reaching Dandridge's degree of connection with the audience. She, on the other hand, chooses the camera over the dressmaker so consistently that the other actress gives up and turns her attention elsewhere.

White's performance has been faulted as smacking of minstrelsy, and there is some validity to that critique. It's a style developed for the theater, not the camera, adapted from a long and then still-popular tradition of variety shows and revues.[14] (William D. Alexander's 1949 film *Burlesque in Harlem* documents one such show.) White had been a cast member of *Jump for Joy*, the Duke Ellington revue that adamantly refuted stereotypical thinking about Black American life and culture. Another White Soundie, *Bli-Blip* (Coslow-Berne, 1942), was adapted from *Jump for Joy*, and his work in that film (with Marie Bryant) is, if anything, more exaggerated and stylized.

From a performance perspective, *A Zoot Suit* is most interesting when Dandridge and White come together, showing off their new clothes. At that point

Dandridge switches strategies, turning from the camera and modulating her performance to White's—not by ratcheting up the gestures, as Bryant does in *Bli-Blip*, but by focusing on White almost exclusively. Only in the closing two-shot does Dandridge shift her gaze away from him toward the camera. That attentiveness forces White to soften his style, so that his one burst of physicality—a little leap of delight after her line "Here comes my walking rainbow"—appears as a genuine response rather than a mere flourish. What comes through in this sequence, too, is Dandridge's artful performing. She makes it seem as though she really had been waiting all week for the joy of dancing with White in their new clothes. His suit is predictably exaggerated—though not at all zoot—but for Dandridge, *A Zoot Suit* is another glamorous turn. In Los Angeles, young Mexican American women adopted long, broad-shouldered "juke jackets" as the female version of the zoot silhouette, but that's hardly the look Dandridge models here. The new ensemble fits like a second skin and, with its shimmering skirt, peaked shoulders, and high-brimmed hat, makes an eye-catching fashion statement, especially in comparison to White's more broadly styled outfit.

Glamour flies out the window, literally, in *Blackbird Fantasy* (Coslow-Moulton, 1942), which puts Dandridge and her co-star, comedian Billy Mitchell, in feathered bird costumes. Hers is fluffy and nondescript, but Mitchell's outfit, complete with spats, is reminiscent of the rooster costume that Black entertainer Bert Williams—"the most famous and greatest droll comedian in the world"—wore in his renowned "Chanticleer" routine in the Ziegfeld Follies of the 1910s.[15] The film's setting, with its cartoonish, two-dimensional cabin, recalls the one in the short film *Yamekraw* (1929), and the choice of song is also something of a throwback. Dandridge opens with a line or two of poetry and a few bars of the Civil War–era tune "Listen to the Mockingbird." Then she and Mitchell launch into a boogie version of "Titwillow," a song from Gilbert and Sullivan's *The Mikado*. Mitchell made two Soundies, both of them *Mikado* updates with vaudeville or minstrel-show referents. The films draw on audiences' presumed familiarity with the two Black-cast, swing versions of *The Mikado* that played on Broadway in 1939, and on Soundies' own penchant for swinging the classics or anything that might be perceived as such. *Billboard* approved. "Production department fell short here, but the performers do an amusing job," it declared in its mini-review, singling out Dandridge as "the cutest colored dancer and singer on the Soundie pay roll."[16]

In *Blackbird Fantasy*, Dandridge again connects directly with the camera. For Soundies' emphatically close-up visual style, it's arguably her greatest performative strength. As Despina Kakoudaki writes, the sexual allure of the two-dimensional pin-up was largely based on a direct eyeline connection with the viewer and the imagined intimacy that it implied. Dandridge was a master at transposing that dynamic to film, and her skilled use of her own camera close-ups embodies that intimate gaze. Small wonder Sam Coslow prized her performances so highly.

COWGIRL KICKS AND A PERPLEXING *DOLL*

On YouTube and other digital platforms, *Cow Cow Boogie* (Coslow-Berne, 1942) is the most popular of Dandridge's Soundies, garnering more than a quarter-million views to date. Even more than with *A Zoot Suit*, in *Cow Cow Boogie* Coslow and Berne get it right. The film is well structured, smoothly choreographed, and smartly framed and shot. It's a showcase for Dandridge that doesn't resort to racist clichés, placing her in the appealing context of a Wild West saloon—a setting that, for some viewers, may have recalled the popular race-film Westerns of the late 1930s. The tune, a savvy hybrid of Western swing and boogie, reflects the cross-genre playfulness that is one of Soundies' most distinctive traits.

The song's history is a case study in the symbiotic relationship between the movie and music industries during the war years. It was originally performed by Ella Fitzgerald for her screen debut in the Abbott and Costello movie *Ride 'Em Cowboy* (1942), but was cut in favor of her other number, "A-Tisket, A-Tasket." At the time it was common for studios to embargo a film's songs until a few weeks before the movie's release, whether those songs made it into the final film or not. *Ride 'Em Cowboy* was shot in August 1941—Fitzgerald's version of "Cow Cow Boogie" included—but the movie wasn't released until March 1942, and the song stayed out of circulation until then. After the movie went into distribution, songwriter Johnny Mercer—on the hunt for material for his new record company, Capitol—came across the tune, forgotten and now available. With lyrics about a "swing half-breed" with a "Harlem touch" who was "raised on locoweed" (sometimes written as "local weed"—in either case a coded reference to marijuana), "Cow Cow Boogie" was a big hit for white singer Ella Mae Morse, who recorded it for Capitol with Freddie Slack and His Orchestra in May 1942.[17] Morse's version is artfully done, buttercream-smooth with a bluesy lilt. Hollywood came calling, and the following year she performed it in the swing-revue movie *Reveille with Beverly* (1943). Fitzgerald herself recorded it on disc in 1943, but Dandridge's Soundie came ahead of both Fitzgerald's record release and Morse's screen performance, and in *Cow Cow Boogie* she makes the song her own.

Interestingly, IMDb lists Dandridge as an uncredited dancer in *Ride 'Em Cowboy*.[18] If that's accurate, she may have been on the set for the filming of Fitzgerald's original version in 1941, which would have made her familiar with that staging of the number as well as Fitzgerald's styling of the song. This could be one reason she appears so completely at ease with the material. Too, *Cow Cow Boogie* was her ninth Soundie, and her fifth with Coslow and Berne. The cast included comedian Dudley Dickerson and Eugene "Pineapple" Jackson, an early member of the *Our Gang* comedies, who had worked with Dandridge, her sister, and Etta Jones when they were kids.[19] His presence and Dickerson's may have contributed to a relaxed, easy professionalism on the set.

Cow Cow Boogie demonstrates the strengths of early West Coast Soundies production. For one, there's enough money. It's visible in every frame, from the deftly staged opening action to the sheer number of performers on screen. The film has a fluidity that only experienced production and editorial teams can bestow. Unlike New York Soundies producers, who often filmed in the aging former Edison studio in the Bronx, West Coast producers had their pick of independent and B-studio facilities in Los Angeles, including Selznick International, Hal Roach, Goldwyn, Monogram, and others. Rentals may have included not only sound stages but production personnel and a certain amount of prop material.[20] That film-industry polish supports Dandridge's work in *Cow Cow Boogie*.

Cow Cow Boogie makes smart use of a tightly defined performance space, buttressed by frequent, sustained close-ups of Dandridge. After opening on a two-shot of a dance-hall girl and Jackson as the saloon pianist—most likely miming someone else's performance—the camera slowly pulls back to reveal a compact set bordered by a bar at the back, the piano at left, and a tableful of cowboys at left foreground. Only when this framing has been established and the opening-shot action completed does Dandridge start singing off-camera. At her voice, all actors turn frame right, anticipating her entrance. She appears in a wide shot, dancing along the bar to the center of the performance area. From that point, the film smoothly alternates between close-ups of Dandridge and wide shots of the set, which, despite its minimal floor space, manages to accommodate not only the cowboys, pianist, bartender, and Dandridge, but six dancers who fall into step behind her.

Within such a tight space the choreography is largely performed in place or close to it, and the style suits Dandridge well. Her own hip and shoulder shimmies are subtle moves that don't overtake her performance, but she lets loose in a wide shot, kicking her cowgirl boots in an exuberant full-body shake. The camera and her cowboy audience are appreciative, but no one seems to enjoy the performance more than Dandridge herself. Framed from the side, one shot

Figure 8.3. Dandridge (*right*) with dancers in *Cow Cow Boogie* (1942). Courtesy Mark Cantor Archive.

shows the other women dancing into formation behind her; she looks over her shoulder and smiles, seemingly invigorated by their presence (fig. 8.3). At the instrumental break the camera cuts to a lone cowboy at the bar—Dickerson, who with some difficulty manages to fire his six-guns in the air and yell "Yippee! Solid man, solid!" Barring that moment and a few cutaways, the film is Dandridge's entirely.[21]

Cow Cow Boogie cuts against conventional expectations about sexuality and gender roles, starting with putting a "cowgirl"—rather than the usual masculine Western hero—at the center of the action. More than that, Dandridge's cowgirl is an active, sexually self-possessed figure, moving confidently among tables full of appreciative but passive men (and Dickerson at the bar, with his problematic six-guns). In *Cow Cow Boogie* she puts her skill in connecting with the viewer to its most explicit use, repeatedly making eye contact with the camera as she suggestively thrusts her hips or gives them a teasing swing. Even as she presents herself as an object of desire, Dandridge's command of her own sexuality confounds the expectation of easy accessibility. She is the essence of stardom, irresistible and unattainable.

That embodiment of sexuality, self-possession, and power is conspicuously missing from Dandridge's final Soundie. In *Paper Doll* (Coslow-Berne, 1942), she shares star billing with the Mills Brothers, appearing as a dancer silently accompanying their vocals. The film is a Soundies classic—a poignant, beautifully sung reflection of wartime yearnings and anxieties—but is in its own way disturbing. It opens on a wide front porch and garden, where three of the singers sit in rocking chairs with women in their laps—a display of easy intimacy that gains impact as it repeats across the couples. The fourth vocalist, seated off to the right, sings of wanting a paper doll who will be faithful instead of a "real live girl" who isn't. As he sings, he cuts out a newspaper picture of Dandridge, identified as a USO entertainer, and stands it on a low table in front of him.[22] Her figure comes alive in miniature, and the second part of the film is devoted to her performance.

Dandridge's "paper doll" is a good example of how Soundies' visual concepts were defined and often limited by the lyrics they interpreted. In the 1940s, paper dolls were popular playthings for girls, with outfits cut out by hand and hung on them by means of fold-over tabs. The dolls themselves were commonly depicted as prepubescent girls in their underwear. This probably accounts for Dandridge's juvenile-looking costume—not what one would expect to see on a USO dancer in World War II, and nothing like her appearance in previous Soundies. In most shots she's tiny, a childlike figure in more ways than one. The camera peers down at her over the shoulders of the full-sized (and fairly bulky) men, who watch her perform as they sing. Tiny in the film frame, with movements that bear little relationship to the music, Dandridge's dancing has a manic quality—strenuous arm waving, frantic kicks, and even a few toe-touches that turn her into a miniature human semaphore (fig. 8.4). Eventually the camera cuts to medium close-ups that restore her to adult size, but only briefly and intermittently. In these shots Dandridge works to establish eye contact with the viewer, throwing in an adult shoulder shimmy or two along with the calisthenics. But that kind of sensuality is not what this Soundie is about. The miniature "doll" shots predominate, giving the film a surreal, dreamlike atmosphere, and arguably introducing a note of pedophilia. For film theorist Amy Herzog, the film's imagery interprets the song so literally that it overshoots the intent of the lyrics, exposing the assumptions behind the fantasy by presenting its impossible embodiment.[23] Sentimental and unsettling, *Paper Doll* exemplifies the psychological and sexual undercurrents that often run through the most resonant of these films. Speaking only of Dandridge's performance, however, for her final Soundie one might have wished for more.

Figure 8.4. The Mills Brothers watch a miniature Dorothy Dandridge perform in
Paper Doll (1942). Courtesy Mark Cantor Archive.

THE CAMERA AND THE SPACE

With her work in Soundies, Dandridge laid a foundation for her screen persona as an adult musical-entertainment performer. The further evolution of
that persona may be traced through the three Hollywood specialty numbers
that followed in 1943, 1944, and 1945. These productions are also a useful point
of comparison between Soundies' visual treatment of musical numbers and
Hollywood's.

In *Hit Parade of 1943* (1943), Dandridge makes a brief appearance with Count
Basie and His Orchestra, in an extended song-and-dance sequence that runs not
quite seven minutes. Here she is a vocalist only, appearing roughly 40 seconds
into the sequence to sing "Harlem Sandman." On screen for less than two minutes, she cuts a striking figure in a form-fitting, full-length gown. The camera
catches her in a few medium close-ups, but rather than acknowledging the viewer,
she directs her glances to Basie or nearby guests in the nightclub setting, maintaining the closed, audience-ignoring "fourth wall" of classic Hollywood film.

After Dandridge's Soundies, the dimensions of the "Harlem Sandman" performance space are something of a shock. In Soundies, even supposedly grand nightclubs are surprisingly petite, scaled to the dimensions of the Panoram screen. In *Hit Parade*, the space is enormous as only a Hollywood sound stage can be—expansive enough to accommodate Basie and his full orchestra, along with featured dancers Jack Williams and the acrobatic tap-dance team of Pops and Louie (Albert Whitman and Louis Williams), plus a dozen more dancers. Interestingly, the area that Dandridge herself performs in is relatively contained, and her movement through it is natural and graceful.

Not so her brief appearance in *Atlantic City* (1944). The performance space of her "Harlem on Parade" number is scaled to the Hollywood screen, and so is the choreography. Instead of the sensuous movements she uses in her Soundies work, in this sequence Dandridge is all angles, throwing out her elbows and jutting her hips to commandeer as much space as possible. It's a movement style more akin to James Cagney's strutting in *Yankee Doodle Dandy* (1942) than to her own leisurely stroll down *Easy Street*. For jazz and film scholar Krin Gabbard, Dandridge in *Atlantic City* is "unrestrained in her erotic body language," but I would argue the opposite.[24] This is one of her least sensual performances of the 1940s, just above the manic semaphoring of *Paper Doll*.

Like the earlier "Harlem Sandman," "Harlem on Parade" runs approximately seven minutes, with Dandridge on screen for perhaps two and in the spotlight for barely one. She opens the number, and the final section of her vocal is an introduction to Louis Armstrong, who comes on to perform "Ain't Misbehavin'." Despite a personal acquaintance dating back to the Dandridge Sisters' work with Armstrong in *Going Places* (1939) if not earlier, their time on screen together yields scant interaction. Dandridge dances over to Armstrong to lead him into the spotlight, but she's limited to the big, stylized gestures of large-screen choreography, and there's little sense of connection between them. Striking and holding an exaggerated pose of interest, she backs off out of the frame, leaving him alone for his solo. After a dance-and-piano routine by entertainers Buck and Bubbles (Ford Washington Lee and John William Sublett), Dandridge returns to close the number with them, finishing at the center of an extreme wide shot, which catches not only the other performers but the orchestra and the patrons in the nightclub setting as well.

Dandridge's performance is most Soundies-like in the last of these musical numbers, which appears in the white-cast romantic comedy *Pillow to Post* (1945). She again pairs with Armstrong, in this case on the tune "Whatcha Say?". Unlike the numbers in *Hit Parade of 1943* or *Atlantic City*, the camera work here, as in Soundies, consists mostly of two-shots that underscore the performers' easy rapport. Half a minute or so into her performance, the camera cuts to a close-up of Dandridge that, in a Soundie, would have had her singing directly to the viewer through the camera. Instead, her eyeline is slightly askance, frame right, and she sings and winks to the nightclub audience before her. For the most part, though, her performance is directed toward Armstrong, much as her performance in *A Zoot Suit* is directed to Paul White. As she sings "Do I get that little kiss? Must you let me down like this?" her approach is lightly flirtatious, with a touch of teasing humor. Armstrong responds in kind, with a playful mock-shyness that ends in a cheerfully acquiescing "Well, all reet!" Though it runs little over a minute, it's a memorable sequence, and it clearly speaks of Dandridge's time in front of the Soundies cameras—sensuous and sexy but wholesome, simultaneously flirtatious and refined. That description also fits the wartime pinup—or its more family-friendly aspects—and in some ways Dandridge's duet with Armstrong is a coda to that waning sensibility. Though her persona is otherwise much the same as in her Soundies, the direct eyeline connection with the viewer, which defined the pinup and gave Dandridge's Soundies such intimacy and impact, is gone. By the time *Pillow to Post* was released in June 1945, the war was winding down and the massive shift to postwar life was already gathering momentum. Though her performance in "Whatcha Say?" evocatively recalls Dandridge's Soundies persona, at this point those films were already long behind her. She was all of 22 years old.

THE WHAT-IFS

"It's weekend television time," Margo Jefferson writes of her 1950s childhood in her memoir *Negroland*. "Sammy Davis Jr. is going to be on *The Milton Berle Show*. Dorothy Dandridge is going to be on *The Jerry Lewis Colgate Comedy Hour*. Lena Horne is going to be on *The Frank Sinatra Timex Show*. These are seminal moments in the viewing mores of the nation."[25]

Anyone with a passing knowledge of Dandridge's later career will likely recall its high point. Three years after portraying an African queen in the B-movie *Tarzan's Peril* (1951), she shot to stardom in Otto Preminger's *Carmen Jones* (1954), a Black-cast adaptation of the 1875 opera *Carmen* set in 1950s America. In the process Dandridge scored a fistful of notable firsts, including the first Black woman nominated for a best actress Oscar and the first on the cover of *Life* magazine. Television appearances followed. But the brilliant career that the film foretold did not materialize. Dandridge made a scant five movies after *Carmen Jones*. Only one—Samuel Goldwyn's big-budget version of *Porgy and Bess* (1959), also directed by Preminger—brought her back into the Hollywood spotlight, to emphatically mixed reviews. Six years later she was dead, most likely of a barbiturate overdose, at 42. At the time, her bank account balance was reportedly $2.14.[26]

The factors behind Dandridge's thwarted career are several and complex, and Bogle's biography explores them in compassionate detail. Racism in the film industry and the culture took an overwhelming toll, and Dandridge's personal life was at times a source of debilitating grief. But her Soundies work suggests, obliquely, another factor: the notions of female sexuality and its representation that dominated the 1950s, particularly with respect to Black actresses. The postwar cultural imperatives that produced "sex symbols" like Marilyn Monroe, Ava Gardner, and Sophia Loren left little room for the playful sensuality that Dandridge embodied in her Soundies and Hollywood specialty numbers. Even before *Carmen Jones*, the sexual iconography of the postwar era had been crucial in molding Dandridge's performances on the nightclub circuit. Publicity for her 1953 booking at the Mocambo nightclub in Hollywood, for instance, made a point of linking her to *Sexual Behavior in the Human Female*, one of two volumes in the so-called "Kinsey Report" on America's sex life that was then titillating the popular imagination. Advertising for the show proclaimed Dandridge "a volume of sex with the living impact of the Kinsey report," and opening night saw the club's roving cigarette girls selling copies of the book at $15 a pop.[27]

Despite the breakthrough that it represented for Dandridge, *Carmen Jones* did not debut to universal acclaim in either the Black community or the culture at large. Its racial and gender politics are so confused, and its melding of opera and big-screen moviemaking is so awkward that the result can be described, accurately, as "cultural schizophrenia."[28] In adapting the Bizet opera, lyricist Oscar Hammerstein II drew heavily on stereotyped associations of Black people with violence, physicality, and unbridled sexuality, and for many viewers the film was—and is—extremely hard to watch. "The tone of *Carmen Jones* is stifling," James Baldwin wrote, "a wedding of the blank, lofty solemnity with which Hollywood so often approaches 'works of art' and the really quite helpless condescension with which Hollywood has always handled Negroes."[29] The *New York Times* review was scathing. "In essence, it is a poignant story," wrote Bosley Crowther. "But here it is not so much poignant as lurid and lightly farcical, with the Negro characters presented by Mr. Preminger as serio-comic devotees of sex."[30]

Bogle writes with conviction about Dandridge's portrayal of Carmen Jones as a mold-breaking role model for Black women—vibrant, independent, and comfortable in expressing an unambiguously adult sexuality.[31] Not everyone embraced that view. "Carmen was a wanton," Jefferson writes in *Negroland*, "which we resent seeing Negro women play since most people think that's what Negro women are."[32]

From either perspective, Dandridge as Carmen obscures the cinematic persona that came earlier, lighter and in some ways more sophisticated than Carmen Jones and the roles that followed. In her Soundies, her dance with the Nicholas Brothers, and the flirtatious duet with Louis Armstrong, Dandridge's sexual presentation is the antithesis of the predatory femme fatale of *Carmen Jones*: collaborative, confiding, fun, and on an equal footing with her partners. There is a refinement in many of Dandridge's early musical appearances that is not only missing but, one might argue, deliberately wrung out of her later roles. "One feels—perhaps one is meant to feel—that here is a *very* nice girl making her way in the movies by means of a bad-girl part," Baldwin writes, "and the glow thus caused, especially since she is a colored girl, really must make up for the glow which is missing from the performance she is clearly trying very hard at."[33] Cultural critic Hilton Als describes Dandridge's Carmen as "performance hysteria—that is to say, Dandridge gave more than she had as an artist and then gave even more."[34]

Carmen Jones shares a technical trait frequently seen in many Soundies: a mismatch of performers on the screen and the soundtrack. In Soundies this was largely a haphazard occurrence driven by deadline, budget, a feckless disregard for the unity of image and sound, and a loose approach to their synchronicity. In *Carmen Jones* the mismatch is intentional. As in most musical film numbers, including Soundies, the visual performances are shaped by their prerecorded soundtracks, with the actors on screen performing to a playback of the track. Usually the result is a perceived unity between singer and song, but not in *Carmen Jones*. Dandridge speaks her lines herself but when she sings, it is in the voice of white soprano Marilyn Horne. Hearing that voice apparently coming from Dandridge's mouth, articulating with full operatic technique the "dems" and "dats" of Hammerstein's lyrics, only heightens the film's pervasive sense of dissociation. As Herzog observes, Dandridge and her costar Harry Belafonte "perform both as actors and as listeners who carefully time their movements based on the nuances of the voices they, and we, hear."[35] At the same time, they must respond to "the need to perform Blackness," as Als puts it, that the film— with its extremes of character, plot, and faux-dialect—demands of them.[36]

The emergence of performers like Eartha Kitt, Lena Horne, and Dandridge into the 1950s entertainment mainstream brought a broader validation of Black women, but as a breakthrough it carried its own constraints. If anything, roles for Black "sex symbols" were more limiting than for their white counterparts, and less open to nuanced interpretation. Dandridge struggled with this. At the height of her success she was cast as the rebellious young lover Tuptim in *The King and I* (1956)—as far removed from Carmen Jones as 1950s Hollywood could imagine—but she ultimately rejected the role as being the equivalent of a slave. ("What misbegotten scruples!" Jefferson writes.[37]) Dandridge did not appear in another Hollywood movie until 1957, and didn't regain the spotlight until two years later with *Porgy and Bess*—only to be nailed by critics for being too refined, too "sinuous and sleek" for the role.[38] Other films after *Carmen Jones* saw Dandridge variously cast as the libidinous wife of a shipboard cook (*The Decks Ran Red*, 1958), half of a contemporary interracial couple (*Island in the Sun*, 1957, and *Malaga*, 1960), and—paradoxically, given *The King and I*—a slave in sexual thrall to a cruel ship captain (*Tamango*, 1958).

It is tantalizing to imagine an alternate career path for Dandridge—roles that, had racism and gender politics not weighed so heavily, she might have claimed. According to Bogle, she had hoped to play the saloon singer Cherie in *Bus Stop* (1956), a character that combined vulnerability, sex appeal, and a touch of comedy; it ultimately became a breakthrough role for Marilyn Monroe. One of Dandridge's competitors for the 1955 Oscar was Audrey Hepburn for *Sabrina* (1954), and it's easy to envision Dandridge in any number of Hepburn roles, from the errant princess in *Roman Holiday* (1953) to the chic widow opposite Cary Grant in *Charade* (1963). With its living-room intimacy, television would have been an ideal medium for tapping her Soundies-honed skill in connecting with viewers. Gale Storm, the white Soundies performer whom Coslow considered Dandridge's equal in drawing power, went on to star in two long-running TV series. Conceivably Dandridge could have done the same, perhaps in a variety show like Nat "King" Cole's (1956–57) or a sitcom like Diahann Carroll's *Julia* (1968–71). Relieved of the obligatory wantonness that seemed to freight all roles for attractive Black women in the 1950s and early 1960s, Dandridge's more sophisticated, more collaborative persona could have conceivably had greater impact and influence than her role as Carmen Jones.

In this sense, Dandridge's Soundies offer a glimpse of the performer she might have become, had she not been confronted with the racism and sexual politics of that era. Under vastly different circumstances she might have had a long, prolific career playing cosmopolitan women of the world—mature, sophisticated versions of the co-ed in *Swing for Your Supper*. Instead she had little opportunity to define on her own terms what it meant to be a Black woman on screen. Among Dandridge's Soundies are some that foreshadow all too acutely the limitations she would grapple with throughout her career. But there are also Soundies in which she expresses herself as a performer in ways that all but vanished as her career progressed. On a certain level, the femme fatale of *Carmen Jones* may be understood as both a misreading and a suppression of the collaborative, playful screen persona that Dandridge articulated in Soundies like *Swing for Your Supper* and *A Zoot Suit,* and the sexual self-possession she conveyed in *Cow Cow Boogie.* The fact that those films were among Soundies' biggest hits underscores Dandridge's influence in shaping Soundies as an entertainment form and as an arena for representing Black women on screen.

9

VISUAL MUSIC

Big Bands, Combos, Solo Musicians

IN DOCUMENTING THE POP MUSIC of the 1940s, Soundies went well beyond the movie industry's usual practices, not only in the attention to Black talent but in a willingness to let the structure of the music dictate the structure of the film. Exploring the breadth of music documented in Black-cast Soundies throws a spotlight on less well-known musicians, including some not recorded beyond these films. It also underscores the music-driven structures of specific Soundies, revealed in quick shot-by-shot analyses. Tighter budgets, the nationwide musicians' strike, and changing musical tastes all left their mark on Black-cast music-performance Soundies and on pop music's postwar path. Close consideration of a few key films brings those influences to light, along with a performance-documentation style that is one of Soundies' most distinctive contributions to music on film.

The war years were probably the first time that dance floors were basic equipment in factory break rooms, and workers on round-the-clock shifts routinely energized themselves with a jitterbug or two.[1] Once regular Soundies production began in late 1940, big bands quickly became a mainstay of the weekly releases. In fact, the second reel to reach the screen (Program 1002) featured no fewer than five bands—six, counting the full-scale philharmonic orchestra in *Blue Danube* (Feher-unknown, 1941).[2] None of these groups was African American. It took almost a year of full-time production for a big band of Black musicians to appear in Soundies. The absence was immediately noted in the Black press. *Pittsburgh Courier* columnist Earl J. Morris was among the journalists covering the gala September 1940 roll-out for Panoram Soundies headlined by President Roosevelt's son, producer James Roosevelt. "To be very popular among Negroes, the 'soundies' will have to make a direct appeal by presenting colored personalities," Morris wrote, adding that "Jimmy Roosevelt has overlooked the fact that Count Basie, Fats Waller, Jimmy Lunceford, right here in Hollywood, have had ofay jitterbugs eating out of their hands."[3] Eleven months after regular Soundies distribution began in January 1941, the *Courier* triumphantly announced the release of Soundies starring Lucky Millinder and His Orchestra, with Count Basie's coming soon and others slated to follow. "'Juke Box' Soundies Opening New Outlet for Colored Bands," the headline proclaimed.[4]

Millinder made four films in his 1941 Soundies session, which followed Dorothy Dandridge's two films in spring 1941 and overlapped with films by two vocal groups, the Charioteers and the Delta Rhythm Boys. By that point more than fifty Soundies featuring white and Latin bands had already been released. A distinctive visual language, structured around the music, was emerging to document these performances, incorporating footage of the bandleader, different instrument sections, close-ups of hands on instruments, and other shots, edited to parallel the music. The approach was not unlike some Hollywood-movie big-band numbers, but the effect was radically different—smaller, less spectacular, more intimate. Soundies generally didn't aspire to and certainly didn't achieve "the inaccessible sheen of the glitzy, big-budget numbers found in the typical feature-length musical," Amy Herzog writes, and for her, the lack of pretense makes Soundies performances "seem more spontaneous and sincere."[5]

Herzog's description applies to Soundies as a whole, but it's especially apropos of the Millinder films. A limited range of bandstand shots are used in *Four or Five Times* and *The Lonesome Road* (Barry-Primi, 1941), two of the Soundies featuring Sister Rosetta Tharpe, who became the band's vocalist in early 1941.[6] Solos by piano and horn players are shot at oblique angles, and there are quick shots of the band in call-and-response with Tharpe. Although Millinder gets top billing, Tharpe's riveting performances consistently draw the camera, and Millinder usually ends up sharing a two-shot with her: "I hear you talking, Sister!" he exclaims in *Four or Five Times* (fig. 3.1, p. 54). In both films, the narrative context is minimal: the same nightclub setting, with the camera tight on Tharpe and the bandstand. At times the frame is jammed with dancers, and the visual music takes a more physical turn.

Narrative emerges more clearly in the two other films from this session. Perhaps as a nod to the rural roots shared by many Soundies viewers—or the need to maximize the use of an already standing set—*Shout! Sister, Shout!* and *I Want a Big Fat Mama* (both Barry-Primi, 1941) take place in a barn, with everyone in farm attire. (Released on the same reel as *Four or Five Times*, the Charioteers' *The Darktown Strutters' Ball* [Barry/Waller-Murray, 1941] appears to have been filmed there too.) Despite the setting, *Shout! Sister, Shout!* succeeds more than the two nightclub films in interweaving Tharpe's performance with that of the band. *Shout!* opens with a roughly ten-second instrumental intro, with the camera panning left across the saxophone section to catch the pianist and guitarist, then panning back to the open doorway, where Millinder and Tharpe enter with a clapping crowd. Millinder is a vivid presence here, more than in the nightclub films, and his hayseed straw-chewing is a sly performance in itself. Eventually a few dancers hit the floor, but they don't obscure the band or command much screen time. Millinder shares the last verse with Tharpe, in a humorous exchange that ends with her exclaiming, "Well, fill me full of rhythm, can you understand that?" The final frame is an exuberant wide shot, with the two of them surrounded by singers, dancers, and musicians.

I Want a Big Fat Mama—the only film of the four that doesn't feature Tharpe—adds a basic storyline to the barn setting, with Millinder suggesting potential partners to a small man searching for the woman of the title. Once he finds her, the focus shifts to jitterbugging and, as in the nightclub films, the band and their performance recede into the background. Only in the brief opening shot are the musicians shown actually playing their instruments. In the few quick cutaways that follow, they merely supply vocal backup for the solo singer, band guitarist Trevor Bacon. As with all Soundies, there are few metrics for gauging the popularity of *I Want a Big Fat Mama*, but the song itself was a solid hit—to the point that in New York, the Apollo Theater turned a Millinder booking into "Big Fat Mama" week, offering free admission for women over 250 pounds ("as the guests of Lucky, gratis") and a fifty-dollar prize at week's end to "the most versatile 'mama.'"[7]

It's worth considering how the Millinder Soundies fit into the trajectory of his and Tharpe's careers. Millinder assembled his band in 1940, with Tharpe joining a few months later. Soon after, the group started making regular appearances at the Savoy Ballroom, the pre-eminent Harlem dance floor. Their performances were broadcast on radio, further lifting the band's national profile. As a solo act and as Millinder's vocalist, Tharpe drew a wide audience, from Black and white southerners to urbanites and European blues fans. Her Pentecostal church and gospel background gave her earthiness a spiritual fervor: she could, as one writer put it, "sing about the evils of worldliness with irreverent pleasure."[8] In *Shout! Sister, Shout!*, Tharpe brings a gospel touch to what is essentially a good-humored complaint about men. Almost a year later, the tune was still a jukebox hit. A July 1942 *Billboard* column reported that although it might "appear to be strictly a race item, it has all the qualities that mean broader phono success," adding that "the Negro spiritual theme of the song makes it all the more attractive to many white nickel-droppers."[9]

In late 1943, Tharpe left Millinder for a solo career. Continuing on the gospel circuit, she was also a force in early R&B and, as a 2011 documentary called her, "the godmother of rock 'n' roll."[10] She'd been a major draw for the band, but Millinder was a formidable show-business figure himself, perhaps more than his Soundies suggest. A debonair performer with a deceptively casual air, he assembled top-notch swing bands and turned in performances that kept wartime dance floors jumping. He was also a generous mentor. A former member of the Prairie View Co-Eds, a Black all-woman big band, recalled Millinder rehearsing the relatively inexperienced group before their big opening at the Apollo. "When it came to show business," she said, "that Lucky Millinder! He knew what to do."[11]

Millinder and his band performed around the country throughout the war, but the musicians' strike of mid-1942 ended their appearances before Soundies cameras. They'd been such a hit that five additional performances, all clipped from films by other producers, were released as Soundies in 1942 and 1946. *Because I Love You* and *Harlem Serenade* (both Goldberg-Seiden, 1942), with vocals by Mamie Smith and Edna Mae Harris, respectively, were taken from the 1939 race film *Paradise in Harlem*; the postwar Soundies were clipped from a film by producer William D. Alexander. By the time Millinder's *Paradise in Harlem* Soundies were released at the end of 1942, other Black big bands had gone into the studios to create some of the biggest hits in the Soundies repertoire.

A VISUAL VOCABULARY

A few weeks after the last of Millinder's 1941 Soundies was released, two films by Count Basie and his band debuted that December. In *Air Mail Special* and *Take Me Back, Baby* (both Barry/Waller-Snody, 1941), the narrative storyline is a stronger element than in the Millinder films. Paradoxically, *Air Mail Special* also ramps up the focus on the band itself, visually parceling out the music among different instrument sections to build a dynamic portrait of the band at work.

The film opens with a medium close-up on Basie as he explains, in a spoken intro, the premise of the plot—a dance marathon with the winners chosen "As you know / By the speed and the class they show / Let's go!" As he turns to the band, the film cuts to a wide shot of the musicians, followed almost immediately by shots of the trombone, trumpet, and saxophone sections. Each shot carries a few notes of the mounting musical crescendo, ending on drummer Jo Jones as the band shifts tempo and launches into the song's thirty-two-bar theme. Dancing is a visual element too, as well as the hinge for the storyline. The camera cuts to a wide shot of the dancers—Whitey's Lindy Hoppers in a relatively low-key performance—taking the floor with the band behind them. It then shifts to a closer shot of several dancers swinging out in jitterbug moves. A quick montage of the trombones, trumpets, and saxophones follows, intercut with a shot of Basie leading the band. Variations on these shots, plus shots of the guitarist and bass player, Jones on drums, and Basie at the piano, build into short sequences that emphasize the band and the music as the driving force of the film. The storyline unfolds on the dance floor, but the real action is on the bandstand.

The montages of musicians propel that dynamic. The horn and reed sections are filmed from the side, with the musicians and their instruments creating ascending and descending diagonals—an approach frequently used in filming big bands in the 1940s.[12] A later shot of tired dancers dropping to the floor is immediately countered by one of the trombones standing up for a section solo (though in true Soundies fashion, the soundtrack under the shot is a single saxophone). In a later montage the trombone players swing their instruments toward and away from the camera, a typical bandstand move that adds eye-catching motion to the frame. Dynamically edited, Basie and the band are more than a match for the movement on the dance floor—a feat that few big-band Soundies managed to pull off, and rarely with such finesse.

In late 1941, one band that might have outdrawn Basie's was Duke Ellington's, and his first Soundie was copyrighted three weeks after Basie's last. It's plausible to think that, with their energy and verve, the Basie films had set a template for Soundies' visual interpretation of big-band music. But that doesn't take into account the decentralized nature of Soundies production, the number of different makers involved in the films, or the influence that performers themselves sometimes wielded, especially a luminary like Ellington.

Ellington's Soundies were made by RCM, the Soundies Corporation's West Coast production house. When they were recorded and shot in November 1941, Ellington had recently wrapped the three-month run of *Jump for Joy*, the "revue-sical" of Black life that he'd created with a team of collaborators (including white Soundies orchestra leader and music arranger Hal Borne). With some thirty numbers and sketches, *Jump for Joy* was envisioned, as Ellington later put it, as "a show that would take Uncle Tom out of the theater, eliminate the stereotyped image that had been exploited by Hollywood and Broadway, and say things that would make the audience think."[13]

Jump for Joy had been staged in Los Angeles, and there was talk of opening in New York. It never got there, largely because of the country's sudden plunge into war that December. But in November, as he headed into the Soundies studio, Ellington would have likely seen the films as an opportunity to promote *Jump for Joy*, cultivate its East Coast audience, and document a few of the performances on film. The Soundies *Bli-Blip* and *I Got It Bad and That Ain't Good* (both Coslow-Berne, 1942) are adapted directly from *Jump for Joy*. (Ellington and his band do not appear in *Bli-Blip* but are heard on the soundtrack.) The show's influence is felt in other ways too. The opening shots of *Hot Chocolate ("Cottontail")* (Coslow-Berne, 1941) include a poster advertising Ellington "With the Stars of *Jump for Joy*." Among them are vocalists Ivie Anderson and Herb Jeffries, who appear in two of the Ellington Soundies—Anderson in *I Got it Bad* and Jeffries in *Flamingo* (Coslow-Berne, 1942). Other *Jump for Joy* performers appear as uncredited actors in *Hot Chocolate ("Cottontail")*, *I Got It Bad*, and *Jam Session* (Coslow-Berne, 1942).

MUSIC VERSUS STORY

With a stage revue as their starting point, the Ellington Soundies are generally driven by narrative storylines rather than musical performance and its documentation. *Hot Chocolate ("Cottontail")* and *Flamingo* are the only ones in which the orchestra appears on a bandstand, and in both, most of the screen time is given over to dancers. In *I Got It Bad*, the focus is on Anderson as she enacts a lyric-driven "song story," with only occasional shots of Ellington in the role of her indifferent lover. The film unfolds on an urban rooftop, with a few band members casually lounging with women friends rather than playing music. Only *Jam Session* emphasizes musicianship, but even there, it's embedded in the context of an after-hours get-together.

The films' producer, Sam Coslow, had worked with Ellington in the 1930s and was enthusiastic about the Ellington Soundies, especially *Jam Session*. In a memo to Soundies Corporation president Gordon Mills listing the week's productions, Coslow described the film as "the first time on any screen an honest-to-God picturization of what a Jam Session is really like. There is a great deal of public curiosity about these things, and with Ellington's famous instrumentalists this should attract a lot of attention."[14]

Ellington was known for keeping a firm grip on projects he was involved with, commercially as well as creatively.[15] The agreement with the Soundies Corporation specified that none of the five Ellington films could be rereleased: once their initial Panoram runs were over, they were no longer available for distribution as Soundies. For Ellington it was a smart business decision, but for the Soundies Corporation it eliminated what would have been a highly productive long-term revenue stream. Coslow was right that *Jam Session* would attract attention: if online traffic is any indication, it may be the most popular film in the entire Soundies catalog (fig. 9.1). Uploaded to YouTube under its own title and as "C Jam Blues"—the tune performed in the film—as of this writing *Jam Session* has had more than 2.7 million views.[16]

The entire Ellington orchestra is heard on the soundtrack in *Jam Session*, but not all the musicians appear on camera. Half a dozen are spotlighted in a succession of solos and identified by name in lower-third titles—a rarity in Soundies, reflecting Ellington's practice of crediting his top players, and perhaps Coslow's enthusiasm for them as well. (Ellington does something similar in *Hot Chocolate*, verbally announcing Ben Webster just before his solo.) The track for *Jam Session* begins with Ellington, accompanied by bassist Junior Raglin, playing under the title credits and first few shots. The film opens on a sign reading "Harlem Cats Eatery," followed by a clock reading 3:03. The camera tilts down to another sign ("No credit to strangers / Welcome, stranger"), then pans left to a counterman wiping down the bar where two male customers are seated. The camera continues across a stairway at the center of the set, past a few tables with stacked-up chairs, before coming to rest on Ellington and Raglin. Musicians drift in one by one, uncasing their instruments and taking short solos, beginning with Ray Nance on violin, followed by Rex Stewart on cornet. The film cuts to three stylish women descending the stairs, then to Ben Webster—the customer at the front of the counter—as he picks up the tune with a saxophone solo. As he plays, he takes a few steps to stand in front of the stairs with the women in the background. Two more musicians appear behind them and come down the stairs, while another two pause on the landing above them. The film cuts to trombonist Joe Nanton, seated at a nearby booth, who takes the solo after Webster. In a wide shot, Barney Bigard joins the musicians around Ellington's piano, contributing a clarinet solo. A shot of the three women—Louise Franklin, Millie Monroe, and an unidentified performer—shows them listening from the stairs. The counterman—drummer Sonny Greer—crosses in front of them, greets Ellington, and takes his place for the final solo. The full band plays several bars before Ellington leaves them to join the women on the stairs. Flanked by Franklin and Monroe, he smiles and winks to the camera as the film fades out.

By the closing sequence there are nine musicians clustered around Ellington's piano, including some, like guitarist Fred Guy and bassist Raglin, not singled out for solos or on-screen identification. That's a significant percentage of the full orchestra, and of the fifteen musicians, including Ellington, who play

Figure 9.1. From *Jam Session* (1942; *from top*): Ray Nance and Rex Stewart arrive; Ben Webster plays his way across the room; drummer Sonny Greer (*in white jacket*) greets Ellington before taking his place with the band. Courtesy Mark Cantor Archive.

on the soundtrack.[17] But the entire group is seen in only that one brief shot. The jam session is presented as a more intimate gathering, focusing for the most part on Ellington and the six musicians who solo. The basement setting of the "Harlem Cats Eatery" is intimate too, and tightly defined: as the musicians take their places, their movements through the space seem, by necessity, almost choreographed. There's a visual pleasure in the camera discovering Webster as the patron at the counter and then Greer as the group's drummer. The editing, for a Soundie, is exceptionally smooth, with audio on several solos continuing over the picture cuts, weaving together the action aurally as well as visually. Even so, it's something of a shock to see ten musicians, including Ellington, crowded into the final wide shot.

Black big bands remained a visible Panoram presence through much of 1942. Ellington's Soundies overlapped a set of four by Cab Calloway (*Blues in the Night, Minnie the Moocher, Virginia, Georgia and Caroline*, and *The Skunk Song*, all Barry/Waller-Snody, 1942), with the last of these copyrighted at the end of March 1942. Calloway's films were produced by the same Minoco team that made the Basie Soundies, and a similar visual sensibility motivates these films. In all four, Calloway takes the vocals, usually backed by a male quartet, the Cabaliers (aka the Palmer Brothers). Filmed at the bandstand, these are music-focused Soundies—only *Virginia, Georgia and Caroline* includes a narrative interlude, and it gets relatively little screen time. Of the four, *Blues in Night* is the most economical in its camera set-ups, repeatedly cutting from Calloway and the Cabaliers to the same five shots of the band. Used as quick cutaways, these shots become a visual shorthand for *big band*, underscoring Calloway as bandleader without distracting from his vocal performance.

Minnie the Moocher, on the other hand, is the epitome of the quick-cut, music-driven style. There are sixty-four shots in the film, perhaps a record for a three-minute Soundie. (*Blues in the Night* uses lavish intercutting, too, but tops out at forty-six shots.) The number of camera set-ups in *Minnie* is also extravagant: twelve, including the five bandstand angles used in *Blues in the Night*, plus shots of individual musicians, a two-shot of Calloway with pianist Benny Payne, and more (fig. 9.2). Instead of the Cabaliers, the musicians themselves take the call-and-response vocals on Calloway's "hi-de-hi-de-ho" choruses, throwing more emphasis on the bandstand.[18] Though his singing drives the film, Calloway appears on screen half the time at most, as shots of musicians and instrument sections knit the band together within the space and establish visual identities for individual players.

Less than a month after Calloway's last 1942 Soundie was copyrighted, four Soundies with Les Hite and His Orchestra started appearing on Panoram

Figure 9.2. Four of the twelve camera set-ups in *Minnie the Moocher* (1942). (*From top left*) Calloway singing with pianist Benny Payne; band members responding in unison. Courtesy Mark Cantor Archive.

screens. Though made by the same Minoco team that produced the Basie and Calloway Soundies, the Hite films depart from the music-structured bandstand approach. These Soundies are solidly narrative: two focus on vocalist Savannah Churchill, including one with a poolside setting, and Hite himself carries the story line in the gym-themed *Pudgy Boy* (Barry/Waller-Snody, 1942). Though they're arguably handled with an ironic touch, tenacious stereotypes turn up in Hite's *That Ol' Ghost Train* (Barry/Waller-Snody, 1942) and—minus the irony—in Louis Armstrong's *Sleepy Time Down South* and *Shine* (both Coslow-Berne, 1942), which followed Hite's Soundies into Panoram release. Kevin Young has praised Armstrong's interpretation of the song "Sleepy Time Down South," which in other hands "is nostalgic and even problematic in evoking a kind of pure plantation past." Armstrong's interpretation, he writes, showcases a "scat virtuosity" that "fights against the words, creating a tension between the South he is singing and the South he is scatting from."[19] But Armstrong's scatting is conspicuously absent from his Soundies performance of "Sleepy Time Down

South," and so is the productive tension that Young describes. For this filmed rendition, "nostalgic and even problematic" is probably a fairer description.

Armstrong's last Soundie, *Swingin' on Nothin'* (Coslow-Berne, 1942) is notable for a display of body positivity that easily surpasses the jitterbugging woman in Lucky Millinder's *I Want a Big Fat Mama*. Vocalist Velma Middleton, a woman of considerable size, performs a quick jitterbug with vocalist George Washington before moving on to an energetic solo dance that ends in a series of rolling splits. Though physically quite different, Middleton is akin to Dorothy Dandridge in her self-possession and bodily presence, and Armstrong readily makes room for her on the dance floor.

By the time *Swingin' on Nothin'* debuted in August 1942, the musicians' strike had swept the entertainment industry. Copyrighted at the end of December 1942, the two Soundies clipped from Lucky Millinder's 1939 *Paradise in Harlem* were the last big-band Soundies with Black musicians until early 1945.

TRAVELING LIGHT

Even without the musicians' strike, the war years were tough on big bands. Military service made it hard to keep the bandstand full, and gas and rubber rationing turned regional tours into logistical nightmares, especially for Black bands traveling in the South. The shellac that would have gone into records was channeled into the defense industry. The musicians' strike—which for some record companies lasted a full two years—helped turn vocalists from big-band afterthoughts into hit-making stars in their own right. Rock 'n' roll was incubating. In New York, progressive musicians were already immersed in bebop.

In Soundies, several of these trends converged in the person of Louis Jordan. In the late 1930s, Jordan had been a member of the Savoy Ballroom orchestra under the leadership of drummer Chick Webb, but the group that he put together for himself was anything but a big band. Widely known as the Tympany Five—regardless of how many musicians were actually on the bandstand—his combo exemplified what came to be known as jump bands.[20] Instead of the full trumpet, trombone, and saxophone sections that typically powered big bands, Jordan's 1942 Soundies featured only himself on saxophone and Eddie Roane on trumpet. It was a nimbler version of the big-band sound, with a driving beat, repeating riffs, a strong blues flavor, and irreverent lyrics, many of them courtesy of Jordan himself.

Jordan made a total of fourteen Soundies in 1942, 1944, and 1945, including one (*The Outskirts of Town*, Coslow-Berne, 1942) in which he appears on the soundtrack only. Four were clipped from *Caldonia*, the featurette that Crouch directed in 1945.[21] Jordan's Soundies are rich with cultural references, but his greatest impact was arguably on pop music itself. Playing with five musicians, Jordan "ruined the big bands," blues singer Dwight "Gatemouth" Moore once remarked. "He could play just as good and just as loud with five as seventeen. And it was cheaper."[22] A fresh sound and cost-effective logistics were an unbeatable combination, and jump bands, Jordan's in particular, sparked the transition from swing to rock 'n' roll. "As a Black musician, I'd like to say one thing," Jordan told a writer shortly before his death in 1975. "Rock 'n' roll was not a marriage of rhythm and blues [to] country and western. That's white publicity. Rock 'n' roll was just a white imitation, a white adaptation of Negro rhythm and blues."[23]

The Tympany Five wasn't the first small combo to appear in Soundies, but it was among the first to have an emphatic bandstand presence. On screen, Jordan's relationship to his band is like Cab Calloway's in *Minnie the Moocher*. Jordan takes the vocals, and the band provides back-up vocals and call-and-response as needed. But with only five players, Jordan is essential as a musician too. *Five Guys Named Moe* (Crouch-Graham, 1942) is a bandstand film, and Jordan is often framed with the entire group or with pianist Arnold Thomas behind him. He sings in the opening and closing sequences, but most of the film shows off his saxophone work. The same is true for many of his other Soundies, including ones that feature dancers, like *Jordan Jive* (Crouch-Crouch, 1944), or incorporate nonbandstand footage, like the department-store vignettes in *Down, Down, Down* (Crouch-Graham, 1942). Occasionally the spotlight falls on another band member too, notably the forty-five-second solo by drummer Rossiere "Shadow" Wilson in the frenetic *Jumpin' at the Jubilee* (Crouch-Graham, 1942).[24]

WARTIME BOOGIE WOOGIE

With the musicians' strike choking production, no Jordan Soundies were produced in 1943, and solo vocalists and dancers featured strongly in the Panoram reels that year. But a vein of boogie piano runs through Soundies—principally in the Meade "Lux" Lewis Soundies of 1942 and 1944—and this musical style also fed the emergence of rock 'n' roll. In 1943 a set of films by pianist Lynn Albritton managed to slip past the musicians' strike. While they feature extended dance sequences, her three Soundies—*Block Party Revels, Backstage Blues*, and *Dispossessed Blues* (all Crouch-Crouch, 1943)—showcase Albritton's masterful boogie style, on the soundtrack if not always on screen. Although her music drives the films, Albritton's placement in the frame is sometimes marginal, making her an awkward afterthought to the dancers. She may be the only

Figure 9.3. Lynn Albritton in *Dispossessed Blues* (1943). Courtesy Mark Cantor Archive.

Soundies pianist obliged to perform looking over her shoulder, turning away from the keyboard to try to catch the camera's eye. In *Backstage Blues*, Albritton is seen only in wide shots (at frame right), with no cutaways to identify her or showcase her playing. She fares better in *Block Party Revels*, which repeatedly shows her at the piano, surrounded by energized partiers and making clear eye contact with the camera, though at an odd angle. She's spotlighted, finally, as the central character in *Dispossessed Blues*, defiantly playing as her belongings are put out on the street (fig. 9.3). Here she's filmed from the side, in close-ups and medium shots that offer the most sustained attention to her playing.

Albritton was an established entertainer in Harlem but did not record extensively. It's possible that she wasn't a union musician, which may have allowed her to make Soundies during the strike. In any case, little of her music survives beyond Soundies. "Excellent pianist," *Billboard* reported in its review of *Block Party Revels*, noting that the film "presents hot music in a highly acceptable way."[25] The reel for the following week included another Albritton title, and *Billboard* was again enthusiastic: "Lynn Albritton really gives in *Backstage*

Blues, and jive fans should eat it up." Though the film had little in the way of a storyline, *Billboard* wrote, "the pianist is good enough so that it's not missed."[26]

Occasionally musicians who didn't normally play together were shoehorned into a Soundies session, and it could be an awkward fit. In the three-film set headlined by pianist Gene Rodgers, his costars are the all-woman combo known as the Vs (Ivern Whittaker, Ivy Ann Glasko, Willie Lee Floyd, and Lady Will Carr). Rodgers was a solid jazz musician, active since the mid-1920s, best known for his memorable four-bar piano intro on Coleman Hawkins's 1939 "Body and Soul." But he was also a variety-show entertainer and "comedy pianist," and in that vein he favored an up-tempo approach that drew on boogie and stride styles.[27] The Vs, on the other hand, were an accomplished jazz combo, well known in Los Angeles's Central Avenue club district, with their own pianist, the redoubtable Lady Will Carr. Perhaps producer Ben Hersh and director Dave Gould thought they were booking Gene Rodgers the jazz pianist; what they got was the variety-show performer. In *Big Fat Butterfly* (Hersh-Gould, 1944), Rodgers mugs, shrugs, and eye-rolls his way through a routine with dancer Marie Bryant before bumping Carr from the piano for a short round of boogie-inspired riffs. He does much the same, minus Bryant, in *My, My, Ain't That Somethin'* (Hersh-Gould, 1944), with the Vs gamely supporting him with music and vocals. In *Juke Box Boogie* (Hersh-Gould, 1944), Rodgers is at the piano from beginning to end, filling the soundtrack with a fluid, rolling style. As noted earlier, the set for *Juke Box Boogie* is stunningly racist—a barn filled with oversized slices of watermelon—and the backdrop for *Big Fat Butterfly* is an offensive caricature. (*My, My, Ain't That Somethin'* uses the same set as *Big Fat Butterfly*, minus the caricature.) If it were possible to look past these settings—a formidable *if*—it would be less for Rodgers's piano, perhaps, than for the Vs.[28] The women have the screen to themselves for almost a minute at the start of *Big Fat Butterfly*, and Lady Will Carr's piano solo opens *My, My, Ain't That Somethin'*.

For other performers, boogie was a springboard into a different music. The musicians' strike ended for the Soundies Corporation in late 1943, and by December, the company had copyrighted four films by pianist Maurice Rocco: *Rock It for Me, Beat Me Daddy, Rhumboogie*, and *Rocco Blues* (all Crouch-Crouch, 1943). Rocco was a well-known nightclub performer, and in the late 1930s he'd appeared in two Hollywood movies.[29] After his Soundies he had a role—with a showstopping number—in the 1945 Technicolor feature *Incendiary Blonde*.[30] Like Jordan, Rocco was a forerunner of rock 'n' roll: in one of his 1943 Soundies he was already singing, "I'm all through with this thing called swing / Oh, oh, oh, rock it for me!" His influence was not as pervasive as

Jordan's, but his energetic, stand-at-the-piano style was echoed by early rockers like Little Richard and Jerry Lee Lewis.

For many Soundies performers—including the young Liberace—a mirrored piano backboard was de rigueur for showing off keyboard technique, and it is standard equipment in all four of Rocco's Soundies. In two of them, Crouch pushes the visual multiplication further, filming Rocco with a prismatic lens that fills the screen with his repeated image. In *Rocco Blues*, it's multiple hands on keyboards; in *Beat Me Daddy*, five or six of him stand at their pianos. Prismatic shots are rare in Soundies, particularly for performance documentation, and in that context they're associated mostly with boogie music. Boogie harpist LaVilla Tullos gets the prismatic treatment in *Swanee Swing* (Crouch-Crouch, 1944; fig. 9.4), and so does another stand-up proto-rocker, white pianist Harry "The Hipster" Gibson, in his Soundie *Opus 12EEE* (Blake-Blake, 1944).

But prismatic shots weren't a universal response to a boogie beat. The multiple-image treatment had no part, for instance, in Meade "Lux" Lewis's Soundies. Made on the West Coast, his three films—*Roll 'Em*, *Boogie Woogie*, and *Low Down Dog* (all Gould-Gould, 1944)—are more narrative than performance focused. In one, Lewis is a piano-playing moving man, and in the others, a musical bystander to long-running romantic tiffs. Crouch also opted against using prismatic shots for Una Mae Carlisle's films. As a teenager, Carlisle had been a protégé of Fats Waller, but her own style was more decorous. The tunes in her three Soundies— *'Tain't Yours*, *I Like It 'Cause I Love It*, and *I'm a Good, Good Woman* (all Crouch-Crouch, 1944)—share a sedate, steady rhythm. The films showcase her piano playing on the instrumental breaks (though not always in sync), but her husky vocals and easy on-camera persona are a big part of their appeal.

JUMP AND JAZZ

As the war continued, the increasing emphasis on vocalists and small combos pushed pop music in other directions. In 1944, drummer Roy Milton and his group made three Soundies with singer June Richmond that took the jump sound deeper into blues territory. If not pure rhythm-and-blues themselves, the songs in *47th Street Jive* and *Ride On, Ride On* herald its imminent arrival, buttressed by Richmond's signature *Hey, Lawdy Mama* (all Hersh-Berne, 1944). Set in an intimate space that could be an after-hours club, all three films are firmly focused on the music, anchored by Richmond's assured vocals and appealing screen presence. The band plays tightly behind her, with individual musicians—especially Milton and pianist Camille Howard—adding strong solos. Two years later, as Roy Milton and His Solid Senders, the group (minus Richmond) reached the charts with the

Figure 9.4. Musician and composer LaVilla Tullos in *Swanee Swing* (1944).
Courtesy Mark Cantor Archive.

single "R. M. Blues," the first of many R&B hits. While continuing with the band,
Camille Howard also built a solo career as an R&B singer and pianist.

In other groups, a combination of piano, guitar, and bass produced a cool, under-
stated sound that leaned toward jazz. The King Cole Trio—Nat "King" Cole on
piano and vocals, Oscar Moore on guitar, and Johnny Miller on bass—were among
the most influential exponents of this low-key style. The group made seven Soundies
in 1944 and 1946. The first two feature vocalist Ida James, dueting with Cole in *Is You
Is or Is You Ain't My Baby?* and soloing in *Who's Been Eating My Porridge?* (both Hersh-
Berne, 1944), with the group effectively acting as her backup band. In the humorously self-reflexive *Frim Fram Sauce* (Crouch-Crouch, 1945), Cole performs with
himself: While he sings as a customer in a crowded café, he—along with Moore and
Miller—is also shown performing on a nearby Panoram. On the screen and in the
café, the two Coles acknowledge each other, staring intently as, one after the other,
each takes a few lines of lyrics, never singing together (figs. I.3 and 1.1, pp. 14 and 25).

Although Cole takes all vocals after the two Soundies with Ida James, it's the
trio, rather than Cole himself, that gets star billing in the films. Cole biographer

Will Friedwald writes that guitarist Moore "was much more than a secondary voice" in the music, providing "very specific chordal underpinnings to what Cole was playing; and in doing so, he helped distinguish the Trio from a simple jam session group to something more like a true chamber music ensemble." Friedwald describes bassist Miller's work with the group as "sleek, solid, and supportive," noting that "he consistently plays in a way that allows him to express himself while at the same time underscoring the group's central narrative." *Frim Fram Sauce* notwithstanding, the King Cole Trio Soundies generally open on a wide shot of the group, and Moore and Miller get a good amount of screen time, particularly on the instrumental breaks.[31]

Other combos followed their lead. The Counts and the Countess—leader Alma Smith on piano and vibes, John Faire on guitar, and Curtis Wilder on bass—had the same configuration and an intentionally similar style. "We were a takeoff on Nat King Cole," Smith later told a music historian. "Everything that he did, we did."[32] Smith was still a teenager when they made their three Soundies for RCM in Los Angeles, including *Five Salted Peanuts* and *I've Got to Be a Rug Cutter* (both Hersh-Berne, 1945). Though not widely available online they're worth seeking out, especially for Smith's sure touch on the keyboard. Set in a café, all three films are emphatically music-focused—there's not a dancer in sight and few cutaways to the audience. Instead, there are satisfying shots of the musicians at work. The trio's harmonizing vocals are light and crisp, occasionally breaking into a scat style. Smith played vibes as well as piano (though not in these Soundies), and one popular story has her stopping a show in LA with her virtuoso performance, prompting the emcee to shout, "Lionel Hampton, take off that dress!"[33] After the Counts and the Countess disbanded in the late 1940s, Smith returned to her hometown, Detroit, where she was an important figure in the music community until her death in 2012.

Another Soundies trio offered a different take on the standard set-up, swapping an accordion for the piano. Performing in suits and tasseled fezzes, the Ali Baba Trio (Cleveland Nickerson, Calvin Ponder, and "Big" Mike McKendrick) appear in four films. On their own in *E-Bob-O-Lee-Bop* and *Your Feet's Too Big* (both Hersh-Gould, 1946), they're typical of a lighter, jazz-inflected sound that gained popularity after the war. In the other two, *Patience and Fortitude* and *If You Only Knew* (both Hersh-Gould, 1946), they serve as capable backup for then-renowned performer Valaida Snow.

At the time of her Soundies, Snow had been in show business for more than twenty-five years. An accomplished singer and dancer who'd appeared with Ethel Waters and Josephine Baker, she was also a music arranger and trumpeter. She'd been nicknamed "Little Louis" after Louis Armstrong, and Armstrong himself affectionately called her the world's second-best trumpet player.[34] Snow spent much of the 1930s performing in Europe, and in 1942 was reportedly held for several months by the Nazis in Denmark, an experience that left her deeply scarred.[35] Made in 1946, her Soundies were part of a professional comeback that began after her return to the United States. The films present her as a vocalist, entertainer, and, in *Patience and Fortitude*, trumpet soloist.

Trios were not the only musical units to rethink swing. When Dallas Bartley, the bassist in Louis Jordan's 1942 Soundies, left Jordan's band to form his own group in 1943, he called it Dallas Bartley and His Orchestra. But *orchestra* was a stretch: Bartley's group was a jump-band unit not unlike Jordan's Tympany Five, in this case a sextet. Along similar lines, Tiny Grimes and His Orchestra were in fact a quintet—saxophone, piano, bass, and drums backing Grimes on guitar. Despite the orchestra labeling, neither group relied on the kind of high-powered horn sections that drove the big-band sound. Instead, both groups delivered a lighter take on jump music, in Soundies like Bartley's *Ya Fine and Healthy Thing* (Crouch-Crouch, 1945) and Grimes's *Never Too Old to Swing* (Crouch-Crouch, 1945). Each group made five Soundies in 1945, most released throughout late summer and fall (with one Bartley film copyrighted in 1946). Redefining the concept of orchestra for a new musical era, these agile, scaled-down units and others like them played to the changing tastes of postwar audiences.

STEPPING OFF THE BANDSTAND

The end of the big-band era more or less coincided with Soundies' commercial decline. Neither happened overnight. On Panorams, 1945 saw the return of Cab Calloway and His Orchestra in five new releases—including the vibrant scat-and-jitterbug *Foo, A Little Ballyhoo* (Crouch-Crouch, 1945)—along with four films by jazz reedman Cecil Scott and His Orchestra. In 1946, the sixteen numbers clipped from William D. Alexander's films provided a stream of classic swing: Lucky Millinder and His Orchestra, Henri Woode and His Orchestra, the International Sweethearts of Rhythm, and crooner Billy Eckstine and His Orchestra. Aside from a set of five films with Noble Sissle and His Orchestra (a compact, seven-person unit), Alexander's clips were the only Black-cast big-band Soundies to reach the screen in 1946.

As the year progressed it became clear that time was running out for the Soundies Corporation. Production and music licensing budgets hit rock bottom, and big-band-sized payrolls were no longer an option. One late Soundie, *Boogiemania* (Crouch-Crouch, 1946), not only reused a soundtrack (identified by Mark Cantor as Cecil Scott's 1945 Soundie *Mr. X. Blues*) but had Sun Tan

Studio head Fritz Pollard—not widely known as a musician—on camera as a pianist and bandleader.[36] (In his honor, the on-screen combo is called the Sun Tan Four.) Soon after, Pollard appeared again in *Sun Tan Strut* (Crouch-Crouch, 1946).

Despite the company's downward spiral, production continued on Black-cast Soundies in quantities that suggest an active market. Of 270 films copyrighted in 1946, fifty-five starred Black performers—roughly 20 percent, somewhat higher than the proportion of Black-cast Soundies in the overall total. Most of them featured groups like the King Cole and Ali Baba Trios, and solo vocalists like June Richmond and Vanita Smythe, whose eight Soundies were all released that year. Jazz trumpeter Henry "Red" Allen and his combo contributed five films, including *House on 52nd Street* and *Mop* (both Crouch-Crouch, 1946), and pianists Pat Flowers and Phil Moore (with the Phil Moore Four) appear in one apiece.

This outpouring was especially notable in that, as of January 1946, for the first time in Soundies history, Black-cast films were excluded from the weekly eight-film reels and shifted entirely into the category of M films. This meant they were available to Panoram operators exclusively by request. Until 1946, M films had been extras, produced for Panoram operators eager to add more Black-cast Soundies to their programs. That year, M-film release became the sole distribution channel for Black-cast Soundies.

As an attempt to navigate a splintering postwar market, it was not a winning strategy. In 1947, as Crouch attempted to keep the enterprise afloat, Black-cast films returned to the general-release reels. Copyrighted on December 31, 1946, but released the following March, Pat Flowers's *Coalmine Boogie* (Crouch-Crouch, 1946) has the distinction of being "the last Soundie"—the final film in the last reel to be released by a Soundies company.[37]

In this survey of music- and performance-focused films, what perhaps emerges most clearly is the breadth of music that Black-cast Soundies encompass—swing, boogie, jump, jazz, and proto-R&B and rock, among others, along with one-off outliers like country-western music (*Along the Navajo Trail*, Hersh-Berne, 1945, starring John Shadrack Horance and Johnnie Moore's 3 Blazers) and barbershop quartet–style harmonizing (*Love Grows on a White Oak Tree*, Crouch-Crouch, 1944, starring the Little Four Quartet). It's also worth mentioning a music that, for the most part, does not figure in these films, namely bebop.[38] Anchored in pop music and pop culture, Soundies would have been an unlikely site for such a radical, disruptive style. Bebop was "not only a reaction to the white-dominated, melody-obsessed 'swing jazz,'" writes Cornel West, "it was also a creative musical response to the major shift in sensibilities and moods in Afro-America after World War II." Through their invention and virtuosity, West says, "bebop jazz musicians expressed the heightened tensions, frustrated aspirations and repressed emotions of an aggressive yet apprehensive Afro-America."[39] If, as Eric Lott has argued, the course of postwar Black music was shaped by the collisions and divergences of R&B and bebop, it is clear—from the number of Louis Jordan Soundies, if nothing else—which side of the musical divide Soundies came down on.[40] Distant echoes of bebop may be heard in a few spots—the unison vocal phrasing near the end of *Five Salted Peanuts*, for instance, or the Charlie Parker–influenced sax solo by John "Flap" Dungee in Dallas Bartley's *All Ruzzit Buzzitt* (Crouch-Crouch, 1945).[41] But for Soundies the determining framework, musical and otherwise, was always popular culture, and the musics that emerge most clearly in postwar Soundies are mainstream forms like R&B and early rock 'n' roll. From this perspective, Soundies' most radical contribution may have been the fundamental insistence on documenting Black music performance on film and developing the visual vocabulary with which to do it. It was perhaps no less radical—though more budget driven—to extend the films' reach to performers rarely seen elsewhere on screen. On both counts, the result is a broader understanding of wartime music trajectories and the musicians who shaped them.

10

BACKING INTO INTEGRATION

IN ONLY A FEW SOUNDIES—perhaps three dozen of roughly 1,880—do Black performers share screen time with white performers. This small subset of films is where, in Soundies, white America's profound discomfort with racial integration was expressed most acutely, especially as the war got underway. It is also where, in one area at least, change was most clearly charted as the decade progressed.

Black-and-white-cast Soundies generally fall into two categories: films that include Black characters in largely white-cast narratives, which were made mostly in 1941 and 1942; and films that document the real-life integration of certain bands and combos in 1945 and 1946. Coming early and late in the Soundies Corporation's production history, these films bookend the company's output. The later Soundies are straightforward performance films that document the integrated status of the groups they depict without making it a major focus. The early narratives, on the other hand, use Hollywood-style stereotypes and visual language, usually to reinforce the racist status quo. In a few cases, the on-screen interpretations are so extreme—dream-like, illogical, sexually charged—that they demand a deeper look.

Even with a scant three minutes of running time, some early Black-and-white-cast Soundies followed the Hollywood practice of marginalizing Black performers in isolated segments. In films like *Once Over Lightly*, *Barnyard Bounce* (both Oliphant/Leonard-Leonard, 1941), and *Night Train to Memphis* (Hersh-Gould, 1944), all-white crowd scenes are punctuated by solo or duo performances by Black actors who—cast as waiters, porters, golf caddies, and other service workers—contribute quick dances, often set apart from the main action and usually limited to the song's instrumental break.

In other films, these performances continue into the sequences that follow. *Bundle of Love* (Ratoff-McNulty, 1943) unfolds in a confectioner's shop, in what are essentially two segregated sets: a sales area populated by white showgirls in tiny organza pinafores, and the kitchen, where a quartet of Black male candy chefs (the Dreamers, aka the Jones Boys) comment in song on the goings-on in the front of the store. In this case, the men's voices continue on the soundtrack, and late in the film a quick cutaway knits them back into the narrative. In *Alabamy Bound* (Coslow-Murphy, 1941), the (credited) vocal group Five Spirits of Rhythm, cast as train porters, take the instrumental break with a percussion riff on shoeshining, then reappear at the film's close to provide the visual punchline, wreathing their white costar in hands outstretched for tips. *The Outline of Jitterbug History* (Coslow-Berne, 1942) allots a full third of its footage to Whitey's Lindy Hoppers. Presented as the highest level of jitterbug achievement, their modern-day performance caps a string of white jitterbugs in historical settings, from the Stone Age to seventeenth-century France and beyond. In Soundies like these, racial integration is more often achieved in the editing room than on the film set, almost invariably reinforcing the racial status quo.

One Mills Brothers film takes a different approach. In six of their seven Soundies, the singers appear with Black supporting players—the women on their laps in *Paper Doll*, the farmyard dancers in *Caravan*—but in *Till Then* (Crouch-Crouch, 1944), they perform in a living room filled with white listeners. The Mills Brothers had enormous crossover appeal and the song was a Top Ten hit for them, but *Till Then* is one of the few Soundies in which Black performers play to a white living-room audience. Why this situation so rarely appears in Soundies is unclear, but given how closely Soundies executives tracked audience responses to the films, feedback from viewers—Black, white, or both—may have been a factor.

It's difficult to fathom what Panoram viewers might have thought about *Lazybones* (Coslow-Murphy, 1941). The film's visualization of its song is extreme enough to expose the racist assumptions behind it and then layer on more of its own. *Lazybones* stars white composer Hoagy Carmichael, introduced in an opening text crawl as "one of the country's foremost songwriters."[1] After a quick piano rendition of his classic "Stardust," Carmichael drawls out the title tune—about a rural type who prefers dozing in the sun to doing chores—seated at a living-room piano, flanked by two women.

Written in 1933 with lyricist Johnny Mercer, "Lazy Bones" was an immediate hit, with the sheet music alone selling an estimated fifteen thousand copies a day in its first few months. By the time Carmichael made the Soundie in 1941,

"Lazy Bones" was an American songbook standard. More recently, at least one writer has criticized the song for naturalizing "Black sloth" and relegating Black men to an antebellum past.[2] Those assumptions take a surreal turn in the film's visuals. If Carmichael is the ostensible star, the action belongs to dancer Peter Ray. In the role of a servant, Ray negotiates the path between kitchen and piano in slow motion, balancing a tray holding a silver coffee pot, creamer, and sugar bowl—on his head.

It's a dream-like performance that defies logic: there's no conceivable reason to carry a coffee set into a living room that way. The absurdity of the task exposes the film's racist associations, starting with the trope of a Black person carrying a burden on his head—or, following the logic of the lyrics, finding a way to perform a task as slowly as possible. Ray's deliberate movements match Carmichael's lugubrious tempo, but his performance cuts against the lyrics: his artful balancing act is the opposite of indolence, requiring concentrated effort and physical skill. He intentionally comes close to spilling the load, to the visible horror of Dorothy Dandridge, who, as a short-skirted maid, dances along with him. When he finally places the tray and its contents on Carmichael's piano, Dandridge's relief seems exaggerated but genuine. Ray's dance cannot overcome the racist underpinnings of its premise, but in its exaggerated caricature and the grace and control of his performance, it calls into question the stereotype that the song and film are looking to impose. Dudley Murphy, the film's director, made several other Soundies with Black performers, including Dandridge, and earlier in his career he'd directed Bessie Smith in her screen debut, Duke Ellington in his sound-film debut, and Paul Robeson in *The Emperor Jones* (1933). Given Murphy's interest in showcasing Black performers, *Lazybones* is a distinct throwback, and an indication of how difficult it was, in 1941, for white interpreters to envision racially integrated scenarios that did not rest on racist assumptions.

Copyrighted in December 1941, *Lazybones* was included in Soundies Program 1046, an eight-film reel that also featured Fats Waller's star turn in *Ain't Misbehavin'* (Barry/Waller-Murray, 1941). The description of *Lazybones* in the Soundies catalog is oblivious to both the strangeness of Ray's performance and its racist stereotyping—oblivious, in fact, to the performance itself. Carmichael was a prestigious name for Soundies and Dandridge had already built an enthusiastic fan base, and the brief description focuses on them exclusively. It hails Carmichael as "Indiana's famous composer," noting that his "piano playing, plus some comedy dancing by Dorothy Dandridge, add much to this subject."[3] Despite the centrality of Ray's performance and his credit in the film, the description does not mention him.

In *I Don't Want to Walk without You* (Barry/Waller-Owen Murphy, 1942), Frank Wilcox, a Black performer cast as a waiter (uncredited), also does a dance with a tray, deftly keeping the refreshments away from one hungry guest in particular.[4] Although he's on screen for a third of the film, his dance is not the focus, as Ray's is in *Lazybones*, but comic relief. Wilcox's movements are so exaggerated that his performance becomes another caricature, like Ray's absurdist labor in *Lazybones*.

A LITTLE MORE LIBIDO

Shoeshiners and Headliners (Feher-unknown, 1941) was one of the earliest Soundies releases—the lead-off film on Program 1002, the second eight-film reel to be distributed after full-time production began in late 1940. The maker, Frederick Feher Productions, was one of the small Los Angeles companies that helped Jimmy Roosevelt's Globe Productions—the nominal producer of all West Coast Soundies—to fulfill its weekly quota. A classically trained orchestra conductor, Feher was more comfortable doing formal interpretations like *The Blue Danube* (also on that reel) than the latest tunes from the hottest swing bands. His attempts at reaching Soundies audiences produced some odd disconnects: for him, pop music meant a vocalist in a tuxedo, backed by a full orchestra, singing a Stephen Foster tune (*Jeannie with the Light Brown Hair*, Feher-unknown, 1941), or showgirls awkwardly making their way through a flock of pianists (*Grand Pianos and Gals*, Feher-unknown, 1941).

Shoeshiners and Headliners is off-kilter in a different way. The film opens on a row of Black shoeshine men attending a row of white male horn players in suits and derbies, seated in elevated shoeshine chairs. In bending over the musicians' shoes, the shine men are angled so that, half a minute into the film, their backsides are presented somewhat provocatively to the camera in a leisurely pan right to left. Above them, the seated musicians perform, raising their instruments in the air (fig. 10.1). The shine men mime a percussion performance, snapping their cloths and tap dancing in place. Their backs are to the viewer; throughout the sequence, the face of the shine man nearest the camera is occasionally visible in profile, but the faces of the others are never shown, objectifying them further.

A troupe of white showgirls enters, dressed as newsboys and holding up papers, led by the film's star, Florence Pepper. The women do their own song and dance, with Pepper taking most of the screen time. The shoeshiners and newsgirls share the performance space but remain separate, not relating to each other—for the most part. Near the end of their dance the women line up, facing

Figure 10.1. A frame of the right-to-left pan across the shoeshine men and their white clientele in *Shoeshiners and Headliners* (1941). Library of Congress, Motion Picture, Broadcasting and Recorded Sound Division.

away from the row of shoeshiners leaning over their customers. Bending slightly forward, the women dance back toward the men, hips swaying. Ultimately, it's unclear if white and Black backsides actually meet, but the final distance between them, shown in a wide shot taken from the side, is negligible (fig. 10.2).

Even for Soundies, the repository of some audacious flights of libido, it's a remarkable moment: sexually multivalent, a little surreal, and slightly shocking in its casual disregard for the social norms of the day. Seeing the shoeshiners' backsides at the feet of the white musicians, the connotations evoked by Black men in a servile posture are layered with homoerotic overtones. The white women's derrières moving toward them introduce a heterosexual current that expands the sexual energy rather than redirecting it. In the space of a few moments, the film sketches the rigidity and constraints of mid-twentieth-century American race relations and the sexual tensions straining against them. The women are the most dynamic choreographic element, and their moves reference, invert, and destabilize one of the most potent and enduring interracial tropes—Black men supposedly lusting for white women—using the visual language of the pinup and the choreography of the chorus line.

Figure 10.2. White chorus-line dancers back into and away from Black shoeshine men in an uncensored print of *Shoeshiners and Headliners* (1941). They then back in again, filmed from another angle. Library of Congress, Motion Picture, Broadcasting and Recorded Sound Division.

The singularity of this moment is reflected in the fact that, although the print of the film held by the Library of Congress is intact, roughly eighteen seconds of footage, including the backside-to-backside shot, is missing from the print held by stock footage company Historic Films—for many years the only online posting of the film.[5] The film was censored in Ohio and the objectionable footage deleted—a testament to the evocative power of that sequence. Given its early spot in the catalog, *Shoeshiners and Headliners* may well have been the first Soundie to come up against a state censorship board. Had the Soundies Corporation been, at that point, more practiced in dealing with these issues, they might have found a way of sidestepping the deletion beyond Ohio. As it was, it's likely that, despite the disruptive effect on the visuals and the soundtrack, the company chose to distribute the film nationally with the sequence deleted. Even with the edits, it was popular enough to be rereleased twice—almost immediately in April 1941 and in January 1944, most likely in its censored version.

Like the catalog description for *Lazybones*, the description for *Shoeshiners and Headliners* ignores the racial and sexual undercurrents beneath its perky surface. "A fast tempo dance number," the description reads. "Girls in shorts and sweaters dancing. Attractive Florence Pepper does the vocal."[6] The film's unusual staging may have contributed to some Soundies historians identifying Pepper, a white performer, as a Black singer and dancer, and by implication, her fellow showgirls as well.[7] Given how the action unfolds, the assumption is understandable, but Pepper and her colleagues, although brunettes, clearly read as white. Played against the provocative positioning of the Black men and their white male clientele, the women's whiteness intensifies what is already an extraordinarily charged depiction for this era, embedded in three minutes of musical fluff.

It's worth a moment to consider *Shoeshiners and Headliners* in the context of the minstrel show. Other Soundies take minstrelsy as a setting or as an obvious reference, but with *Shoeshiners and Headliners* the commonality is more basic. At their most uninhibited, Soundies and the mid-nineteenth-century minstrel show share what Eric Lott describes as an unrestrained tendency "to air from behind the mask, as though live and direct from the white unconscious, just about anything that chances to surface."[8] White male desire for Black men "was everywhere to be found in minstrel acts," he writes, and something of that desire animates the film's opening sequence.[9] Lott argues that those repressed desires emerge as fantasy, and this Freudian "return of the repressed" is evident in *Shoeshiners and Headliners*, as it was in the rowdy, raunchy minstrel shows of a hundred years earlier.[10]

Whether inadvertent or deliberate, these ambiguous, sexualized, and surreal undercurrents set Soundies apart from much of the moving-image media of their day. Despite being censored in a few states, the films did not come under review by the federal Office of War Information, which strongly pressured Hollywood to stay on-message with the war effort. Nor were they subject to the Hays Office, the film-industry watchdog that maintained tight standards of moral behavior in studio-produced films. Even with state censorship, Soundies generally took a looser approach to sexuality and libido than Hollywood could get away with, and that comparative freedom—coupled with a need to keep experimenting with the three-minute film form—arguably led to a more open-minded outlook overall. As Herzog observes, in Soundies "that which is threatening need not be resolved or punished, as it often is in narrative forms. Within Soundies there is room for irrationality, transformation, eruption— even a joy in difference."[11] The visual language of *Shoeshiners and Headliners* is pure movie musical, but what it has to say is far beyond the Hollywood norm, and is left that way with no need for resolution.

Though they'd always been few in number, by 1943 Black-and-white-cast narratives had all but vanished from the weekly Soundies reels, as social changes set into motion by the war continued to gather momentum. When Black and white performers next appeared together on Panoram screens, Hollywood-style stereotypes and film language had very little to do with it. Instead, the focus was on the bandstand and the changes taking place there.

IN PLAIN SIGHT

Straightforward and unembellished, the Black-and-white-cast Soundies of 1945 and 1946 are solid examples of performance documentation. There are no storylines to speak of, and the soundtracks take priority over the visuals, which focus almost exclusively on the musicians as they perform. Performance documentation was one of the earliest Soundies formats, and its visual language was quickly codified. It was reasonably cost-effective, and that became increasingly important as the company's finances soured. All of which left Soundies well positioned to record the integration taking place in a small number of bands and orchestras.[12]

During the war, racial integration was rarely a factor in musical-performance Soundies. This more or less reflected the music scene at the time. Although Black musicians might occasionally appear as guest performers with white bands, big-band orchestras and small groups were rarely integrated—at least not in terms that publicly acknowledged the fact. White musicians in Black bands touring the South sometimes declared themselves Black, rather than deal with the challenges of touring as a mixed-race group.[13]

In Soundies, an unlikely exception to this status quo was Borrah Minevitch's Harmonica Rascals. At least one of the group's Soundies, *Bugle Call Rag* (Oliphant/Leonard-Leonard, 1942), featured its sole Black member, Ernie Morris, as an uncredited leader in the on-screen action. A more prominent exception was Gene Krupa and His Orchestra, the first and most high-profile integrated big band to appear on Panoram screens. "Gene Krupa is, of all ofay ork [white orchestra] leaders, about the fairest on the color question we have yet watched and enjoyed," wrote the *Chicago Defender*.[14] "As an example, take a peek at his band appearing on the 'Soundies' machines." Krupa's group made two Soundies released in 1942 and recorded the soundtrack for another (used, with a different band on screen, in *Sugar Hill Masquerade*). "Krupa uses Roy Eldridge in a solo part and Roy and Gene's vocalist, who is white, do a little skit together," the *Defender* wrote.[15] Both *Let Me Off Uptown* and *Thanks for the Boogie Ride* (both Waller-Snody, 1942) feature an easy, pleasurable rapport between trumpeter Eldridge and vocalist Anita O'Day—a rarity on wartime film screens. But the camaraderie on camera belied mounting offscreen tensions. According to O'Day, by 1942 Eldridge was barely speaking to her, convinced that she was upstaging him during his solos. The band broke up in 1943 following Krupa's arrest and ninety-day jail sentence for marijuana possession, on charges that were later dropped.[16]

The Krupa films are the only Soundies in which a Black musician appears as a member of a predominantly white big band or combo. After that, integration in Soundies moved in the other direction, with white musicians appearing in predominantly Black groups. Again, this reflected developments taking place in the music industry. The first of these films did not appear until after the war, in late 1945 and early 1946, with a series starring Black bandleader Phil Moore and the Phil Moore Four.

Moore was a music-industry powerhouse: a performer, arranger, songwriter, and musical director who worked for MGM and went on to shape nightclub acts for stars like Lena Horne and Dorothy Dandridge.[17] With Crouch as producer-director, Moore and his band made four Soundies: *I Want a Little Doggie*, *Lazy Lady*, *Who Threw the Whiskey in the Well?* (all Crouch-Crouch, 1945), and *The Chair Song* (Crouch-Crouch, 1946). All feature white guitarist Chuck Wayne. In wide shots of the full combo he appears at frame right, playing or chatting with the band's drummer.

As expected, Moore himself gets most of the screen time, but Wayne and trumpeter John Letman are given generous solos. With Wayne, the camerawork concentrates on close-ups of his hands on the guitar. Somewhat unusually, there are no close or medium shots showing his face. That's a fair indication of

Figure 10.3. Band leader Anna Mae Winburn conducts the International Sweethearts of Rhythm in *She's Crazy with the Heat* (1946). Courtesy Mark Cantor Archive.

where things stood right after the war: integrated bands were starting to appear on tour and on Panorams but not yet in Hollywood movies.[18] In Soundies, the presentation was low-key and straightforward, with Black and white musicians shown together on the bandstand, primarily in wide shots. There was neither evasion nor fanfare, particularly in depicting bands that toured the South.

In 1946, Black filmmaker William D. Alexander produced two musical shorts starring integrated bands, which furnished the clips for six of his sixteen Soundies. One of the films starred the International Sweethearts of Rhythm (fig. 10.3). Founded in 1937, the Sweethearts were the most successful Black all-woman big band of the 1940s. From the start, the group included light-skinned, mixed-race musicians whose heritage legally defined them as Black under the "one drop" rule that prevailed through much of the South.[19] After 1943, the band also included a few members who were legally white. Headed by bandleader and vocalist Anna Mae Winburn (fig. 3.3, p. 62), the Sweethearts were, as Sherrie Tucker writes, a "vision of an interracial group of women where white women do not dominate, where Blackness has room for all the different Black women that there are" and "group identity has room for difference."[20] As one fan recalled, the music was terrific. "Their arrangements were always first rate, the ensembles well executed, and solos always interesting," said Thomas Jefferson Anderson, who heard the band in 1940. "Here I sat in a segregated audience and was witnessing a performance by women who looked like they were from all over the world. This was my first visual experience with integration."[21]

In the three Soundies excerpted from Alexander's film—*Jump Children, That Man of Mine*, and *She's Crazy with the Heat* (all Alexander-Sandiford, 1946)—the band's "international" aspect is not always immediately evident. In some shots, white saxophonist Roz Cron is visible at the extreme left of the frame, and according to Tucker, white trumpet player Toby Butler holds the fourth trumpet chair in the back row.[22] But most of the screen time and close-ups deservedly go to the magnetic Winburn and tenor saxophonist Vi Burnside, both of whom present as Black. (*She's Crazy with the Heat* showcases other musicians as well, including drummer Pauline Brady and pianist Johnnie Mae Rice.) Even saxophonist Willie Mae Wong—whose mixed Chinese ancestry was regularly touted in the band's press coverage—is often obscured by Winburn as she stands in front of the bandstand. As Tucker observed, the footage was shot and edited "not to offend segregationists yet crafted with enough ambiguity so as not completely to obscure the possibility that the band is mixed, for those to whom this aspect is important."[23]

Alexander's second integrated film featured Lucky Millinder and His Orchestra. Millinder was no stranger to Soundies, having done a session in 1941 that yielded four Panoram hits. But the postwar version of Millinder's orchestra was a departure from his previous groups, and the three Soundies excerpted from Alexander's film—*Big Fat Mamas, Hello Bill*, and *I Want a Man* (all Alexander-Sandiford, 1946)—reflect the bandleader's deliberate decision to integrate his orchestra. According to the *Pittsburgh Courier*, Millinder felt it was time "'to do away with the jim-crow attitude of Negroes as well as whites,'" and in 1946 he added the band's first "non-Negro" members. "Before his rebuilding program was over," the *Courier* wrote, "he had literally put together an 'all nations' crew, with an Italian, an Armenian, an Irishman, a Jew, and an East Indian, along with a number of Negroes," who "played all through the South without incident."[24] A sense of that purposeful camaraderie is apparent in *Hello Bill*. A bandstand number, it opens with Millinder on vocals, with lyrics that have him greeting an old friend. On the line "Shake my hand / It's solid, man / Just jiving with the boys," a band member approaches on either side and he shakes hands with one, then the other. Behind them the other musicians repeatedly shake and slap hands as they join in a call-and-response on the chorus. Arguably, a case might be made for a homosexual subtext to this masculine bonhomie, but given the "all nations" nature of Millinder's band, the overall effect is generous, conciliatory, and affirming.[25]

Looking more broadly at bandstand integration, the Armed Forces Radio Service program *Jubilee* may have set a precedent for later postwar efforts. Conceived in 1942 as a showcase for Black talent, as early as 1944 *Jubilee* featured occasional appearances by white performers, including top names like Bing Crosby and Frank Sinatra.[26] With these episodes, *Jubilee* sidestepped the restrictions that the music industry placed on integrated bands.[27] But while some *Jubilee* programs were racially integrated, the military services that broadcast them were not. The armed forces remained officially segregated until July 26, 1948, when President Harry S. Truman signed Executive Order 9981, and informally for some years after.

Under the circumstances it was courageous for Millinder to publicly integrate his band in 1946, in a postwar moment when racial prejudice was widespread and white terrorism remained a real and formidable threat.[28] It was also remarkable for William D. Alexander to put Millinder's band and the International Sweethearts on film at that time, several years before integrated music groups began appearing in mainstream movies and TV. Media scholar Catherine Squires notes the "glacial pace" of racial integration by even the most progressive white television executives, since the industry depended on commercial advertising and had to contend with affiliate stations in the South.[29]

In this context, it is no less remarkable that at least ten Soundies with integrated bands—the six excerpted from Alexander's two films plus the four starring Phil Moore and his combo—appeared on postwar Panorams. There's a sad irony in the fact that, as it was producing or purchasing the films for distribution, the Soundies Corporation was actively limiting the audiences who would see them. With the exception of three Phil Moore films copyrighted in 1945—*I Want a Little Doggie, Lazy Lady,* and *Who Threw the Whiskey in the Well?*—the integrated-band Soundies were released as M films, available by special order only, not in the weekly reels. Ahead of its time in documenting Black bandleaders' efforts at integration, the Soundies Corporation fell short in putting those films before its viewers. (For more on M films, see chap. 3.)

It is reasonable to assume that as a commercial enterprise, the company made its decisions based on its reading of the marketplace. When it set aside the stereotypes and racial fictions of the early Black-and-white-cast Soundies, it was most likely doing so in response to perceived market demand—and again, a few years later, when it opted to feature Soundies that documented Black and white musicians performing together. As always, the need to produce films quickly and cheaply cannot be overlooked as a rationale for any decision. But the end of the war signaled a new phase in the nation's social history, and intentionally or inadvertently, Soundies responded to this shift. The integrated performance-documentation films are notable, especially in that era, for their willingness to encompass difference without framing it as a threat. This small subset of late films is a visual record of not only performers and their music but the social change that these individuals were quietly putting into effect. Even so, the decision to produce and distribute the films cannot be separated from the decision to limit their audience exposure.

Despite their contradictions and limitations, Soundies could be a space of fluidity and experimentation, where Black performers often functioned as active collaborators, and the changing image of Black people on screen was worked out on an almost week-by-week basis. As the business foundered, a postwar cultural sensibility overtook the wartime climate of urgency and possibility. Even before the war ended, a different type of small-screen entertainment began making its presence known in the bars and taverns that Soundies had claimed as their home turf. As the Soundies Corporation approached its final decline, America entered the television era.

11

—⁓⁓—

UNPLUGGED, WITH AN AFTERLIFE

THE END OF THE WAR brought abrupt changes for Soundies and their audiences. As the economy prepared to absorb some twelve million returning GIs, defense plants across the country downsized, closed, or retooled for commercial production. Many Soundies viewers were hard hit, especially Black workers. "The Negroes' greatest employment advances have been made in precisely those occupations, industries, and areas in which the postwar adjustment will be most severe," warned *The Negro Handbook, 1946–1947*, adding that Black people, generally among the last to be hired, were more likely to be laid off.[1] The GI Bill, signed into law in 1944, gave returning servicemen support for education, small business loans, mortgage insurance, and other programs, laying the foundation for a postwar middle class. But the racial discrimination embedded in the bill's structure and administration has been documented in detail, and on the whole, Black GIs realized substantially fewer benefits than their white counterparts.[2]

The drop in Soundies viewership extended across its audience segments. While many Black people struggled with the postwar economy, significant numbers of white southerners reversed their wartime migrations, leaving industrial hubs for rural hometowns, where Panorams were less likely to be located.[3] Across the board, Americans in 1946 were more intent on home and family—and new cars and refrigerators—than entertainment. But a shifting, shrinking audience was only one of Soundies' postwar problems. A total of 270 films were copyrighted in 1946—slightly more than in 1944 or 1945, but nowhere near the 400-plus needed to fill a year's worth of eight-film reels.[4] With the armistice, patriotic and war-related Soundies were immediately obsolete, taking dozens of potential rereleases out of circulation.

The shift to a postwar economy might have been enough to trigger Soundies' collapse, but other factors came into play. The expansion of commercial television broadcasting had been largely put on hold during the war, and with peacetime the industry quickly picked up again. Bars and taverns were among the first venues to host the resurgent technology, with TV sets appearing in a few locations even before the war ended.[5] In response, jukebox manufacturers hurriedly experimented with coin-operated televisions like the Solotone, which gave audiences six minutes of viewing per turn, and hybrid machines that combined a television with radio and/or jukebox capabilities. Large-screen TV sets were produced specifically for bars. The Tavern Tele-Symphonic, for instance, had a screen more than double the size of typical home models and, at 19 by 25 inches, slightly larger than the Panoram's.

None of these experiments caught on. Customers might pay for a jukebox tune or a Soundie but not TV air time, and for many bar owners, the Tele-Symphonic's hefty price tag—$2,000 in 1947 dollars (more than $24,000 in 2021)—would have been hard to justify.[6]

In 1945, American Federation of Musicians president James Petrillo—who led the 1942–43 strike that had hamstrung Soundies production for more than a year—barred union musicians from appearing on television for a full three years, on the grounds that the medium had not matured enough to warrant professional musicians' participation.[7] The ban made television less of a direct competitor to Soundies than it might have been. When the final Soundies reel was released in March 1947, union musicians were still officially prohibited from appearing on TV. Had Soundies been in the position to produce enough new, high-quality films to fill its weekly reels, conceivably the business might have survived, at least until live music hit the TV airwaves in 1948. At that point a more robust Soundies organization might have shifted to making films for television. In reality, there was no competition. The novelty of television and the immediacy of what it offered—especially live news and sports events—were powerful draws, particularly against the music of what was rapidly becoming a bygone era.

FOR PERFORMERS, A NEW MEDIUM

As the television industry began experimenting with various programming formats in the late 1940s and early 1950s, it both reiterated and departed from the racial stereotypes of earlier entertainment forms. In sitcoms like *Beulah*

(1950–52) and *Amos 'n' Andy* (1951–53), Black actors had to contend with stereo-typical "prewar images in a postwar era," as Donald Bogle put it, and on some local TV stations even minstrel shows flourished for a time.[8] But other early programs made a point of presenting Black entertainers in glamorous settings, using visual language taken from movie musicals and more immediately from Soundies.[9] While Ethel Waters, the first star of *Beulah*, grappled with the challenges of portraying a loyal domestic worker to a white family—leaving the show after a single season—Hazel Scott was an evening-gowned sophisticate at the piano.[10] Sharply contradicting Hollywood's habit of marginalizing and deleting Black performance, the *Hazel Scott Show* (1950) and other early TV programs made Black entertainers the stars.

Several Soundies performers moved into the new medium as hosts and guest performers, and their experiences underscore how Soundies differed from commercial television as an arena for Black talent. In part, those differences sprang from the two mediums' divergent business models and comparative scales—one relying on viewers' dimes flowing into a limited number of machines, the other on advertising and commercial sponsorship to reach an expanding, theoretically limitless audience.

Bob Howard was among the first Soundies stars to appear on television, and one of the first Black performers to host his own TV show. From 1948 to 1950, the fifteen-minute *Bob Howard Show* aired Monday through Friday on the regional CBS affiliate in New York. It was essentially a one-man operation, with Howard at the piano playing, singing, chatting to the camera between tunes, and handling the commercial announcements. "For later generations, Howard's act would hardly look offbeat or unusual," Bogle writes, but the impact was substantial: whether in corner bars or their own living rooms, a broad swath of viewers could "*see* a Black man hosting the proceedings, calling the shots, and literally running the show."[11] Howard was a capable pianist and raconteur in the Fats Waller style, with a seemingly inexhaustible songbook of standards and old favorites. CBS touted his informal, unscripted approach, and his show had an appealing spontaneity. Howard's run at CBS ended in late 1950. By February 1951 he was back on the air with WOR-TV, another regional New York broadcaster, doing two fifteen-minute shows a day, Monday through Friday.

Howard's affable persona and ease on camera are evident in his four Soundies, produced and directed by Crouch in 1944. He's at the piano in a sheet-music store in *Dinah*, playfully responding to a chorus line in *She's Too Hot to Handle*, doing a supposedly live radio broadcast with his orchestra in *Shine*, and paying tribute to Black servicemen in battle in *Hey! Tojo, Count Yo' Men*. As performances filmed to prerecorded music, Howard's Soundies couldn't fully exploit the spontaneity, improvisation, and ad-lib chat that were his strengths on live TV. With its reliance on repeat viewings, Soundies' business model was, in fact, the antithesis of the constantly changing flow that defined Howard's television work. But his Soundies and TV broadcasts did have one trait in common, and that was low overhead. Howard's Soundies were modest productions at best, and the advertising-industry magazine *Sponsor* made a point of praising his TV show for its cost-effectiveness. On the revenue side, the *Bob Howard Show* was more of a moneymaker for CBS than his films ever were for the Soundies Corporation. Each fifteen-minute broadcast usually included three commercial spots. Going for three to four hundred dollars each, they brought in as much as six thousand dollars a week for the show—the equivalent, per week, of sixty thousand Soundie plays, dime by dime, over a more than two-year period.[12]

On the other hand, it's unlikely that Howard's television repertoire would have included a tune like "Hey! Tojo" or its postwar equivalent, with a similarly explicit focus on Black Americans' role in national events. His TV playlist had a determinedly mainstream profile: the premiere show included the songbook standard "As Time Goes By" (made famous by Black pianist Arthur "Dooley" Wilson in the 1942 MGM classic *Casablanca*), and later sing-along segments featured everything from "Tea for Two" to "I've Been Working on the Railroad."

The *Nat King Cole Show* had a rockier broadcast history. Debuting on NBC in November 1956, as the civil rights movement was gathering momentum, Cole's show is widely regarded as the first nationally broadcast program hosted by a Black performer. (That distinction actually goes to the *Hazel Scott Show*, which briefly aired nationwide on the DuMont network in 1950.[13]) By then, television had moved into middle-class living rooms as it solidified its presence in neighborhood bars and taverns. Despite critical acclaim, the *Nat King Cole Show* ran into problems with advertisers and audiences—Bogle cites viewer ratings of 19 percent versus 50 percent for a hit show like *Adventures of Robin Hood*—and lost its only national sponsor a few weeks into its run.[14] Many NBC affiliates, particularly in the South, refused to air the program, contributing to its low ratings. And the audience hostility could get personal. As one southern station manager told *Ebony* magazine: "I like Nat Cole, but they told me if he came back on they would bomb my house and my station."[15] A few months before the show's premiere, Cole himself had been viciously attacked by white supremacists during a performance in Birmingham, Alabama.[16] (He responded in part by recording a stirring version of "We Are Americans Too," which Crouch had made as a Soundie in 1943.[17]) A little over a year after its premiere, the *Nat King Cole Show* ended its run in December 1957.[18]

Like the television show, Cole's seven Soundies—made in 1943 and 1945 and released in 1944, 1945, and 1946—highlight his low-key style, on-camera ease, and unmistakable voice. In the Soundies, though, he's not a solo performer but part of the King Cole Trio (with Oscar Moore on guitar and Johnny Miller on bass), acclaimed as much for his jazz-inflected piano as his vocals. If anything, he's more relaxed in the Soundies, without the pressure of carrying a live, fifty-minute show that was struggling to find its audience. Cole's easy connection with the camera anchors Soundies like *I'm a Shy Guy* and *Come to Baby Do* (both Crouch-Crouch, 1946), and a decade later it's a large part of his appeal in *The Nat King Cole Show*.

In the years between making his Soundies and hosting his show, Cole had honed his on-camera persona in guest appearances on the *Ed Sullivan Show*, *Jackie Gleason Show*, *Colgate Comedy Hour*, and other musical variety programs. Other Soundies performers did the same. In an appearance on the short-lived *Frank Sinatra Show* (CBS, 1951–52), Louis Armstrong visibly put his host at ease after a chaotic, seltzer-spraying comedy sketch with the Three Stooges left Sinatra somewhat rattled. The two had appeared together on a *Jubilee* radio program in 1945, with Armstrong adding a hot trumpet half-chorus to Sinatra's rendition of "Blue Skies." On the TV show, seated side by side at the piano amid the wreckage of the set, the two delivered a relaxed, thoroughly professional performance.[19] In his four 1942 Soundies, Armstrong had appeared with his band, vocalists, and other performers in settings that could be painfully stereotyped, as in *Sleepy Time Down South* (Coslow-Berne, 1942). On television he was a solo act, performing a version of his own cosmopolitan persona, or joined by the All Stars, his combo of top musicians. Armstrong was a frequent guest star throughout the 1950s and 1960s, making repeat appearances on the *Ed Sullivan Show*, the *Danny Kaye Show*, the *Tonight Show Starring Johnny Carson*, and the quiz show *What's My Line?* (Cole also appeared on that show, twice). As early as 1948, Cab Calloway was guest-starring too, on shows like *Ed Sullivan*, *Cavalcade of Stars*, and the *Gulf Road Show Starring Bob Smith* (and on *What's My Line?* in 1951). Dorothy Dandridge was another early guest performer, appearing in 1951 on the *Colgate Comedy Hour* and in 1952 on the *Ed Sullivan Show*, *Cavalcade of Stars*, and *Songs for Sale*. With Soundies' low-budget, single-take approach to filming, performing in them was not that different from live TV, and the on-camera personas of Bob Howard, Nat King Cole, and other television stars may be seen, in nascent form, in their Soundies work. Scaled to the intimacy of the living room, musical performance on early television was a ready match for the small-screen, "be yourself" aesthetic that Soundies had pioneered.

FOR THE MAKERS, MORE FILM

While notable Soundies performers made their way into the new industry, television offered fewer opportunities for Soundies makers. On the West Coast, a few producers and directors did go on to successful television careers, but Soundies filmmakers who'd worked extensively with Black talent were not among them. (The closest was West Coast director Dave Gould, who lasted four weeks as choreographer on *Fireball Fun-For-All*, a 1949 comedy-variety show on NBC.[20]) In New York, the informal entertainment–industry network that had coalesced around Black-cast Soundies moved toward a broader independent film scene rather than broadcast TV. As early as 1946, an article in the *Chicago Defender* heralded an upsurge in Black-cast film production, under the headline "Negroes Due for Break in Films with New York as Own Hollywood."[21]

In the New York entertainment community, musicians and dancers who were already affected by the postwar downturn in nightclubs, stage shows, and live music events felt the loss of Soundies production.[22] Sun Tan Studio continued into the 1950s, but it was no longer a filmmaking hub. A 1948 article in the *Chicago Defender* heralded the studio's recently established modeling agency and a new school of exotic dance.[23] Little more than a year later, an article in the *New York Amsterdam News* described Sun Tan as a "training ground for undeveloped talent," pointing to its discovery of Soundies star Mable Lee, "who captured the imagination of the critics in this country then went on to Europe where she won the hearts of the nightlife public."[24] Both articles positioned Fritz Pollard as Sun Tan's driving force, but also identified Johnny "Trala" Walker—an entertainer who'd reportedly started out with Duke Ellington—as studio manager. The final *Amsterdam News* mention of Sun Tan Studio appeared in December 1954. In an article about a cocktail benefit organized by the Sigma Wives of New York (a women's organization linked to the Phi Beta Sigma fraternity), "Fritz Pollard's Sun Tan beauties and singers" were listed among the entertainers.[25] By that point Pollard had already embarked on a career as an independent financial consultant, and he soon left the entertainment industry. He died in 1986. In 2005, he was posthumously inducted into the Pro Football Hall of Fame.

With Soundies' collapse, producer William D. Alexander lost a reliable source of revenue for his music performance films. Despite the setback, Alexander continued to produce Black-cast films through 1949, through his independent companies Associated Producers of Negro Motion Pictures and Alexander Productions. In 1946 he produced *Jivin' in Be-Bop*, a fifty-eight-minute performance documentary starring Dizzy Gillespie and a revue cast of dancers, singers, and other performers. It was not excerpted into Soundies, but internal Soundies Corporation memos suggest that the process was underway when the company folded.[26] Other Alexander productions of 1946 include a short cabaret film, *The Vanities*, and *The Call of Duty* and *The Highest Tradition*, short films about Black servicemen in the army and navy, respectively.[27] In 1948, Alexander produced *The Fight Never Ends*, a dramatic feature about juvenile delinquency that starred boxing champ Joe Louis and a young Ruby Dee (with a musical performance by the Mills Brothers). The following year he teamed up with writer-director Powell Lindsay—"the muse of Black social realism on film"—for *Souls of Sin* (1949), a feature-length drama recounting the lives and dreams of three Harlem roommates.[28] That year, Alexander also made *Burlesque in Harlem*, a fifty-five-minute movie of a stage revue with more than twenty singers, dancers, exotic dancers, and other performers.[29] Also in 1949, the New York–based producer-distributor Transvideo released four ten-minute shorts clipped from Alexander's 1946 music films.

Alexander's output was part of the last, prolific phase of Black-cast film production heralded in the 1946 *Chicago Defender* article, which flourished in New York as Soundies were winding down. Describing an active nationwide circuit of movie houses showing "all-Negro films," the *Defender* story spotlighted upcoming releases by Astor Pictures, Hollywood Pictures, and Toddy Pictures—three of the independent New York companies that produced and distributed Black-cast shorts and features in the late 1940s. Others included Herald Pictures, Century Productions, All-American, and Transvideo. With few exceptions, they were largely white-run: one historian identifies Alexander's late-1940s projects with director Powell Lindsay as "the end of Black-controlled race-film production companies."[30]

In 1953, Alexander began production on *By-Line News*, theatrical newsreels on African American topics that were released through 1956.[31] (*By-Line Newsreel #1* is accessible online and features Alexander himself as narrator and, in a later segment, as on-camera interviewer.[32]) Alexander then moved to London, where he began making documentaries about the emerging nation-states of sub-Saharan Africa.[33] The *New York Times* identified him as the official film producer for Liberia and later for Ethiopia, and in the mid-1960s, documentaries he produced in these countries won citations at the Cannes and Venice Film Festivals.[34] In the early 1970s, Alexander became one of the few Black filmmakers of the era to produce a big-budget Hollywood project: *The Klansman* (1974). A drama of racial conflict in a Southern town, it starred Lee Marvin, Richard Burton, Lola Falana, and, in his big-screen debut, O. J. Simpson.

From all reports it was a tense, difficult shoot, and the film was not a hit. Nevertheless, the following year Alexander began work on *Jackpot*, another major production starring Burton. That movie wasn't completed, and Alexander is not credited on further productions. He died in 1991.[35]

As Soundies sputtered to an end, William Forest Crouch—producer of more than half the Black-cast Soundies—joined the New York independent production circuit. In 1945 he'd directed *Caldonia*, an eighteen-minute short that was the source for Louis Jordan's last four Soundies. Two years later, after the Soundies Corporation folded, Crouch directed *Reet, Petite, and Gone* (1947), a sixty-seven-minute featurette starring Jordan and Soundies regulars June Richmond, Vanita Smythe, and Mable Lee. Like *Caldonia*, *Reet* was produced by Louis Jordan Productions, with Jordan's manager, Berle Adams, credited as producer on both films. Shot at Crouch's old Filmcraft studio in the Bronx, it was filmed by Don Malkames, the cinematographer on most of the Black-cast Soundies shot in New York and most Black-cast films produced in New York between 1946 and 1950.

In 1947, Crouch also produced and directed a pair of one-reel shorts, *Open the Door Richard* (written by Soundies performer Claude DeMetrius) and what was most likely a follow-up, *I Ain't Gonna Open That Door*. The following year he produced and directed *The Dreamer*, a half-hour compendium of Black-cast Soundies linked by comic interludes with Mantan Moreland and Mable Lee. As with Crouch's other films, production credits on *The Dreamer* affirm the close ties among the New York independent Black-cast-film community, with a script by Claude DeMetrius, cinematography by Don Malkames, and editing by Leonard Anderson, who had directed three of Alexander's music films and edited *Reet, Petite, and Gone*. *The Dreamer* was one of Crouch's last projects: on IMDb, no films are attributed to him after 1948.[36] According to a brief, unsourced Wikipedia entry, in the early 1960s Crouch emigrated to Australia with his interracial family.[37] He died in 1968 at the age of sixty-four.

Malkames and Anderson went on to careers in film and television—Anderson as an editor of *The Honeymooners*, the classic TV sitcom starring Jackie Gleason, and Malkames as cinematographer for programs like *Man Against Crime* (1952–54) and *Show Time at the Apollo* (1955).[38] Other Soundies makers who'd worked with Black talent pursued different career paths. Fred Waller, the producer and inventor who'd worked on most of the Minoco Black-cast films, left Soundies in late 1942 to develop equipment for the US Armed Forces. His Waller Flexible Gunnery Trainer was later described as essential to the war effort, and he went on to adapt its technology for film. The resulting wide-screen projection system, Cinerama, debuted in the early 1950s, earning Waller an Academy Award in 1954.[39]

Minoco chief Jack Barry left Soundies in 1944 with the aim of producing for television, a logical step for someone so attuned to the dynamics of small-screen performance. He reportedly became president of an independent company, Eagle Productions, but professionally, he more or less vanished: nothing more about him appeared in *Billboard,* other trade papers, or IMDb.[40] In the 1944 L.O.L. Productions lawsuit, Soundies Corporation vice president George Ulcigan testified that Barry had left film production and was working with the advertising firm Young & Rubicam in their motion picture division, but no more was heard of him in that capacity either.[41] Josef Berne directed two low-budget independent features before falling off the industry radar; Dudley Murphy set up a movie studio in Mexico, then returned to Los Angeles to open a beachfront restaurant and hideaway in Malibu. After the 1944 lawsuit—which had been prompted in part by the Soundies that L.O.L. made with white actors in blackface—L.O.L. partner Arthur Leonard went on to direct two Black-cast features for Herald Pictures: *Sepia Cinderella* and *Boy! What a Girl* (both 1947).[42] Leaving Soundies, Sam Coslow worked again for Paramount—and, according to Ulcigan, for MGM and then silent-screen star turned producer Mary Pickford.[43] Like Fritz Pollard, Coslow eventually turned to financial consulting, in his case as an investor, advisor, and investment analyst.[44] Over the years, his songs have been heard on countless movie and television soundtracks, including episodes of *Mad Men* and *The Tonight Show Starring Jimmy Fallon.* For the films themselves, the future unfolded somewhat differently.

AN AFTERLIFE OR TWO

Although Soundies were made primarily for play on Panorams, the Soundies Corporation had always been open to other possibilities. Shot in 35 mm and reduced to 16 mm for Panoram distribution, the films had the cinematic resolution required for theatrical projection. According to Soundies archivist Mark Cantor, after their initial Panoram runs, selected films were sometimes packaged into compilation reels, roughly ten minutes in length, and screened as pre-feature shorts in movie houses. In late 1944, as commercial television geared up for its postwar takeoff and the first few TV sets started to appear in bars and taverns, Soundies caught the attention of the television industry.

"'Soundies' Getting Air-Pix Test" was the headline for *Billboard's* Radio Television section on November 11, 1944—repeated, in the same inch-high letters, with the story's continuation some forty pages later. "Big name backlog means 16mm. box film available when video starts rolling," both pages proclaimed.[45] The nugget of news buried deep in the story was that W6XAO—an

early Hollywood television station that eventually became a CBS affiliate—
was testing Soundies for possible broadcast.

It was an enticing proposition for all concerned. In the article, executives at
RCM, the Soundies Corporation's West Coast production arm, claimed that
fifteen hundred films were completed and available for broadcast. Television
producers readily grasped the affinities between the two media. "Trade figures
that 'soundie' film could be used for television, as most of the productions stick
to close-ups so necessary for the small screen on juke box movies," *Billboard*
wrote. "As far as production is concerned, RCM uses practically the same technique as is now used for television. In other words, talent is concentrated in [a]
small area, therefore making action suitable for television screens." The article
speculated that "when the new medium finally breaks through commercially,"
RCM would divide its production between Soundies and television.[46]

Promising as the possibility was, it didn't happen. It may have been that
the two sides were unable to come to terms, or the cost of converting the films
proved too high. Screening a Soundie on the Panoram involved projecting the
film onto mirrors inside the Panoram cabinet—which meant that, for Panoram
play, Soundies were printed backward, left to right, in order to appear in the correct orientation on screen. Television broadcast would have required reprinting
the films in reverse, a time-consuming and expensive process for even a fraction
of the available titles. In any event, no further developments were reported, and
Soundies remained a strictly celluloid phenomenon.

And a waning one. With the war's end, Soundies' parent firm, Mills Novelty Company—by then renamed Mills Industries—stumbled badly. Panoram
Soundies had consumed investment capital that hadn't been recouped. The
slot-machine market, long a Mills mainstay, had fallen off during the war and
postwar legislation would hobble it further. In 1946 the slot business was spun
off into a separate company, the Bell-O-Matic Corporation, diverting significant revenue. By the late 1940s, Mills Industries had run into financial difficul-
ties and petitioned the federal court for time to pay off its debts. According to
one source, the Soundies Distributing Corporation of America—referred to
throughout this book as the Soundies Corporation—ceased operations in 1946,
and Crouch continued the business himself under another company name.[47]
Corporate memos suggest otherwise, indicating that the Soundies Corporation
remained in operation to the end.[48] In either case, by the close of 1946, Crouch
was Soundies' sole producer and director. The last few titles—including Pat
Flowers's *Coalmine Boogie*—were released in March 1947.

By then, the films had embarked on a life beyond the Panoram. As early
as 1942, Soundies had been licensed for nontheatrical use, marketed to small

film-rental companies and the general public. The home-movie market picked up after the war, and classified newspaper ads reflect a brisk trade among collectors. "16MM Soundies exchanged, 50 cents; best subjects; list free," read a typical ad in the *New York Times*.[49] In 1945, the distributor Castle Films began packaging Soundies for home viewing, releasing them in themed medley reels, generally three to a reel. Of the thirty-four Castle reels, only three include Soundies by Black performers. In the medley Jazz and Jitters, the Three Chefs' *Breakfast in Rhythm* appears with the white-cast Soundies *Jiveroo* and *Jazz Etude*; in Musical Medley, the Deep River Boys' *Hark! Hark! The Lark* is sandwiched between the white-cast *MacNamara's Band* and Liberace's *Tiger Rag*; and in Songs of Yesterday, Bob Howard's *Dinah* is positioned between white-cast films *How Come You Do Me Like You Do* and *The Bowery*. After Universal Pictures acquired Castle Films in 1947, the Soundies catalog went to a rival distributor, Official Films. Official compiled more than sixty new medley reels for the 16 mm home-movie market. Nine showcase Black performers, with individual reels devoted to Billy Eckstine, the Mills Brothers, and Day, Dawn, and Dusk, and multi-artist compilations featuring Fats Waller, Count Basie, and Maurice Rocco, among others.[50]

In the late 1940s, Soundies finally made it to television. Radio hosts, experimenting with adapting the disc-jockey format to TV, were among the first to air the films. On shows like *Requestfully Yours*, individual Soundies were presented as moving-image versions of the records being played, often with a shot of a spinning record dissolving into the opening of the film. (This approach reportedly confused inexperienced TV viewers who, as *Billboard* and *Variety* reported, thought the films were somehow contained on the discs along with the music.[51])

With a rapidly aging songbook, by 1950 Soundies had more or less run their course as disc-jockey fodder. Rather than disappearing, they went into broader distribution. A brief article in the February 3, 1951, issue of *Billboard* noted that, the year before, Official Films had begun syndicating Soundies to television under the package title Music Hall Varieties.[52] According to *Billboard*, Official Films had grossed $700,000 to date on Soundies sales to TV stations looking for between-show filler material, on an investment of $300,000 in copyright clearances and reprocessing costs. A dozen stations around the country had reportedly bought the package. "Deals have been made with WCBS-TV for 100G; WNAC-TV, Boston, for 75G; WFIL-TV, Philadelphia for 90G; WNGQ-TV, Chicago, for 90G; KTTV, Los Angeles, 90G; WNBK-TV, Cleveland, 75G; WNBW-TV, Washington, 50G; and WBTV, Charlotte, N.C., 40G," *Billboard* recounted, with additional half-packages purchased by stations in Providence,

San Francisco, and Houston. Together, stations in Havana and Mexico City bought a joint package "at a rate estimated to be 25G."[53]

If Soundies had an afterlife apart from the Panoram, the machines, too, had one separate from Soundies—primarily (though not exclusively) as the Solovue-Peep. "Appropriately enough," writes Andrea J. Kelley, "these modified Panoram machines migrated to arcades, were given larger coin slots (for quarters rather than dimes), and showed films ranging in degrees of illicit content from burlesque striptease to pornography."[54]

Having run their course on TV sets and home-movie screens, by the late 1950s Soundies disappeared from the cultural landscape.

Decades later, the Black-cast films were among the first to re-emerge. In 1984, the European label Storyville released four LP record albums of soundtracks from selected Black-cast Soundies, under the series title Harlem Roots. Storyville then followed with the films themselves, releasing four Harlem Roots VHS cassettes in 1988. In 2004, the company rereleased two of the Harlem Roots video programs, *The Big Bands* and *The Headliners*, on DVD. In 2007, they rereleased volume 3, *Rhythm in Harmony*, following a year later with volume 4, *Jivin' Time*.[55]

Soon after the Harlem Roots VHS cassettes appeared in the late 1980s, film historian and critic Leonard Maltin—a dedicated Soundies fan—wrote, produced, and served as host on Leonard Maltin's Movie Memories–Soundies, a four-cassette VHS series. Released for the home market in 1991, the programs showcased his top picks from the Soundies catalog. Performers like Nat "King" Cole and Cab Calloway appeared throughout the series, which concluded with the cassette *Harlem Highlights*, a full program of Black-cast Soundies.[56] In March 2007, the documentary *Soundies: A Musical History*, hosted by singer Michael Feinstein—a champion of the American popular songbook—fueled public television fundraising drives around the country, and has occasionally reappeared in that capacity in one PBS market or another.

A more spontaneous, wide-ranging revival has taken hold online. In the early 2000s, Soundies began appearing on the internet. Posted by individual enthusiasts on MySpace and then YouTube, Soundies are also available for viewing on websites like Mark Cantor's Celluloid Improvisations and archive-footage sites like Historic Films and Prelinger Archives. Early on, the films were sometimes treated as found footage, with individual uploaders deleting credits and adding their own titles, digital collages, and other embellishments.[57] It's more common now for Soundies to be posted in their entirety, with respect for their cinematic integrity, and image quality has improved dramatically.

Figure 11.1. William Forest Crouch (*center, seated, leaning forward*) with cast and crew on the set of *Tuxedo Junction* (1942). The film's star, Edna Mae Harris, is next to Crouch at left, wearing a wide-brimmed hat; the cast also includes the Lenox Lindy Hoppers dance troupe, including the women seated at front. From the Soundies Distributing Corporation of America photographs of the Margaret Herrick Library, Academy of Motion Picture Arts and Sciences.

Not surprisingly, Soundies with Black performers are among the most consistently popular and searched-for titles. Stars like Dorothy Dandridge and Count Basie have drawn hundreds of thousands of views, and Duke Ellington, millions. In classics like *Jam Session* and *Cow Cow Boogie*, what Soundies had to offer wartime audiences is overwhelmingly evident, but the impulse to share these films has brought a much broader range of Black-cast Soundies online (fig. 11.1). Many of June Richmond's films are available on YouTube or other sites, and the same is true for Soundies by Tiny Grimes, the Delta Rhythm Boys, Edna Mae Harris, and other performers whose cultural currency may have diminished over the decades. The availability of Black-cast Soundies online goes a long way toward restoring this overlooked chapter of American entertainment history. (Most of the Soundies discussed in this book have been gathered for convenient screening online; for details, see susandelson.com.)

How the films are likely to be viewed there is revealing in itself. In the past decade, cell-phone cameras, YouTube videos, and Zoom meetings have reshaped media aesthetics. Soundies' "be yourself" style and casual approach to film technique are immediately familiar to viewers today: we're less likely to reject them for their unpolished quality and more likely to appreciate their glitches. But viewing Soundies online is most often a solitary pleasure—a reminder of the stark contrast between the intensely public and communal nature of leisure in the World War II years and the markedly different character of twenty-first-century life. These days, sharing a Soundie is likely to mean forwarding the link or posting the film on social media, where it's viewed by an audience that's both collective and fragmentary. Most often what's shared is the experience of watching it alone. Too, Soundies weren't necessarily intended for intense, focused viewing, but for intermittent screening in diffuse, noisy, highly social environments. Short of streaming them as background for a party, it would be difficult to approach, much less duplicate, the sort of ambience that they were part of and helped create.

Despite these differences, Black-cast Soundies have much to say about the current moment and the history that has brought us here. Considering them in the context of their own era allows us to read them as a continuously unfolding, pop-culture chronicle of their time, and as meaningful markers of change. In *Stony the Road*, historian Henry Louis Gates Jr. outlines a broad cultural project, begun just after the Civil War, to collectively shape a Black counter-narrative to white supremacist thought and imagery; seen in this context, the films are more than entertainment history. Some Soundies bring the attitudes of the World War II era into sharper focus—tuneful, eye-catching, and undeni-ably racist—underscoring the persistence of those attitudes in our own time. Other Soundies register the shifts that took place as the war continued: the jagged back-and-forth of advancement and denial, of change coming fast and nowhere near fast enough. But the greatest number of Black-cast Soundies embody something far rarer in 1940s America: a vision of Black agency as a basis for the nation's postwar future.

As with the ongoing counternarrative that Gates describes, that vision is a work of collective imagination. At a 1991 conference on Black popular culture, Stuart Hall reminded his listeners that popular culture, though commodified and stereotyped, is a "*profoundly* mythic" arena, "a theater of popular desires, a theater of popular fantasies. It is where we discover and play with the identifica-tions of ourselves, where we are imagined, where we are represented, not only to the audiences out there who do not get the message, but to ourselves for the first time."[58] It is highly unlikely that in 1991, Hall had Black-cast Soundies in mind. Yet his description speaks to the films as a vehicle of collective imagination and to their significance in the cultural landscape of the 1940s, for Black Americans and all Americans. As the products of a largely forgotten media phenomenon, the films have the capacity to clarify and complicate—in the most productive sense of the term—our understanding of the World War II home front and the years that followed. The racial mix of makers, performers, and audiences associated with Soundies was unique in the US film industry in the 1940s, and the resulting depictions not only reflected the state of American race relations but moved meaningfully beyond that status quo. It is rich material for investigation from a range of perspectives, and for a broader conversation about the films and the significance they might hold for our own moment.

—⁂—

ACKNOWLEDGMENTS

WHEN I FIRST BEGAN RESEARCHING Soundies in 2007, I couldn't have predicted how immersed I would become in the films and the histories they contain. As this book developed, it enjoyed the support of many who share my view of Soundies as a unique repository of American cultural history, and the Black-cast Soundies above all.

First among them is Soundies historian Mark Cantor. Mark and I have enjoyed a long and fruitful dialogue about the films—appreciating them, unearthing the circumstances of their production, attempting to resolve their persistent conundrums. His archive contains indispensable documentation of Soundies as a business, and over the years he has generously shared information, expertise, hard-to-find films, and more, all to the book's immense benefit. I am indebted to Mark for most of the images in this volume—sourced from films in his collection—and for his collaboration on the lists of films, performers, and actors in the book's appendixes. His close reading of the manuscript greatly enriched its depth and accuracy. Mark brings a wide-ranging knowledge of American music history and jazz on film to his own writing, and his forthcoming book, *Music for the Eyes: Soundies and Jukebox Shorts of the 1940s* (McFarland, 2022), will be an invaluable resource for anyone with an interest in this field.

As work on *Soundies and the Changing Image of Black Americans on Screen* neared completion, the Robert B. Silvers Foundation generously awarded the project a Work in Progress grant for image research and reproduction. The foundation's funding made an enormous difference in the number and quality of images I was able to include, and I'm deeply appreciative of its support.

Much of the project's early research was done at the Library of Congress, which holds one of the largest public collections of Soundies in the United States. The librarians of the Moving Image Section, especially reference specialist Zoran Sinobad, lent their sustained and enthusiastic support at a time when relatively few Soundies were accessible online. Thanks, too, to Zoran for coordinating the video transfer of Soundies in the library's collection. Research was also conducted at (and remotely with) the Margaret Herrick Library of the Academy of Motion Picture Arts and Sciences, which holds a large repository of Soundies film stills, and at the New York Public Library's Schomburg Center for Research in Black Culture and Library for the Performing Arts at Lincoln Center. Many thanks to these institutions and their staffs.

As I began to develop the book, residencies at the Ucross Foundation and the Brown Foundation's Dora Maar House in 2011, and at Art Omi in 2012, provided time and space for sustained, uninterrupted thought. Thanks to Sharon Dynak, president and executive director of the Ucross Foundation; Ruth Salvatore, Ucross residency manager during my time there; Gwen Strauss, director of Dora Maar House; and D W Gibson, director of Art Omi: Writers for making my stays enjoyable as well as productive. Over the years, the writers' space Paragraph provided an essential and welcoming base for the project in New York. Many thanks to Joy Parisi and the Paragraph staff.

As the manuscript took shape, colleagues read chapters and drafts, offered feedback and suggestions, and advanced the project in other ways. I am indebted to Mark Nelson, who carved time from an overflowing work schedule—and his own beautifully conceived book, *Hollywood Arensberg: Avant-Garde Collecting in Midcentury L.A.*, published by the Getty Research Institute—to become one of the manuscript's most attentive readers. Mark's insights, clarity, and subtlety of thought are reflected in these pages, and I am deeply grateful for his involvement. Heartfelt thanks as well to Beth Kracklauer for her essential input in the book's early stages, and to Bruce Posner, J M Stifle, Missy Sullivan, Barbara London, Joanne Popkin, Pamela Haag, and Peter Agree for their efforts on the book's behalf. For her friendship and encouragement in bringing the book to its readership, warm thanks to Faith Childs. I am especially indebted to the manuscript's academic readers, whose thoughtful assessments and suggestions substantially deepened and expanded the scope of the text.

Even with a subject as obscure as Soundies, other scholars have gotten there first, and the book has benefited greatly from their work. Scott MacGillivray and Ted Okuda's *The Soundies Book*, a primary index of the films and their performers, was a cornerstone of my research. Writings on Soundies by Ellen

C. Scott, Amy Herzog, and Andrea J. Kelley were immensely valuable. Broader scholarship by Paula Massood, Miriam J. Petty, Jacqueline Najuma Stewart, and Cara Caddoo, and the pioneering work of Pearl Bowser, Donald Bogle, and Thomas Cripps deepened my understanding of Soundies within the scope of Black film history. In particular, I would like to thank Michele Wallace, whose CUNY Graduate Center course, "Imitations of Life: Images of Race and Gender in Visual Culture 1929–1961," posed the questions that sparked my interest in racial representation on film and its implications for what was happening on the other side of the camera.

At Indiana University Press, special thanks to acquisitions editor Allison Blair Chaplin, whose support for the book was immediate and sustained. Others at the press took the book through copy editing, design, and production, and their professionalism is much appreciated. Several publishers and presses kindly granted permission to excerpt the works quoted in this book, and I thank them all—especially Dr. Carlos R. Handy, president and CEO of Handy Brothers Music Co., Inc., for the lyrics of "We Are Americans Too"; and David Dunkin of Wrights Media for the excerpts from *Billboard*.

I count myself fortunate to have worked with designer Vivian Selbo on my website, susandelson.com, especially in tackling how to best present all those Soundies online. I am indebted to Vivian for her expertise, patience, and sense of creative play. With 16 mm film prints as old and reduplicated as Soundies, it can be a challenge to transform them into sharp, clear videos—a necessary step in creating most of the images in this book. Thanks to the teams at Film and Video Transfers, Inc., and at the Library of Congress for their care in ensuring the best transfers possible, and to Nick Spark of Periscope Film for test runs and consultation. Thanks as well to Bruce Lawton and Helge Bernhard for the rare shot of William Forest Crouch before the camera. Many other individuals contributed in small but significant ways, and I am grateful to them all.

My husband, Jeffrey Ehrlich, was among the manuscript's earliest, most constant, and most perceptive readers, and his comments and suggestions have been invaluable in bringing the book to completion. More than that, he lived with this project for years, combining vast reserves of patience and humor with just enough inquisitiveness. Jeff has an unerring ability to find the music in any situation, and that—and so much else—has made him an indispensable partner on this journey. As I've written elsewhere, when it comes to Jeff, whatever gratitude I've expressed so far should be moved many, many decimal places to the right. That hasn't changed.

For bringing Alice Barker and her Soundies to worldwide attention on YouTube, and for generously sharing his knowledge, my thanks to Dave Shuff. I'm especially grateful to Gail Campbell, who never gave up on the search for those films and who introduced me to Alice. Finally, my thanks to Alice Barker and her colleagues, the hundreds of performers who make these Soundies such a joy to watch. May they continue to entertain and inspire us all, on whatever technologies the future holds.

PART III

FOLLOWING UP

APPENDIX 1:
DIRECTORY OF
BLACK-CAST SOUNDIES

Films Starring or Featuring Black Performers

Compiled by SUSAN DELSON *and* MARK CANTOR

This list includes all Black-cast and Black-and-white-cast Soundies in which Black performers are credited and/or have significant time on screen. It includes some films in which performers appear in stereotyped roles.

Films are listed in alphabetical order. The date for each film is its copyright registration, which is usually (but not always) its release date. "Cat. no." is the number assigned to the film in the Soundies catalog. Films with M in their catalog numbers were released as limited-distribution M films and were not listed in Soundies catalogs prior to the 1946 edition.

In this list, the names of credited musicians and performers, as they appear on screen, are <u>underlined</u>. *Uncredited performers are listed next, followed by performers who appear on the soundtrack only.*

Every effort has been made to ensure accuracy based on available data. Errors will be corrected in future editions.

The information on uncredited performers is by no means exhaustive and pertains primarily to films and performers discussed in the book. Complete listings of performers, including musicians and uncredited actors, are given in Mark Cantor's Music for the Eyes: Soundies and Jukebox Shorts of the 1940s, *scheduled for publication in 2022.*

For additional information on individual films, see The Soundies Book *by Scott MacGillivray and Ted Okuda.*

1. ADVENTURE
[Excerpted from the film *Love in Syncopation*, 1946]
December 30, 1946

Cat. no. 27805
Production company: An Alexander Production, New York
Producer: William D. Alexander
Director: Leonard Anderson
Performers: <u>Henri Woode and His Orchestra</u>, <u>Harrell Tillman</u>

2. **AIN'T MISBEHAVIN'**
December 15, 1941
Cat no. 4607
Production company: Minoco Productions, New York
Executive Producer: Jack Barry
Producer: Fred Waller
Director: Warren Murray
Performers: <u>Fats Waller</u>; His Rhythm (Al Casey, John Hamilton, Slick
Jones, Gene Sedric, Cedric Wallace); Vivian Brown, Hilda "Hibby" Brown,
Winnie Johnson, Mable Lee [uncredited]; Myra Johnson [soundtrack only,
uncredited]

3. **AIN'T MY SUGAR SWEET**
December 6, 1943
Cat. no. 14408
Production company: Soundies Films, Inc., New York
Producer-Director: William Forest Crouch
Performers: <u>The Chanticleers</u>; Francine Everett, Bea Griffith, Laverne
Keane [uncredited]

4. **AIN'T SHE PRETTY**
November 20, 1944
Cat. no. 18908
Production company: Filmcraft Productions, New York
Producer-Director: William Forest Crouch
Performers: <u>The Three Peppers</u> (Bob Bell, Roy Branker, Walter Williams)

5. **AIR MAIL SPECIAL**
December 8, 1941
Cat. no. 4501
Production company: Minoco Productions, New York
Executive Producer: Jack Barry
Producer: Fred Waller
Director: Robert Snody
Performers: <u>Count Basie and His Orchestra</u>; Jimmy Rushing, Winnie
Johnson, Whitey's Lindy Hoppers [uncredited]

6. ALABAMY BOUND
December 22, 1941
Cat. no. 4707
Production company: RCM Productions, Los Angeles
Producer: Sam Coslow
Director: Dudley Murphy
Performers: The Five Spirits of Rhythm; Jackie Greene [white]

7. ALL-AMERICAN NEWS #1
Date unknown
Cat. no. 3M1
Production company: All-American News, New York
Producer: Unknown, possibly Emanuel M. Glucksman
Director: Unknown
Performers: Unknown; Bill Robinson, Hazel Scott and others are probably
mentioned in "newsreel" fashion and may be pictured on screen

8. ALL-AMERICAN NEWS #2
Date unknown
Cat. no. 3M2
Production company: All-American News, New York
Producer: Unknown, possibly Emanuel M. Glucksman
Director: Unknown
Performers: Seaman Len Bowden [exact credit unknown]

9. ALL RUZZITT BUZZITT
July 16, 1945
Cat. no. 88908
Production company: Filmcraft Productions, New York
Producer-Director: William Forest Crouch
Performers: Dallas Bartley and His Orchestra; Bill Martin [uncredited]

10. ALONG THE NAVAJO TRAIL
October 15, 1945
Cat. no. 21708
Production company: RCM Productions, Los Angeles
Producer: Ben Hersh
Director: Josef Berne
Performers: John Shadrack Horance, Johnny Moore's 3 Blazers

11. AM I LUCKY
October 28, 1946
Cat. no. 24M5

Production company: RCM Productions, Los Angeles
Producer: Ben Hersh
Director: Dave Gould
Performers: Dusty Brooks and His Four Tones

12. **BABBLING BESS**
August 30, 1943
Cat. no. 13108
Production company: Soundies Films, Inc., New York
Producer-Director: William Forest Crouch
Performers: The Chanticleers; Francine Everett, Mable Lee [uncredited]

13. **BABY, ARE YOU KIDDIN'?**
August 12, 1946
Cat. no. 22M2
Production company: RCM Productions, Los Angeles
Producer: Ben Hersh
Director: Dave Gould
Performers: Dusty Brooks and His Four Tones; Mildred Boyd

14. **BABY DON'T GO 'WAY FROM ME**
February 4, 1946
Cat. no. 16M1
Production company: Filmcraft Productions, New York
Producer-Director: William Forest Crouch
Performers: Mable Lee, Lincoln Perry (aka Stepin Fetchit), Derek
Sampson's Orchestra (aka Deryck Sampson and His Band)

15. **BABY DON'T YOU CRY**
December 13, 1943
Cat. no. 14508
Production Company: Soundies Films, Inc., New York
Producer-Director: William Forest Crouch
Performers: Warren Evans

16. **BABY, DON'T YOU LOVE ME ANYMORE**
November 26, 1945
Cat. no. 13M2
Production company: Filmcraft Productions, New York
Producer-Director: William Forest Crouch
Performers: June Richmond

17. BACK DOOR MAN
June 3, 1946
Cat. no. 19M4
Production company: Filmcraft Productions, New York
Producer-Director: William Forest Crouch
Performers: Vanita Smythe; Dan Burley [soundtrack only, uncredited]

18. BACKSTAGE BLUES
June 1, 1943
Cat. no. 11905
Production company: Soundies Films, Inc., New York
Producer-Director: William Forest Crouch
Performers: Lynn Albritton, Llewelyn Crawford (aka Lou Ellen), The Harlem Cuties

19. BEAT ME DADDY
December 29, 1943
Cat. no. 15008
Production company: Soundies Films, Inc., New York
Producer-Director: William Forest Crouch
Performers: Maurice Rocco; Mable Lee [uncredited]

20. BECAUSE I LOVE YOU
[Excerpted from the film *Paradise in Harlem*, 1939]
December 30, 1942
Cat. no. 2M1
Production company: Jubilee Productions, New York
Producer: Jack Goldberg
Director: Joseph Seiden
Performers: Lucky Millinder and His Orchestra, Mamie Smith

21. BIG FAT BUTTERFLY
December 31, 1944
Cat. no. 89908
Production company: RCM Productions, Los Angeles
Producer: Ben Hersh
Director: Dave Gould
Performers: Gene Rodgers and the Vs (Lady Will Carr, Willie Lee Floyd, Ivy Ann Glasko, Ivern Whittaker); Marie Bryant [uncredited]

22. BIG FAT MAMAS
August 19, 1946
Cat. no. 22M3
Production company: An Alexander Production, New York
Producer: William D. Alexander
Director: Ray Sandiford[1]
Performers: <u>Lucky Millinder and His Orchestra</u>, Benjamin Clarence "Bull Moose" Jackson [credit unverified]

23. BLACKBIRD FANTASY
August 31, 1942
Cat. no. 8302
Production company: RCM Productions, Los Angeles
Producer: Sam Coslow
Director: Herbert Moulton
Performers: <u>Dorothy Dandridge</u>, <u>Billy Mitchell</u>

24. BLI-BLIP
January 5, 1942
Cat. no. 4904
Production company: RCM Productions, Los Angeles
Producer: Sam Coslow
Director: Josef Berne
Performers: <u>Paul White</u>, <u>Marie Bryant</u>; <u>Duke Ellington and His Orchestra</u> [soundtrack only]

25. BLITZKREIG BOMBARDIER
December 31, 1944
Cat. no. 9M1
Production company: Filmcraft Productions, New York
Producer-Director: William Forest Crouch
Performers: <u>Skeets Tolbert and His Orchestra</u>

26. BLOCK PARTY REVELS
May 17, 1043
Cat. no. 11802
Production company: Soundies Films, Inc., New York
Producer-Director: William Forest Crouch
Performers: <u>Lynn Albritton</u>, <u>Billy and Ann</u>, <u>The Six Knobs</u>, <u>The Harlem Cuties</u>, Edna Mae Harris [uncredited]

27. BLOWTOP BLUES
October 29, 1945
Cat. no. 21808
Production company: Filmcraft Productions, New York
Producer-Director: William Forest Crouch
Performers: Cab Calloway and His Orchestra

28. BLUES IN THE NIGHT
January 26, 1942
Cat. no. 5201
Production company: Minoco Productions, New York
Executive Producer: Jack Barry
Producer: Fred Waller
Director: Robert Snody
Performers: Cab Calloway and His Orchestra

29. BOOGIE WOOGIE
April 24, 1944
Cat. no. 16308
Production company: Dave Gould Film Associates, Los Angeles
Producer-Director: Dave Gould
Performers: Meade "Lux" Lewis, Dudley Dickerson; Leonard "Lennie"
Bluett, Avanelle Harris [uncredited]

30. BOOGIE WOOGIE DREAM
[Excerpted from the film *Boogie Woogie Dream*, 1941]
December 31, 1944
Cat. no. 20008
Production company: B&W Film Shorts, Inc., New York
Producer: Mark Marvin
Director: Hans Burger
Performers: Lena Horne, Albert Ammons, Pete Johnson

31. BOOGIEMANIA
April 29, 1944
Cat. no. 18M6
Production company: Filmcraft Productions, New York
Producer-Director: William Forest Crouch
Performers: Nicky O'Daniel, The Sun Tan Four, Helen Bangs, Albert
Reese Jones; Fritz Pollard [uncredited]

32. BOOGLIE WOOGLIE PIGGY
November 10, 1941
Cat. no. 4102
Production company: Minoco Productions New York
Executive Producer: Jack Barry
Producer: Fred Waller
Director: Robert Snody
Performers: <u>The Deep River Boys</u> (Vernon Gardner, George Lawson,
Harry Douglass, Edward "Mumbles" Ware); Vivian Brown, Hilda "Hibby"
Brown, Winnie Johnson [uncredited]

33. BREAKFAST IN RHYTHM
October 29, 1943
Cat. no. 6M3
Production Company: Atlas Enterprises, Los Angeles
Executive Producer: Louis Weiss
Producer: Adrian Weiss
Director: Clarence Bricker
Performers: <u>The Three Chefs</u> (Benny "Smiley" Johnson, George "Smiley"
McDaniel, Sammy Warren); Barry Paige and His Orchestra [white;
uncredited]

34. BROADWAY
[Excerpted from the film *Love in Syncopation*, 1946]
December 30, 1946
Cat. no. 28M3
Production company: An Alexander Production, New York
Producer: William D. Alexander
Director: Leonard Anderson
Performers: <u>Henri Woode and His Orchestra</u>; Tops & Wilder [credit
unverified]

35. BROADWAY AND MAIN
February 4, 1946
Cat. no. 22505
Production company: Filmcraft Productions, New York
Producer-Director: William Forest Crouch
Performers: Lincoln Perry (aka <u>Stepin Fechit</u>); <u>Gloria Parker and Her
Orchestra</u> [white]

36. BROTHER BILL

March 5, 1945
Cat. no. 20108
Production company: Filmcraft Productions, New York
Producer-Director: William Forest Crouch
Performers: The Jubalaires

37. BUGLE CALL RAG

March 8, 1943
Cat. no. 10805
Production company: L.O.L. Productions, New York
Executive producer: Samuel Oliphant
Producer-director: Arthur Leonard
Performers: Ernie Morris [uncredited]; Borrah Minevich's Harmonica Rascals [white, with the exception of Morris]

38. BUNDLE OF LOVE

May 3, 1945
Cat. no. 11608
Production company: Song-O-Graf Productions, Los Angeles (1941)
Producer: Peter Ratoff
Director: George McNulty
Performers: The Dreamers [aka The Jones Boys]; Gene Grounds [white]

39. BUZZ ME

April 2, 1945
Cat. no. 20108
Production company: An Adams Production, New York
Producer: Berle Adams
Director: William Forest Crouch
Performers: Louis Jordan and His Tympany Five

40. BY AN OLD SOUTHERN RIVER

March 16, 1942
Cat. no. 5907
Production company: Minoco Productions, New York
Executive Producer: Jack Barry
Producer: Fred Waller
Director: Robert Snody
Performers: Bill Robinson

41. CAB CALLOWAY MEDLEY
April 24, 1944 [unverified]
Cat. no. 1M
Production company: Minoco Productions, New York
Executive Producer: Jack Barry
Producer: Fred Waller
Director: Robert Snody
Performers: Cab Calloway and His Orchestra

42. CALDONIA
[Excerpted from the film *Caldonia*, 1945]
June 11, 1945
Cat. no. 20808
Production company: An Adams Production, New York
Producer: Berle Adams
Director: William Forest Crouch
Performers: Louis Jordan and His Tympany Five; Roxie Joynes [uncredited]

43. CAN'T SEE FOR LOOKIN'
December 30, 1944
Cat. no. 19608
Production company: Filmcraft Productions, New York
Producer-Director: William Forest Crouch
Performers: Ida James

44. CARAVAN
October 12, 1942
Cat. no. 8907
Production company: RCM Productions, Los Angeles
Producer: Sam Coslow
Director: Josef Berne
Performers: The Mills Brothers (Donald Mills, Harry Mills, Herbert Mills, John H. Mills); Lucille (Lucy) Battle [uncredited]

45. CASE O' THE BLUES
April 27, 1942
Cat. no. 6501
Production company: RCM Productions, Los Angeles
Producer: Sam Coslow

Director: Josef Berne
Performers: <u>Maxine Sullivan</u>; Benny Carter and His Orchestra [uncredited]

46. CATS CAN'T DANCE
December 31, 1945
Cat. no. 87608
Production company: Filmcraft Productions, New York
Producer-Director: William Forest Crouch
Performers: <u>Mable Lee</u>; Deryck Sampson and His Band [uncredited]

47. CHA-CHI MAN
November 13, 1944
Cat. no. 18808
Production company: Filmcraft Productions, New York
Producer-Director: William Forest Crouch
Performers: <u>The Little Four Quartet</u>

48. THE CHAIR SONG
February 18, 1046
Cat. no. 16M3
Production company: Filmcraft Productions, New York
Producer-Director: William Forest Crouch
Performers: <u>Phil Moore and the Phil Moore Four</u> (Wallace Bishop, Doles Dickens, John Letman, Chuck Wayne [aka Charles Jagelka; white])

49. CHATTER
November 29, 1944
Cat. no. 14308
Production company: Soundies Films, Inc., New York
Producer-Director: William Forest Crouch
Performers: <u>Cook and Brown</u> (Charles Cook, Ernest Brown); <u>The Sepia Steppers</u> [including Alice Barker, uncredited]

50. CHICKEN SHACK SHUFFLE
September 21, 1943
Cat. no. 5M1
Production company: WFC Productions, New York
Producer-Director: William Forest Crouch
Performers: <u>Mable Lee</u>

51. CHILLY 'N COLD
April 16, 1945
Cat. no. 10M
Production company: Filmcraft Productions, New York
Producer-Director: William Forest Crouch
Performers: <u>The Little Four Quartet</u>

52. CIELITO LINDO
December 31, 1944
Cat. no. 19708
Production company: Filmcraft Productions, New York
Producer-Director: William Forest Crouch
Performers: <u>The Mills Brothers</u> (Donald Mills, Herbert Mills, John H. Mills, Gene Smith[2]); Nellie Hill, Bea Griffith [uncredited]

53. CLOSE SHAVE
November 30, 1942
Cat. no. 9608
Production company: RCM Productions, Los Angeles
Producer: Sam Coslow
Director: Josef Berne
Performers: <u>LeRoy Broomfield</u>, <u>Aurora Greeley</u>; John Kirby Sextet [soundtrack only; uncredited]

54. COALMINE BOOGIE
December 30, 1946
Cat. no. 29M2
Production company: Filmcraft Productions, New York
Producer-Director: William Forest Crouch
Performers: <u>Pat Flowers</u>, <u>Mable Lee</u>, <u>The Ebonettes</u> [credit unverified]

55. COME TO BABY DO
February 25, 1946
Cat. no. 16M4
Production company: Filmcraft Productions, New York
Producer-Director: William Forest Crouch
Performers: <u>The King Cole Trio</u> (Nat "King" Cole, Johnny Miller, Oscar Moore)

56. CONGO CLAMBAKE
August 3, 1942
Cat. No. 7906

Production company: RCM Productions, Los Angeles
Producer: Sam Coslow
Director: Josef Berne
Performers: <u>Dorothy Dandridge</u>; <u>Stan Kenton and His Orchestra</u> [white; soundtrack only]

57. CONTRAST IN RHYTHM
June 4, 1945
Cat. no. 11M1
Production company: Filmcraft Productions, New York
Producer-Director: William Forest Crouch
Performers: <u>Cecil Scott and His Orchestra</u>, <u>Robinson and Hill</u>

58. CORN PONE
March 16, 1945
Cat. no. 9M2
Production company: Filmcraft Productions, New York
Producer-Director: William Forest Crouch
Performers: <u>Skeets Tolbert and His Orchestra</u>, <u>Lupe Carterio</u>

59. COUNT ME OUT
June 24, 1946
Cat. no. 20M3
Production company: Filmcraft Productions, New York
Producer-Director: William Forest Crouch
Performers: <u>Henry "Red" Allen and His Band</u>, <u>J. C. Higginbotham</u>, <u>Johni Weaver</u>, <u>Harry Turner</u>

60. COW COW BOOGIE
October 26, 1942
Cat. no. 9104
Production company: RCM Productions, Los Angeles
Producer: Sam Coslow
Director: Josef Berne
Performers: <u>Dorothy Dandridge</u>; Dudley Dickerson, Eugene "Pineapple" Jackson [uncredited]

61. CRAWL RED CRAWL
May 13, 1946
Cat. no. 19M2
Production company: Filmcraft Productions, New York

Producer-Director: William Forest Crouch
Performers: <u>Henry "Red" Allen and His Band</u>, <u>J. C. Higginbotham</u>, <u>Johni Weaver</u>

62. CRYIN' AND SINGIN' THE BLUES
October 8, 1945
Cat. no. 88208
Production company: Filmcraft Productions, New York
Producer-Director: William Forest Crouch
Performers: <u>Dallas Bartley and His Orchestra</u>

63. CUBAN EPISODE
July 20, 1942
Cat. no. 7703
Production company: RCM Productions, Los Angeles
Producer: Sam Coslow
Director: Josef Berne
Performers: <u>Katherine Dunham and Her Dancers</u>; <u>Hal Borne and His Orchestra</u> [white; soundtrack only]

64. DANCE REVELS
December 30, 1944
Cat. no. 24507
Production Company: Filmcraft Productions, New York
Producer-Director: William Forest Crouch
Performers: Merrita Moore and Her Dancing Darlings

65. DANCE YOUR OLD AGE AWAY
December 31, 1944
Cat. no. 19908
Production company: Filmcraft Productions, New York
Producer-Director: William Forest Crouch
Performers: <u>Tosh Hammed and Company</u>

66. DANCEMANIA
September 21, 1943
Cat. no. 4M4
Production company: WFC Productions, New York
Producer-Director: William Forest Crouch
Performers: <u>Nicky O'Daniel</u>, <u>Mable Lee</u>, <u>Shim Sham</u> (aka Shim Sham Sam), <u>Sun Tan Four</u> [including Fritz Pollard, uncredited]

67. THE DARKTOWN STRUTTERS' BALL

October 6, 1941
Cat. no. 3603
Production company: Minoco Productions, New York
Executive Producer: Jack Barry
Producer: Fred Waller
Director: Warren Murray
Performers: The Charioteers; Hilda "Hibby" Brown, Vivian Brown, Deanie Gordon, Jackie Lewis, Tweedie Mason [uncredited]

68. DEAR OLD SOUTHLAND

December 8, 1941
Cat. no. 4507
Production company: Minoco Productions, New York
Producer: Fred Waller
Director: Robert Snody
Performers: Smalls Boytins, Vivian Brown, Hilda "Hibby" Brown, Robert (Bobby) Johnson, Julius Puillys, Ella Bessie Smook [uncredited]; The Dixairs [white]; Ray Bloch and His Orchestra [white; soundtrack only]

69. THE DEVIL SAT DOWN AND CRIED

April 20, 1942
Cat. no. 6408
Production company: Minoco Productions, New York
Executive Producer: Jack Barry
Producer: Fred Waller
Director: Warren Murray
Performers: Savannah Churchill, Les Hite and His Orchestra

70. DINAH

July 3, 1944
Cat. no. 27308
Production company: Filmcraft Productions, New York
Producer-Director: William Forest Crouch
Performers: Bob Howard

71. DISPOSSESSED BLUES

July 5, 1943
Cat. no. 12408
Production company: Filmcraft Productions, New York

Producer-Director: William Forest Crouch
Performers: <u>Lynn Albritton</u>, <u>The Four Knobs</u>

72. DIXIE RHYTHM
April 23, 1945
Cat. no. 89308
Production company: Filmcraft Productions, New York
Producer-Director: William Forest Crouch
Performers: <u>Pat Flowers</u>

73. DO I WORRY?
October 11, 1943
Cat. no. 13708
Production company: Soundies Films, Inc., New York
Producer-Director: William Forest Crouch
Performers: <u>Patterson and Jackson</u> (Warren Patterson and Al Jackson)

74. DOES YOU DO, OR DOES YOU DON'T
August 5, 1946
Cat. no. 22M1
Production company: Filmcraft Productions, New York
Producer-Director: William Forest Crouch
Performers: <u>Vanita Smythe</u>; Dan Burley [soundtrack only, uncredited]

75. DON'T BE LATE
April 21, 1945
Cat. no. 89208
Production company: Filmcraft Productions, New York
Producer-Director: William Forest Crouch
Performers: <u>Warren Evans</u>, <u>Cecil Scott and His Orchestra</u>

76. DOWN, DOWN, DOWN
December 31, 1942
Cat. no. 10904
Production company: Soundies Films, Inc., New York
Producer: William Forest Crouch
Director: John C. Graham
Performers: <u>Louis Jordan and His Band</u>

77. DRINK HEARTY
March 11, 1946
Cat. no. 17M2

Production company: Filmcraft Productions, New York
Producer-Director: William Forest Crouch
Performers: <u>Henry "Red" Allen and His Band</u>, J. C. Higginbotham

78. DRY BONES
April 30, 1945
Cat. no. 20508
Production company: Filmcraft Productions, New York
Producer: William Forest Crouch
Director: Josef Berne
Performers: <u>The Delta Rhythm Boys</u> (Traverse Crawford, Otho "Lee" Gaines, Clinton Holland, Harry Lewis); Rene DeKnight [pianist; uncredited]

79. E-BOB-O-LEE-BOP
March 25, 1946
Cat. no. 18M1
Production company: RCM Productions, Los Angeles
Producer: Ben Hersh
Director: Dave Gould
Performers: <u>The Ali Baba Trio</u> ("Big" Mike McKendrick, Cleveland Nickerson, Calvin Ponder)

80. EASY STREET
December 29, 1941
Cat. no. 4805
Production company: RCM Productions, Los Angeles
Producer: Sam Coslow
Director: Dudley Murphy
Performers: <u>Dorothy Dandridge</u>; <u>Jess Brooks</u>; <u>The Five Spirits of Rhythm</u>

81. EMILY BROWN
June 14, 1943
Cat. No. 12108
Production company: Glamourettes Productions, Los Angeles
Producer: Sydney M. Williams
Director: Dave Gould
Performers: <u>Bob Parrish</u>, <u>Chinky Grimes</u>

82. ERRAND BOY FOR RHYTHM
May 27, 1946
Cat. no. 19M3
Production company: Filmcraft Productions, New York

Producer-Director: William Forest Crouch
Performers: <u>The King Cole Trio</u> (Nat "King" Cole, Johnny Miller, Oscar Moore)

83. EVERY DAY IS SATURDAY IN HARLEM
May 22, 1944
Cat. no. 16608
Production company: Filmcraft Productions, New York
Producer-Director: William Forest Crouch
Performers: <u>Hilda Rogers</u>; Claude DeMetrius [aka Claude Demetrius, Claude Demetruis; uncredited]

84. EVERYBODY'S JUMPIN' NOW
December 30, 1946
Cat. no. 28M2
Production company: Filmcraft Productions, New York
Producer-Director: William Forest Crouch
Performers: <u>Mable Lee</u>, <u>Noble Sissle and His Orchestra</u>

85. FARE THEE WELL
July 9, 1945
Cat. no. 21008
Production company: Filmcraft Productions, New York
Producer: William Forest Crouch
Director: Josef Berne
Performers: <u>Day, Dawn, and Dusk</u> (Robert Caver, Ed Coleman, and Augustus "Gus" Simons)

86. FATS WALLER MEDLEY
Date unknown
Cat. no. 4M
Production company: Minoco Productions, New York
Producer: Fred Waller
Director: Warren Murray
Performers: <u>Fats Waller</u>; His Rhythm (Al Casey, John Hamilton, Slick Jones, Gene Sedric, Cedric Wallace), Vivian Brown, Hilda "Hibby" Brown [uncredited]

87. FAUST
May 14, 1945
Cat. no. 20608
Production company: Filmcraft Productions, New York

Producer: William Forest Crouch
Director: Josef Berne
Performers: <u>Day, Dawn, and Dusk</u> (Robert Caver, Ed Coleman, Augustus "Gus" Simons)

88. FIVE GUYS NAMED MOE
December 31, 1942
Cat no. 11108
Production company: Soundies Films, Inc., New York
Producer: William Forest Crouch
Director: John C. Graham
Performers: <u>Louis Jordan and His Band</u>

89. FIVE SALTED PEANUTS
October 22, 1945
Cat. no. 88108
Production company: RCM Productions, Los Angeles
Producer: Ben Hersh
Director: Josef Berne
Performers: <u>The Counts and the Countess</u> (Alma Smith, John Faire, Curtis Wilder)

90. FLAMINGO
January 5, 1942
Cat. no. 4907
Production company: RCM Productions, Los Angeles
Producer: Sam Coslow
Director: Josef Berne
Performers: <u>Duke Ellington and His Orchestra</u>, <u>Herb Jeffries</u>, <u>Janet Collins</u>, <u>Talley Beatty</u>

91. FOO, A LITTLE BALLYHOO
September 17, 1945
Cat. no. 21508
Production company: Filmcraft Productions, New York
Producer-Director: William Forest Crouch
Performers: <u>Cab Calloway and His Orchestra</u>, <u>Rusty Stanford</u> (aka Rusti Sanford)

92. FOOLIN' AROUND
November 1, 1943
Cat. no. 14008

Production company: Soundies Films, Inc., New York
Producer-Director: William Forest Crouch
Performers: Harris and Hunt, Mable Lee, The Harlem Honeys

93. 47TH STREET JIVE
August 28, 1944
Cat. no. 17908
Production company: RCM Productions, Los Angeles
Producer: Ben Hersh
Director: Josef Berne
Performers: June Richmond, Roy Milton and His Band

94. FOUR OR FIVE TIMES
October 5, 1941
Cat. no. 5608
Production company: Minoco Productions, New York
Producer: Jack Barry
Director: John Primi
Performers: Sister Rosetta Tharpe (aka Sister Tharpe), Lucky Millinder and His Orchestra

95. FRIM FRAM SAUCE
December 31, 1945
Cat. no. 87408
Production company: Filmcraft Productions, New York
Producer-Director: William Forest Crouch
Performers: The King Cole Trio (Nat "King" Cole, Johnny Miller, Oscar Moore); Shirley Johnson

96. FUZZY WUZZY
December 31, 1942
Cat. no. 10305
Production company: Soundies Films, Inc., New York
Producer: William Forest Crouch
Director: John C. Graham
Performers: Louis Jordan and His Band; Ruby Richards [uncredited]

97. G. I. JIVE
March 30, 1944
Cat. no. 15708
Production company: Soundies Films, Inc., New York

Producer-Director: William Forest Crouch
Performers: <u>Louis Jordan and His Band</u>

98. GEE
December 18, 1944
Cat. no. 19308
Production company: RCM Productions, Los Angeles
Producer: Ben Hersh
Director: Dave Gould
Performers: <u>Mabel Scott</u>, <u>The Flennoy Trio</u> (Lorenzo Flennoy, Robert Lewis, Eugene Phillips)

99. GET IT OFF YOUR MIND
September 2, 1946
Cat. no. 23M1
Production company: Filmcraft Productions, New York
Producer-Director: William Forest Crouch
Performers: <u>Vanita Smythe</u>, <u>Claude DeMetrius</u> (aka Claude Demetrius, Claude Demetruis)

100. GET WITH IT
November 22, 1943
Cat. no. 6M5
Production Company: WFC Productions, New York
Producer-Director: William Forest Crouch
Performers: <u>The Bye Trio</u>

101. GIT IT
December 28, 1943
Cat. no. 14808
Production company: Soundies Films, Inc., New York
Producer-Director: William Forest Crouch
Performers: <u>Patterson and Jackson</u> (Warren Patterson and Al Jackson)

102. GIVE ME SOME SKIN
December 30, 1046
Cat. no. 26M3
Production company: Transfilm Productions, probably New York
Producer: Unknown
Director: Unknown
Performers: <u>The Delta Rhythm Boys</u> (Traverse Crawford, Otho "Lee" Gaines, Clinton Holland, Harry Lewis); Rene DeKnight [pianist; uncredited]

8

PPENDIX 1

103. GOD'S HEAVEN

[Excerpted from the British film *He Found a Star*, 1941]
July 19, 1943
Cat. no. 12607
Production company: John Corfield Productions
Producer: John Corfield
Director: John Paddy Carstairs
Performers: <u>George Washington Brown</u> (aka Uriel Porter)

104. GOOD-NITE ALL

July 12, 1943
Cat. no. 12508
Production company: L.O.L. Productions, New York
Executive producer: Samuel Oliphant
Producer-director: Arthur Leonard
Performers: <u>Johnny Taylor</u>; "Hot-Cha" [uncredited]

105. GOT A PENNY BENNY

April 22, 1946
Cat. no. 18M5
Production company: Filmcraft Productions, New York
Producer-Director: William Forest Crouch
Performers: <u>The King Cole Trio</u> (Nat "King" Cole, Johnny Miller, Oscar Moore)

106. HALF PAST JUMP TIME

December 30, 1945
Cat. no. 22408
Production company: Filmcraft Productions, New York
Producer-Director: William Forest Crouch
Performers: <u>Mable Lee</u>; Deryck Sampson and His Band [uncredited]

107. HAREM REVELS

August 28, 1944
Cat. no. 8M1
Production company: WFC Productions, New York
Producer-Director: William Forest Crouch
Performers: <u>Roberta Harris</u>, <u>Ferrabee Purnell</u>, <u>Rusti Stanford</u> (aka Rusty Sanford)

108. HARK! HARK! THE LARK

December 8, 1941
Cat. no. 4505
Production company: Minoco Productions, New York
Producer: Fred Waller
Director: Robert Snody
Performers: The Deep River Boys (Harry Douglass, Vernon Gardner, George Lawson, Edward "Mumbles" Ware); Vivian Brown, Hilda "Hibby" Brown, Winnie Johnson [uncredited]

109. HARLEM HOTCHA

December 21, 1943
Cat. no. 20M1
Production company: Filmcraft Productions, New York
Producer-Director: William Forest Crouch
Performers: Nicky O'Daniel, Harry Turner, Tops & Wilder (Thomas "Tops" Lee and Wilda Crawford), Sun Tan Four [including Fritz Pollard, uncredited]; Cecil Scott and His Orchestra [soundtrack only]

110. HARLEM HOTCHA

June 10, 1946
Cat. no. 7M4
Production company: WFC Productions, New York
Producer-Director: William Forest Crouch
Performers: Tops & Wilder (Thomas "Tops" Lee and Wilda Crawford), The Harlem Queens

111. HARLEM RHUMBA

December 21, 1942
Cat. no. 9902
Production company: RCM Productions, Los Angeles
Producer: Sam Coslow
Director: Josef Berne
Performers: The Chocolateers

112. HARLEM SERENADE

[Excerpted from the film *Paradise in Harlem*, 1939]
December 31, 1942
Cat. no. 11204
Production company: Jubilee Productions, New York

Producer: Jack Goldberg
Director: Joseph Seiden
Performers: <u>Lucky Millinder and His Orchestra</u>; Edna Mae Harris [uncredited]

113. A HARLEMESQUE REVIEW

[Excerpted from the British film *Everything Is Rhythm*, 1936]
March 8, 1943
Cat. no. 10806
Production company: Joe Rock Productions, London
Producer: Joe Rock
Director: Alfred J. Goulding
Performers: <u>Mabel Mercer</u>; <u>Harry Roy</u> [white]

114. HELLO BILL

[Excerpted from the film *Lucky Millinder and His Orchestra*, 1946]
September 9, 1946
Cat. no. 23M2
Production company: An Alexander Production, New York
Producer: William D. Alexander
Director: Ray Sandiford
Performers: <u>Lucky Millinder and His Orchestra</u>

115. HERE 'TIS HONEY, TAKE IT

December 21, 1943
Cat. no. 7M3
Production company: WFC Productions, New York
Producer-Director: William Forest Crouch
Performers: <u>Myra Johnson</u>, <u>Dewey Brown</u>

116. HEY, LAWDY MAMA

June 5, 1944
Cat. no. 16808
Production company: RCM Productions, Los Angeles
Producer: Ben Hersh
Director: Josef Berne
Performers: <u>June Richmond</u>, <u>Roy Milton and His Band</u>

117. HEY! TOJO, COUNT YO' MEN

May 29, 1944
Cat. no. 16708
Production company: Filmcraft Productions, New York

Producer-Director: William Forest Crouch
Performers: <u>Bob Howard;</u> Claude DeMetrius [aka Claude Demetrius, Claude Demetruis; uncredited]

118. HIS ROCKIN' HORSE RAN AWAY
October 23, 1944
Cat. no. 18608
Production company: RCM Productions, Los Angeles
Producer: Sam Coslow
Director: Josef Berne
Performers: <u>Ida James</u>

119. HIT THAT JIVE JACK
August 9, 1043
Cat. no. 12908
Production company: Soundies Films, Inc., New York
Producer-Director: William Forest Crouch
Performers: <u>The Musical Madcaps</u>

120. HONEY CHILE
[Excerpted from the film *Caldonia*, 1945]
January 29, 1945
Cat. no. 19808
Production company: An Adams Production, New York
Producer: Berle Adams
Director: William Forest Crouch
Performers: <u>Louis Jordan and His Tympany Five</u>

121. HONEYSUCKLE ROSE
November 3, 1941
Cat. no. 4001
Production company: Minoco Productions, New York
Producer: Fred Waller
Director: Warren Murray
Performers: <u>Fats Waller;</u> His Rhythm (John Hamilton, Gene Sedric, Al Casey, Cedric Wallace, Slick Jones), Vivian Brown, Hilda "Hibby" Brown, Winnie Johnson, Mable Lee [uncredited]

122. HOT CHOCOLATE ("COTTONTAIL")
December 31, 1941
Cat. no. 5304
Production company: RCM Productions, Los Angeles

Producer: Sam Coslow
Director: Josef Berne
Performers: <u>Duke Ellington and His Orchestra</u>, <u>Whitey's Lindy Hoppers</u>

123. HOT IN THE GROOVE
[Excerpted from the film *Deviled Hams*, 1937]
December 14, 1942
Cat. no. 9808
Production company: Milton Schwarzwald/Nu-Atlas Productions
Producer-Director: Milton Schwarzwald
Performers: <u>Erskine Hawkins and His Jive Sepia Scorchers</u>

124. HOUSE ON 52ND STREET
July 29, 1946
Cat. no. 21M5
Production company: Filmcraft Productions, New York
Producer-Director: William Forest Crouch
Performers: <u>Henry "Red" Allen and His Band</u>, J. C. Higginbotham

125. I CAN'T DANCE
July 31, 1944
Cat. no. 17508
Production company: RCM Productions, Los Angeles
Producer: Ben Hersh
Director: Josef Berne
Performers: <u>Cliff Allen</u>, <u>Billie Haywood</u>

126. I CAN'T GIVE YOU ANYTHING BUT LOVE
June 19, 1944
Cat. no. 17008
Production company: Filmcraft Productions, New York
Producer-Director: William Forest Crouch
Performers: <u>Hilda Rogers</u>; Claude DeMetrius [aka Claude Demetrius, Claude Demetruis; uncredited]

127. I CRIED FOR YOU
[Excerpted from the film *Rhythm in a Riff*, 1946]
December 30, 1946
Cat. no. 27903
Production company: An Alexander Production, New York
Producer: William D. Alexander

Director: Leonard Anderson
Performers: Billy Eckstine and His Orchestra; Ann Baker

128. I DON'T WANT TO WALK WITHOUT YOU
April 13, 1942
Cat. no. 6301
Production company: Minoco Productions, New York
Producer: Jack Barry
Director: Owen Murphy
Performers: Frank Wilcox [uncredited]; Kay Lorraine [white], Merle Pitt and His Five Shades of Blue [white]

129. I DREAMT I DWELT IN HARLEM
September 29, 1941
Cat. no. 3506
Production company: Minoco Productions, New York
Producer: Jack Barry
Director: Warren Murray
Performers: The Delta Rhythm Boys (Traverse Crawford, Otho "Lee" Gaines, Clinton Holland, Harry Lewis); Rene DeKnight [pianist; uncredited]

130. I GOT IT BAD AND THAT AIN'T GOOD
January 19, 1942
Cat. no. 5105
Production company: RCM Productions, Los Angeles
Producer: Sam Coslow
Director: Josef Berne
Performers: Ivie Anderson, Duke Ellington and His Orchestra; Louise Franklin, Millie Monroe [uncredited]

131. I GOTTA GO TO CAMP TO SEE MY MAN
July 26, 1943
Cat. no. 12708
Production company: Soundies Films, Inc., New York
Producer-Director: William Forest Crouch
Performers: Edna Mae Harris

132. I HAD A DREAM
July 16, 1945
Cat. no. 88708
Production company: Filmcraft Productions, New York

Producer-Director: William Forest Crouch
Performers: <u>Johnny and George</u> (Johnny "Baby Face" Macklin, George MacLean)

133. I LIKE IT 'CAUSE I LOVE IT
September 18, 1944
Cat. no. 18108
Production company: Filmcraft Productions, New York
Producer-Director: William Forest Crouch
Performers: <u>Una Mae Carlisle</u>

134. I MISS YOU SO
December 21, 1943
Cat. no. 7M1
Production company: WFC Productions, New York
Producer-Director: William Forest Crouch
Performers: <u>Warren Evans</u>

135. I NEED A PLAYMATE
October 14, 1946
Cat. no. 24M3
Production company: Filmcraft Productions, New York
Producer-Director: William Forest Crouch
Performers: <u>Vanita Smythe</u>

136. I WANT A BIG FAT MAMA
October 20, 1941
Cat. no. 3807
Production company: Minoco Productions, New York
Producer: Jack Barry
Director: John Primi
Performers: <u>Lucky Millinder and His Orchestra</u>; Trevor Bacon [uncredited]

137. I WANT A LITTLE DOGGIE
November 12, 1945
Cat. no. 21908
Production company: Filmcraft Productions, New York
Producer-Director: William Forest Crouch
Performers: <u>Phil Moore and the Phil Moore Four</u> (Wallace Bishop, Doles Dickens, John Letman, Chuck Wayne [aka Charles Jagelka; white])

138. I WANT A MAN
[Excerpted from the film *Lucky Millinder and His Orchestra*, 1946]
October 21, 1946
Cat. no. 24M4
Production company: An Alexander Production, New York
Producer: William D. Alexander
Director: Ray Sandiford
Performers: Lucky Millinder and His Orchestra, Annisteen Allen

139. I WANT TO TALK ABOUT YOU
[Excerpted from the film *Rhythm in a Riff*, 1946]
December 30, 1946
Cat. no. 28M4
Production company: An Alexander Production, New York
Producer: William D. Alexander
Director: Leonard Anderson
Performers: Billy Eckstine and His Orchestra

140. I WAS HERE WHEN YOU LEFT ME
October 1, 1945
Cat. no. 21608
Production company: Filmcraft Productions, New York
Producer-Director: William Forest Crouch
Performers: Cab Calloway and His Orchestra, Dotty Saulter

141. I WON'T MISS YOU
[Excerpted from the film *Paradise in Harlem*, 1939]
December 30, 1942
Cat. no. 2M2
Production company: Jubilee Productions, New York
Producer: Jack Goldberg
Director: Joseph Seiden
Performers: Unknown; opening credits unverifiable

142. IF YOU CAN'T SMILE AND SAY YES
May 8, 1944
Cat. no. 16408
Production company: Filmcraft Productions, New York
Producer-Director: William Forest Crouch
Performers: Louis Jordan and His Tympany Five

143. **IF YOU ONLY KNEW**
July 8, 1946
Cat. no. 21M2
Production company: RCM Productions, Los Angeles
Producer: Ben Hersh
Director: Dave Gould
Performers: <u>Valaida Snow</u>, <u>The Ali Baba Trio</u> ("Big" Mike McKendrick, Cleveland Nickerson, Calvin Ponder)

144. **IF YOU TREAT ME TO A HUG**
December 29, 1943
Cat. no. 14608
Production company: Soundies Films, Inc., New York
Producer-Director: William Forest Crouch
Performers: <u>The Chanticleers</u>; Laverne Keane, Francine Everett [uncredited]

145. **I'LL BE GLAD WHEN YOU'RE DEAD YOU RASCAL YOU**
July 27, 1942
Cat. no. 7803
Production company: RCM Productions, Los Angeles
Producer: Sam Coslow
Director: Josef Berne
Performers: <u>Louis Armstrong and His Band</u>; Velma Middleton, Lawrence Lucie [uncredited]

146. **I'M A GOOD, GOOD WOMAN**
August 28, 1944
Cat. no. 8M2
Production company: Filmcraft Productions, New York
Producer-Director: William Forest Crouch
Performers: <u>Una Mae Carlisle</u>

147. **I'M A SHY GUY**
February 11, 1946
Cat. no. 16M2
Production company: Filmcraft Productions, New York
Producer-Director: William Forest Crouch
Performers: <u>The King Cole Trio</u> (Nat "King" Cole, Johnny Miller, Oscar Moore)

148. I'M MAKING BELIEVE
March 19, 1945
Cat. no. 20208
Production company: Filmcraft Productions, New York
Producer-Director: William Forest Crouch
Performers: <u>Warren Evans</u>, <u>Cecil Scott and His Orchestra</u>

149. I'M TIRED
August 21, 1944
Cat. no. 17808
Production company: Filmcraft Productions, New York
Producer-Director: William Forest Crouch
Performers: <u>Apus and Estrellita</u> (Montrose Morse and Estrellita Bernier)

150. IS YOU IS OR IS YOU AIN'T MY BABY
February 21, 1944
Cat. no. 15408
Production company: RCM Productions, Los Angeles
Producer: Ben Hersh
Director: Josef Berne
Performers: <u>The King Cole Trio</u> (Nat "King" Cole, Johnny Miller, Oscar Moore), <u>Ida James</u>

151. IT'S ME, OH LORD
November 20, 1945
Cat. no. 87908
Production company: RCM Productions, Los Angeles
Producer: Ben Hersh
Director: Josef Berne
Performers: <u>John Shadrack Horance</u>, <u>Johnnie Moore's 3 Blazers</u>

152. I'VE GOT A LITTLE LIST
September 21, 1942
Cat. no. 8608
Production company: Herbert Moulton Productions, Los Angeles;
released by RCM Productions, Los Angeles
Producer: Sam Coslow
Director: Herbert Moulton
Performers: <u>Billy Mitchell</u>; Vivian Dandridge, Florence O'Brien
[uncredited]

153. I'VE GOT TO BE A RUG CUTTER
November 26, 1945
Cat. no. 22008
Production company: RCM Productions, Los Angeles
Producer: Ben Hersh
Director: Josef Berne
Performers: The Counts and the Countess (Alma Smith, John Faire, Curtis Wilder)

154. JACK, YOU'RE PLAYING THE GAME
November 17, 1941
Cat. no. 4207
Production company: Minoco Productions, New York
Executive Producer: Jack Barry
Producer: Fred Waller
Director: Robert Snody
Performers: The Delta Rhythm Boys (Traverse Crawford, Otho "Lee" Gaines, Clinton Holland, Harry Lewis); Rene DeKnight [pianist; uncredited]; Steve Schultz and His Orchestra [white; soundtrack only]

155. JACKPOT
December 21, 1943
Cat. no. 7M6
Production company: WFC Productions, New York
Producer-Director: William Forest Crouch
Performers: Peggy Backus, The Harlem Honeys

156. JAM SESSION
February 16, 1942
Cat. no. 5503
Production company: RCM Productions, Los Angeles
Producer: Sam Coslow
Director: Josef Berne
Performers: Duke Ellington and His Orchestra; Louise Franklin, Millie Monroe [uncredited]

157. JIM
November 24, 1941
Cat. no. 4308
Production company: RCM Productions, Los Angeles
Producer: Sam Coslow

Director: Dudley Murphy
Performers: Judy Carroll; Johnny Thomas [uncredited]

158. JIVE COMES TO THE JUNGLE
November 16, 1942
Cat. no. 9406
Production company: Minoco Productions, New York
Producer: Jack Barry
Director: John C. Graham
Performers: Slim Thomas, Ze Zulettes; Edna Mae Harris [uncredited; identified in the Soundies catalog entry as Edna Mae Jones], Alice Barker [uncredited]

159. JOE, JOE
December 16, 1946
Cat. no. 26M5
Production company: Filmcraft Productions, New York
Producer-Director: William Forest Crouch
Performers: Noble Sissle and His Orchestra, Pat Rainey

160. THE JOINT IS JUMPIN'
December 1, 1941
Cat. no. 4403
Production company: Minoco Productions, New York
Producer: Fred Waller
Director: Warren Murray
Performers: Fats Waller; Myra Johnson, His Rhythm (Al Casey, John Hamilton, Slick Jones, Gene Sedric, Cedric Wallace), Vivian Brown, Hilda "Hibby" Brown, Winnie Johnson, Mable Lee [uncredited]

161. JONAH AND THE WHALE
April 10, 1944
Cat. no. 16108
Production company: RCM Productions, Los Angeles
Producer: Ben Hersh
Director: Josef Berne
Performers: The Shadrach Boys

162. JORDAN JIVE
August 14, 1944
Cat. no. 17708

Production company: Filmcraft Productions, New York
Producer-Director: William Forest Crouch
Performers: <u>Louis Jordan and His Orchestra</u>, <u>The Swing Maniacs</u>

163. JORDAN MEDLEY #1
Date unknown
Cat. no. 3M
Production information unknown
Performers: <u>Louis Jordan and His Tympany Five</u>

164. JORDAN MEDLEY #2
Date unknown
Cat. no. $2M^3$
Production information unknown
Performers: <u>Louis Jordan and His Tympany Five</u>

165. JOSEPH 'N HIS BRUDDERS
July 16, 1945
Cat. no. 88808
Production company: Filmcraft Productions, New York
Executive Producer: William Forest Crouch
Director: Leonard Weiss
Performers: <u>June Richmond</u>; Claude Demetrius [aka Claude Demetrius, Claude Demetruis, uncredited]; Tiny Grimes and His Orchestra [soundtrack only, uncredited]

166. JUKE BOX BOOGIE
December 30, 1944
Cat. no. 19508
Production company: RCM Productions, Los Angeles
Producer: Ben Hersh
Director: Dave Gould
Performers: <u>Gene Rodgers and the Vs</u> (Lady Will Carr, Willie Lee Floyd, Ivy Ann Glasko, Ivern Whittaker); Marie Bryant [uncredited]

167. JUMP CHILDREN
[Excerpted from the film *The International Sweethearts of Rhythm featuring Anna Mae Winburn*, 1946]
August 26, 1946
Cat. no. 22M4
Production company: An Alexander Production, New York

Producer: William D. Alexander
Director: Ray Sandiford
Performers: <u>Anna Mae Winburn</u>, <u>The International Sweethearts of Rhythm</u>

168. JUMP IN
[Excerpted from the film *Mystery in Swing*, 1940]
December 31, 1942
Cat. no. 10605
Production company: Aetna Films Corporation, Los Angeles
Producer: Jack Goldberg
Director: Arthur Dreifuss
Performers: <u>The Four Toppers</u>, <u>Cee Pee Johnson and His Orchestra</u>

169. JUMPIN' AT THE JUBILEE
April 17, 1944
Cat. no. 16208
Production company: Soundies Films, Inc., New York
Producer-Director: William Forest Crouch
Performers: <u>Louis Jordan and His Band</u>, <u>The Swing Maniacs</u>

170. JUMPIN' JACK FROM HACKENSACK
October 25, 1943
Cat. no. 13908
Production company: Soundies Films, Inc., New York
Producer-Director: William Forest Crouch
Performers: <u>The Chanticleers</u>, <u>Tommy Thompson</u>

171. JUNGLE JAMBOREE
October 4, 1943
Cat. no. 13608
Production company: Soundies Films, Inc., New York
Producer-Director: William Forest Crouch
Performers: <u>Pauline Bryant</u>, <u>Cook and Brown</u> (Charles Cook and Ernest Brown); Alice Barker [uncredited]

172. JUNGLE JIG
June 2, 1941
Cat. no. 1802
Production company: Cameo Productions, Los Angeles
Producer: Sam Coslow

Director: Josef Berne
Performers: <u>Dorothy Dandridge</u>; <u>Cee Pee Johnson and His Orchestra</u>

173. JUST A SITTIN' AND A ROCKIN'
April 20, 1945
Cat. no. 21308
Production company: Filmcraft Productions, New York
Producer-Director: William Forest Crouch
Performers: <u>The Delta Rhythm Boys</u> (Traverse Crawford, Otho "Lee" Gaines, Clinton Holland, Harry Lewis); Rene DeKnight [pianist; uncredited]

174. KEEP SMILING
August 23, 1943
Cat. no. 13008
Production company: Soundies Films, Inc., New York
Producer-Director: William Forest Crouch
Performers: <u>The Four Ginger Snaps</u> (Ruth Christian, Charles Ford, Ethel E. Harper, Leona Virginia Hemingway)

175. KEEP WAITIN'
[Excerpted from the film *He Found a Star*, 1941]
June 7, 1943
Cat. no. 12008
Production company: John Corfield Productions
Producer: John Corfield
Director: John Paddy Carstairs
Performers: <u>George Washington Brown</u> (aka Uriel Porter)

176. KNOCK ME OUT
March 16, 1945
Cat. no. 89508
Production company: Filmcraft Productions, New York
Producer-Director: William Forest Crouch
Performers: <u>Apus and Estrellita</u> (Montrose Morse and Estrellita Bernier); Dewey Brown [uncredited]; Louis Jordan and His Tympany Five [soundtrack only; uncredited]

177. LAZY LADY
December 24, 1945
Cat. no. 22208
Production company: Filmcraft Productions, New York
Producer-Director: William Forest Crouch

Performers: <u>Phil Moore and the Phil Moore Four</u> (Wallace Bishop, Doles Dickens, John Letman, Chuck Wayne [aka Charles Jagelka; white])

178. LAZY RIVER
February 28, 1944
Cat. no. 15508
Production company: RCM Productions, Los Angeles
Producer: Ben Hersh
Director: Josef Berne
Performers: <u>The Shadrach Boys</u>

179. LAZY RIVER
December 4, 1944
Cat. no. 19108
Production company: Filmcraft Productions, New York
Producer-Director: William Forest Crouch
Performers: <u>The Mills Brothers</u> (Donald Mills, Herbert Mills, John H. Mills, Gene Smith)

180. LAZYBONES
December 15, 1941
Cat. no. 4602
Production company: RCM Productions, Los Angeles
Producer: Sam Coslow
Director: Dudley Murphy
Performers: <u>Dorothy Dandridge</u>, <u>Peter Ray</u>; <u>Hoagy Carmichael</u> [white]; Bob Crosby and His Orchestra [white; soundtrack only, uncredited]

181. LEGS AIN'T NO GOOD
December 28, 1942
Cat. no. 10006
Production company: Minoco Productions, New York
Executive Producer: Jack Barry
Producer: Fred Waller
Director: John C. Graham
Performers: <u>Edna Mae Harris</u>, <u>Slim Thomas</u>; Alice Barker [uncredited]; Peggy Mann [white; soundtrack only, uncredited]

182. LET ME OFF UPTOWN
January 12, 1942
Cat. no. 5001
Production company: Minoco Productions, New York

Producer: Fred Waller
Director: Robert Snody
Performers: <u>Roy Eldridge</u>, <u>Anita O'Day</u> [white], <u>Gene Krupa and His Orchestra</u> [white, with the exception of Eldridge]

183. LET'S BEAT OUT SOME LOVE
October 29, 1943
Cat. no. 5M3
Production company: WFC Productions, New York
Producer-Director: William Forest Crouch
Performers: <u>Warren Evans</u>

184. LET'S GET DOWN TO BUSINESS
September 21, 1943
Cat. no. 5M2
Production company: WFC Productions, New York
Producer-Director: William Forest Crouch
Performers: <u>Myra Johnson</u>, <u>Dewey Brown</u>

185. LET'S GO
[Excerpted from the film *Mystery in Swing*, 1940]
December 31, 1942
Cat. no. 11305
Production company: Aetna Films Corporation, Los Angeles
Producer: Jack Goldberg
Director: Arthur Dreifuss
Performers: <u>The Four Toppers</u>, <u>Cee Pee Johnson and His Orchestra</u>

186. LET'S SCUFFLE
January 12, 1942
Cat. no. 5006
Production company: Minoco Productions, New York
Executive Producer: Jack Barry
Producer: Fred Waller
Director: Robert Snody
Performers: <u>Bill Robinson</u>

187. LINDA BROWN
September 6, 1943
Cat. no. 13208
Production company: Soundies Films, Inc., New York

Producer-Director: William Forest Crouch
Performers: The Musical Madcaps

188. LONESOME LOVER BLUES
[Excerpted from the film *Rhythm in a Riff*, 1946]
December 30, 1946
Cat. no. 28M1
Production company: An Alexander Production, New York
Producer: William D. Alexander
Director: Leonard Anderson
Performers: Billy Eckstine and His Orchestra

189. THE LONESOME ROAD
November 10, 1941
Cat. no. 4106
Production company: Minoco Productions, New York
Executive Producer: Jack Barry
Producer: Fred Waller
Director: John Primi
Performers: Sister Rosetta Tharpe (aka Sister Tharpe), Lucky Millinder and His Orchestra

190. LOVE GROWS ON A WHITE OAK TREE
December 28, 1944
Cat. no. 19408
Production company: Filmcraft Productions, New York
Producer-Director: William Forest Crouch
Performers: The Little Four Quartet

191. LOVIN' UP A SOLID BREEZE
August 2, 1943
Cat. no. 12808
Production company: Soundies Films, Inc., New York
Producer-Director: William Forest Crouch
Performers: The Chanticleers

192. LOW DOWN DOG
May 15, 1944
Cat. no. 16508
Production company: Dave Gould Film Associates, Los Angeles
Producer-Director: Dave Gould

Music Director: Billy McDonald
Performers: <u>Meade "Lux" Lewis</u>, <u>Dudley Dickerson</u>; Avanelle Harris,
Leonard "Lennie" Bluett [uncredited]; <u>Joe Turner</u> [soundtrack only]

193. LOW, SHORT AND SQUATTY
December 2, 1946
Cat. no. 26M1
Production company: Filmcraft Productions, New York
Producer-Director: William Forest Crouch
Performers: <u>Vanita Smythe</u>; "Shorty" Jackson, Dan Burley Trio (Dan
Burley, Carl Lynch, Ivan "Loco" Rolle) [uncredited]

194. MAMA, I WANNA MAKE RHYTHM
December 30, 1943
Cat. no. 15108
Production company: Soundies Films, Inc., New York
Producer-Director: William Forest Crouch
Performers: <u>Patterson and Jackson</u> (Warren Patterson and Al Jackson)

195. MARY HAD A LITTLE LAMB
October 9, 1944
Cat. no. 18408
Production company: Filmcraft Productions, New York
Producer-Director: William Forest Crouch
Performers: <u>The Three Peppers</u> (Bob Bell, Roy Branker, Walter Williams)

196. MELODY TAKES A HOLIDAY
October 29, 1943
Cat. no. 6M2
Production company: WFC Productions, New York
Producer-Director: William Forest Crouch
Performers: <u>The Harlem Honeys</u>

197. MINNIE THE MOOCHER
February 9, 1942
Cat. no. 5405
Production company: Minoco Productions, New York
Executive Producer: Jack Barry
Producer: Fred Waller
Director: Robert Snody
Performers: <u>Cab Calloway and His Orchestra</u>

198. MISTLETOE
[Excerpted from the film *Love in Syncopation*, 1946]
December 30, 1946
Cat. no. 29M1
Production company: An Alexander Production, New York
Producer: William D. Alexander
Director: Leonard Anderson
Performers: Henri Woode and His Orchestra, Tops & Wilder (Thomas "Tops" Lee and Wilda Crawford)

199. MOP
April 15, 1946
Cat. no. 18M4
Production company: Filmcraft Productions, New York
Producer-Director: William Forest Crouch
Performers: Henry "Red" Allen and His Band, J. C. Higginbotham

200. MR. JACKSON FROM JACKSONVILLE
June 4, 1945
Cat. no. 89108
Production company: Filmcraft Productions, New York
Producer: William Forest Crouch
Director: Leonard Weiss
Performers: June Richmond; Claude DeMetrius [aka Claude Demetrius, Claude Demetruis; uncredited]

201. MR. X BLUES
June 4, 1945
Cat. no. 11M3
Production company: Filmcraft Productions, New York
Producer-Director: William Forest Crouch
Performers: Cecil Scott and His Orchestra

202. MY BOTTLE IS DRY
October 7, 1946
Cat. no. 24M2
Production company: Filmcraft Productions, New York
Producer-Director: William Forest Crouch
Performers: June Richmond

203. MY, MY, AIN'T THAT SOMETHIN'
October 30, 1944
Cat. no. 18708
Production company: RCM Productions, Los Angeles
Producer: Ben Hersh
Director: Dave Gould
Performers: <u>Gene Rodgers and the Vs</u> (Lady Will Carr, Willie Lee Floyd, Ivy Ann Glasko, Ivern Whittaker)

204. MY NEW GOWN
[Excerpted from the film *Boogie Woogie Dream*, 1941]
December 30, 1944
Cat. no. 21M1
Production company: B&W Film Shorts, Inc., New York
Producers: Mark Marvin
Director: Hans Burger
Performers: <u>Lena Horne</u>, <u>Albert Ammons</u>, <u>Pete Johnson</u>

205. NEVER TOO OLD TO SWING
November 5, 1945
Cat. no. 88008
Production company: Filmcraft Productions, New York
Producer-Director: William Forest Crouch
Performers: <u>Tiny Grimes and His Orchestra</u>

206. NO, NO, BABY
March 16, 1946
Cat. no. 89608
Production company: Filmcraft Productions, New York
Producer-Director: William Forest Crouch
Performers: <u>Skeets Tolbert and His Orchestra</u>, <u>The Sun Tan Sweeties</u>

207. NOAH
January 28, 1946
Cat. no. 15M1
Production company: Filmcraft Productions, New York
Producer-Director: William Forest Crouch
Performers: <u>The Jubalaires</u>

208. OH, SUSANNAH
September 22, 1941
Cat. no. 3402

Production company: Minoco Productions, New York
Executive Producer: Jack Barry
Producer: Fred Waller
Director: Warren Murray
Performers: The Charioteers; Vivian Brown, Hilda "Hibby" Brown
[uncredited]; George Steiner and His Orchestra [white; soundtrack only, uncredited]

209. OH-H-E-E, MY, MY
December 3, 1945
Cat. no. 87808
Production company: RCM Productions, Los Angeles
Producer: Ben Hersh
Director: Josef Berne
Performers: The Counts and the Countess (Alma Smith, John Faire, Curtis Wilder)

210. OLD DAN TUCKER
March 4, 1946
Cat. no. 17M1
Production company: Filmcraft Productions, New York
Producer-Director: William Forest Crouch
Performers: The Jubalaires

211. OLD MAN MOSE
December 31, 1942
Cat. no. 10506
Production company: Soundies Films, Inc., New York
Producer: William Forest Crouch
Director: John C. Graham
Performers: Louis Jordan and His Band

212. THE OUTLINE OF JITTERBUG HISTORY
March 23, 1942
Cat. no. 6005
Production company: RCM Productions, Los Angeles
Producer: Sam Coslow
Director: Josef Berne
Performers: Whitey's Lindy Hoppers; Tom Herbert [white]; Stan Kenton and His Orchestra [white; soundtrack only]

213. THE OUTSKIRTS OF TOWN
October 19, 1942
Cat. no. 9005
Production company: RCM Productions, Los Angeles
Producer: Sam Coslow
Director: Josef Berne
Performers: <u>Dudley Dickerson</u>, <u>Theresa Harris</u>; Louis Jordan and His
Band [soundtrack only, uncredited]

214. PAPER DOLL
December 7, 1942
Cat. no. 9706
Production company: RCM Productions, Los Angeles
Producer: Sam Coslow
Director: Josef Berne
Performers: <u>Dorothy Dandridge</u>, <u>The Mills Brothers</u> (Donald Mills, Harry
Mills, Herbert Mills, John H. Mills); Avanelle Harris, Lucille (Lucy)
Battle, Juanita Moore [uncredited]

215. PARDON ME, BUT YOU LOOK JUST LIKE MARGIE
June 28, 1943
Cat. no. 12408
Production Company: Atlas Enterprises, Los Angeles
Executive Producer: Louis Weiss
Producer: Adrian Weiss
Director: Clarence Bricker
Performers: <u>The Three Chefs</u> (Benny "Smiley" Johnson, George "Smiley"
McDaniel, Sammy Warren); <u>Barry Paige and His Orchestra</u> [white]

216. PATIENCE AND FORTITUDE
April 8, 1946
Cat. no. 18M3
Production company: RCM Productions, Los Angeles
Producer: Ben Hersh
Director: Dave Gould
Performers: <u>Valaida Snow</u>, <u>The Ali Baba Trio</u> ("Big" Mike McKendrick,
Cleveland Nickerson, Calvin Ponder)

217. PECKIN'
November 9, 1942
Cat. no. 9303

Production company: RCM Productions, Los Angeles
Producer: Sam Coslow
Director: Josef Berne
Performers: <u>The Chocolateers</u>

218. PIGMEAT THROWS THE BULL

December 24, 1945
Cat. no. 14M1
Production company: Filmcraft Productions, New York
Producer-Director: William Forest Crouch
Performers: <u>Dewey "Pigmeat" Markham</u>, <u>Mable Lee</u>

219. THE POLLARD JUMP

April 1, 1946
Cat. no. 18M2
Production company: Filmcraft Productions, New York
Producer-Director: William Forest Crouch
Performers: <u>Nicky O'Daniel</u>, <u>The Sun Tan Four</u> (including Fritz Pollard; uncredited)

220. POPPIN' THE CORK

June 21, 1943
Cat. no. 12208
Production company: Soundies Films, Inc., New York
Producer-Director: William Forest Crouch
Performers: <u>Billy and Ann</u>, <u>The Sepia Steppers</u>

221. PRANCING IN THE PARK

December 21, 1943
Cat. no. 7M2
Production company: Filmcraft Productions, New York
Producer-Director: William Forest Crouch
Performers: <u>Tops & Wilder</u> (Thomas "Tops" Lee and Wilda Crawford)

222. THE PREACHER AND THE BEAR

April 16, 1945
Cat. no. 20408
Production company: Filmcraft Productions, New York
Producer-Director: William Forest Crouch
Performers: <u>The Jubalaires</u>

223. PRISONER OF LOVE
[Excerpted from the film *Rhythm in a Riff*, 1946]
December 30, 1946
Cat. no. 28003
Production company: An Alexander Production, New York
Producer: William D. Alexander
Director: Leonard Anderson
Performers: <u>Billy Eckstine and His Orchestra</u>

224. PUDGY BOY
May 11, 1942
Cat. no. 6707
Production company: Minoco Productions, New York
Executive Producer: Jack Barry
Producer: Fred Waller
Director: Robert Snody
Performers: <u>Les Hite and His Orchestra</u>

225. PUT YOUR ARMS AROUND ME, HONEY
September 21, 1943
Cat. no. 4M1
Production company: WFC Productions, New York
Producer-Director: William Forest Crouch
Performers: <u>Virgil Van Cleve</u>, <u>Ruby Hill</u>

226. QUARRY ROAD
March 8, 1943
Cat. no. 10802
Production company: L.O.L. Productions, New York
Executive producer: Samuel Oliphant
Producer-director: Arthur Leonard
Performers: <u>Sam Manning</u>, <u>Belle Rosette</u> (Beryl McBurnie)

227. QUICK WATSON, THE RHYTHM
October 29, 1943
Cat. no. 5M5
Production company: WFC Productions, New York
Producer-Director: William Forest Crouch
Performers: <u>Myra Johnson</u>, <u>The Harlem Honeys</u>

228. RATION BLUES
March 27, 1944
Cat. no. 15908
Production company: Soundies Films, Inc., New York
Producer-Director: William Forest Crouch
Performers: Louis Jordan and His Orchestra

229. RHAPSODY OF LOVE
July 24, 1944
Cat. no. 17408
Production company: Filmcraft Productions, New York
Producer-Director: William Forest Crouch
Performers: Hilda Rogers

230. RHUMBOOGIE
December 31, 1943
Cat. no. 15308
Production company: Soundies Films, Inc., New York
Producer-Director: William Forest Crouch
Performers: Maurice Rocco

231. RHYTHM IN A RIFF
[Excerpted from the film *Rhythm in a Riff*, 1946]
December 30, 1946
Cat. no. 27M3
Production company: An Alexander Production, New York
Producer: William D. Alexander
Director: Leonard Anderson
Performers: Billy Eckstine and His Orchestra; Hortence Allen [aka Hortence, Hortence "The Body" Allen; uncredited]

232. RHYTHM MAD
October 29, 1943
Cat. no. 6M4
Production company: WFC Productions, New York
Producer-Director: William Forest Crouch
Performers: The Musical Madcaps

233. RHYTHM OF THE RHYTHM BAND
September 20, 1943
Cat. no. 13408

Production company: Soundies Films, Inc., New York
Producer-Director: William Forest Crouch
Performers: <u>The Musical Madcaps</u>

234. RHYTHM SAM
June 17, 1946
Cat. no. 20M2
Production company: Filmcraft Productions, New York
Producer-Director: William Forest Crouch
Performers: <u>The Lennox Trio</u> (Carl Lynch, Ivan "Loco" Rolle, pianist unidentified), <u>The Three Peppers</u> (Roy Branker, Bob Bell, Walter Williams)

235. RHYTHMANIA
October 29, 1943
Cat. no. 5M4
Production company: WFC Productions, New York
Producer-Director: William Forest Crouch
Performers: <u>Harris and Hunt</u>, <u>Mable Lee</u>, <u>The Harlem Honeys</u>

236. RIDE ON, RIDE ON
June 26, 1944
Cat. no. 17108
Production company: RCM Productions, Los Angeles
Producer: Ben Hersh
Director: Josef Berne
Performers: <u>June Richmond</u>, <u>Roy Milton and His Band</u>

237. RIDE, RED, RIDE
September 8, 1941
Cat. no. 3203
Production company: Minoco Productions, New York
Executive Producer: Jack Barry
Producer: Fred Waller
Director: Warren Murray
Performers: <u>The Charioteers</u>

238. RIGOLETTO
June 25, 1945
Cat. no. 20908
Production company: Filmcraft Productions, New York
Producer: William Forest Crouch

Director: Josef Berne
Performers: <u>Day, Dawn, and Dusk</u> (Robert Caver, Ed Coleman, Augustus "Gus" Simons)

239. RIGOLETTO BLUES

November 3, 1941
Cat. no. 4005
Production company: Minoco Productions, New York
Executive Producer: Jack Barry
Producer: Fred Waller
Director: Robert Snody
Performers: <u>The Delta Rhythm Boys</u> (Traverse Crawford, Otho "Lee" Gaines, Clinton Holland, Harry Lewis); Rene DeKnight [pianist, uncredited], Winnie Johnson [uncredited]; Steve Schultz and His Orchestra [white; soundtrack only, uncredited]

240. RINKA TINKA MAN

June 12, 1944
Cat. no. 16908
Production company: RCM Productions, Los Angeles
Producer: Ben Hersh
Director: Josef Berne
Performers: <u>Cliff Allen</u>, <u>Billie Haywood</u>

241. ROCCO BLUES

December 31, 1943
Cat. no. 15608
Production company: Soundies Films, Inc., New York
Producer-Director: William Forest Crouch
Performers: <u>Maurice Rocco</u>

242. ROCK IT FOR ME

December 27, 1943
Cat. no. 14708
Production company: Soundies Films, Inc., New York
Producer-Director: William Forest Crouch
Performers: <u>Maurice Rocco</u>

243. ROCKIN' CHAIR

November 2, 1941
Cat. no. 9202
Production company: RCM Productions, Los Angeles

Producer: Sam Coslow
Director: Josef Berne
Performers: <u>The Mills Brothers</u> (Donald Mills, Harry Mills, Herbert Mills, John H. Mills)

244. ROLL 'EM

April 3, 1944
Cat. no. 16008
Production company: Dave Gould Film Associates, Los Angeles
Producer-Director: Dave Gould
Performers: <u>Meade "Lux" Lewis</u>, <u>Dudley Dickerson</u>; Avanelle Harris [uncredited]; <u>Joe Turner</u> [soundtrack only]

245. ROMANCE WITHOUT FINANCE

December 31, 1945
Cat. no. 87508
Production company: Filmcraft Productions, New York
Producer-Director: William Forest Crouch
Performers: <u>Tiny Grimes and His Orchestra</u>

246. RUG CUTTERS HOLIDAY

March 1, 1943
Cat. no. 10704
Production company: L.O.L. Productions, New York
Executive producer: Samuel Oliphant
Producer-director: Arthur Leonard
Performers: <u>Freddie and Flo</u> (Fernando "Freddie" Robinson and Florence Brown), <u>Slap and Happy</u>, <u>Snap and Snappy</u>

247. SANDIN' JOE

September 10, 1945
Cat. no. 12M2
Production company: Filmcraft Productions, New York
Producer-Director: William Forest Crouch
Performers: <u>Dallas Bartley and His Orchestra</u>; Milton Woods, Rudy Tombs [uncredited]

248. SATCHEL MOUTH BABY

July 22, 1946
Cat. no. 21M4
Production company: RCM Productions, Los Angeles
Producer: Ben Hersh

Director: Dave Gould
Performers: <u>Dusty Brooks and His Four Tones</u>, <u>Mildred Boyd</u>

249. SCOTCH BOOGIE

September 10, 1945
Cat. no. 88508
Production company: Filmcraft Productions, New York
Producer-Director: William Forest Crouch
Performers: <u>Pat Flowers</u>

250. SHADRACH

October 27, 1941
Cat. no. 3903
Production company: Minoco Productions, New York
Executive Producer: Jack Barry
Producer: Fred Waller
Director: Robert Snody
Performers: <u>The Deep River Boys</u> (Harry Douglass, Vernon Gardner, George Lawson, Edward "Mumbles" Ware)

251. SHE'S CRAZY WITH THE HEAT

[Excerpted from the film *The International Sweethearts of Rhythm featuring Anna Mae Winburn*, 1946]
November 3, 1946
Cat. no. 25M1
Production company: An Alexander Production, New York
Producer: William D. Alexander
Director: Ray Sandiford
Performers: <u>Anna Mae Winburn</u>, <u>The International Sweethearts of Rhythm</u>

252. SHE'S TOO HOT TO HANDLE

September 25, 1944
Cat. no. 18208
Production company: Filmcraft Productions, New York
Producer-Director: William Forest Crouch
Performers: <u>Bob Howard</u>

253. SHINE

June 29, 1942
Cat. no. 7403
Production company: RCM Productions, Los Angeles

Producer: Sam Coslow
Director: Josef Berne
Performers: <u>Louis Armstrong and His Band</u>, <u>Nicodemus</u> (Nick Stewart)

254. SHINE
September 4, 1944
Cat. no. 18008
Production company: Filmcraft Productions, New York
Producer-Director: William Forest Crouch
Performers: <u>Bob Howard</u>

255. SHO HAD A WONDERFUL TIME
November 18, 1946
Cat. no. 25M3
Production company: Filmcraft Productions, New York
Producer-Director: William Forest Crouch
Performers: <u>Vanita Smythe</u>, <u>Claude DeMetrius</u> (aka Claude Demetrius, Claude Demtruis)

256. SHOESHINERS AND HEADLINERS
January 31, 1941
Cat. no. 201
Production company: Frederic Feher Productions, Los Angeles
Producer: Frederic Feher
Director: Unknown
Performers: Unidentified Black dancers [uncredited]; Florence Pepper [white]; unidentified white dancers [uncredited]

257. SHOOT THE RHYTHM TO ME
September 21, 1943
Cat. no. 4M3
Production company: WFC Productions, New York
Producer-Director: William Forest Crouch
Performers: <u>The Musical Madcaps</u>

258. SHOUT, BROTHER, SHOUT
September 16, 1946
Cat. no. 23M3
Production company: RCM Productions, Los Angeles
Producer: Ben Hersh
Director: Dave Gould
Performers: <u>Dusty Brooks and His Four Tones</u>

259. SHOUT! SISTER, SHOUT!
October 13, 1941
Cat. no. 3701
Production company: Minoco Productions, New York
Executive Producer: Jack Barry
Producer: Fred Waller
Director: Robert Snody
Performers: Sister Rosetta Tharpe (aka Sister Tharpe); Lucky Millinder and His Orchestra [credits unverified]

260. SIZZLE WITH SISSLE
December 9, 1946
Cat. no. 26M2
Production company: Filmcraft Productions, New York
Producer-Director: William Forest Crouch
Performers: Noble Sissle and His Orchestra, Mable Lee

261. THE SKUNK SONG
March 30, 1942
Cat. no. 6105
Production company: Minoco Productions, New York
Executive Producer: Jack Barry
Producer: Fred Waller
Director: Robert Snody
Performers: Cab Calloway and His Orchestra; The Cabaliers (aka the Palmer Brothers), Tyree Glenn [uncredited]

262. SLEEP KENTUCKY BABE
September 3, 1945
Cat. no. 21408
Production company: Filmcraft Productions, New York
Producer: William Forest Crouch
Director: Josef Berne
Performers: Day, Dawn, and Dusk (Robert Caver, Ed Coleman, Augustus "Gus" Simons)

263. SLEEPY TIME DOWN SOUTH
May 25, 1942
Cat. no. 6906
Production company: RCM Productions, Los Angeles
Producer: Sam Coslow
Director: Josef Berne

Performers: <u>Louis Armstrong and His Band</u>; Velma Middleton,
Nicodemus (Nick Stewart) [uncredited]

264. SNOQUALOMIE JO JO
June 4, 1945
Cat. no. 89008
Production company: Filmcraft Productions, New York
Producer: William Forest Crouch
Director: Josef Berne
Performers: <u>The Delta Rhythm Boys</u> (Traverse Crawford, Otho "Lee"
Gaines, Clinton Holland, Harry Lewis); Rene DeKnight [pianist;
uncredited]; Augustus "Gus" Simons [uncredited]

265. SOLID JIVE
August 19, 1946
Cat. no. 25201
Production company: Dave Gould Film Associates, Los Angeles
Producer-Director: Dave Gould
Performers: <u>Charles Whitty, Jr.</u>, <u>Ray Bauduc and His Band</u> [white]

266. SOME OF THESE DAYS
April 6, 1942
Cat. no. 6205
Production company: Minoco Productions, New York
Executive Producer: Jack Barry
Producer: Fred Waller
Director: John Primi
Performers: <u>Maxine Sullivan</u>

267. A SONG AND DANCE MAN
November 22, 1943
Cat. no. 14208
Production company: Soundies Films, Inc., New York
Producer-Director: William Forest Crouch
Performers: <u>Taps Miller</u> (Marion Joseph Miller); Claude DeMetrius
(aka Claude Demetrius, Claude Demetruis), Rosetta Davis, Jeanne Bayer
[uncredited]

268. SPIRIT OF BOOGIE WOOGIE
August 17, 1942
Cat. no. 8103

Production company: RCM Productions, Los Angeles
Producer: Sam Coslow
Director: Josef Berne
Performers: <u>Meade "Lux" Lewis</u>, <u>Katherine Dunham and Her Dancers</u>

269. STEAK AND POTATOES
November 27, 1944
Cat. no. 19008
Production company: RCM Productions, Los Angeles
Producer: Ben Hersh
Director: Dave Gould
Performers: <u>Mabel Scott</u>, <u>The Flennoy Trio</u> (Lorenzo Flennoy, Robert Lewis, Eugene Phillips)

270. STEPPING ALONG
November 8, 1943
Cat. no. 14108
Production company: Soundies Films, Inc., New York
Producer-Director: William Forest Crouch
Performers: <u>Evelyn Keyes</u>, <u>The Sepia Steppers</u> [including Alice Barker, uncredited]

271. SUGAR BABE
December 30, 1946
Cat. no. 27M4
Production company: Filmcraft Productions, New York
Producer-Director: William Forest Crouch
Performers: <u>Mable Lee</u>, <u>Noble Sissle and His Orchestra</u>

272. SUGAR HILL MASQUERADE
November 23, 1942
Cat. no. 9505
Production company: Minoco Productions, New York
Executive Producer: Jack Barry
Producer: Fred Waller
Director: Robert Snody
Performers: <u>Whitey's Lindy Hoppers</u>, <u>Walter Fuller and His Band</u> [film only]; Gene Krupa and His Band with Roy Eldridge [white, with the exception of Eldridge; soundtrack only, uncredited]; Alice Barker [uncredited]

273. SUN TAN STRUT
September 30, 1946
Cat. no. 24M1
Production company: Filmcraft Productions, New York
Producer-Director: William Forest Crouch
Performers: The Sun Tan Band, Hortence (aka Hortence Allen, Hortence "The Body" Allen); Nicky O'Daniel, Fritz Pollard [uncredited]

274. SWANEE SMILES
[Excerpted from the 1937 film *Rhythm Saves the Day*]
May 10, 1943
Cat. no. 11704
Production company: Skibo Productions, New York
Producer: E. W. Hammons
Director: Raymond Kane
Performers: The Cabin Kids (Ruth Hall, Helen Hall, James "Darling" Hall, Winifred "Sugar" Hall, Frederick Hall)

275. SWANEE SWING
July 10, 1944
Cat. no 17308
Production company: Filmcraft Productions, New York
Producer-Director: William Forest Crouch
Performers: LaVilla Tullos

276. SWEET KISSES
December 21, 1943
Cat. no. 7M5
Production company: WFC Productions, New York
Producer-Director: William Forest Crouch
Performers: Evelyn Keyes, The Mitchell Brothers, The Sepia Steppers

277. SWING CAT'S BALL
December 28, 1943
Cat. no. 14908
Production company: Soundies Films, Inc., New York
Producer-Director: William Forest Crouch
Performers: Evelyn Purvis, Rusti Sanford (aka Rusty Stanford)

278. SWING FOR SALE
August 11, 1941
Cat. no. 2802

Production company: Minoco Productions, New York
Executive Producer: Jack Barry
Producer: Fred Waller
Director: Robert Snody
Performers: The Charioteers; Vivian Brown, Hilda "Hibby" Brown [uncredited]

279. SWING FOR YOUR SUPPER
April 5, 1941
Cat. no. 1406
Production company: Cameo Productions, Los Angeles
Producer: Sam Coslow
Director: Josef Berne
Performers: Dorothy Dandridge, Cee Pee Johnson and His Orchestra

280. SWINGIN' IN THE GROOVE
October 22, 1945
Cat. no. 13M1
Production company: Filmcraft Productions, New York
Producer-Director: William Forest Crouch
Performers: Tiny Grimes and His Orchestra

281. SWINGIN' ON NOTHIN'
August 10, 1942
Cat. no. 8004
Production company: RCM Productions, Los Angeles
Producer: Sam Coslow
Director: Josef Berne
Performers: Louis Armstrong and His Band; Velma Middleton; George Washington

282. 'TAIN'T YOURS
August 7, 1944
Cat. no. 19608
Production company: Filmcraft Productions, New York
Producer-Director: William Forest Crouch
Performers: Una Mae Carlisle

283. TAKE EVERYTHING
April 23, 1945
Cat. no. 89408
Production company: Filmcraft Productions, New York

Producer-Director: William Forest Crouch
Performers: The Three Peppers (Bob Bell, Roy Branker, Walter Williams)

284. TAKE ME BACK, BABY
December 1, 1941
Cat. no. 4406
Production company: Minoco Productions, New York
Executive Producer: Jack Barry
Producer: Fred Waller
Director: Robert Snody
Performers: Count Basie and His Orchestra; Jimmy Rushing, Winnie
Johnson [uncredited]

285. TAKE THE 'A' TRAIN
October 20, 1941
Cat. no. 3803
Production company: Minoco Productions, New York
Executive Producer: Jack Barry
Producer: Fred Waller
Director: Robert Snody
Performers: The Delta Rhythm Boys (Traverse Crawford, Otho "Lee"
Gaines, Clinton Holland, Harry Lewis); Rene DeKnight [pianist;
uncredited]; Winnie Johnson [uncredited]

286. TAP HAPPY
December 13, 1943
Cat. no. 15208
Production company: Soundies Films, Inc., New York
Producer-Director: William Forest Crouch
Performers: Slim and Sweets (Luther Preston and Lucille Preston)

287. TEN THOUSAND YEARS AGO
May 28, 1945
Cat. no 20708
Production company: Filmcraft Productions, New York
Producer-Director: William Forest Crouch
Performers: The Jubalaires

288. T. G. BOOGIE WOOGIE
December 17, 1945
Cat. no. 87708

Production company: Filmcraft Productions, New York
Producer-Director: William Forest Crouch
Performers: Tiny Grimes and His Orchestra

289. THANKS FOR THE BOOGIE RIDE
February 9, 1942
Cat. no. 5407
Production company: Minoco Productions, New York
Producer: Fred Waller
Director: Robert Snody
Performers: Roy Eldridge, Anita O'Day [white], Gene Krupa and His Orchestra [white, with the exception of Eldridge]

290. THAT MAN OF MINE
[Excerpted from the film *The International Sweethearts of Rhythm featuring Anna Mae Winburn*, 1946]
September 23, 1946
Cat. no. 23M4
Production company: An Alexander Production, New York
Producer: William D. Alexander
Director: Ray Sandiford
Performers: Anna Mae Winburn, The International Sweethearts of Rhythm

291. THAT OL' GHOST TRAIN
June 1, 1942
Cat. no. 7006
Production company: Minoco Productions, New York
Executive Producer: Jack Barry
Producer: Fred Waller
Director: Robert Snody
Performers: Les Hite and His Orchestra

292. THERE ARE EIGHTY-EIGHT REASONS WHY
September 10, 1945
Cat. no. 88408
Production company: Filmcraft Productions, New York
Producer-Director: William Forest Crouch
Performers: Johnny and George (Johnny "Baby Face" Macklin, George MacLean)

293. THEY RAIDED THE JOINT
July 15, 1946
Cat. no. 21M3
Production company: Filmcraft Productions, New York
Producer-Director: William Forest Crouch
Performers: Vanita Smythe; Dan Burley [soundtrack only, uncredited]

294. TILL THEN
October 2, 1944
Cat. no. 18308
Production company: Filmcraft Productions, New York
Producer-Director: William Forest Crouch
Performers: The Mills Brothers (Donald Mills, Herbert Mills, John H.
Mills, Gene Smith)

295. TILLIE
July 23, 1945
Cat. no. 21108
Production company: An Adams Production, New York
Producer: Berle Adams
Director: William Forest Crouch
Performers: Louis Jordan and His Tympany Five

296. TIME TAKES CARE OF EVERYTHING
November 10, 1946
Cat. no. 25M2
Production company: Filmcraft Productions, New York
Producer-Director: William Forest Crouch
Performers: June Richmond

297. 'TIS YOU, BABE
September 10, 1945
Cat. no. 12M1
Production company: Filmcraft Productions, New York
Producer-Director: William Forest Crouch
Performers: Skeets Tolbert and His Orchestra

298. TOOT THAT TRUMPET!
December 22, 1941
Cat. no. 4703
Production company: Minoco Productions, New York
Executive Producer: Jack Barry

Producer: Fred Waller
Director: Robert Snody
Performers: The Deep River Boys (Harry Douglass, Vernon Gardner, George Lawson, Edward "Mumbles" Ware); Vivian Brown, Hilda "Hibby" Brown, Winnie Johnson [uncredited]

299. TOOT THAT TRUMPET
October 18, 1943
Cat. no. 13808
Production company: Soundies Films, Inc., New York
Producer-Director: William Forest Crouch
Performers: Francine Everett, Cook and Brown (Charles Cook and Ernest Brown); The Sepia Steppers, including Alice Barker [uncredited]

300. TUXEDO JUNCTION
December 31, 1942
Cat. no. 10206
Production company: Soundies Films, Inc., New York
Producer: William Forest Crouch
Director: John C. Graham
Performers: Edna Mae Harris, The Lenox Lindy Hoppers; Lillian Randolph [soundtrack only, uncredited]

301. TWAS LOVE
December 30, 1946
Cat. no. 27M1
Production company: Filmcraft Productions, New York
Producer-Director: William Forest Crouch
Performers: Noble Sissle and His Orchestra, Gwen Tynes

302. TWEED ME
December 31, 1942
Cat. no. 10107
Production company: RCM Productions, Los Angeles
Producer: Sam Coslow
Director: Josef Berne
Performers: The Chocolateers; John Kirby Sextet [soundtrack only, uncredited]

303. UNEXPECTED KISS
[Excerpted from the film *Love in Syncopation*, 1946]
Date unknown

Cat. no. unknown; possibly 29M2[4]
Production company: An Alexander Production, New York
Producer: William D. Alexander
Director: Leonard Anderson
Performers: <u>Henri Woode and His Orchestra</u>; Harrell Tillman [uncredited]

304. UNLUCKY WOMAN
[Excerpted from the film *Boogie Woogie Dream*, 1941]
December 31, 1944
Cat. no. 19208
Production company: B&W Film Shorts, Inc., New York
Producer: Mark Marvin
Director: Hans Burger
Performers: <u>Lena Horne</u>, <u>Teddy Wilson and His Orchestra</u>

305. VIRGINIA, GEORGIA AND CAROLINE
February 23, 1942
Cat. no. 5606
Production company: Minoco Productions, New York
Executive Producer: Jack Barry
Producer: Fred Waller
Director: Robert Snody
Performers: Cab Calloway and His Orchestra; The Cabaliers [aka the Palmer Brothers, uncredited]; Vivian Brown, Marion Egbert, Venna (aka Verna, Vearna) Smith [uncredited]

306. WALKING WITH MY HONEY
August 6, 1945
Cat. no. 21208
Production company: Filmcraft Productions, New York
Producer-Director: William Forest Crouch
Performers: <u>Cab Calloway and His Orchestra</u>, <u>Dotty Saulter</u>

307. THE WALLS KEEP TALKING
April 13, 1942
Cat. no. 6306
Production company: RCM Productions, Los Angeles
Producer: Sam Coslow
Director: George Cunningham

Performers: Artie Brandon, Paul White; Hal Borne and His Orchestra [white; soundtrack only, uncredited]

308. WE ARE AMERICANS TOO
October 29, 1943
Cat. no. 6M1
Production company: Soundies Films, Inc., New York
Producer-Director: William Forest Crouch
Performers: The Chanticleers

309. WE PITCHED A BOOGIE WOOGIE
March 18, 1946
Cat. no. 17M3
Production company: Filmcraft Productions, New York
Producer-Director: William Forest Crouch
Performers: Johni Weaver, Llewelyn Crawford (aka Lou Crawford), Dallas Bartley and His Orchestra [soundtrack only]

310. WE THE CATS SHALL HEP YA
December 10, 1945
Cat. no. 22108
Production company: Filmcraft Productions, New York
Producer-Director: William Forest Crouch
Performers: Cab Calloway and His Orchestra

311. WE'RE STEPPING OUT TONIGHT
September 10, 1945
Cat. no. 88308
Production company: Filmcraft Productions, New York
Executive Producer: William Forest Crouch
Director: Leonard Weiss
Performers: June Richmond

312. WHAM
September 13, 1943
Cat. no. 13308
Production company: Soundies Films, Inc., New York
Producer- Director: William Forest Crouch
Performers: The Four Ginger Snaps (Ruth Christian, Charles Ford, Ethel E. Harper, Leona Virginia Hemingway)

313. WHAT GOOD AM I WITHOUT YOU
December 23, 1946
Cat. no. unknown, possibly 26M4
Production company: Filmcraft Productions, New York
Producer-Director: William Forest Crouch
Performers: Vanita Smythe

314. WHAT TO DO
May 4, 1942
Cat. no. 6601
Production company: Minoco Productions, New York
Executive Producer: Jack Barry
Producer: Fred Waller
Director: Robert Snody
Performers: Savannah Churchill, Les Hite and His Orchestra

315. WHEN JOHNNY COMES MARCHING HOME
September 27, 1943
Cat. no. 13508
Production company: Soundies Films, Inc., New York
Producer- Director: William Forest Crouch
Performers: The Four Ginger Snaps (Ruth Christian, Charles Ford, Ethel
E. Harper, Leona Virginia Hemingway)

316. WHO DUNIT TO WHO
November 25, 1946
Cat. no. 25M4
Production company: Filmcraft Productions, New York
Producer-Director: William Forest Crouch
Performers: June Richmond

317. WHO THREW THE WHISKEY IN THE WELL?
December 30, 1945
Cat. no. 22308
Production company: Filmcraft Productions, New York
Producer-Director: William Forest Crouch
Performers: Phil Moore and the Phil Moore Four (Wallace Bishop, Doles
Dickens John Letman, Chuck Wayne [aka Charles Jagelka; white])

318. WHO'S BEEN EATING MY PORRIDGE?
March 30, 1944
Cat. no. 15808

Production company: RCM Productions, Los Angeles
Producer: Ben Hersh
Director: Josef Berne
Performers: Ida James, The King Cole Trio (Nat "King" Cole, Johnny Miller, Oscar Moore)

319. WILLIE WILLIE
February 1, 1943
Cat. no. 10406
Production company: L.O.L. Productions, New York
Executive producer: Samuel Oliphant
Producer-director: Arthur Leonard
Performers: Sam Manning, Belle Rosette (Beryl McBurnie)

320. WRITE THAT LETTER TONIGHT
June 4, 1945
Cat. no. 11M2
Production company: Filmcraft Productions, New York
Producer-Director: William Forest Crouch
Performers: Johnny and George (Johnny "Baby Face" Macklin, George MacLean)

321. YA FINE AND HEALTHY THING
September 10, 1945
Cat. no. 88608
Production company: Filmcraft Productions, New York
Producer-Director: William Forest Crouch
Performers: Dallas Bartley and His Orchestra

322. YANKEE DOODLE NEVER WENT TO TOWN
December 31, 1944
Cat. no. 89808
Production company: RCM Productions, Los Angeles
Producer: Ben Hersh
Director: Dave Gould
Performers: Mabel Scott, The Flennoy Trio (Lorenzo Flennoy, Robert Lewis, Eugene Phillips)

323. YES, INDEED!
November 24, 1941
Cat. no. 4304
Production company: RCM Productions, Los Angeles

Producer: Sam Coslow
Director: Dudley Murphy, Josef Berne
Performers: <u>Dorothy Dandridge</u>, <u>The Five Spirits of Rhythm</u>

324. YOU ALWAYS HURT THE ONE YOU LOVE
October 16, 1944
Cat. no. 18508
Production company: Filmcraft Productions, New York
Producer-Director: William Forest Crouch
Performers: <u>The Mills Brothers</u> (Donald Mills, Herbert Mills, John H. Mills, Gene Smith)

325. YOU CALL IT MADNESS
[Excerpted from the film *Rhythm in a Riff*, 1946]
December 30, 1946
Cat. no. 27703
Production company: An Alexander Production, New York
Producer: William D. Alexander
Director: Leonard Anderson
Performers: <u>Billy Eckstine and His Orchestra</u>

326. YOU CAN'T FOOL ABOUT LOVE
[Excerpted from the film *Mystery in Swing*, 1940]
September 21, 1943
Cat. no. 4M2
Production company: Aetna Films Corporation, Los Angeles
Producer: Jack Goldberg
Director: Arthur Dreifuss
Performers: <u>The Four Toppers</u>; <u>Josephine Edwards</u>, <u>Cee Pee Johnson and His Orchestra</u>

327. YOUR FEET'S TOO BIG
November 17, 1941
Cat. no. 4203
Production company: Minoco Productions, New York
Executive Producer: Jack Barry
Producer: Fred Waller
Director: Warren Murray
Performers: <u>Fats Waller</u>; His Rhythm (Al Casey, John Hamilton, Slick Jones, Gene Sedric, Cedric Wallace), Vivian Brown, Hilda "Hibby" Brown, Winnie Johnson, Mable Lee [uncredited]

328. YOUR FEET'S TOO BIG
May 6, 1946
Cat. no. 19M1
Production company: RCM Productions, Los Angeles
Producer: Ben Hersh
Director: Dave Gould
Performers: The Ali Baba Trio ("Big" Mike McKendrick, Cleveland
Nickerson, Calvin Ponder)

329. A ZOOT SUIT
March 9, 1942
Cat. no. 5801
Production company: RCM Productions, Los Angeles
Producer: Sam Coslow
Director: Josef Berne
Performers: Dorothy Dandridge, Paul White; Ted Fio Rito and His
Skylined Music [white; soundtrack only, uncredited]

APPENDIX 2:
PERFORMERS AND THEIR FILMS

Compiled by Susan Delson and Mark Cantor

Performers are listed as credited in their Soundies. Their original names, names they're also known by, and the names of individual musicians in groups appear in parentheses after their credited names.

Performers who did not receive screen credit for their appearances are listed as "uncredited." If more than one Soundie was made with the same title, the production company for that film is also listed.

Every effort has been made to ensure accuracy based on available data. Errors will be corrected in future editions.

Complete listings of performers, including musicians and uncredited actors, will be included in Mark Cantor's Music for the Eyes: Soundies and Jukebox Shorts of the 1940s, *scheduled for publication in 2022. The Soundies Book by Scott MacGillivray and Ted Okuda is also a valuable resource for information on films and performers.*

Lynn Albritton

Backstage Blues
Block Party Revels
Dispossessed Blues

The Ali Baba Trio *("Big" Mike McKendrick, Cleveland Nickerson, Calvin Ponder)*

E-Bob-O-Lee-Bop
If You Only Knew
Patience and Fortitude
Your Feet's Too Big [RCM Productions]

Annisteen Allen

I Want a Man

Cliff Allen

I Can't Dance
Rinka Tinka Man

Henry "Red" Allen

Count Me Out
Crawl Red Crawl
Drink Hearty
House on 52nd Street
Mop

Hortence Allen *(Hortence, Hortence "The Body" Allen)*

Rhythm in a Riff [uncredited]
Sun Tan Strut

Albert Ammons and Pete Johnson

Boogie Woogie Dream
My New Gown

Ivie Anderson

I Got It Bad and That Ain't Good

Apus and Estrellita *(Montrose Morse and Estrellita Bernier)*

I'm Tired
Knock Me Out

Louis Armstrong and His Band

I'll Be Glad When You're Dead You Rascal You
Shine [RCM Productions]
Sleepy Time Down South
Swingin' on Nothin'

Peggy Backus

Jackpot

Helen Bangs

Boogiemania

Alice Barker *[uncredited]*

Chatter
Jive Comes to the Jungle
Jungle Jamboree

Legs Ain't No Good
Stepping Along
Sugar Hill Masquerade
Toot That Trumpet [Soundies Films]

Dallas Bartley and His Orchestra

All Ruzzit Buzzit
Cryin' and Singin' the Blues
Sandin' Joe
We Pitched a Boogie Woogie
Ya Fine and Healthy Thing

Count Basie and His Orchestra

Air Mail Special
Take Me Back, Baby

Lucille Battle *(Lucy Battle)* *[uncredited]*

Caravan
Paper Doll

Talley Beatty

Flamingo

Billy and Ann

Block Party Revels
Poppin' the Cork

Leonard "Lennie" Bluett *[uncredited]*

Boogie Woogie
Low Down Dog

Mildred Boyd

Baby, Are You Kiddin'? [uncredited]
Satchel Mouth Baby

Smalls Boytins *[spelling unverified; uncredited]*

Dear Old Southland

Artie Brandon

The Walls Keep Talking

Dusty Brooks and His Four Tones

Am I Lucky
Baby, Are You Kiddin'?

Satchel Mouth Baby
Shout, Brother, Shout

Jess Brooks

Easy Street

LeRoy Broomfield

Close Shave

Dewey Brown

Here 'Tis Honey, Take It
Knock Me Out [uncredited]
Let's Get Down to Business

Ernest Brown *[See Charles Cook and Ernest Brown]*

George Washington Brown *(Uriel Porter)*

God's Heaven
Keep Waitin'

Hilda "Hibby" Brown *[uncredited]*

Ain't Misbehavin'
Booglie Wooglie Piggy
The Darktown Strutters' Ball
Dear Old Southland
Fats Waller Medley
Hark! Hark! The Lark
Honeysuckle Rose
The Joint is Jumpin'
Oh, Susannah
Swing for Sale
Toot That Trumpet! [Minoco Productions]
Your Feet's Too Big [Minoco Productions]

Vivian Brown *[uncredited]*

Ain't Misbehavin'
Booglie Wooglie Piggy
The Darktown Strutters' Ball
Dear Old Southland
Fats Waller Medley
Hark! Hark! The Lark
Honeysuckle Rose

The Joint is Jumpin'
Oh, Susannah
Swing for Sale
Toot That Trumpet! [Minoco Productions]
Virginia, Georgia and Caroline
Your Feet's Too Big [Minoco Productions]

Marie Bryant

Big Fat Butterfly [uncredited]
Bli-Blip
Juke Box Boogie [uncredited]

Pauline Bryant

Jungle Jamboree

Dan Burley *[uncredited]*

Back Door Man [soundtrack only]
Does You Do, or Does You Don't [soundtrack only]
They Raided the Joint [soundtrack only]

Dan Burley Trio *(Dan Burley, Carl Lynch, Ivan "Loco" Rolle)*

Low, Short and Squatty [uncredited]

The Bye Trio

Get With It

The Cabaliers *(The Palmer Brothers)*

The Skunk Song
Virginia, Georgia and Caroline

The Cabin Kids *(Ruth Hall, Helen Hall, James "Darling" Hall, Winifred "Sugar" Hall, Frederick Hall)*

Swanee Smiles

Cab Calloway and His Orchestra

Blowtop Blues
Blues in the Night
Cab Calloway Medley
Foo, A Little Ballyhoo
I Was Here When You Left Me
Minnie the Moocher
The Skunk Song
Virginia, Georgia and Caroline

Walking With My Honey
We the Cats Shall Hep Ya

Una Mae Carlisle

I Like It 'Cause I Love It
I'm a Good, Good Woman
'Tain't Yours

Judy Carroll

Jim

Benny Carter and His Orchestra *[uncredited]*

Case O' The Blues

Lupe Carterio

Corn Pone

The Chanticleers

Ain't My Sugar Sweet
Babbling Bess
If You Treat Me to a Hug
Jumpin' Jack from Hackensack
Lovin' Up a Solid Breeze
We Are Americans Too

The Charioteers

The Darktown Strutters' Ball
Oh, Susannah
Ride, Red, Ride
Swing for Sale

The Chocolateers

Harlem Rhumba
Peckin'
Tweed Me

Savannah Churchill

The Devil Sat Down and Cried
What To Do

The King Cole Trio *(Nat "King" Cole, Johnny Miller, Oscar Moore)*

Come to Baby Do
Errand Boy for Rhythm

Frim Fram Sauce
Got a Penny Benny
I'm a Shy Guy
Is You Is or Is You Ain't My Baby?
Who's Been Eating My Porridge?

Janet Collins

Flamingo

Cook and Brown *(Charles Cook, Ernest Brown)*

Chatter
Jungle Jamboree
Toot That Trumpet [Soundies Films]

The Counts and the Countess *(Alma Smith, John Faire, Curtis Wilder)*

Five Salted Peanuts
I've Got to Be a Rug-Cutter
Oh-H-E-E, My, My

Lou Crawford *(Llewelyn Crawford, aka Lou Ellen)*

Backstage Blues
We Pitched a Boogie Woogie

Dorothy Dandridge

Blackbird Fantasy
Congo Clambake
Cow Cow Boogie
Easy Street
Jungle Jig
Lazybones
Paper Doll
Swing for Your Supper
Yes, Indeed!
A Zoot Suit

Vivian Dandridge *[uncredited]*

I've Got a Little List

Day, Dawn, and Dusk *(Robert Caver, Ed Coleman, Augustus "Gus" Simons)*

Fare Thee Well
Faust

Rigoletto
Sleep Kentucky Babe
Snoqualomie Jo Jo [Augustus "Gus" Simons only; uncredited]

The Deep River Boys *(Harry Douglass, Vernon Gardner, George Lawson, Edward "Mumbles" Ware)*

Booglie Wooglie Piggy
Hark! Hark! The Lark
Shadrach
Toot That Trumpet! [Minoco Productions]

The Delta Rhythm Boys *(Traverse Crawford, Otho "Lee" Gaines, Clinton Holland, Harry Lewis; Rene DeKnight, pianist)*[1]

Dry Bones
Give Me Some Skin
I Dreamt I Dwelt in Harlem
Jack, You're Playing the Game
Just A-Sittin' and A-Rockin'
Rigoletto Blues
Snoqualomie Jo Jo
Take the 'A' Train

Claude DeMetrius *(aka Claude Demetrius, Claude Demetruis)*

Everyday is Saturday in Harlem [uncredited]
Get It Off Your Mind
Hey! Tojo, Count Yo' Men [uncredited]
I Can't Give You Anything But Love [uncredited]
Joseph 'n His Brudders [uncredited]
Mr. Jackson from Jacksonville [uncredited]
Sho Had A Wonderful Time
A Song And Dance Man [uncredited]

Dudley Dickerson

Boogie Woogie
Cow Cow Boogie [uncredited]
Low Down Dog
The Outskirts of Town
Roll 'Em

The Dreamers *(aka The Jones Boys)*

Bundle of Love

Katherine Dunham and Her Dancers

Cuban Episode
Spirit of Boogie Woogie

The Ebonettes

Coalmine Boogie [credit unverified]

Billy Eckstine and His Orchestra

I Cried for You
I Want to Talk About You
Lonesome Lover Blues
Prisoner of Love
Rhythm in a Riff
You Call It Madness

Josephine Edwards

You Can't Fool About Love

Marion Egbert *[uncredited]*

Virginia, Georgia and Caroline

Roy Eldridge

Let Me Off Uptown
Sugar Hill Masquerade [soundtrack only; uncredited]
Thanks for the Boogie Ride

Lou Ellen *[see Lou Crawford]*

Duke Ellington and His Orchestra

Bli-Blip [soundtrack only]
Flamingo
Hot Chocolate ("Cottontail")
I Got It Bad and That Ain't Good
Jam Session

Estrellita *[See Apus and Estrellita]*

Warren Evans

Baby Don't You Cry
Don't Be Late
I Miss You So
I'm Making Believe
Let's Beat Out Some Love

Francine Everett

Ain't My Sugar Sweet [uncredited]
Babbling Bess [uncredited]
If You Treat Me to a Hug [uncredited]
Toot That Trumpet [Soundies Films]

The Five Spirits of Rhythm

Alabamy Bound
Easy Street
Yes, Indeed!

The Flennoy Trio (*Lorenzo Flennoy, Robert Lewis, Eugene Phillips*)

Gee
Steak and Potatoes
Yankee Doodle Never Went to Town

Pat Flowers

Coalmine Boogie
Dixie Rhythm
Scotch Boogie

The Four Ginger Snaps

Keep Smiling
Wham
When Johnny Comes Marching Home

The Four Knobs [*See also The Six Knobs*]

Dispossessed Blues

The Four Toppers

Jump In
Let's Go
You Can't Fool About Love

Louise Franklin [*uncredited*]

I Got It Bad And That Ain't Good
Jam Session

Freddie and Flo (*Fernando Robinson and Florence Brown*)

Rug Cutters' Holiday

Walter Fuller and His Band

Sugar Hill Masquerade [film only]

Deanie Gordon *[uncredited]*

The Darktown Strutters' Ball

Aurora Greeley

Close Shave

Bea Griffith

Ain't My Sugar Sweet [uncredited]
Cielito Lindo

Chinky Grimes

Emily Brown

Tiny Grimes and His Orchestra

Joseph 'n His Brudders [soundtrack only; uncredited]
Never Too Old To Swing
Romance Without Finance
Swingin' in the Groove
T. G. Boogie

Tosh Hammed and Company

Dance Your Old Age Away

The Harlem Cuties

Backstage Blues
Block Party Revels

The Harlem Honeys

Foolin' Around
Jackpot
Melody Takes a Holiday
Quick Watson, the Rhythm
Rhythmania

The Harlem Queens

Harlem Hotcha [Filmcraft Productions]

Harris and Hunt

Rhythmania
Foolin' Around

Avanelle Harris *[uncredited]*

Boogie Woogie
Low Down Dog

Paper Doll
Roll 'Em

Edna Mae Harris

Block Party Revels [uncredited]
Harlem Serenade [uncredited]
I Gotta Go to Camp and See My Man
Jive Comes to the Jungle [identified in catalogue as Edna Mae Jones]
Legs Ain't No Good
Tuxedo Junction

Roberta Harris

Harem Revels

Theresa Harris

The Outskirts of Town

Erskine Hawkins and His Jive Sepia Scorchers

Hot in the Groove

Billie Haywood

I Can't Dance
Rinka Tinka Man

J. C. Higginbotham

Count Me Out
Crawl Red Crawl
Drink Hearty
House on 52nd Street
Mop

Ruby Hill

Put Your Arms Around Me Honey

Les Hite and His Orchestra

The Devil Sat Down and Cried
Pudgy Boy
That Ol' Ghost Train
What to Do

His Rhythm (*Al Casey, John Hamilton, Slick Jones, Gene Sedric, Cedric Wallace*) [*uncredited*]

Ain't Misbehavin'
Fats Waller Medley

Honeysuckle Rose
The Joint Is Jumpin'
Your Feet's Too Big [Minoco Productions]

John Shadrack Horance

Along the Navajo Trail
It's Me, Oh Lord

Lena Horne

Boogie Woogie Dream
My New Gown
Unlucky Woman

"Hot-Cha" *[uncredited]*

Good-Nite All

Bob Howard

Dinah
Hey! Tojo, Count Yo' Men
She's Too Hot to Handle
Shine [Filmcraft Productions]

International Sweethearts of Rhythm with Anna Mae Winburn

Jump Children
She's Crazy with the Heat
That Man of Mine

Benjamin Clarence "Bull Moose" Jackson

Big Fat Mamas [credit unverified]

Eugene "Pineapple" Jackson *[uncredited]*

Cow Cow Boogie

"Shorty" Jackson *[uncredited]*

Low, Short and Squatty

Ida James

Can't See for Lookin'
His Rockin' Horse Ran Away
Is You Is or Is You Ain't My Baby
Who's been Eating My Porridge?

Herb Jeffries

Flamingo

Johnny and George *(Johnny "Baby Face" Macklin, George MacLean)*

> I Had a Dream
> There Are Eighty-Eight Reasons Why
> Write That Letter Tonight

Cee Pee Johnson and His Orchestra

> Jump In
> Jungle Jig
> Let's Go
> Swing for Your Supper
> You Can't Fool About Love

Myra Johnson

> Ain't Misbehavin' [soundtrack only; uncredited]
> Here 'Tis Honey, Take It
> The Joint is Jumpin'
> Let's Get Down to Business
> Quick Watson, the Rhythm

Pete Johnson *[See Albert Ammons and Pete Johnson]*

Robert (Bobby) Johnson *[uncredited]*

> Dear Old Southland

Shirley Johnson

> Frim Fram Sauce

Winnie Johnson *[uncredited]*

> Ain't Misbehavin' [Minoco Productions]
> Booglie Wooglie Piggy
> Hark! Hark! The Lark
> Honeysuckle Rose
> The Joint Is Jumpin'
> Rigoletto Blues
> Take Me Back, Baby
> Take the 'A' Train
> Toot That Trumpet! [Minoco Productions]
> Your Feet's Too Big [Minoco Productions]

Albert Reese Jones

> Boogiemania

The Jones Boys *[See The Dreamers]*

Louis Jordan and His Band

Down, Down, Down
Five Guys Named Moe
Fuzzy Wuzzy
GI Jive
Jumpin' at the Jubilee
Old Man Mose
The Outskirts of Town [soundtrack only; uncredited]

Louis Jordan and His Orchestra

Ration Blues
Jordan Jive

Louis Jordan and His Tympany Five

Buzz Me
Caldonia
Honey Chile
If You Can't Smile and Say Yes
Jordan Medley #1
Jordan Medley #2
Knock Me Out [soundtrack only; uncredited]
Tillie

Roxie Joynes *[uncredited]*

Caldonia

The Jubalaires

Brother Bill
Noah
Old Dan Tucker
The Preacher and the Bear
Ten Thousand Years Ago

Laverne Keane *[uncredited]*

Ain't My Sugar Sweet
If You Treat Me to a Hug

Evelyn Keyes

Stepping Along
Sweet Kisses

John Kirby Sextet

  Close Shave [soundtrack only; uncredited]
  Tweed Me [soundtrack only; uncredited]

Mable Lee

  Ain't Misbehavin' [uncredited]
  Babbling Bess [uncredited]
  Baby Don't Go 'Way from Me
  Beat Me Daddy [uncredited]
  Cats Can't Dance
  Chicken Shack Shuffle
  Coalmine Boogie
  Dancemania
  Everybody's Jumpin' Now
  Foolin' Around
  Half Past Jump Time
  Honeysuckle Rose [uncredited]
  The Joint Is Jumpin' [uncredited]
  Pigmeat Throws the Bull
  Rhythmania
  Sizzle with Sissle
  Sugar Babe
  Your Feet's Too Big [Minoco Productions; uncredited]

The Lenox Lindy Hoppers

  Tuxedo Junction

The Lennox Trio (*Carl Lynch, Ivan Rolle, pianist unidentified*)

  Rhythm Sam

Jackie Lewis *[uncredited]*

  The Darktown Strutters' Ball

Meade "Lux" Lewis

  Boogie Woogie
  Low Down Dog
  Roll 'Em
  Spirit of Boogie Woogie

The Little Four Quartet

  Cha-Chi Man
  Chilly 'n Cold
  Love Grows on a White Oak Tree

Lawrence Lucie *[uncredited]*

I'll Be Glad When You're Dead You Rascal You

Sam Manning

Quarry Road
Willie Willie

Dewey "Pigmeat" Markham

Pigmeat Throws the Bull

Tweedie Mason *[uncredited]*

The Darktown Strutters' Ball

Beryl McBurnie *[See Belle Rosette]*

Mabel Mercer

A Harlemesque Revue

Velma Middleton

I'll Be Glad When You're Dead You Rascal You [uncredited]
Sleepy Time Down South [uncredited]
Swingin' on Nothin'

Taps Miller *(Marion Joseph Miller)*

A Song and Dance Man

Lucky Millinder and His Orchestra

Because I Love You
Big Fat Mamas
Four or Five Times
Harlem Serenade
Hello Bill
I Wasn't a Big Fat Mama
I Want a Man
The Lonesome Road
Shout! Sister, Shout!

The Mills Brothers *(Donald Mills; Harry Mills, Herbert Mills, John H. Mills, Gene Smith[2])*

Caravan
Cielito Lindo
Lazy River [Filmcraft Productions]
Paper Doll
Rockin' Chair

Till Then
You Always Hurt the One You Love

Roy Milton and His Band

47th Street Jive
Hey, Lawdy Mama
Ride On, Ride On

Billy Mitchell

Blackbird Fantasy
I've Got a Little List

The Mitchell Brothers

Sweet Kisses

Millie Monroe [*uncredited*]

I Got It Bad and That Ain't Good
Jam Session

Johnny Moore's 3 Blazers

Along the Navajo Trail
It's Me, Oh Lord

Juanita Moore [*uncredited*]

Paper Doll

Merrita Moore and Her Dancing Darlings

Dance Revels

Phil Moore and the Phil Moore Four (*Wallace Bishop, Doles Dickens, John Letman, Chuck Wayne [aka Charles Jagelka; white]*)

The Chair Song
I Want a Little Doggie
Lazy Lady
Who Threw the Whiskey in the Well?

Ernie Morris [*uncredited*]

Bugle Call Rag

The Musical Madcaps

Hit That Jive, Jack
Linda Brown
Rhythm Mad

Rhythm of the Rhythm Band
Shoot the Rhythm to Me

Nicodemus *(Nick Stewart)*

Shine [RCN Productions]
Sleepy Time Down South [uncredited]

Florence O'Brien *[uncredited]*

I've Got a Little List

Nicky O'Daniel

Dancemania
Harlem Hotcha [WFC Productions]
The Pollard Jump
Sun Tan Strut

Bob Parrish

Emily Brown

Patterson and Jackson *(Warren Patterson, Al Jackson)*

Do I Worry?
Git It
Mama, I Wanna Make Rhythm

Lincoln Perry *[See Stepin Fetchit]*

Frederick Douglass "Fritz" Pollard *[uncredited]*

Boogiemania
Sun Tan Strut

Julius Puillys *[uncredited]*

Dear Old Southland

Ferrabee Purnell

Harem Revels

Evelyn Purvis

Swing Cat's Ball

Pat Rainey

Joe, Joe

Peter Ray

Lazybones

Ruby Richards *[uncredited]*

Fuzzy Wuzzy

June Richmond

Baby Don't You Love Me Anymore
47th Street Jive
Hey, Lawdy Mama
Joseph 'n His Brudders
Mr. Jackson from Jacksonville
My Bottle Is Dry
Ride On, Ride On
Time Takes Care of Everything
We're Stepping Out Tonight
Who Dunit to Who

Robinson and Hill

Contrast in Rhythm

Bill Robinson

By an Old Southern River
Let's Scuffle

Maurice Rocco

Beat Me Daddy
Rhumboogie
Rocco Blues
Rock It for Me

Gene Rodgers and the Vs *(Lady Will Carr, Willie Lee Floyd, Ivy Ann Glasko, Ivern Whittaker)*

Big Fat Butterfly
Juke Box Boogie
My, My, Ain't That Somethin'

Hilda Rogers

Every Day Is Saturday in Harlem
I Can't Give You Anything But Love
Rhapsody of Love

Belle Rosette *(Beryl McBurnie)*

Quarry Road
Willie Willie

Jimmy Rushing *[uncredited]*

Air Mail Special
Take Me Back, Baby

Derrick Sampson and His Band *(Deryck Sampson and His Band)*

Baby, Don't Go 'Way From Me
Cats Can't Dance [uncredited]
Half Past Jump Time [uncredited]

Rusti Sanford *(aka Rusty Stanford, Rusti Stanford)*

Foo, A Little Ballyhoo
Harem Revels
Swing Cat's Ball

Dotty Saulter *(Dorothy Saulter)*

I Was Here When You Left Me
Walking With My Honey

Cecil Scott and His Orchestra

Contrast in Rhythm
Don't Be Late
Harlem Hotcha [Filmcraft Productions; soundtrack only]
I'm Making Believe
Mr. X Blues

Mabel Scott

Gee
Steak and Potatoes
Yankee Doodle Never Went to Town

The Sepia Steppers

Chatter
Poppin' the Cork
Stepping Along
Sweet Kisses
Toot That Trumpet [Soundies Films]

The Shadrach Boys

Jonah and the Whale
Lazy River [RCM Productions]

Shim Sham *(aka Shim Sham Sam)*

Dancemania

Noble Sissle and His Orchestra

Everybody's Jumpin' Now
Joe, Joe
Sizzle with Sissle
Sugar Babe
Twas Love

The Six Knobs *[See also The Four Knobs]*

Block Party Revels

Slap and Happy

Rug Cutters Holiday

Slim and Sweets

Tap Happy

Mamie Smith

Because I Love You

Venna Smith *(aka Verna Smith, Vearna Smith)* *[uncredited]*

Virginia, Georgia and Caroline

Ella Bessie Smook *[uncredited]*

Dear Old Southland

Vanita Smythe

Back Door Man
Does You Do or Does You Don't
Get It Off Your Mind
I Need a Playmate
Low, Short and Squatty
Sho Had a Wonderful Time
They Raided the Joint
What Good Am I Without You

Snap and Snappy

Rug Cutters Holiday

Valaida Snow

If You Only Knew
Patience and Fortitude

Nick Stewart *[See Nicodemus]*

Maxine Sullivan

Case o' the Blues
Some of These Days

The Sun Tan Band

Sun Tan Strut

The Sun Tan Four *[including Fritz Pollard]*

Boogiemania
Dancemania
Harlem Hotcha [WFC Productions]
The Pollard Jump

The Swing Maniacs

Jordan Jive
Jumpin' at the Jubilee

Johnny Taylor

Good-Nite All

Sister Tharpe *(Sister Rosetta Tharpe)*

Four or Five Times
The Lonesome Road
Shout! Sister, Shout!

Slim and Sweets

Tap Happy

Slim Thomas

Jive Comes to the Jungle
Legs Ain't No Good

Tommy Thompson

Jumpin' Jack from Hackensack

Stepin Fetchit *(Lincoln Perry)*

Baby Don't Go 'Way from Me
Broadway and Main

The Three Chefs *(Benny "Smiley" Johnson, George "Smiley" McDaniel, Sammy Warren)*

Breakfast in Rhythm
Pardon Me, But You Look Just Like Margie

The Three Peppers *(Bob Bell, Roy Branker, Walter Williams)*

Ain't She Pretty
Mary Had a Little Lamb
Rhythm Sam
Take Everything

Harrell Tillman

Adventure
Unexpected Kiss [uncredited]

Skeets Tolbert and His Orchestra

Blitzkrieg Bombardier
Corn Pone
No, No, Baby
'Tis You, Babe

Tops & Wilder *(Thomas "Tops" Lee, Wilda Crawford)*

Broadway [credit unverified]
Harlem Hotcha [WFC Productions]
Mistletoe
Prancing in the Park

LaVilla Tullos

Swanee Swing

Joe Turner *(aka Big Joe Turner)*

Lowdown Dog [soundtrack only]
Roll 'Em [soundtrack only]

Harry Turner

Count Me Out
Harlem Hotcha [WFC Productions]

Gwen Tynes

Twas Love

The Vs *[See Gene Rodgers and the Vs]*

Virgil Van Cleve

Put Your Arms Around Me Honey

Fats Waller

Ain't Misbehavin'
Fats Waller Medley
Honeysuckle Rose
The Joint Is Jumpin'
Your Feet's Too Big [Minoco Productions]

Johni Weaver

Count Me Out
Crawl Red Crawl
We Pitched a Boogie Woogie

Paul White

Bli-Blip
The Walls Keep Talking
A Zoot Suit

Whitey's Lindy Hoppers

Airmail Special [uncredited]
Hot Chocolate ("Cottontail")
The Outline of Jitterbug History
Sugar Hill Masquerade

Charles Whitty Jr.

Solid Jive

Frank Wilcox *[uncredited]*

I Don't Want to Walk Without You

Teddy Wilson and His Orchestra

Unlucky Woman

Anna Mae Winburn *[See International Sweethearts of Rhythm]*

Henri Woode and His Orchestra

Adventure
Broadway

Mistletoe
Unexpected Kiss

Ze Zulettes

Jive Comes to the Jungle

[Unknown]

I Won't Miss You [credits unverifiable]

APPENDIX 3:
MAKERS AND THEIR FILMS

Compiled by SUSAN DELSON and MARK CANTOR

Filmmakers' roles in their productions are indicated in brackets after their names. If more than one Soundie was made with the same title, the production company for that film is also listed.

Detailed listings of production personnel for each film are included in Mark Cantor's Music for the Eyes: Soundies and Jukebox Shorts of the 1940s, *scheduled for publication in 2022.*

Every effort has been made to ensure accuracy based on available data. Errors will be corrected in future editions.

Berle Adams *[producer]*

Buzz Me
Caldonia
Honey Chile
Tillie

William D. Alexander *[producer]*

Adventure
Big Fat Mamas
Broadway
Hello Bill
I Cried for You
I Want a Man
I Want to Talk About You
Jump Children
Lonesome Lover Blues

Mistletoe
Prisoner of Love
Rhythm in a Riff
She's Crazy with the Heat
That Man of Mine
Unexpected Kiss
You Call It Madness

Leonard Anderson [*director*]

Adventure
Broadway
I Cried for You
I Want to Talk About You
Lonesome Lover Blues
Mistletoe
Prisoner of Love
Rhythm in a Riff
Unexpected Kiss
You Call It Madness

Jack Barry [*executive producer; producer as noted*]

Ain't Misbehavin'
Air Mail Special
Blues in the Night
Booglie Wooglie Piggy
By an Old Southern River
Cab Calloway Medley
The Darktown Strutters Ball
The Devil Sat Down and Cried
Four or Five Times [producer]
I Don't Want to Walk Without You [producer]
I Dreamt I Dwelt in Harlem [producer]
I Want a Big Fat Mama [producer]
Jack, You're Playing the Game
Jive Comes to the Jungle [producer]
Legs Ain't No Good
Let's Scuffle
The Lonesome Road
Minnie the Moocher
Oh, Susannah
Pudgy Boy

Ride, Red, Ride
Rigoletto Blues
Shadrach
Shout! Sister, Shout!
The Skunk Song
Some of These Days
Sugar Hill Masquerade
Swing for Sale
Take Me Back, Baby
Take the 'A' Train
That Ol' Ghost Train
Toot That Trumpet! [Minoco Productions]
Virginia, Georgia and Caroline
What to Do
Your Feet's Too Big [Minoco Productions]

Josef Berne *[director]*

Along the Navajo Trail
Bli-Blip
Caravan
Case o' the Blues
Close Shave
Congo Clambake
Cow Cow Boogie
Cuban Episode
Dry Bones
Fare Thee Well
Faust
Five Salted Peanuts
Flamingo
47th Street Jive
Harlem Rhumba
Hey Lawdy Mama
His Rockin' Horse Ran Away
Hot Chocolate ("Cottontail")
I Can't Dance
I Got It Bad and That Ain't Good
I'll Be Glad When You're Dead You Rascal You
Is You Is or Is You Ain't My Baby
It's Me, Oh Lord
I've Got to Be a Rug Cutter

Jam Session
Jonah and the Whale
Jungle Jig
Lazy River [RCM Productions]
Oh-H-E-E, My, My
The Outline of Jitterbug History
The Outskirts of Town
Paper Doll
Peckin'
Ride On, Ride On
Rigoletto
Rinka Tinka Man
Rockin' Chair
Shine [RCM Productions]
Sleep Kentucky Babe
Sleepy Time Down South
Snoqualomie Jo Jo
Spirit of Boogie Woogie
Swing for Your Supper
Swingin' on Nothin'
Tweed Me
Who's Been Eating My Porridge?
Yes, Indeed! [codirected with Dudley Murphy]
A Zoot Suit

Clarence Bricker *[director]*

Breakfast in Rhythm
Pardon Me, But You Look Just Like Margie

Hans Burger *[director]*

Boogie Woogie Dream
My New Gown
Unlucky Woman

John Paddy Carstairs *[director]*

God's Heaven
Keep Waitin'

Albert Cornfield *[producer]*

God's Heaven
Keep Waitin'

Sam Coslow *[producer]*

Alabamy Bound
Blackbird Fantasy
Bli-Blip
Caravan
Case o' the Blues
Close Shave
Congo Clambake
Cow Cow Boogie
Cuban Episode
Easy Street
Flamingo
Harlem Rhumba
His Rockin' Horse Ran Away
Hot Chocolate ("Cottontail")
I Got It Bad and That Ain't Good
I'll Be Glad When You're Dead You Rascal You
I've Got a Little List
Jam Session
Jim
Jungle Jig
Lazybones
The Outline of Jitterbug History
The Outskirts of Town
Paper Doll
Peckin'
Rockin' Chair
Shine [RCM Productions]
Sleepy Time Down South
Spirit of Boogie Woogie
Swing for Your Supper
Swingin' on Nothin'
Tweed Me
The Walls Keep Talking
Yes, Indeed!
A Zoot Suit

William Forest Crouch *[producer-director; producer and director as noted]*

Ain't My Sugar Sweet
Ain't She Pretty

All Ruzzit Buzzit
Babbling Bess
Baby Don't Go 'Way from Me
Baby, Don't You Cry
Baby, Don't You Love Me Anymore
Back Door Man
Backstage Blues
Beat Me Daddy
Blitzkrieg Bombardier
Block Party Revels
Blowtop Blues
Boogiemania
Broadway and Main
Brother Bill
Buzz Me [director]
Caldonia [director]
Can't See for Lookin'
Cats Can't Dance
Cha-Chi Man
The Chair Song
Chatter
Chicken Shack Shuffle
Chilly 'n Cold
Cielito Lindo
Coalmine Boogie
Come to Baby Do
Contrast in Rhythm
Corn Pone
Count Me Out
Crawl Red Crawl
Cryin' and Singin' the Blues
Dance Revels
Dance Your Old Age Away
Dancemania
Dinah
Dispossessed Blues
Dixie Rhythm
Do I Worry?
Does You Do or Does You Don't
Don't Be Late
Down, Down, Down [producer]

Drink Hearty
Dry Bones [producer]
Errand Boy for Rhythm
Every Day is Saturday in Harlem
Everybody's Jumpin' Now
Fare Thee Well [producer]
Faust [producer]
Five Guys Named Moe [producer]
Foo, A Little Ballyhoo
Foolin' Around
Frim Fram Sauce
Fuzzy Wuzzy [producer]
G.I. Jive
Get It Off Your Mind
Get with It
Git It
Got a Penny Benny
Half Past Jump Time
Harem Revels
Harlem Hotcha [1943 + 1946]
Here 'Tis Honey, Take It
Hey! Tojo, Count Yo' Men
Hit That Jive Jack
Honey Chile [director]
House on 52nd Street
I Can't Give You Anything But Love
I Gotta Go to Camp to See My Man
I Had a Dream
I Like It 'Cause I Love It
I Miss You So
I Need a Playmate
I Want a Little Doggie
I Was Here When You Left Me
If You Can't Smile and Say Yes
If You Treat Me to a Hug
I'm a Good, Good Woman
I'm a Shy Guy
I'm Making Believe
I'm Tired
Jackpot
Joe, Joe

Jordan Jive
Joseph 'n His Brudders [executive producer]
Jumpin' at the Jubilee
Jumpin' Jack from Hackensack
Jungle Jamboree
Just A-Sittin' and A-Rockin'
Keep Smiling
Knock Me Out
Lazy Lady
Lazy River [Filmcraft Productions]
Let's Beat Out Some Love
Let's Get Down to Business
Linda Brown
Love Grows on a White Oak Tree
Lovin' Up a Solid Breeze
Low, Short and Squatty
Mama, I Wanna Make Rhythm
Mary Had a Little Lamb
Melody Takes a Holiday
Mop
Mr. Jackson from Jacksonville [producer]
Mr. X. Blues
My Bottle Is Dry
Never Too Old to Swing
No, No, Baby
Noah
Old Dan Tucker
Old Man Mose [producer]
Pigmeat Throws the Bull
The Pollard Jump
Poppin' the Cork
Prancing in the Park
The Preacher and the Bear
Put Your Arms Around Me Honey
Quick Watson, the Rhythm
Ration Blues
Rhapsody of Love
Rhumboogie
Rhythm Mad
Rhythm of the Rhythm Band
Rhythm Sam

Rhythmania
Rigoletto [producer]
Rocco Blues
Rock It for Me
Romance Without Finance
Sandin' Joe
Scotch Boogie
She's Too Hot to Handle
Shine [Filmcraft Productions]
Sho Had a Wonderful Time
Shoot the Rhythm to Me
Sizzle with Sissle
Sleep Kentucky Babe [producer]
Snoqualomie Jo Jo [producer]
A Song and Dance Man
Stepping Along
Sugar Babe
Sun Tan Strut
Swanee Swing
Sweet Kisses
Swing Cat's Ball
Swingin' in the Groove
'Tain't Yours
Take Everything
Tap Happy
Ten Thousand Years Ago
T. G. Boogie Woogie
There Are Eighty-Eight Reasons Why
They Raided the Joint
Till Then
Tillie [director]
Time Takes Care of Everything
'Tis You Babe
Toot That Trumpet [Soundies Films]
Tuxedo Junction [producer]
Twas Love
Walking with My Honey
We Are Americans Too
We Pitched a Boogie Woogie
We the Cats Shall Hep Ya
We're Stepping Out Tonight [executive producer]

Wham
What Good Am I Without You
When Johnny Comes Marching Home
Who Dunit to Who
Who Threw the Whiskey in the Well?
Write That Letter Tonight
Ya Fine and Healthy Thing
You Always Hurt the One You Love

George Cunningham *[director]*

The Walls Keep Talking

Arthur Dreifuss *[director]*

Jump In
Let's Go
You Can't Fool About Love

Frederick Feher *[producer]*

Shoeshiners and Headliners

Emanuel M. Glucksman *[producer]*

All American Newsreel #1 [unverified]
All American Newsreel #2 [unverified]

Jack Goldberg *[producer]*

Because I Love You
Harlem Serenade
I Won't Miss You
Jump In
Let's Go
My New Gown
You Can't Fool About Love

Dave Gould *[director; producer-director as noted]*

Am I Lucky
Baby, Are You Kiddin'?
Big Fat Butterfly
Boogie Woogie [producer-director]
E-Bob-O-Lee-Bop
Emily Brown
Gee
If You Only Knew

Juke Box Boogie
Low Down Dog [producer-director]
My, My, Ain't That Somethin'
Patience and Fortitude
Roll 'Em [producer-director]
Satchel Mouth Baby
Shout, Brother, Shout
Solid Jive [producer-director]
Steak and Potatoes
Yankee Doodle Never Went to Town
Your Feet's Too Big [RCM Productions]

Alfred J. Goulding [*director*]

A Harlemesque Review

John C. Graham [*director*]

Down, Down, Down
Five Guys Named Moe
Fuzzy Wuzzy
Jive Comes to the Jungle
Legs Ain't No Good
Old Man Mose
Tuxedo Junction

E. W. Hammons [*producer*]

Swanee Smiles

Ben Hersh [*producer*]

Along the Navajo Trail
Am I Lucky
Baby, Are You Kiddin'?
Big Fat Butterfly
E-Bob-O-Lee-Bop
Five Salted Peanuts
47th Street Jive
Gee
Hey, Lawdy Mama
I Can't Dance
If You Only Knew
Is You Is or Is You Ain't My Baby
It's Me, Oh Lord
I've Got to Be a Rug Cutter

Jonah and the Whale
Juke Box Boogie
Lazy River [RCM Productions]
My, My, Ain't That Somethin'
Oh-H-E-E, My, My
Patience and Fortitude
Ride On, Ride On
Rinka Tinka Man
Satchel Mouth Baby
Shout, Brother, Shout
Steak and Potatoes
Who's Been Eating My Porridge?
Yankee Doodle Never Went to Town
Your Feet's Too Big [RCM Productions]

Raymond Kane *[director]*

Swanee Smiles

Arthur Leonard *[producer-director]*

Bugle Call Rag
Good-Nite All
Quarry Road
Rug Cutters Holiday
Willie Willie

Mark Marvin *[producer]*

Boogie Woogie Dream
My New Gown
Unlucky Woman

Billy McDonald *[music director]*

Low Down Dog

George McNulty *[director]*

Bundle of Love

Herbert Moulton *[director]*

Blackbird Fantasy
I've Got a Little List

Dudley Murphy *[director]*

Alabamy Bound
Easy Street

Jim

Lazybones

Yes, Indeed! [codirected with Josef Berne]

Owen Murphy [director]

I Don't Want to Walk Without You

Warren Murray [director]

Ain't Misbehavin'

The Darktown Strutters' Ball

The Devil Sat Down and Cried

Fats Waller Medley

Honeysuckle Rose

I Dreamt I Dwelt in Harlem

The Joint Is Jumpin'

Oh, Susannah

Ride, Red, Ride

Your Feet's Too Big [Minoco Productions]

Samuel Oliphant [executive producer]

Bugle Call Rag

Good-Nite All

Quarry Road

Rug Cutters Holiday

Willie Willie

John Primi [director]

Four or Five Times

I Want a Big Fat Mama

The Lonesome Road

Some of These Days

Peter Ratoff [producer]

Bundle of Love

Joe Rock [producer]

A Harlemesque Review

Ray Sandiford [director]

Big Fat Mamas

Hello Bill

I Want a Man

Jump Children

She's Crazy with the Heat
That Man of Mine

Milton Schwarzwald *[producer-director]*

Hot in the Groove

Joseph Seiden *[director]*

Because I Love You
Harlem Serenade
I Won't Miss You

Robert Snody *[director]*

Air Mail Special
Blues in the Night
Booglie Wooglie Piggy
By an Old Southern River
Cab Calloway Medley
Dear Old Southland
Hark! Hark! The Lark
Jack, You're Playing the Game
Let Me Off Uptown
Let's Scuffle
Minnie the Moocher
Pudgy Boy
Rigoletto Blues
Shadrach
Shout! Sister, Shout!
The Skunk Song
Sugar Hill Masquerade
Swing for Sale
Take Me Back, Baby
Take the 'A' Train
Thanks for the Boogie Ride
That Ol' Ghost Train
Toot That Trumpet! [Minoco Productions]
Virginia, Georgia and Caroline
What to Do

Fred Waller *[producer]*

Ain't Misbehavin'
Air Mail Special
Blues in the Night

Booglie Wooglie Piggy
By an Old Southern River
Cab Calloway Medley
The Darktown Strutters' Ball
Dear Old Southland
The Devil Sat Down and Cried
Fats Waller Medley
Hark! Hark! The Lark
Honeysuckle Rose
Jack, You're Playing the Game
The Joint Is Jumpin'
Legs Ain't No Good
Let Me Off Uptown
Let's Scuffle
The Lonesome Road
Minnie the Moocher
Oh, Susannah
Pudgy Boy
Ride, Red, Ride
Rigoletto Blues
Shadrach
Shout! Sister, Shout!
The Skunk Song
Some of These Days
Sugar Hill Masquerade
Swing for Sale
Take Me Back, Baby
Take the 'A' Train
Thanks for the Boogie Ride
That Ol' Ghost Train
Toot That Trumpet! [Minoco Productions]
Virginia, Georgia and Caroline
What to Do
Your Feet's Too Big [Minoco Productions]

Adrian Weiss [*producer*]

Breakfast in Rhythm
Pardon Me, But You Look Just Like Margie

Louis Weiss [*executive producer*]

Breakfast in Rhythm
Pardon Me, But You Look Just Like Margie

Leonard Weiss [*director*]

Joseph 'n His Brudders
Mr. Jackson from Jacksonville
We're Stepping Out Tonight

Sydney M. Williams [*producer*]

Emily Brown

Unknown

Give Me Some Skin [producer, director]
Jordan Medley #1 [producer, director]
Jordan Medley #2 [producer, director]
Shoeshiners and Headliners [director]

NOTES

1. A full-page ad appearing in a 1941 issue of *Variety* lists a number of filmmakers working on Soundies in New York. Among the producers, directors, art directors, and other staffers, the sole editor is identified as Shirley Stone. IMDb lists Stone as "Actress, Editor," and credits her with editing the 1946 Black-cast featurette *Tall, Tan, and Terrific*. At the time, *Shirley* was not exclusively a woman's name, but if Stone was indeed a woman—as IMDb seems to believe—then the *Variety* ad is the only public documentation I've found of a female film professional in a nonsecretarial position working in Soundies. Stone's one appearance as an actress was an uncredited part ("Girl in Photo") in the 1938 feature *Port of Missing Girls*. The IMDb entry for the film lists her with several other uncredited actors, many of them Black; her own racial identity is a question, as no images of Stone are available online. "Minoco Productions Presents a Star-Spangled Program" (advertisement), *Variety*, October 1, 1941, 66; "Shirley Stone," IMDb, accessed January 30, 2021, https://www.imdb.com/name/nm0832172/.

2. Maynard Reuter, "The Future of Juke Box Pictures," *Billboard 1944 Music Yearbook*, September 1944, 124.

3. For Vallee and Vis-o-Graph, see MacGillivray and Okuda, *The Soundies Book*, 380; and Austen, *TV-a-Go-Go*, 196. For DeMille and Talkitones, see Lukow, "The Archaeology of Music Video," 37; and Douglas Churchill, "News of the Screen," *New York Times*, October 2, 1940, 18.

4. The Violano Virtuoso was a complicated device and maintaining it under arcade-use conditions was undoubtedly a headache. A three-minute video of a Violano Virtuoso in action, playing a theme by Johann Sebastian Bach, is

accessible on YouTube. "Mills Bow Front Violano Virtuoso Playing 'Air on the
G String,'" YouTube, video, 03:18, February 4, 2009, https://www.youtube.com
/watch?v=y5i1sRc_CSk.

5. Mills Novelty reportedly teamed up with Charles Fey, the inventor of the
original machine, to produce the "Mills Liberty Bell" slot machine. See "Mills
Novelty Company History," Mills Novelty, accessed January 30, 2021, https://
millsnovelty.com/index.php/mills-novelty-history/mills-novelty-company
-history.

As of the late 1960s, a later offshoot of Mills Novelty, the Reno, Nevada–based
Mills Bell-O-Matic Company, led by later-generation family member Tony
Mills, was manufacturing slot machines for the Nevada market. Harpster, *King of
the Slots*, 85.

6. A twenty-two-minute documentary about Mills Novelty Company,
made in 1935, details the considerable scope of its industrial and coin-machine
production, which required three separate manufacturing plants in Chicago.
"Mills Novelty Company Latest Factory Tour (1935)," YouTube, video, 21:59,
September 29, 2016, https://www.youtube.com/watch?time_continue=1296&v=
Zzy-agUgxxA.

7. For the full list of Mills Novelty Company personnel, see "Music Machine
Manufacturers Facts and Personnel," *Billboard Band Year Book*, September 26,
1942, 84. As president of the Soundies Distributing Corporation of America,
Gordon Mills was not a Mills Novelty executive and not mentioned in the article.

8. "Soundies Panoram," spiral-bound sales booklet (Chicago: Mills Novelty
Company, 1940), unpaged. A copy is archived in the New York Public Library's
Lincoln Center Library for the Performing Arts.

9. "Goon Violence Flares in Rich Juke Box Field," *Chicago Daily Tribune*,
September 20, 1941, 11.

10. For "mob's accountant," see Madinger, *Money Laundering*, 23. For jukebox
announcement: "Lansky-Smith New Wurlitzer N. Y., N. J., Conn. Distribs,"
Billboard, March 13, 1943, 59.

11. The assumption of syndicate involvement was seconded by Soundies
business partner and early producer James Roosevelt. In a 1987 interview
by Mark Cantor, Roosevelt strongly implied (without going on record)
that organized crime in Chicago had invested in Panoram Soundies. Phone
conversation with the author, December 12, 2012.

12. The primary machinery in the Panoram was a standard RCA 16 mm
projector, known for performing well under a variety of screening conditions.
In designing the Panoram, Mills Novelty added a continuous-loop film pathway
engineered to handle a reel of 850 feet or more. Unlike 35 mm film, 16 mm film
was made of triacetate, or "safety" film, a less combustible base than the celluloid
nitrate commonly used at the time for 35 mm films.

13. Gerald G. Gross, "Mahomet and Mountain Now Boon Companions," *Washington Post,* February 26, 1940, 14.

14. See Lukow, "Archaeology of Music Video," 38. Mills Novelty approached Warner Bros. about excerpting clips from their Vitaphone Varieties, Pepper Pot, and other brands of short films, produced from 1926 through 1939, which originally used the Vitaphone sound-on-disc system.

15. Douglas Churchill, "Hollywood Strikes Back," *New York Times,* September 29, 1940, 121. For a more caustic commentary on James Roosevelt's involvement with Soundies, see "The White House and the Green Pastures," *Chicago Tribune,* February 27, 1940, 10.

16. "Jimmy's Got It Again," *Look,* November 19, 1940, 14.

17. MacGillivray and Okuda, *Soundies Book,* 378–379.

18. "Are Juke Boxes Arms?," *Chicago Daily Tribune,* October 20, 1941, 14.

19. For a detailed discussion of unusual Panoram locations, particularly related to war bond and recruitment drives, see Kelley, "A Revolution in the Atmosphere," 72–93. Kelley incorporates this research into a broader analysis of Panoram use, Soundies exhibition practices, Soundies aesthetics, and the transition to other screening practices in *Soundies Jukebox Films and the Shift to Small-Screen Culture.*

20. The Alaska Panoram was sighted by war correspondent Joseph Driscoll, as reported in his book, *Pacific Victory 1945,* 107–108. For the Guatemala sighting, see Leonard Spinrad, "Movie Going Down Guatemala Way," *New York Times,* July 7, 1946, 41.

21. "OWI Pics for Soundies Fans," *Billboard,* June 17, 1944, 68. To screen free of charge, the OWI film was not given the usual notch in the triacetate that caused the Panoram projector to stop running until another dime was inserted.

At least one Hollywood studio had reportedly tried something similar. Paramount Pictures used Soundies to promote its movie *The Fleet's In* (1942), producing preview clips that appeared on weekly reels as free ninth films. The three Paramount clips were not listed in the Soundies catalog. Mark Cantor, email to author, April 27, 2018.

22. Douglas W. Churchill, "Hollywood Strikes Back," *New York Times,* September 29, 1940, 121. By comparison, the average cost of a movie ticket in 1940 was 24 cents ($4.47 in 2021 dollars). See "Cost of Products in the 1940s," in Sickels, *The 1940s,* 237. For contemporary dollar figures, see Dollar Times Inflation Calculator, accessed January 30, 2021, https://www.dollartimes.com /inflation/inflation.php?amount=7&year=1940.

23. "L.O.L. Productions, Inc., Plaintiff-Respondent, against Soundies Distributing Corporation of America, Inc., Defendant-Appellant." New York State Supreme Court Trial Term Part XVI, 1944. Included in the 1945 records of the New York Supreme Court Appellate Division—First Department, digitized under public

domain fair use by Google Books. Witness testimonies begin on page 72. https://
books.google.com/books?id=d_Eb-tbjfeIC&pg=RA1-PA71&lpg=RA1-PA71&dq
=LOL+Productions+Supreme+Court+Trial+Term+Part+XVI+1944&source=bl
&ots=rIO5adp_K9&sig=ACfU3U3ircyVgSy66DsQxkSMaQgH4UdNIQ&hl=en
&sa=X&ved=2ahUKEwi6z46jpNX0AhWzgnIEHasJB3oQ6AEwAHoECAwQKA
#v=onepage&q=LOL%20Productions%20Supreme%20Court%20Trial
%20Term%20Part%20XVI%201944&f=false (Ulcigan), 357. In a 1943 *Billboard*
article, Soundies Corporation president Gordon Mills corroborated Ulcigan's
assessment, stating that "the censorship problem has been bothersome only in
Ohio, Pennsylvania and New York." Gordon Mills, "Movie Jukeboxes: What about
Them?," *Billboard 1943 Music Yearbook*, September 25, 1943, 73.

24. "L.O.L." (Ulcigan), 362–363.

25. The six cities are New York, Philadelphia, Pittsburgh, Cleveland,
Columbus, and Cincinnati. For all figures cited in this paragraph, see Gibson and
Jung, "Historical Census Statistics on Population Totals by Race, 1790 to 1990,
and by Hispanic Origin, 1790 to 1990."

26. "L.O.L." (Crouch), 334.

27. "L.O.L." (Crouch), 465. Letter from William Forest Crouch to Arthur
Leonard, L.O.L. Productions, Inc. dated March 26, 1943.

28. Earl J. Morris, "Grand Town Day and Night," *Pittsburgh Courier*,
September 28, 1940, 21; Al Monroe, "Swinging the News," *Chicago Defender*, June
26, 1943.

29. "Play Goes Upward on Movie Machines," *Billboard*, September 19, 1942, 62.

30. "L.O.L." (Crouch), 473.

31. "L.O.L." (Crouch), 347. Created in 1928, "Amos 'n Andy" was written and
performed by white actors. The 1950s television show starred Black actors.

32. Don De Leighbur, "'Soundies' Open the Way for Our Talent," *New York
Amsterdam News*, August 11, 1945, A14. "Don De Leighbur" was a pseudonym for Dan
Burley, a journalist and musician who held several editorial positions at the newspaper.

33. See the Hall and Gates entries in the Bibliography and other writings; also
the writings of historians Glenda Gilmore and Lauren Rebecca Sklaroff.

34. Bogle, *Toms, Coons, Mulattoes, Mammies, and Bucks*, 37.

35. Rajchman, "Thinking with Shiraga," 273.

CHAPTER 1

1. In 1940, the US government census reported a continental US population
of 131,669,275, with an additional 2,477,023 living in other American territories.
Official 1940 Census Website, National Archives, accessed March 8, 2021,
https://1940census.archives.gov/about/.

2. Schatz, *Boom and Bust*, 65–66. For rerelease date, see IMDb, "*Gone with the Wind* Release Info," accessed January 30, 2021, http://www.imdb.com/title/tt0031381/releaseinfo.

3. Petty, *Stealing the Show*, 4. Petty's book, and the chapter on McDaniel in particular, offer insightful analyses of the problematic stardom that confronted successful Black performers of the 1930s.

4. Tolson, "*Gone with the Wind* Is More Dangerous Than *Birth of a Nation*," 215.

5. "*Gone with the Wind* is a product of its time and depicts some of the ethnic and racial prejudices that have, unfortunately, been commonplace in American society," an HBO Max statement read. "These racist depictions were wrong then and are wrong today, and we felt that to keep this title up without an explanation and a denouncement of those depictions would be irresponsible." Daniel Victor, "HBO Max Pulls 'Gone with the Wind,' Citing Racist Depictions," *New York Times*, June 11, 2020, C3, https://www.nytimes.com/2020/06/10/business/media/gone-with-the-wind-hbo-max.html?searchResultPosition=1.

A few days later, Black film scholar Jacqueline Stewart argued in a CNN op-ed that "'Gone with the Wind' is a prime text for examining expressions of white supremacy in popular culture" and on that basis "should stay in circulation and remain available for viewing, analysis and discussion." She added that "HBO Max will bring 'Gone with the Wind' back to its line-up, and when it appears, I will provide an introduction placing the film in its multiple historical contexts. For me, this is an opportunity to think about what classic films can teach us." Jacqueline Stewart, "Why We Can't Turn Away from 'Gone with the Wind,'" CNN, June 13, 2020, https://www.cnn.com/2020/06/12/opinions/gone-with-the-wind-illuminates-white-supremacy-stewart/index.html.

On March 4, 2021, Turner Classic Movies (TCM) debuted "Reframed: Classics in the Rearview Mirror," a month-long series of movies that "have stood the test of time in several ways" but "when viewed by contemporary standards" have "troubling and problematic" aspects. Stewart was among the TCM hosts and writers who participated in the screening discussions; *Gone with the Wind* was the first film on the schedule (https://www.tcm.com/articles/Programming-Article/020930/reframed-classic-films-in-the-rearview-mirror).

6. The term "blacking up" was widely used to reference the process of applying burnt cork to the face and hands in preparation for a minstrel-style performance. Mickey Rooney joined Garland in blacking up for the minstrel number in *Babes on Broadway* (1941), an encore to their earlier blackface appearance in *Babes in Arms* (1939). In 1942, Bing Crosby and much of the cast blacked up for the Lincoln's Birthday number in *Holiday Inn*—deleted from most later television broadcasts—and Crosby appeared in blackface again in *Dixie*

(1943). Other actors also appeared in blackface in early 1940s films, including Betty Grable (*Coney Island*, 1943, and *The Dolly Sisters*, 1945).

7. Koppes and Black, "Blacks, Loyalty, and Motion-Picture Propaganda in World War II," 401.

8. See Sklaroff, *Black Culture and the New Deal*; Katznelson, *Fear Itself*; and Bateman, Katznelson, and Lapinski, *Southern Nation*.

9. The OWI's Bureau of Motion Pictures was led by liberal white journalists Lowell Mellett and his second-in-command, Nelson Poynter. Neither had significant film industry experience. See Koppes and Black, "What to Show the World: The Office of War Information and Hollywood, 1942–1945"; and Koppes, "Regulating the Screen: The Office of War Information and the Production Code Administration," 262–281.

10. OWI report quoted in Koppes and Black, "Blacks, Loyalty, and Motion-Picture Propaganda in World War II," 399. In spring 1943, the OWI "largely abandoned its efforts to change the portrayal of Blacks. The agency was under sharp attack in Congress, in part because its stand on race relations, however mild, excited the ire of southern racists and the conservative coalition.... Hollywood for the duration continued to treat Blacks as a people essentially apart." Koppes and Black, "Blacks, Loyalty, and Motion-Picture Propaganda in World War II," 400.

11. Muse was among those who praised McDaniel for her role in *Gone with the Wind* but not the film itself, stating that "There are many THINGS about the story that will not SATISFY our people," but that "IT MEANS a great DEAL when our THESPIANS can rise above distasteful things and turn in a FINE PERFORMANCE." (Uppercase in original.) Clarence Muse, "What's Going On in Hollywood," *Chicago Defender*, December 23, 1939, 21. For organizations joining the NAACP pressure campaign, see Cripps, *Slow Fade*, 378–379.

12. "For those actors in Hollywood who can play only comic servant roles," White wrote in 1942, "I trust they will not let their own interests spoil the opportunity we now have to correct a lot of things from which Negroes have suffered in the past in movies." Letter from Walter White to Will Hays, president of the Motion Picture Producers and Distributors of America. Cited in Petty, *Stealing the Show*, 218.

13. Ryan Jay Friedman has posited that this market sector was a significant factor in determining studio productions in the early sound period. Friedman, *Hollywood's African American Films*, 52–53.

14. See Massood, "The Antebellum Idyll and Hollywood's Black-Cast Musicals," in *Black City Cinema*, 11–43.

15. See Sklaroff, *Black Culture and the New Deal*, 238. For feature film releases 1941 to 1945, see Schatz, "Number of Feature Films Released in the United States, 1940–1949," in *Boom and Bust*, 463.

16. See Sklaroff, *Black Culture and the New Deal*, 194.

17. Petty, *Stealing the Show*, 220. Pressure from the OWI and NAACP, she wrote, obligated the studios "to do little besides stop casting Blacks in general to cut down on stereotypical representations."

18. Koppes and Black, "Blacks, Loyalty, and Motion-Picture Propaganda in World War II," 404. In "I Tried to Crash the Movies," the cover story in the August 1946 issue of *Ebony*, Soundies performer Avanelle (also spelled Avenelle) Harris discussed her largely unsuccessful attempts to break into the Hollywood film industry.

19. See Stewart, *Migrating to the Movies*, and Caddoo, *Envisioning Freedom*.

20. Stewart, *Migrating to the Movies*, 117.

21. See Massood, "Harlem Is Heaven: City Motifs in Race Films from the Early Sound Era," in *Black City Cinema*, 45–77.

22. Massood, *Black City Cinema*, 69, 61.

23. Jeffries's four films are *Harlem on the Prairie* (1937), *Two-Gun Man from Harlem* (1938), *Harlem Rides the Range*, and *The Bronze Buckaroo* (both 1939).

24. Massood, *Black City Cinema*, 56, 78.

25. "Negroes Due for a Break in Films with New York as Own Hollywood," *Chicago Defender*, April 27, 1946, 17. Film historian Thomas Doherty has estimated the number of theaters serving Black audiences at a somewhat lower but still significant 450. Thomas Doherty, "Documenting the 1940s," in Schatz, *Boom and Bust*, 398.

26. Barry Ulanov, "The Jukes Take Over Swing," *American Mercury*, October 1940, 172.

27. "Program 1047," Movie Machine Reviews, *Billboard*, January 3, 1942, 73.

28. Knight, "Star Dances: African-American Constructions of Stardom, 1925–1960," 386–414.

29. Savage, *Broadcasting Freedom*, 6.

30. Savage, *Broadcasting Freedom*, 11.

31. For more on the impact of BMI and other changes in the music industry in the 1930s and 1940s, see Green, *Selling the Race*, 54–58.

32. "The Billboard's Harlem Hit Parade," *Billboard*, October 24, 1942, 25. The chart was based on sales reports from Rainbow Music Shop, Harvard Radio Shop, Lehman Music Company, Harlem De Luxe Music Store, Ray's Music Shop, and Frank's Melody Music Shop.

33. "Most Played Juke Box Race Records," *Billboard*, March 3, 1945, 100.

34. "The Billboard Music Popularity Charts Part VII: Rhythm & Blues Records," *Billboard*, June 25, 1949, 30.

35. Sklaroff, *Black Culture*, 177.

36. Giddins, "The Mirror of Swing," 120.

37. Scott, "Black Movement Impolitic: Soundies, Regulation, and Black Pleasure," 222.

38. For the complete list of Soundies in which Barker has been identified
to date, see her entry in the appendix "Performers and Their Films." Over the
course of her career Barker also danced at the Cotton Club and the Apollo
Theater in Harlem. The 2006 documentary *Been Rich All My Life*, directed by
Heather MacDonald, features some of Barker's colleagues and contemporaries
from those years, though not Barker herself.

CHAPTER 2

1. Gordon Mills, "Movie Jukeboxes: What about Them?" *Billboard 1943 Music
Yearbook*, September 25, 1943, 73.

2. Maynard Reuter, "The Future of Juke Box Pictures," *Billboard 1944 Music
Yearbook*, September 1944, 124.

3. Soundies Corporation president Gordon Mills also testified, but his
testimony was brief and focused on establishing dates and times of specific
events in May 1943.

4. Leonard directed and/or coproduced *Gang Smashers* (1938) and *The Devil's
Daughter* (1939), both with McKinney, and *Straight to Heaven* (1939). For Warner
Bros. reference, see Leonard's testimony on page 74 of "L.O.L. Productions, Inc.,
Plaintiff-Respondent, against Soundies Distributing Corporation of America,
Inc., Defendant-Appellant."

5. "L.O.L." (Leonard), 225.

6. "L.O.L." (Ulcigan), 359.

7. "L.O.L." (Leonard), 195.

8. "L.O.L." (Appellant's Brief), 10.

9. "L.O.L." (Crouch), 312.

10. "L.O.L." (Crouch), 317, 318.

11. The rejected L.O.L. Soundies also included *Fiddlin' Around*, starring
comedian Henny Youngman in a monologue-driven routine, and *Casa Casa*,
which reportedly showed a murder on screen. "L.O.L." (Crouch), 272, 283.
Plenty of King features an obese white man in blackface playing a "native" ruler,
appearing with Black dancers from the Ubangi Club, a New York City night club.
Interestingly, footage from this Soundie is included in the Black-cast film *Murder
with Music*, where it is presented as a television broadcast. An excerpt from *Murder
with Music* that includes the *Plenty of King* clip has been uploaded to YouTube.
"Noble Sissle + Bob Howard - Murder with Music -1 1948 excerpt," YouTube,
video, 12:31, July 15, 2013, https://www.youtube.com/watch?v=cfglTCNHvwQ.

Confoundingly, L.O.L.'s final set of films included a witty, urbane Black-cast
Soundie, *Good-Nite All* (Oliphant/Leonard-Leonard, 1943). One of the stars of
that film, uncredited on screen and identified in the Soundies catalog only as
"Hot Cha," is a vocalist and lead dancer in *Plenty of King*.

12. "L.O.L." (Crouch), 257.

13. "L.O.L." (Ulcigan), 355.

14. "L.O.L." (Ulcigan), 357; "L.O.L." (Crouch), 251.

15. "L.O.L." (Ulcigan), 357.

16. "L.O.L." (Ulcigan), 357.

17. According to Soundies Corporation documents held by Mark Cantor, Armstrong and his group were paid $2,500. Email to author, October 8, 2019. MacGillivray and Okuda put the figure at double that, $5,000. MacGillivray and Okuda, *The Soundies Book*, 8.

18. For the Soundies Corporation, the strike was settled in late October 1943. According to an article in the November 6 issue of *Billboard*, the company received a telegram from union head James Petrillo announcing that the recording ban had been lifted for Soundies. This prompted Crouch to resume production in New York with some thirty films on the schedule. "Petrillo Lifts Ban on Hiring of Union Men by Soundies," *Billboard*, November 6, 1943, 62. The strike lasted longest for the Columbia and RCA Victor record companies, which settled more than a year later in November 1944.

19. "L.O.L." (Ulcigan), 393.

20. The four L.O.L. films with Black performers are *Good-Nite All, Rug Cutters Holiday* (starring African American performers) and *Quarry Road* and *Willie Willie* (starring performers from Trinidad). In addition, *Bugle Call Rag* prominently features Ernie Morris, the only Black member of the group Borrah Minevitch and His Harmonica Rascals, in an uncredited performance. The four L.O.L. films with white performers in blackface are *Meetin' Time, Ask Dad, Two-of-a-Kind*, and the rejected *Plenty of King* (all films Oliphant/Leonard-Leonard, 1943).

21. Reuter, "Future of Juke Box Pictures."

22. "L.O.L." (Leonard), 233, 234.

23. "L.O.L." (Crouch), 494; memo from William Forest Crouch to George Ulcigan, March 24, 1943, submitted as Defendant's Exhibit Q during the trial.

24. "L.O.L." (Crouch), 252.

25. "L.O.L." (Crouch), 472; letter from William Forest Crouch to Arthur Leonard, May 3, 1943.

26. "L.O.L." (Bowers), 353.

27. "L.O.L." (Crouch), 495.

28. For more on McBurnie and the two Soundies, see Ray Funk, "Beryl McBurnie: The Flowering of La Belle Rosette," *Caribbean Beat*, November/December 2008, https://www.caribbean-beat.com/issue-94/flowering -la-belle-rosette-beryl-mcburnie#axzz5mzSVNLNm.

29. "L.O.L." (Crouch), 495.

30. "L.O.L." (Crouch), 497.

31. "L.O.L." (Crouch), 489.

32. "L.O.L." (Crouch), 472. In addition to *Ask Dad*, the four L.O.L. films (all white-cast) included *Hip Hip Hooray*, *Our Teacher* (with comedian Henny Youngman), and *Sh! Sh! Somebody Blabbed* (all Oliphant/Leonard-Leonard, April 1943).

33. "L.O.L." (Appellant's Brief), 20.

34. "L.O.L." ("Verdict. Polling the Jury"), 444–445.

35. "L.O.L." (Crouch), 265–266; "L.O.L." (Ulcigan), 362.

36. "L.O.L." (Ulcigan), 382.

37. "L.O.L." (Crouch), 499; letter from William Forest Crouch to Arthur Leonard, May 20, 1943.

38. "L.O.L.," 459; letter to L.O.L. Productions from Soundies Corporation treasurer R. P. McNamara, May 26, 1943.

39. Scott, "Black Movement Impolitic," 218.

40. Reuter, "Future of Juke Box Pictures."

41. The first edition of the Soundies catalog includes this disclaimer: "Films listed in this catalog are not available for exhibition in any state, municipality or location where they are prohibited by censorship or otherwise restricted by law." *Soundies Parade of Hits*, 1st ed.

42. Scott, "Black Movement Impolitic," 218.

43. Scott, "Black Movement Impolitic," 224n19.

44. For a thorough examination of *Coalmine Boogie* and its production, see Mark Cantor, "Pat Flowers, Mabel Lee and the 'Very Last Soundie,'" Celluloid Improvisations, accessed January 30, 2021, http://www.jazz-on-film.com /patflowers.html#learn.

45. Before the problems with L.O.L. Productions, Crouch testified, the Soundies Corporation had released between eight- and nine hundred films without rejecting any on the basis of poor quality. "L.O.L." (Crouch), 272.

46. "Panoram Soundies," spiral-bound sales booklet for potential franchise purchasers (Chicago: Mills Novelty Company, 1940), unpaginated. Ellipses in original.

47. According to Mark Cantor, memos circulated among Mills Novelty and Soundies Corporation executives suggest that theatrical release was not ruled out in the early years, and Soundies were frequently shown in movie theaters after their initial Panoram runs. However, Panoram play was always the primary object. Email to author, December 31, 2013. Additionally, a *Billboard* article cites the Panoram's capability of externally projecting a large-format film image: "as many as one thousand persons at a time can see the pictures projected on a large screen." See "Soundies for War Plants," *Billboard*, February 13, 1943, 61. See also the discussion of the Panoram's uses in nonleisure settings in Kelley, *Soundies Jukebox Films and the Shift to Small-Screen Culture.*

48. Jack Barry, "This New Showmanship," *Billboard*, January 31, 1942, 89.

49. Media historians Philip Auslander and Murray Forman have pointed out that television production and programming work continued during the war but was severely curtailed in scope and ambition. See Forman, *One Night on TV Is Worth Weeks at the Paramount*, 29.

50. The mid-twentieth-century increase in nontheatrical and transient screening spaces, and the use of small-gauge portable projection equipment, have been explored by several film scholars, including Kelley, Haidee Wasson, Charles Acland, and Anna McCarthy.

51. For more on adapting musical performance to television, see Forman, *One Night on TV Is Worth Weeks at the Paramount*, 173–176.

52. Hazel Scott and Billy Daniels also hosted musical-variety television shows in these years. See McGee, *Some Liked It Hot*, 207.

53. Herzog, *Dreams of Difference, Songs of the Same*, 47.

54. Herzog, *Dreams of Difference, Songs of the Same*, 51.

55. See McCarthy, "TV, Class, and Social Control in the 1940s Neighborhood Tavern," in *Ambient Television*, 29–62.

CHAPTER 3

1. For more about Murphy and his career, see Delson, *Dudley Murphy, Hollywood Wild Card*.

2. Berne's *Dawn to Dawn* is included in "Inverted Narratives: New Directions in Storytelling," Program Four of *Unseen Cinema: Early American Avant-Garde Film 1894–1941* (2005), a seven-part film series and video anthology curated by Bruce Posner and produced for DVD by David Shepard.

3. See "Josef Berne," IMDb, accessed January 30, 2021, http://www.imdb .com/name/nm0076653/?ref_=fn_al_nm_1.

4. Crouch began hands-on Soundies producing in 1942.With the exception of 1943—the year he directed an Oscar-winning short film with Sam Coslow—Berne was active in Soundies from 1941 through 1946.

5. As a point of speculation, it's worth considering whether Day, Dawn, and Dusk's work with Berne might have been a factor in their decision to record the Yiddish song "Mein Stetela Belz" the following year. "Day, Dawn & Dusk–Mein Stetela Belz (Collector Item 806-A) 1946," November 18, 2011, YouTube, video, 02:26, https://www.youtube.com/watch?v=9rAcpn1WK3s. For more on Day, Dawn, and Dusk see chaps. 5–7.

6. "Armstrong Signed," *Los Angeles Times*, May 2, 1942, 9.

7. The two Ellington Soundies adapted from *Jump for Joy* are *I Got It Bad and That Ain't Good* and *Bli-Blip* (both Coslow-Berne, 1942). In the second, Ellington and his band appear on the soundtrack only.

8. Gibson and Jung, "Historical Census Statistics on Population Totals by Race, 1790 to 1990, and by Hispanic Origin, 1790 to 1990," tabulation for California, 1940.

9. McWilliams, *Southern California Country*, 324.

10. Jack Barry, "This New Showmanship," *Billboard*, January 31, 1942, 89.

11. Barry, "This New Showmanship."

12. Fred Waller also directed *Cab Calloway's Hi-De-Ho* (1934) and *Cab Calloway's Jitterbug Party* (1935), as well as Duke Ellington's *A Bundle of Blues* (1933). See "Fred Waller," IMDb, accessed January 30, 2021, https://www.imdb .com/name/nm0909044/?ref_=tt_ov_dr.

13. Mark Cantor, conversation with author, March 6, 2020.

14. "Program 1105," Movie Machine Reviews, *Billboard*, February 27, 1943, 104.

15. "Soundies Company Now Going into Production Field," *Billboard*, March 6, 1943, 71.

16. Ulcigan testified that "Mr. Crouch had been going back and forth between New York and Chicago quite a bit of the time from November or December of 1942 right on through 1943, to produce pictures in different groups." "L.O.L. Productions, Inc., Plaintiff-Respondent, against Soundies Distributing Corporation of America, Inc., Defendant-Appellant," (Ulcigan), 378.

17. "L.O.L." (Leonard), 195.

18. Don De Leighbur [Dan Burley], "'Soundies' Open the Way for Our Talent," *New York Amsterdam News*, August 11, 1945, A14.

19. See "Pick Song Hits for New Film," *New York Amsterdam News*, February 12, 1938, 17. According to Thomas Cripps, Pollard was unable to raise the necessary funding for the venture. Cripps, *Slow Fade to Black*, 338.

20. Active since the 1920s as a performer, choreographer, and producer, Harper had staged *Hot Chocolates* (1929) and other Broadway shows and revues as well as floor shows at the Cotton Club, Connie's Inn, the Apollo Theater, and other venues. When he died of a heart attack, Harper had just finished rehearsing a new revue for Murrain's Cabaret in Harlem. "Last Tribute Paid Leonard Harper," *New York Amsterdam News*, February 13, 1943, 1. See also Harper's biography, written by his grandson: Grant Harper Reid, *Rhythm for Sale*, rev. ed. (New York: Self-published, 2014).

21. Julius J. Adams, "Pollard Inherited Sun Tan Studio after Producer Died," *New York Amsterdam News*, September 10, 1949, 20.

22. "Last Tribute Paid," *Amsterdam News*. As reported in the article, Pollard and Crawford were among Leonard's pallbearers, along with songwriter Andy Razaf, J. C. Johnson, Doc Rhythm Johnson, Charley Davis, and Dewey Weinglass.

23. "22 New Shorts for Soundies Are Completed," *New York Amsterdam News*, August 21, 1943, 15.

24. "22 New Shorts for Soundies Are Completed."

25. Al Monroe, "Swinging the News," *Chicago Defender*, January 22, 1944.

26. Pollard may have been miming, or "sidelining," the soundtrack performance of another pianist, but it's possible that he recorded the music himself. According to his biographer, Pollard was a proficient pianist, if not a professional musician. Carroll, *Fritz Pollard*.

27. According to Carroll, Pollard "signed a contract with Gordon Mills to serve as manager of the New York office of the Soundies Distributing Corporation of America." Carroll, *Fritz Pollard*, 212.

28. In a telephone interview with Thomas Cripps in 1970, Pollard stated that film exhibitors feared the competition that Panoram Soundies and other movie-jukebox ventures represented, and that whites bought up the few Black-owned holdings in the business. See Cripps, *Slow Fade*, 234, 234n37, and 417.

29. De Leighbur [Burley], "'Soundies' Open the Way for Our Talent."

30. "John Doran Succumbs; Soundie Executive," *New York Amsterdam News*, October 26, 1946, 27.

31. "Has 375 Steps," *New York Amsterdam News*, October 16, 1943.

32. "22 New Shorts for Soundies Are Completed."

33. The company was also known as All-American Films and the All-American Newsreel Company.

34. Bowser's figure may count individual newsreel segments rather than multisegment newsreels. For more on Alexander's newsreels and his career in general, see the entry on William Alexander in Moon, *Reel Black Talk*, 3–6; and Bowser, "Pioneers of Black Documentary Film," 25–28.

35. See Doherty, "Documenting the 1940s," 398.

36. In 2018, the Library of Congress made several All-American Newsreels available for viewing in the National Screening Room section of its website. All-American News Inc., National Screening Room Collection, Library of Congress, accessed January 30, 2021, https://www.loc.gov/collections/national-screening-room/?fa=contributor:all+american+news,+inc. Pearl Bowser notes that the entire collection of All-American's newsreels was acquired in the 1990s by the Columbia Broadcasting System (CBS). Bowser, "Pioneers of Black Documentary Film," 27.

37. Two documentaries about the band and its musicians were made in the 1980s: *International Sweethearts of Rhythm* (1986) and *Tiny & Ruby: Hell-Divin' Women* (1989), both by Greta Schiller and Andrea Weiss for Jezebel Productions. See Jezebel Productions, https://jezebelproductions.org/.

38. Mark Cantor, email to author, June 18, 2018.

39. Bowser, "Pioneers of Black Documentary Film," 28. Bowser interviewed Barton in 1990.

40. The Soundie counted here for July 1941, *Just a Little Bit South of North Carolina* (Barry-Waller, 1941), features Black performers in a brief performance as field hands, and is not included in the list of Black-cast films in the Appendixes. The same for *Hot Frogs*, an excerpt from the 1937 MGM cartoon *Swing Wedding*, released as a Soundie in March 1942.

41. Letter dated January 13, 1942, from George P. Ulcigan to John F. Barry, Minoco Productions. Ulcigan sent a similarly worded letter, also dated January 13, to Sam Coslow at RCM Productions. The "necessity" Ulcigan mentions is most likely budget-related, and another indication that Black performers may have been paid less than whites. Thanks to Mark Cantor and the Mark Cantor Archive for sharing the Soundies Corporation documents cited in this section.

The one weekly reel that arguably includes three Black-cast Soundies is #1045, copyrighted December 8, 1941, which has *Air Mail Special* (Coslow-Berne, 1941), *Hark! Hark! The Lark* (Waller-Snody, 1941), and *Dear Old Southland* (Waller-Snody, 1941). In that third film, the white vocal group the Dixiairs is neatly upstaged by a vibrant troupe of uncredited Black performers, including Vivian and Hibby Brown.

42. Soundies Corporation interoffice communication from G. N. Childs to R. P. McNamara, January 17, 1942.

43. Letter to R. P. McNamara from James R. Hudson, assistant sales manager, Panoram division, March 2, 1942, quoting a letter received by Hudson from J. G. Isenhour, district sales manager in District No. 3, Atlanta, GA.

44. Weekly reels released during this time that do not include a Black-cast film: Programs 1068 (May 1942), 1071, 1072, and 1073 (all June 1942), 1075 and 1076 (both July 1942), 1082 (August 1942), 1084 and 1087 (both September 1942), 1088 (October 1942), 1110 (March 1943), and 1114 (April 1943), *Soundies Parade of Hits*, 1st and 2nd eds.

45. Memo from E. R. Crum and V. M. Bowers to Exchange, V. Krupa, Central Laboratory, W. F. Crouch, Production Records, signed by E. R. Crum and dated February 12, 1945.

46. This note appears on the first "Catalog Information" page of the 1946 Soundies catalog (unpaginated), obtained from the Margaret Herrick Library, Academy of Motion Picture Arts and Sciences, Los Angeles.

47. See Koppes and Black, "Blacks, Loyalty, and Motion-Picture Propaganda in World War II"; also Cripps, "The Myth of the Southern Box Office: A Factor in Racial Stereotyping in the American Movies, 1920–1940," 116–144.

48. The Social Science Institute at Fisk University reported 242 racial confrontations in 47 cities. See Sitkoff, "Racial Militancy and Interracial Violence in the Second World War," 661–671; also Wynn, *The African American Experience during World War II*, 73.

49. *Pittsburgh Courier*, June 26, 1943, 1.

CHAPTER 4

1. "Program 1078," Movie Machine Reviews, *Billboard*, July 18, 1942, 71.

2. Set in a fictionalized version of Edo-era Japan, *The Mikado* has been criticized for its crude Asian stereotypes. A 2016–2017 production by the

New York Gilbert and Sullivan Players reimagined the work from an Asian perspective, triggering a mixed response. See Michael Cooper, "The Mikado Returns, and So Do Questions," *New York Times*, December 26, 2016, C1.

3. The expression "Good riddance to bad rubbish" appeared in Charles Dickens's 1848 novel *Dombey and Sons* and quickly became a popular catchphrase—a nineteenth-century equivalent of a meme.

4. Before the draft was enacted in September 1940, an estimated thirty thousand Black people had attempted to enlist and been turned away. Wynn, *The African American Experience*, 27.

5. "116,000 Enlisted Men in Navy; 2,807 Colored!," *Pittsburgh Courier*, February 24, 1940, 24. See also Goodwin, *No Ordinary Time*, 165.

6. Letter to the editor from Byron Johnson, Floyd Owens, Otto Robinson, Shannon Goodwin, et al., *Pittsburgh Courier*, October 5, 1940, 1, 4. The Navy subsequently filed criminal charges against the fifteen men who signed the letter and dismissed them from the service. See "The Philadelphia Fifteen," in Richard E. Miller, *The Messman Chronicles*.

7. The few Black individuals who did receive special training were not always permitted to use it. A 2018 *New York Times* article reported on a 1942 graduate of the Army Officer Candidate School who, at the age of 98, finally received his promotion to the rank of second lieutenant. Rachel L. Swarns, "A Black Soldier Achieves a Dream That the Army Denied, Until Now," *New York Times*, June 30, 2018, A10.

8. See Goodwin, *No Ordinary Time*, 166–167; Koppes and Black, "Blacks, Loyalty, and Motion-Picture Propaganda in World War II," 388; and Dalfiume, "The 'Forgotten Years,'" 91.

9. "Half a Million Workers," *Fortune*, March 1941, 163.

10. Illustrated in Lucy G. Barber, *Marching on Washington: The Forging of an American Political Tradition* (Berkeley: University of California Press, 2002), 113.

11. Dalfiume, "The 'Forgotten Years,'" 93.

12. Dalfiume, "The 'Forgotten Years,'" 95.

13. Office of Facts and Figures, Bureau of Intelligence, "Negroes in a Democracy at War," Philleo Nash Papers, Box 22, Harry S. Truman Library, Independence, MO. Cited in Koppes and Black, "Blacks, Loyalty, and Motion-Picture Propaganda in World War II," 385–386.

14. *Pittsburgh Courier*, June 20, 1942, 4. Cited in Washburn, *The African American Newspaper*, 163.

15. Lee, Table 11: Quarterly Negro Strength and Total Strength of the Army, December 1941–December 1945, in "Manpower and Readjustments," chap. 14 in *The Employment of Negro Troops*, 415.

16. Toll, "Social Commentary in Late-Nineteenth-Century White Minstrelsy," 94.

17. *The Swing Mikado* was a hit in its Chicago debut, but New York critics were disappointed that the production "swung" only three songs. Opening soon after, Todd's *Hot Mikado* was a swing show throughout. In addition to appearing on Broadway (across the street from *The Swing Mikado*), *The Hot Mikado* was presented at the 1939–1940 World's Fair in New York City. Footage of this production has been uploaded to YouTube. "1939 1940 NY World's Fair Hot Mikado Bill BoJangles Robinson," YouTube, video, 03:16, June 3, 2007, http://www.youtube.com/watch?v=LQ-CcPIU2MY.

For a detailed analysis of *The Swing Mikado* and its competitors—which included a Philadelphia production, *Mikado in Swing*—see Sklaroff, *Black Culture and the New Deal*, 36–80.

18. *I Gotta Go to Camp to See My Man*, Soundie 12708, Program 1127, *Soundies Parade of Hits*, 2nd ed., 127.

19. "Program 1127," Movie Machine Reviews, *Billboard*, July 31, 1943, 97.

20. See "Spotlight on the Ginger Snaps," Vocal Group Harmony, accessed January 30, 2021, https://www.vocalgroupharmony.com/ROWNEW2/TooManyIrons.htm.

21. The Four Ginger Snaps appear on V-Disc No. 579 singing "The Shrimp Man," their first release after signing with RCA Victor in 1945. The disc was released on December 12, 1945. See Tom Lord, *The Jazz Discography* (Chilliwack, Canada: Lord Music Reference, 1997), 15:305. An audio recording has been uploaded to YouTube. "V-Disc 579 Andrews Sisters, 4 Ginger Snaps. Gracie Fields, Cass Daley," YouTube, video, 09:25, October 5, 2009, http://www.youtube.com/watch?v=boGM-CjWKoA.

22. "Frank Palumbo's Theater-Restaurant, Philadelphia," Night Club Reviews, *Billboard*, May 22, 1943, 13.

23. "Program 1135," Movie Machine Reviews, *Billboard*, October 2, 1943, 67.

24. Lee, *Employment of Negro Troops*, 415.

25. Lee, *Employment of Negro Troops*, 410–411.

26. See Sitkoff, "Racial Militancy and Interracial Violence in the Second World War," 668.

27. Dalfiume, "The 'Forgotten Years,'" 96.

28. See Peiss, *Zoot Suit*.

29. See Sitkoff, "Racial Militancy and Interracial Violence in the Second World War," 671–675.

30. Singer, *Black and Blue*, 314.

31. Savage, *Broadcasting Freedom*, 91–92.

32. *Don't Be an Absentee*, Soundie 13406, Program 1134, *Soundies Parade of Hits*, 2nd ed., 134.

33. Letter dated October 29, 1943, submitted to the Register of Copyrights, Library of Congress, by Alice Toman, Production Record Department,

Soundies Distribution Corporation of America, Inc. Obtained from the Motion Picture, Broadcasting and Recorded Sound Division of the Library of Congress.

34. Sitkoff, "Racial Militancy and Interracial Violence in the Second World War," 672. See also Collins, *All Hell Broke Loose*, 164n3.

35. Over the course of the war, some eighty-five million Americans bought more than $185 billion worth of these securities. See "Reflections—Wartime Bond Drives," Army Historical Foundation, https://armyhistory.org /reflections-wartime-bond-drives/.

36. By one estimate, 20 percent of all war bonds were sold in movie theaters. Rose, *Myth and the Greatest Generation*, 117.

37. M. H. Orodenker, "Alvino Rey (Victor 27936)," On the Records, *Billboard*, July 25, 1942, 98.

38. Anti-Japanese propaganda gained traction in 1943, the year *Keep Smiling* was released, after it became known that captured members of the 1942 Doolittle raid (the first US bombing strike on Tokyo) had been tortured. Lingeman, *Don't You Know There's a War On?*, 341.

39. The women-only vocals end about two-thirds through the film, as Ford joins them after a quick solo of his own. Beyond the Ginger Snaps, the Peters Sisters was one notable Black female vocal group of the 1940s. Primarily a nightclub and stage act, they did not make Soundies but did appear in the 1947 Cab Calloway feature *Hi De Ho* (not to be confused with the 1934 short film *Cab Calloway's Hi-De-Ho*). A clip of the Peters Sisters' performance has been uploaded to YouTube. "The Peters Sisters (1947)," YouTube, video, 06:20, October 6, 2014, https://www.youtube.com/watch? v=Anuc4uEG8Zs.

40. See Sklaroff, *Black Culture and the New Deal*, 136–137.

41. "Despite its air of authenticity and its raw emotional power, [*The Negro Soldier*] did not address current racial inequities or the prospects of Black postwar progress," Savage writes. "The conditions Blacks faced at home and in the services were literally blocked from the film's frame of reference." Savage, *Broadcasting Freedom*, 147.

The Negro Soldier has been uploaded in its entirety on two YouTube channels. "The Negro Soldier (1944)," YouTube, video, 42:32, October 26, 2012, https:// www.youtube.com/watch?v=sj4ibGEYRS4; and "The Negro Soldier (1944)," You-Tube, video, 40:21, January 31, 2017, https://www.youtube.com/watch?v=H6YvZy _IsZY.

42. Lee, *Employment of Negro Troops*, 416.

43. For the number of Black servicemen in the Navy, see James, *The Double V*, 191. For the Marines, see Nalty, *Strength for the Fight*, 201.

44. See "Tuskegee Airmen Timeline," in Stentiford, *Tuskegee Airmen*.

45. Thompson, "An Aesthetic of the Cool," 41.

46. Amiri Baraka cited in MacAdams, *Birth of the Cool*, 20. See also Young, *The Grey Album*, 194. Also of interest, the discussion of cool in relation to dance in Seibert, *What the Eye Hears*.

47. "Shoo Shoo Baby" came relatively early in Moore's career, which included lengthy runs as a musician, arranger, composer, vocal coach, and musical director. For more about Moore, see "Phil Moore: The Man Who Made Music," in Bogle, *Bright Boulevards, Bold Dreams*; also Bogle, *Dorothy Dandridge*, 165–176.

48. Jones, *The Songs That Fought the War*, 240.

49. According to *Billboard*, James introduced the song in *Meet the New People*, a theatrical revue that opened in Los Angeles in 1943. See "Civic Groups Bid for Hot Licks to Distract Bobby Socks Following N. C. Lead," *Billboard*, March 4, 1944, 15. In the 1944 movie *Trocadero*, James gives an abbreviated performance of the song, which has been uploaded to YouTube. "Shoo Shoo Baby," YouTube, video, 01:20, August 30, 2009, https://www.youtube.com/watch?v= JprWUCIsjBk.

50. Ake, *Jazz Cultures*, 47.

51. Adams is credited as producer on several Jordan Soundies, features, and featurettes. Ake and Ramsey both cite Jordan's Soundies as a key factor in his success (though Ramsey refers to them as "Nickelodeons"). See Ake, *Jazz Cultures*, 46; Ramsey, *Race Music*, 64.

52. Crouch also directed Jordan in the sixty-seven-minute featurette *Reet, Petite, and Gone* (1947).

53. Soundies by Fats Waller and Cab Calloway were also assembled as solo medley reels, but only one reel was released for each of them. Of all Soundies performers, Waller, Calloway, and Jordan were the only ones whose films were repackaged in this format. A Movie Machine Reviews column in *Billboard* cites *Louis Jordan Medley No. 2* as part of a reel of rereleases, listing its three films as *Old Man Mose, If You Can't Smile and Say Yes*, and *GI Jive*. Movie Machine Reviews, *Billboard*, November 11, 1944, 64.

54. Jordan's cowriters on the song were Antonio Cosey and Collenane Clark. See Jones, *The Songs That Fought the War*, 212; also "Louis Jordan: Ration Blues," Allmusic, accessed January 30, 2021, http://www.allmusic.com/song /ration-blues-mt0011855998.

55. Jones, *The Songs That Fought the War*, 114.

56. Military historian Ulysses Lee notes that "few general circulation dailies carried the normal press releases about the activities of Negro troops." Lee, *Employment of Negro Troops*, 86.

57. "Ration Blues" wasn't Jordan's only double-entendre treatment of wartime shortages. Though not made into a Soundie, his "You Can't Get That No More" is worth searching out.

58. *Jordan Jive,* Soundie 17708, Program 1177, *Soundies Parade of Hits,* 2nd ed., 177.

59. *Hey! Tojo* was written by white songwriters Samuel "Buck" Ram and Clarence Stout, both music-industry veterans. Stout had run a touring minstrel show in the 1920s and 1930s, which may account for the *yo'* in the lyrics. See Hyatt, *A Critical History,* 7.

60. James, *The Double V,* 166.

61. The Twenty-Fourth Infantry was followed at Bougainville by the Twenty-Fifth Infantry, both part of the Ninety-Third Infantry Division. Troops from the Ninety-Second Infantry Division entered Allied lines in Italy in early August 1944. Nalty, *Strength for the Fight,* 169–172.

62. Howard was one of the first Black Americans to host a national television program. See chap. 11.

63. Black women defense workers appear in at least two of the All-American Newsreels on the Library of Congress website.

CHAPTER 5

1. See Massood, *Black City Cinema,* 2003.

2. *Historical Statistics of the United States Colonial Times to 1957,* 181–209.

3. Wynn, *The African American Experience,* 69–70.

4. As the prospect of war set off a new wave of Black migration, artist Jacob Lawrence embarked on *The Migration Series* (1940–41), a cycle of paintings chronicling the Great Migration of the 1910s and 1920s. See Jacob Lawrence: The Migration Series, accessed January 30, 2021, https://lawrencemigration .phillipscollection.org/the-migration-series.

5. For data on southern Black people relocating in California, see Wynn, *The African American Experience,* 69–73.

6. For San Francisco and Oakland, see Fusfeld and Bates, *The Political Economy,* 49. Exact figures for both cities are given in the table accompanying their text. For Los Angeles, see Leonard, "In the Interest of All Races," in de Graaf, Mulroy, and Taylor, 312. Per Leonard, in 1945 the Black population of Los Angeles was at minimum 133,000 — 7.4 percent of the total population of 1.8 million.

7. Wynn, *The African American Experience,* 67.

8. Fusfeld and Bates, *The Political Economy,* 48.

9. For the 2.6 million figure, see Gregory, *The Southern Diaspora,* 16; for white migrants' home states, see Gregory, 23. For Los Angeles and Detroit, see Lipsitz, *Time Passages,* 117. According to Lipsitz, Los Angeles attracted 750,000 white newcomers during the war years, Detroit, 200,000.

10. Details are drawn from descriptions of housing and consumer goods shortages in Lingeman, *Don't You Know There's a War On?,* notably 7–8, 147

("hot beds"), and 252 (thefts of alarm clocks amid other shortages). Lipsitz, *Time Passages*, 117, also cites eight-hour bed rentals, specifically in Beaumont, Texas.

11. Kristin McGee, *Some Liked It Hot*, 147.

12. Ramsey, *Race Music*, 8.

13. Appadurai, *Modernity at Large*, 3.

14. Ramsey, *Race Music*, 101.

15. Street eviction scenes were a common setting for musical numbers with Black performers in stage revues, presenting "an easy, jiving approach to what in real life would be a personal catastrophe." Petty, *Stealing the Show*, 88. See Petty's discussion of the eviction scene in *Hooray for Love* (1935), performed by Bill Robinson and Fats Waller—both of whom later appeared in Soundies—and dancer Jenny LeGon. Petty, 85–92.

16. Scott, "Black Movement Impolitic," 210.

17. In a 1943 *Billboard* article, Mills asserted that "the smaller night club" and "the high-grade restaurant" were Panorams' most successful locations, but in 1944, Crouch testified that bars and taverns were the basis of the business, rather than more upscale locations. Gordon Mills, "Movie Jukeboxes: What about Them?" in *Billboard 1943 Music Yearbook*, September 25, 1943, 73; "L.O.L." (Crouch), 465.

18. The upheaval that came to be called the Harlem Riot took place on March 19, 1935, prompted by rumors that a teenage shoplifter had been beaten by employees of a dime store on 125th Street. Three people died and more than one hundred were wounded, all of them Black. Property damage was estimated at more than $2 million. A New York City investigation concluded that job discrimination, police aggression, and other injustices had been contributing factors. The second uprising took place on August 1–2, 1943, sparked by the shooting of a Black soldier by a white police officer, after the soldier had attempted to intervene in the arrest of a Black woman for disturbing the peace. Six people died and almost five hundred were injured, with property damage estimated at $5 million.

19. Monica L. Miller, *Slaves to Fashion*, 97.

20. Harris appears with Dickerson in *Low Down Dog* and *Roll 'Em* (both Gould-Gould, 1944).

21. Bluett was an uncredited extra in *Gone with the Wind* and went on to appear in *Cabin in the Sky, Stormy Weather,* and several other movies. He was instrumental in desegregating the film set of *Gone with the Wind*. See Ronald E. Franklin, "Clark Gable Desegregated 'Gone With the Wind' Movie Set," Reel Rundown, accessed January 30, 2021, https://reelrundown.com /film-industry/Clark-Gable-Desegregates-Gone-With-The-Wind-Movie-Set (page also includes a short video on Bluett). See also "Lennie Bluett," IMDb, accessed January 30, 2021, https://www.imdb.com/name/nm0089591/.

22. For more on Whitey's Lindy Hoppers, see Crease, "Divine Frivolity," in Gabbard; Caponi-Tabery, "The Lindy Hop Takes to the Air," in *Jump for Joy*, 51–67; and Trenka, *Jumping the Color Line*, 157–198. In 2018, Norma Miller was still active in the swing-dance scene. See Renata Sago, "An Original Lindy Hopper in Her Element," Arts & Leisure, *New York Times*, August 12, 2018, 15. The last of the original troupe, Miller died a few months later. See Robert D. McFadden, "Norma Miller, Lindy-Hopping 'Queen of Swing,' Is Dead at 99," *New York Times*, May 9, 2019, B14.

23. See "Jumpin' at the Jukebox, Dancin' in the Street," in Trenka, 129–155. As a latter-day Lindy-hopper who attended dance workshops with Frankie Manning and Norma Miller in the 1990s and 2000s, Trenka brings her physical experience of 1940s popular dance to a history and analysis of the subject, including this chapter focusing on Black-cast Soundies.

24. Harvey G. Cohen, *Duke Ellington's America* (Chicago: University of Chicago Press, 2010), 187.

25. *Bli-Blip* and *I Got It Bad and That's Not Good* (both Coslow-Berne, 1942) were adapted from *Jump for Joy*.

26. Lott, "Double V, Double Time," 600.

27. Hall, "What Is This 'Black' in Black Popular Culture?," in Dent, 27. Italics in original.

28. *Statistical Abstract of the United States 1968* (Washington, DC: US Department of Commerce), 461, table 663. See also Robert Bangs, "Public and Private Debt in the United States, 1929–40," in *Survey of Current Business*, November 1941, 18–21. During the war, "charge-account shopping was governed by strict regulation; bills had to be paid within two months or the charge account was frozen. Installment buying was drastically limited." Lingeman, *Don't You Know There's a War On?*, 248–249. By 1945, when the war ended, the national total for installment loans was not quite $2.5 million, less than half the 1940 total. *Statistical Abstract*, 461.

29. Peiss, *Zoot Suit*, 94.

30. Scott, "Race and the Struggle for Cinematic Meaning," 287.

31. The program notes for the original 1941 production of *Jump for Joy*, for example, include a glossary of slang used in the show's lyrics, from "all reet" (all right) to "knock a scarf" (eat a good meal) and "furburg" (town far away). Reprinted in Caponi-Tabery, *Jump for Joy*, 100.

32. *New York Amsterdam News* writer and editor Dan Burley, who worked with Vanita Smythe on her Soundies, also published a guide to slang, *Dan Burley's Original Handbook of Harlem Jive* (1944). See Theodore Hamm, "Dan Burley's *Original Handbook of Harlem Jive* (1944)," *Brooklyn Rail*, December 2008–January 2009, https://brooklynrail.org/2008/12/express/dan-burleys-original-handbook-of-harlem-jive-1944.

33. Mark Cantor notes that the Delta Rhythm Boys recorded the song in December 1940 as a 78 rpm release on Decca Records, under the title "Gimme Some Skin." Cantor suspects that the Soundie *Give Me Some Skin* is an outtake from one of the short films that the group made for Universal, where they were under contract from 1943 to 1946. "Certainly the general look of the film," he writes, "with its many wipes and dissolves, suggests a major studio production rather than a second-tier jukebox production." According to his records, the film was purchased (for $800) by the Soundies Corporation from Official Films, which had purchased it from Transfilm, which, he assumes, had originally acquired it from Universal. Email to author, August 1, 2019.

34. John Louis Clarke, "'Black King' Not So Hot, Critic Says of Movie," *Norfolk Journal and Guide*, January 23, 1932. Cited in Friedman, *Hollywood's African American Films*, 192.

35. Friedman, *Hollywood's African American Films*, 105.

36. Lott, *Love and Theft*, 18.

37. Dinerstein, *Swinging the Machine*, 5.

38. Dinerstein, *Swinging the Machine*, 12.

39. Young, *The Grey Album*, 189.

40. "Day, Dawn, and Dusk" in Marv Goldberg's R&B Notebooks, accessed January 30, 2021, http://www.uncamarvy.com/DayDawnAndDusk/daydawnanddusk.html. See also "Day, Dawn, and Dusk Going Strong; Talented Threesome Breaks Records," *New York Amsterdam News*, March 3, 1945, 7B.

41. The record, titled "Rigoletto in Harlem," documents another performance of the tune by the group. "Day, Dawn & Dusk–Rigoletto In Harlem (Collector Item 805-B) 1946," YouTube, video, 02:49, November 11, 2011, https://www.youtube.com/watch?v=wMQNmeoxz6s.

42. The tune, "Buggin' on a Rug," was written by Henry Nemo, a white songwriter and bandleader who wrote several numbers for Soundies produced by L.O.L. Nemo appears on screen with vocalist Kay Penton in the white-cast L.O.L. Soundie *Hip Hip Hooray* (Oliphant/Leonard-Leonard, 1943). A hepster known as "The Neem," Nemo appeared in that persona in the movie *Song of the Thin Man* (1947). His songs have been used in film and television soundtracks ranging from the 1970s series *Sanford and Son* to the 1996 indie movie *Big Night* and a 2017 episode of the TV series *The Marvelous Mrs. Maisel*. See "Henry Nemo," IMDb, accessed January 30, 2021, https://www.imdb.com/name/nm0625977/.

43. "L.O.L. (Leonard)," 102–103.

44. In his testimony Leonard recalled telling Crouch that "I could get the show from the Ubangi Club on Broadway . . . I studied the Club Ubangi girls and we featured a jungle number [*Plenty of King*, which the Soundies Corporation rejected] and also a house party number." "L.O.L. (Leonard)," 95. The performer

identified in *Good-Nite All* as "Hot-Cha" appears to be the lead performer in *Plenty of King*.

45. *Good-Nite All*, Soundie 12508, Program 1125, *Soundies Parade of Hits*, 2nd ed., 125.

46. Scott, "Black Movement Impolitic," 208.

47. Gates, *Stony the Road*, xix.

CHAPTER 6

1. Ramsey, *Race Music*, 29.

2. Written by Black Canadian songwriter Shelton Brooks, "The Darktown Strutters' Ball" was inspired by an annual event in Chicago. See Lasser, *America's Songs II*, 63.

3. Music historian Nelson George, cited in Ramsey, *Race Music*, 64.

4. *The Darktown Revue* is included on Disc 3 of *Pioneers of African-American Cinema*, a five-disc collection curated by Charles Musser and Jacqueline Najuma Stewart, distributed on DVD and Blu-Ray by Kino Lorber.

5. Ma and Pa Kettle were the main characters in a series of movie comedies produced by Universal in the late 1940s and 1950s. As the series began, they lived with their fifteen children on a ramshackle farm and were commonly described as hillbillies. See *Ma and Pa Kettle* (1949) and other entries in the series on IMDb.

6. *Big Fat Butterfly* (Hersh-Gould, 1944), also starring Gene Rodgers and the Vs, features a backdrop of racist caricatures, as do *Satchel Mouth Baby* and *E-Bob-O-Lee-Bop* (both Hersh-Gould, 1946).

7. Crosby wore blackface for a musical number in *Dixie* (1943), a biopic of Daniel Decatur Emmett, widely credited as the author of the tune.

8. "Program 1095," Movie Machine Reviews, *Billboard*, November 14, 1942, 67.

9. Jazz scholars have long credited the track to Krupa and Eldridge, but the attribution was confirmed in 2010 by Mark Cantor, who located definitive documentation of the recording date in the Soundies production files held in his archives.

10. Scott, "Black Movement Impolitic," 209.

11. Appadurai, *Modernity at Large*, 3.

CHAPTER 7

1. Wynn, *The African American Experience*, 68. He writes that "At Lockheed [in Los Angeles] the number of Black female workers had risen from fifty-four in 1941 to seventeen hundred in 1943; at North American the number had risen from eight women to twenty-five hundred."

2. Kakoudaki, "Pinup," in Williams, 336.

3. Hegarty, *Victory Girls, Khaki-Wackies, and Patriotutes*, 7.

4. Scott, "Black Movement Impolitic," 212, 215.

5. For a detailed analysis of *Take Me Back, Baby*, and especially the positioning of the girlfriend in the narrative, see Scott, "Black Movement Impolitic," 213–215.

6. Willis, *Posing Beauty*, xvii. The book includes an image of a woman modeling a Double V hairstyle, taken by Pittsburgh photographer Charles "Teenie" Harris, on p. 142.

7. For a detailed discussion of the Deep River Boys Soundies (and the work of their musical arranger, Charles Ford of the Four Ginger Snaps), see Mark Cantor, "The Deep River Boys," Celluloid Improvisations, accessed on February 1, 2021, http://www.jazz-on-film.com/deepriverboys.html#learn.

8. Vivian Brown's son Eddie Henderson (b. 1940), a jazz trumpeter and clinical psychiatrist, came to music-world prominence in the 1970s as a member of Herbie Hancock's band. He received his first formal trumpet lessons from Louis Armstrong. See "Eddie Henderson (musician)," Wikipedia, last modified December 10, 2020, https://en.wikipedia.org/wiki/Eddie_Henderson_(musician). See also "Eddie Henderson," Oberlin Conservatory of Music (website), accessed February 1, 2021, https://www.oberlin.edu/eddie-henderson.

9. Jack Barry, "This New Showmanship," *Billboard*, January 31, 1942, 89.

10. Dickerson also sidelines Turner's vocals in the Soundie *Roll 'Em* (Gould-Gould, 1944). With typical Soundies economy, Avanelle Harris appears in this film too, in an outfit also seen in *Low Down Dog*.

11. For this song and for "Get It Off Your Mind," which Jordan also cowrote with DeMetrius, Jordan's songwriting credit appears under the name of his wife, Fleecy Moore, as "F. Moore."

12. Sklaroff, *Black Culture and the New Deal*, 185.

13. Petty, *Stealing the Show*, 7. Perry also appears in the Soundie *Broadway and Main* (Crouch-Crouch, 1946), starring white vocalist and bandleader Gloria Parker. Credited on screen as Stepin Fetchit, he appears in a nonspeaking role as a janitor.

14. Bryant also dances with pianist Gene Rodgers in the Soundie *Big Fat Butterfly* (Hersh-Gould, 1944), notable for its female music combo, the Vs, and for the racist caricature on its set backdrop. Elsewhere, see Gjon Milli's 1944 short film *Jammin' the Blues*, with Bryant contributing a sultry vocal performance of "The Sunny Side of the Street" and a bravura jitterbug with Archie Savage, https://www.youtube.com/watch?v=ohCOIPjyXZM. For Bryant as a choreographer for the major studios, see Bogle, *Bright Boulevards, Bold Dreams*, 240–243.

15. Aljean Harmetz, "Lena Horne, Singer and Actress, Dies at 92," *New York Times*, May 10, 2010, A1.

16. Kakoudaki, "Pinup," 339.

17. Scott, "Black Movement Impolitic," 218.

18. Delson, *Dudley Murphy*, 139. Friedman writes that in 1930s Hollywood, the Production Code Administration "used the 'miscegenation clause' to police the 'color line,' steering studios away from any depictions of 'social equality' in the form of 'mixed' contacts not built around clearly marked, hierarchical distinctions." Friedman, *Hollywood's African American Films*, 104–05.

19. Scott, "Race and the Struggle for Cinematic Meaning," 291. See also Kelley, *Soundies Jukebox Films*, 100.

20. It's unclear why Harris, an accomplished vocalist, would lip-sync another singer's performance. One possible explanation is the American Federation of Musicians' strike and recording ban, which began in August 1942. *Legs Ain't No Good* was copyrighted in December 1942, during the ban, and Soundies producers may have opted to use the track—recorded before the strike—because it included not only Mann's vocals but a full band behind her.

21. Sismondo, *America Walks into a Bar*, 242.

22. Moore, *To Place Our Deeds*, 135. Richmond is home to the Rosie the Riveter/WWII Home Front National Historical Park (https://www.nps.gov/rori/index.htm). Established in 2000, the park interprets the wartime home front through the city's shipyards, factories, housing projects, and other historic sites, with an emphasis on the roles of women and Black Americans.

23. "Angeline Featherstone Fleming," transcript #32 in The Real Rosie the Riveter Project, Tamiment Library, New York University, 18, http://dlib.nyu.edu/rosie/interviews/angeline-featherstone-fleming. Featherstone Fleming specifically mentions the Detroit clubs Sam's, Sunny Wilson's, and the Cellar.

CHAPTER 8

1. Coslow, *Cocktails for Two*, 228. Gale Storm made more than a dozen movies in the 1940s and starred in two hit television series of the 1950s: *My Little Margie* (1953–56) and *The Gale Storm Show: Oh! Susanna* (1956–1960).

2. Etta Jones of the Dandridge Sisters was not the well-known blues, R&B, and gospel vocalist of the same name. For details of Dandridge's life and career, see Bogle, *Dorothy Dandridge*; and Dandridge and Conrad, *Everything and Nothing*.

3. As a member of the Dandridge Sisters, Dorothy Dandridge performed musical numbers in such films as *Irene* (1940), *Going Places* (1937), and *Easy to Take* (1936), and as a singer in the Marx Brothers' *A Day at the Races* (1937). Most of these appearances were uncredited. See "Dorothy Dandridge," IMDb, accessed February 1, 2021, http://www.imdb.com/name/nm0199268/?ref_=fn_al_nm_1.

4. For an analysis of Dandridge's Soundies focusing on her as a mulatto figure embodying the concept of "racechange," see Kelley, *Soundies Jukebox Films*, 97–113.

5. Common in times of hardship, rent parties were events held in private homes, with entrance fees that went toward covering the host's rent or other bills.

6. Although Johnson was a well-regarded bandleader and musician, it's probable that he and his group did not record the soundtrack to *Swing for Your Supper* but mimed it in the film. While conga drums (or tom-toms) were a specialty of Johnson's, on *Swing for Your Supper* the drum solo sounds as if it had been performed on a conventional drum kit rather than the drums seen on screen.

7. A telling example of this stereotyping is the 1932 Betty Boop cartoon, *I'll Be Glad When You're Dead You Rascal You*. The film opens with live footage of Louis Armstrong leading his orchestra in the song, then depicts him as the disembodied, singing head of a "native" pursuing two cartoon characters through the jungle. The image cross-fades between the cartoon head and Armstrong's as he sings.

8. Young, *The Grey Album*, 141–142. Young also posits a second reading of the jungle trope, this one "Black-made and -masked," created "not to express a real self or an imagined other but *to conjure an imagined self.*" (Italics in original.) He cites work by later Black artists, such as Kool & the Gang's "Jungle Boogie" and James Brown's album *In the Jungle Groove*.

9. The Soundies catalog includes the 1942 release *Hot Frogs*, a cartoon animation that features caricatured versions of Soundies performers in a swamp setting. Excerpted from the 1937 MGM animation *Swing Wedding*, it includes caricatures of Fats Waller, Bill "Bojangles" Robinson, and the Mills Brothers. It is not included in the list of Black-cast Soundies in this book. *Hot Frogs*, Soundie 5707, Program 1057, *Soundies Parade of Hits*, 1st ed., 57.

10. Cited in Bogle, *Dorothy Dandridge*, 87.

11. See Peiss, *Zoot Suit*, 94.

12. See Peiss, *Zoot Suit*, 126–130.

13. *Frail* was a slang term for a woman hepcat, supposedly derived from the expression "frail sister," meaning a prostitute. Interestingly, it is not included in Cab Calloway's *Hepster's Dictionary*.

14. In the 1940s, Paul White was a frequent performer with white bandleader Ted Lewis's ensemble. "Lewis does okay with his standard bits," one reviewer wrote, "but it was Paul White who got the screams" with his "hilarious" routines. Bill Smith, "Vaudeville Reviews, Strand, New York, Friday June 4," *Billboard*, June 14, 1947, 44.

15. Sylvester Russell, "Bert Williams–Commentary," *Indianapolis Freeman*, August 1, 1914, cited in Sampson, *Blacks in Blackface*, 341. In the Chanticleer skit, Williams made his entrance by emerging from a large papier-mâché egg.

16. "Program 1083," Movie Machine Reviews, *Billboard*, September 5, 1942, 69.

17. "Locoweed" is a type of plant common in the American West that is poisonous to livestock. Thanks to Mark Cantor and the members of the Toast of Broadway listserv group for their help in clarifying the performance history of "Cow Cow Boogie." Mark Cantor, emails to author, January 27 and January 28, 2013.

18. See "Full Cast and Crew: *Ride 'Em Cowboy* (1942)," IMDb, accessed February 1, 2021, http://www.imdb.com/title/tt0035252/fullcredits?ref_=tt_ft.

19. With the Dandridge Sisters trio, Jackson and his brother Freddie became a quintet known as the Five Rhythmatics, which worked together off and on for roughly five years. Etta Jones later recalled that the girls would sing, "Freddie and Eugene would do most of the dancing and we'd have like little skits in between and then we'd do something together, the three of us and the two boys." Bogle, *Dorothy Dandridge*, 40.

20. In his discussion of the King Cole Trio Soundies, Nat "King" Cole biographer Will Friedwald affirms the superior production values of West Coast Soundies. "It's shocking how shoddy these productions look," Friedwald writes of the Cole Soundies produced in New York in 1945, "much more so than the 1943 entries filmed in Hollywood" with vocalist Ida James. Friedwald, *Straighten Up and Fly Right*, 142. Shot in December 1943, the Soundies with James were copyrighted and released in early 1944.

21. Intensifying the focus on Dandridge, cutaway shots of the pianist and the tableful of cowboys have been deleted from the most widely viewed version of *Cow Cow Boogie* online.

22. Established in 1941, the USO (United Service Organizations, Inc.) is a nonprofit organization that provides live entertainment and other programs to members of the armed forces and their families. During World War II the USO ran thousands of local centers for military personnel, but it is best known for a sister organization, USO Camp Shows, Inc., which presented live stage shows at military facilities around the world. By the time USO Camp Shows dissolved in 1947, it had sent some seven thousand performers overseas. William H. Young and Nancy K. Young, *Music of the World War II Era* (Westport, CT: Greenwood Press, 2008), 141.

23. Herzog, *Dreams of Difference, Songs of the Same*, 56–57.

24. Gabbard, *Jammin' at the Margins*, 221.

25. Jefferson, *Negroland*, 64–65.

26. Bogle, *Dorothy Dandridge*, 551.

27. Bogle, *Dorothy Dandridge*, 253.

28. Jeff Smith, cited in Herzog, *Dreams of Difference, Songs of the Same*, 98.

29. Baldwin, "*Carmen Jones*," in *Notes of a Native Son*, 49.

30. Bosley Crowther, review of *Carmen Jones, New York Times,* October 29, 1954, https://www.nytimes.com/1954/10/29/archives /updated-translation-of-bizet-work-bows.html.

31. See Bogle, *Dorothy Dandridge,* 293–294.

32. Jefferson, *Negroland,* 70.

33. Baldwin, "*Carmen Jones,*" 50. Italics in original.

34. Hilton Als, "Working It," *New Yorker,* July 9 and 16, 2019, 75.

35. Herzog, *Dreams of Difference, Songs of the Same,* 104.

36. Als, "Working It," 75.

37. Jefferson, *Negroland,* 70.

38. Bosley Crowther, review of *Porgy and Bess, New York Times,* June 25, 1959, https://www.nytimes.com/1959/06/25/archives/samuel-goldwyns-porgy-and -bess-has-premiere-at-warner-sidney.html. See also review of *Porgy and Bess, Variety,* December 31, 1958, https://variety.com/1958/film/reviews/porgy-and -bess-2-1200419345/.

CHAPTER 9

1. By one estimate, more than two thousand wartime plants had on-site dance facilities, usually with record players. Lingeman, *Don't You Know There's a War On?,* 250. This phenomenon provides the narrative setting for the white-cast Soundie *Swing Shift Swing* (Coslow-Berne, 1942), which opens with documentary footage of defense plants before moving to a factory recreation-hall setting for some 4 a.m. jitterbugging.

2. The orchestra in *The Blue Danube* is identified as the Mills Philharmonic Orchestra, a Soundies-backed group under the baton of the classically trained Frederick Feher. Both Feher and the Mills Philharmonic were gone in a few months, and a quick look at Soundies like *The Blue Danube* or *Jeannie with the Light Brown Hair* (both Feher-unknown, 1941) will demonstrate why.

3. Earl J. Morris, "Grand Town Day and Night," *Pittsburgh Courier,* November 22, 1941, 21. *Ofay* is a term for white people used in the 1940s.

4. "'Juke Box' Soundies Opening New Outlet for Colored Bands," *Pittsburgh Courier,* November 22, 1941, 20.

5. Herzog, *Dreams of Difference, Songs of the Same,* 48.

6. Wald, *Shout, Sister, Shout!,* 54.

7. "Girls, If You Are Heavy the Apollo Will Admit You 'Free,'" *Chicago Defender,* December 13, 1941, 20. A white-cast Soundie of the tune, *Big Fat Mama* (Hersh-Gould, 1944), was produced on the West Coast three years later.

8. Wald, *Shout, Sister, Shout!,* x.

9. "Talent and Tunes on Music Machines," *Billboard,* July 18, 1942, 68.

10. *The Godmother of Rock 'n' Roll: Sister Rosetta Tharpe*, directed by Mick Czacky (2011), documentary, IMDb, http://www.imdb.com/title/tt4544944/.

11. Tucker, *Swing Shift*, 126.

12. Diagonal framing is put to especially effective use in the Count Basie Orchestra's performance of "One O'Clock Jump" in the feature film *Reveille with Beverly*. The film was made in 1943, two years after *Air Mail Special*, and it's conceivable that the extreme use of diagonal "Dutch angles" in *Reveille* was inspired in part by the framing in *Air Mail Special*.

13. Cohen, *Duke Ellington's America*, 187. See also Stratemann, *Duke Ellington*, 169–171. Program notes for the original production of *Jump for Joy* are reprinted in Caponi-Tabery, *Jump for Joy*, 100. A documentary about *Jump for Joy*, produced by Mark Cantor and directed by Robert Clampett, is currently in production.

14. A facsimile of page 1 of this memo is accessible on Celluloid Improvisations, accessed January 30, 2021, http://jazz-on-film.com/dukeellington.html#_.

15. As dance historian Robert P. Crease noted about *Hot Chocolate* (*"Cottontail"*), "Ellington would have insisted on carefully supervising anything with his name on it." Crease, "Divine Frivolity," in Gabbard, 222.

16. Uploaded to YouTube in September 2007 (as "C Jam Blues"), one version of the film has drawn more than 2.6 million views on its own. "Duke Ellington–C Jam Blues (1942)," YouTube, video, 03:04, accessed February 1, 2021, https://www.youtube.com/watch?v=gOlpcJhNyDI. The film has also been uploaded by the Library of Congress and is available for downloading. "Jam Session," Library of Congress, video, 03:23, accessed February 1, 2021, https://www.loc.gov/item/mbrs00078987/.

17. The Library of Congress lists the musicians heard on the soundtrack as Ray Nance, trumpet, violin; Wallace Jones, trumpet; Rex Stewart, cornet; Joe Nanton, Juan Tizol, Lawrence Brown, trombones; Otto Hardwick, Johnny Hodges, alto sax; Barney Bigard, Ben Webster, Harry Carney, reeds; Duke Ellington, piano; Junior Raglin, acoustic double bass; Fred Guy, guitar; Sonny Greer, drums. See "Jam Session Soundie," Library of Congress, accessed February 1, 2021, https://www.loc.gov/item/jots.200021115.

18. Fred Waller, the producer on the 1942 Calloway Soundies, had directed Calloway and his band in *Cab Calloway's Hi De Ho* (1934), a ten-minute Paramount short. It includes a performance of "Zah Zuh Zaz" with a similar call-and-response with the band but substantially fewer shots.

19. Young, *The Grey Album*, 208.

20. In addition to the Tympany Five, Jordan's combo made Soundies under the name of Louis Jordan and His Band and, in two instances, Louis Jordan and His Orchestra. See *Louis Jordan* in Appendix 2: Performers and Their Films.

21. The soundtracks for Jordan's five 1942 Soundies were recorded in Chicago. Four were sent to New York for filming, and Jordan and his band appear in these. The fifth, "The Outskirts of Town," was sent to the Soundies office in Los Angeles, where it became the soundtrack for the Soundie of the same name, with Dudley Dickerson appearing on screen.

22. Quoted in Lauterbach, *The Chitlin' Circuit*, 115.

23. Lauterbach, *The Chitlin' Circuit*, 294.

24. Wilson (1919–1959) was a pivotal figure in the transition from swing to bebop and jazz. He played with several big bands in the late 1930s and 1940s and went on to work with Thelonious Monk, John Coltrane, and Art Blakey, among others. See Ron Wynn, "Shadow Wilson," Allmusic, accessed February 1, 2021, http://www.allmusic.com/artist/shadow-wilson-mn0000130425.

25. "Program 1118," Movie Machine Reviews, *Billboard*, June 5, 1943, 66.

26. "Program 1119," Movie Machine Reviews, *Billboard*, June 5, 1943, 66.

27. "Also Nab Comedy Pianist," Cocktail Combos, *Billboard*, November 13, 1943, 24.

28. See Mark Cantor, "Gene Rodgers and the Vs: My, My, Ain't That Somethin'," Celluloid Improvisations, accessed January 30, 2021, https://www.jazz-on-film.com/aintthatsomething.html#archive.

29. The two films, both produced by Walter Wanger, are *Vogues of 1938* and *52nd Street*. For an evaluation of Rocco's performances in these films, see Mark Cantor, "Maurice Rocco in the 1930s," Celluloid Improvisations, accessed January 30, 2121, http://www.jazz-on-film.com/mauricerocco.html#learn.

30. In this performance, Rocco effectively demolishes and reconstructs "The Darktown Strutters' Ball." "MAURICE ROCCO–The Darktown Strutters Ball (Color Movie Clip) 1945," YouTube, video, 02:08, July 16, 2016, https://www.youtube.com/watch?v=I2Mp_Er8NOM.

31. Friedwald, *Straighten Up and Fly Right*, 131, 133.

32. Jim Gallert, "Alma Smith: The Countess of Swing," All About Jazz, 1992, accessed February 1, 2021, https://musicians.allaboutjazz.com/almasmith.

33. W. Kim Heron, "Remembering Alma Smith, Detroit Music Countess," *Detroit Metro Times*, May 9, 2012, http://www.metrotimes.com/city-slang/archives/2012/05/09/remembering-alma-smith-detroit-music-countess.

34. Kemp, *Early Jazz Trumpet Legends*, 71.

35. See Reed, "Over Here . . . Over There," in *Hot from Harlem*, 64–69; also Clarence Lusane, *Hitler's Black Victims*, 152–160.

36. Pollard might have been miming another musician's performance—or perhaps not. According to his biographer, Pollard did play piano, though not professionally, and in his early days at Sun Tan Studio would occasionally step in as rehearsal pianist. See Carroll, *Fritz Pollard*, 206. For more on the Sun Tan

musical units, see Mark Cantor, "Soundies Mystery: The Sun Tan Four and Sun Tan Band," Celluloid Improvisations, accessed January 30, 2121, http://www .jazz-on-film.com/suntanband.html#learn.

37. For more on Pat Flowers's Soundies, see "Pat Flowers, Mable Lee and the 'Very Last Soundie,'" Celluloid Improvisations, accessed January 30, 2121, http:// www.jazz-on-film.com/patflowers.html#learn.

38. When the Soundies Corporation folded, plans had been underway to clip excerpts from William D. Alexander's 1946 film *Jivin' in Be-Bop*. But bebop numbers by the film's headliner, Dizzy Gillespie, may not have been what Soundies executives had in mind. The film also featured songs by vocalist Helen Humes, a swing piano-and-organ number by *New York Amsterdam News* writer/ editor Dan Burley and another musician, and performances by Sahji, an exotic dancer. The complete film has been uploaded to YouTube. "Jivin' In Be-Bop (1946)," YouTube, video, 57:06, accessed February 1, 2021, https://www.youtube.com/watch?v=iBRygYQCpkw.

39. West, "On Afro-American Music," 475.

40. Lott, "Double V, Double Time," 599.

41. See "Dallas Bartley and His Orchestra: 'All Ruzzitt Buzzitt,'" Celluloid Improvisations, accessed January 30, 2121, http://www.jazz-on-film.com /ruzzittbuzzitt.html.

CHAPTER 10

1. Extended text crawls were a rarity in Soundies, and this one is frequently cut from versions of the film found online. A version with the full text crawl has been uploaded to susandelson.com.

2. See Hewitt, "Black through White," 45: "Johnny Mercer's lyrics often related to 'Black' subject matter, and his collaboration with Carmichael on 'Lazy Bones' displays a view of the young Black male equally inscribed with the antebellum past."

3. *Lazybones*, Soundie 4602, Program 1046, *Soundies Parade of Hits*, 1st ed., 46.

4. Owen Murphy directed thirteen Soundies for Minoco in New York from early to mid-1942. To avoid confusion with director Dudley Murphy, Owen Murphy's full name is used to identify him in these credits. All credits that specify only "Murphy" refer to Dudley Murphy.

5. A video of the uncensored Library of Congress print is available on susandelson.com. The censored *Shoeshiners and Headliners* is the fourth film in the online reel posted by Historic Films Archive. A visible and clearly audible cut occurs at roughly 05:02:28:00, as shown on the timer at the lower right of the film. "F-7756," Historic Films, video, 05:30:02, accessed February 1, 2021, http://

www.historicfilms.com/tapes/7979. Library of Congress print screened by the author on June 11, 2008, and again on August 13, 2018.

6. *Shoeshiners and Headliners*, Soundie 201, Program 1002, *Soundies Parade of Hits*, 1st ed., 2.

7. MacGillivray and Okuda, "Florence Pepper," in *The Soundies Book*, 209.

8. Lott, *Love and Theft*, 193. Arguably the same might be said of some current-day social media sites.

9. Lott, *Love and Theft*, 163.

10. Lott, *Love and Theft*, 149.

11. Herzog, *Dreams of Difference, Songs of the Same*, 57.

12. Thanks to Mark Cantor for sharing his thoughts and research on the topic of integrated bands in Soundies, particularly Phil Moore and the Phil Moore Four and Lucky Millinder and His Orchestra.

13. Trumpeter Joe Wilder, a veteran of several bands, has given a humorous spin to his recollection of one such experience. See Mark Cantor, "Lucky Millinder and His Orchestra," Celluloid Improvisations, accessed January 30, 2021, http://www.jazz-on-film.com/luckymillinder.html#learn.

In *Swing Shift*, Tucker also writes about white musicians passing as Black in relation to the International Sweethearts of Rhythm. Sweethearts band member Roz Cron has reflected on those experiences; see note 22 in this chapter.

In his discussion of the short film *Jammin' the Blues* (1944), Arthur Knight notes that Black bandleader Fletcher Henderson "hired several white players, though he claimed that in the South they had sometimes been forced to wear blackface." Knight, *Disintegrating the Musical*, 206.

14. *Ofay* is a term for whites used by Black people, and the Black press, in the 1940s. *Ork* is a shortened term for "orchestra," used by the entertainment-industry press and some Black newspapers.

15. "Gene Krupa Forgets South, Features Roy," *Chicago Defender*, March 7, 1942, 20.

16. O'Day and Eells, *High Times, Hard Times*, 113. For Krupa's arrest and the band's dissolution, see Yanow, *Swing*, 92.

17. For more about Moore and his career, see note 47 in chap. 4.

18. In a parallel situation, director Gjon Milli required special permission from Warner Bros. to include white guitarist Barney Kessel with Black musicians in *Jammin' the Blues* (1944). Kessel was shot from an oblique side angle, heavily shadowed. His hands, shot in tight close-ups, were reportedly darkened with berry juice (https://www.youtube.com/watch?v=ohCOIPjyXZM).

19. The "one-drop" rule held that one drop of Black blood made a person Black. As a social construct (and in some states a legal ruling), it was widely promulgated during the Jim Crow era and was still a strong influence in the

1940s. See Malcomson, *One Drop of Blood*; and also Davis, "Black Identity in the United States," in Kivisto and Rundblad.

20. Tucker, *Swing Shift*, 182.

21. Cited in Tucker, *Swing Shift*, 182–183.

22. Tucker, 171. Cron has written movingly about the hazards of touring the South during these years. See Rosalind Cron, "Roz Cron and the International Sweethearts of Rhythm," The Girls in the Band, accessed February 1, 2021, http://thegirlsintheband.com/2013/11/roz-cron-and-the-international -sweethearts-of-rhythm/. See also "The International Sweethearts of Rhythm (1937–1955)," Susan Fleet Archives, accessed February 1, 2021, http://archives .susanfleet.com/documents/international_sweethearts_of_rhythm.html.

23. Tucker, *Swing Shift*, 171.

24. "Millinder's Mixed Band Idea Praised," *Pittsburgh Courier*, January 11, 1947, 17. See also "Lucky Millinder and His Orchestra," Celluloid Improvisations, accessed February 1, 2021, http://www.jazz-on-film.com/luckymillinder.html #learn.

25. In a brief note, Scott references "homosocial tensions" at play in *Hello Bill*. Scott, "Black Movement Impolitic," 224n13.

26. Music and pop-culture historian Will Friedwald writes that Crosby, "a lifelong political conservative and unswerving Republican . . . was nonetheless decades ahead of his time in his lifelong support of Black causes and Black artists." Friedwald, *Straighten Up and Fly Right*, 73.

27. Sklaroff, *Black Culture and the New Deal*, 189.

28. Two years later, Millinder generated intense controversy in the Black community by becoming the host and musical director of the NBC radio program *National Minstrels*. See S. W. Garlington, "Radio Row: Producers Assure Public 'Minstrels' Will Be Okay," *New York Amsterdam News*, June 5, 1948, 14; also Forman, "Employment and Blue Pencils," in Hilmes and Henry, 121–122.

29. Squires, *African Americans and the Media*, 217.

CHAPTER 11

1. "Labor and Industry: Defense and Wartime Employment," in Murray, 99, 101, https://archive.org/stream/in.ernet.dli.2015.6221/2015.6221 .The-Negro-Handbook_djvu.txt.

In 1947, the median family income for Black Americans was slightly more than half that of whites. See the chart "Median family income, by race and ethnicity, 1947–2010 (2011 dollars)," in Mishel et al., *The State of Working America*, 12th ed., http://www.stateofworkingamerica.org/chart /swa-income-table-2-5-median-family-income/.

2. See Katznelson, *When Affirmative Action Was White*, 140; also Humes, "How the GI Bill Shunted Blacks into Vocational Training," 92–104.

3. See Gregory, *The Southern Diaspora*, 16.

4. Some 244 films were copyrighted in 1944; 252 in 1945.

5. Media historian Anna McCarthy specifically mentions a television installed around 1944 in Starr's Tavern in Jersey City, New Jersey. McCarthy, *Ambient Television*, 54–62. See also McCarthy, "The Front Row Is Reserved for Scotch Drinkers," 40.

6. For the Tavern Tele-Symphonic and coin-operated TV jukeboxes, see McCarthy, "Scotch Drinkers," 40. For the Tele-Symphonic and combination television devices, see Forman, *One Night on TV Is Worth Weeks at the Paramount*, 104–106.

7. See Fairchild, *Sounds, Screens, Speakers*, 34–35.

8. Bogle, *Primetime Blues*, 26. Regionally broadcast minstrel shows included *Mississippi Minstrels*, broadcast on KTSL-TV, Hollywood, in 1948; *Dixie Show Boat* on KTLA, Los Angeles, in 1950 (picked up by WPIX, New York, later that year); and on KTTV, Los Angeles, *McMahon's Minstrels* in 1950 and *All Star Minstrels* in 1951. On early national television, white performers still blacked up for occasional minstrel numbers. See Forman, *One Night on TV*, 240.

9. Forman and Kelley cite Soundies as a source of the visual language and aesthetics of musical presentation on early television. See Forman, *One Night on TV*, 173, 184; Kelley, *Soundies Jukebox Films*, 84.

10. In *Beulah*, Waters was followed by Hattie McDaniel and then Louise Beavers. See Bogle, *Primetime Blues*, 25–26.

11. Bogle, *Primetime Blues*, 14. Italics in original.

12. Forman, *One Night on TV*, 253. For more on Howard, see Forman, *One Night on TV*, 251–254, and Bogle, *Primetime Blues*, 13–14.

13. After its successful New York debut, the *Hazel Scott Show* was carried nationally on the DuMont network from June to September 1950. It was abruptly canceled over unsubstantiated charges that Scott was a communist sympathizer. Forman, *One Night on TV*, 256–258.

14. Bogle, *Primetime* Blues, 76. The sponsor, Carter Products, manufactured Arrid deodorant, Rise shaving cream, and other personal-care items. Chambers, *Madison Avenue and the Color Line*, 108. As Chambers points out, in contrast to Cole's series, stereotype-laden shows like *Amos 'n' Andy* had no problem securing national sponsorships. Chambers, 109.

15. Louie Robinson, "The Life and Death of Nat King Cole," *Ebony*, April 1965, 128.

16. In the aftermath of the incident, Cole was criticized in the Black community for performing for segregated audiences in the South. See Epstein, *Nat King Cole*, 258–259; Friedwald, *Straighten Up and Fly Right*, 326–327.

17. See Robert Hilburn, "Singing for Civil Rights," *Los Angeles Times*, January 20, 2009, http://articles.latimes.com/2009/jan/20/entertainment /et-backtracking20.

18. Forman, *One Night on TV*, 271. Several episodes of *The Nat King Cole Show* have been uploaded to YouTube.

19. A clip of the performance has been uploaded to YouTube. "Louis Armstrong 1952 Frank Sinatra Show–Lonesome Man Blues / Confessin'," YouTube, video, 05:55, accessed February 2, 2021, https://www.youtube.com /watch?v=9l6iLotFJV4.

20. See "Dave Gould," IMDb, accessed February 2, 2021, http://www.imdb .com/name/nm0332346/.

21. "Negroes Due for Break in Films with New York as Own Hollywood," *Chicago Defender*, April 27, 1946, 17.

22. "Niteclub owners are frantically cutting their budgets in view of the sudden and drastic slump in business." Major Robinson, "Harlem to Broadway," *Chicago Defender*, June 7, 1947, 19.

23. Henry Brown, "Sun Tan Studios Train Nation's New Starlets," *Chicago Defender*, July 31, 1948, 13.

24. Julius J. Adams, "Pollard Inherited Sun Tan Studio after Producer Died," *New York Amsterdam News*, September 10, 1949, 20.

25. "Sigma Wives Stage Swank Basin St. Benefit: Distaff Side of Sigmas Put the Show on the Road," *New York Amsterdam News*, December 11, 1954, 10.

26. It's likely that Soundies clipped from this film would have focused on the revue and burlesque elements rather than Gillespie and bebop.

27. *The Highest Tradition* is viewable online. Internet Archive, video, 13:13, accessed February 2, 2021, https://archive.org/details/22514TheHighest Tradition. *The Vanities* is also viewable online. Tyler, Texas Black Film Collection, SMU Libraries, video, 10:08, accessed March 7, 2021, https://digitalcollections .smu.edu/digital/collection/ttb/id/4.

28. Grant, *Film Genre Reader III*, 482. Actor-filmmaker William Greaves portrayed one of the roommates. For a detailed description of *Souls of Sin*, see Reid, *Black Lenses, Black Voices*, 47–49.

29. *Burlesque in Harlem* is also known as *Rock & Roll Burlesque* and *A French Peep Show*. In addition to 1949, it carries a 1954 release date. See Wikipedia and IMDB entries for *Burlesque in Harlem*. The complete film is viewable on YouTube. "Burlesque in Harlem (1949)," YouTube, video, 55:43, January 19, 2015, https://www.youtube.com/watch?v=TAyoHYzu2qg.

30. Grant, *Film Genre Reader III*, 482.

31. See Otfinoski, "Alexander, William," in *African Americans in the Visual Arts*, rev. ed., 1.

32. Accessible in the Tyler, Texas Black Film Collection housed at Southern Methodist University. Alexander Productions, "By-Line Newsreel #1" (1953).

video, 07:22, accessed March 29, 2021, https://digitalcollections.smu.edu/digital
/collection/ttb/id/2/.

33. See Bowser, "Pioneers of Black Documentary Film," in Klotman and
Cutler, 28. Bowser dates the move to 1950, but given the production of *By-Line
News*, it may have taken place after 1956.

34. "William Alexander, Producer Featuring Blacks, Dies at 75," *New York
Times*, December 6, 1991, D21.

35. "William Alexander," IMDb, accessed February 2, 2021, http://www.imdb
.com/name/nm0018796/?ref_=fn_nm_nm_2.

36. "William Forest Crouch," IMDb, accessed February 2, 2021, http://www
.imdb.com/name/nm0189464/.

37. "William Forest Crouch," Wikipedia, last modified November 25, 2020,
08:37. https://en.wikipedia.org/wiki/William_Forest_Crouch.

38. See "Leonard Anderson," IMDb, accessed February 2, 2021, http://www
.imdb.com/name/nm0027075/?ref_=fn_al_nm_2; and "Don Malkames,"
IMDb, accessed February 2, 2021, http://www.imdb.com/name/nm0539776/?ref
_=nv_sr_1.

39. See Koszarski, *Hollywood on the Hudson*, 393–394; and Hughes, *Catchers of
the Light*, 1194.

40. MacGillivray and Okuda, *The Soundies Book*, 394.

41. "L.O.L.," (Ulcigan), 373–374.

42. For more on these films, see Mark Cantor, "Sepia Cinderella, part one,"
"Sepia Cinderella, part two," and "'Oh What a Tangled Web We Weave': Three
Black Cast Films from the 1940s," Celluloid Improvisations, accessed February 2,
2021, http://jazz-on-film.com/mistakenidentity.html#one.

43. "L.O.L.," (Ulcigan), 373.

44. See Coslow's description of his career as an investment consultant in his
biography. Coslow, *Cocktails for Two*, 1977.

45. "'Soundies' Getting Air-Pix Test," Radio and Television, *Billboard*,
November 11, 1944, 12, 63.

46. "'Soundies' Getting Air-Pix Test."

47. See MacGillivray and Okuda, *Soundies Book*, 397.

48. Mark Cantor, email to author, June 9, 2020.

49. Classified ad appearing under Cameras and Equipment category, *New York
Times*, November 14, 1946.

50. For more about Castle Films, Official Films, and a detailed list of the
compilation reels, see MacGillivray and Okuda, *Soundies Book*, 397, 401–414.

51. See Kelley, *Soundies Jukebox Films*, 119–120; also "Brenner a Disc Jockey
on TV with Soundie Films Instead of Wax," *Variety*, February 2, 1949, 37; and
"'Requestfully Yours' Televised by WATV," *Billboard*, February 5, 1949, 41. See

also Kelley's discussion of the factors involved in Soundies' successful transition to television. Kelley, *Soundies Jukebox Films*, 118.

52. A print of the Cab Calloway Soundie *Minnie the Moocher*, uploaded on YouTube by Prelinger Archives, opens with a credit reading "Official Television Inc. Presents." "Soundie: Minnie the Moocher (Cab Calloway)," YouTube, video, 03:18, January 9, 2017, https://www.youtube.com/watch?v=x_sg7kmoglA.

53. "Old Soundies, Costing 300G, Bring in 700G," *Billboard*, February 3, 1951, 4.

54. Kelley, *Soundies Jukebox Films*, 122. For a broad discussion of Panorams after Soundies, see Kelley, 121–125. For more on Panorams in the adult film industry, see Herzog, "Fetish Machines," in Jacques, 47–89; and Alilunas, *Smutty Little Movies*, 42–50.

55. For detailed descriptions of all four programs, see Yanow, *Jazz on Film*, 60–62.

56. In addition to *Harlem Highlights*, the cassette titles in Maltin's series were *The 1940s Music Machine*, *Singing Stars of the Swing Era*, and *Big Band Swing*. Leonard Maltin's Movie Memories–Soundies (BMG Video, 1991). See Yanow, *Jazz on Film*, 91.

57. The absence of title credits isn't always a by-product of online posting. In compiling their medley reels, Castle and Official Films routinely cut all Soundies identification, including original title credits, from their reels. For Soundies collectors, these later medley reels were among the most widely available prints. See MacGillivray and Okuda, *Soundies Book*, 401.

58. Hall, "What Is This 'Black' in Black Popular Culture?" in Dent, 32. Italics in original.

APPENDIX 1

1. The Library of Congress website lists Leonard Anderson as the director for the 1946 Soundies starring Lucky Millinder and His Orchestra and the Soundies starring the International Sweethearts of Rhythm, all clipped from short films by producer William D. Alexander. However, the screen credits on those films identify Ray Sandiford as director, so he is listed as such on these films.

2. After the Mills Brothers made their 1942 Soundies, Harry Mills was drafted into the military. His place was taken by Gene Smith, who appears in the 1944 Soundies. Harry Mills rejoined the group after the war.

3. Although it would appear that the catalog numbers on these two Jordan Medleys should be reversed, they are in fact correct.

4. Per Mark Cantor, this film clip was licensed by Soundies Films, Inc. but not released. See Mark Cantor, "Henri Woode and His Orchestra," Celluloid Improvisations, accessed April 24, 2017, http://www.jazz-on-film.com/henriwoode.html#learn.

APPENDIX 2

1. *The Soundies Book* by Scott McGillivray and Ted Okuda lists *Don't Get Around Much Anymore* as a ninth Delta Rhythm Boys Soundie. According to Mark Cantor, this is a later Snader Telescription, not a Soundie, so it has not been included in these appendixes. Email to author, December 7, 2019.

2. After the Mills Brothers made their 1942 Soundies (*Caravan, Paper Doll,* and *Rockin' Chair*), Harry Mills was drafted into the military. His place was taken by Gene Smith, who appears in the 1944 Soundies. Harry Mills rejoined the group after the war.

BIBLIOGRAPHY

Ake, David Andrew. *Jazz Cultures*. Berkeley: University of California Press, 2002.

Alilunas, Peter. *Smutty Little Movies: The Creation and Regulation of Adult Video.* Berkeley: University of California Press, 2016.

Appadurai, Arjun. *Modernity at Large: Cultural Dimensions of Globalization.* Minneapolis: University of Minnesota Press, 1996.

Austen, Jake. *TV-a-Go-Go: Rock on TV from American Bandstand to American Idol.* Chicago Review Press, 2005.

Baldwin, James. "*Carmen Jones*: The Dark Is Light Enough." In *Notes of a Native Son*, 49–50. Boston: Beacon, 1955.

Bateman, David A., Ira Katznelson, and John S. Lapinski. *Southern Nation: Congress and White Supremacy after Reconstruction.* Princeton, NJ: Princeton University Press, 2018.

Bogle, Donald. *Bright Boulevards, Bold Dreams: The Story of Black Hollywood.* New York: One World Ballantine Books, 2006.

———. *Dorothy Dandridge*. New York: Amistad, 1997.

———. *Primetime Blues: African Americans on Network Television.* New York: Farrar, Straus & Giroux, 2001.

———. *Toms, Coons, Mulattoes, Mammies, and Bucks: An Interpretive History of Blacks in American Films.* New York: Continuum Publishing, 1994.

Bowser, Pearl. "Pioneers of Black Documentary Film." In *Struggles for Representation: African American Documentary Film and Video,* edited by Phyllis R. Klotman and Janet K. Cutler, 1–33. Bloomington: Indiana University Press, 1999.

Caddoo, Cara. *Envisioning Freedom: Cinema and the Building of Modern Black Life.* Cambridge, MA: Harvard University Press, 2014.

Campbell, Tracy. *The Year of Peril: America in 1942.* New Haven, CT: Yale University Press, 2020.

Cantor, Mark. *Music for the Eyes: Soundies and Jukebox Shorts of the 1940s.* Jefferson, NC: McFarland, 2022 (on press).

Caponi-Tabery, Gena. *Jump for Joy: Jazz, Basketball & Black Culture in 1930s America.* Amherst: University of Massachusetts Press, 2008.

Carroll, John M. *Fritz Pollard: Pioneer in Racial Advancement.* Urbana: University of Illinois Press, 1992.

Chambers, Jason. *Madison Avenue and the Color Line: African Americans in the Advertising Industry.* Philadelphia: University of Pennsylvania Press, 2008.

Cohen, Harvey G. *Duke Ellington's America.* Chicago: University of Chicago Press, 2010.

Collins, Ann V. *All Hell Broke Loose: American Race Riots from the Progressive Era through World War II.* Santa Barbara, CA: Praeger, 2012.

Coslow, Sam. *Cocktails for Two: The Many Lives of Giant Songwriter Sam Coslow.* New Rochelle, NY: Arlington House Publishers, 1977.

Crease, Robert P. "Divine Frivolity: Hollywood Representations of the Lindy Hop, 1937–1942." In *Representing Jazz,* edited by Krin Gabbard, 207–227. Durham, NC: Duke University Press, 1995.

Cripps, Thomas. *Hollywood's High Noon: Moviemaking & Society before Television.* Baltimore, MD: Johns Hopkins University Press, 1997.

———. *Making Movies Black: The Hollywood Message Movie from World War II to the Civil Rights Era.* New York: Oxford University Press, 1993.

———. "The Myth of the Southern Box Office: A Factor in Racial Stereotyping in the American Movies, 1920–1940." In *The Black Experience in America: Selected Essays,* edited by James C. Curtis and Lester L. Gould, 116–144. Austin: University of Texas Press, 1970.

———. *Slow Fade to Black: The Negro in American Film, 1900–1942.* 1977. Reprint, Oxford, UK: Oxford University Press, 1993.

Dalfiume, Richard M. "The 'Forgotten Years' of the Negro Revolution." *Journal of American History* 55, no. 1 (June 1968): 90–106.

Dandridge, Dorothy, and Earl Conrad. *Everything and Nothing: The Dorothy Dandridge Tragedy.* New York: HarperCollins, 2000.

Davis, F. James. "Black Identity in the United States." In *Multiculturalism in the United States: Current Issues, Contemporary Voices,* edited by Peter Kivisto and Georganne Rundblad, 101–111. Thousand Oaks, CA: Pine Forge Press, 2000.

Delson, Susan. *Dudley Murphy, Hollywood Wild Card.* Minneapolis: University of Minnesota Press, 2006.

Dinerstein, Joel. *Swinging the Machine: Modernity, Technology, and African American Culture between the World Wars.* Amherst: University of Massachusetts Press, 2003.

Doherty, Thomas. "Documenting the 1940s." In *Boom and Bust: American Cinema in the 1940s,* edited by Thomas Schatz, 397–421. Berkeley: University of California Press, 1999.

Driscoll, Joseph. *Pacific Victory 1945.* Philadelphia: J. B. Lippincott, 1944.

Epstein, Daniel Mark. *Nat King Cole.* New York: Farrar, Straus and Giroux, 1999.

Fairchild, Charles. *Sounds, Screens, Speakers: An Introduction to Music and Media.* London: Bloomsbury, 2019.

Forman, Murray. "Employment and Blue Pencils: NBC, Race, and Representation, 1926–55." In *NBC: America's Network,* edited by Michele Hilmes and Michael Lowell Henry, 117–134. Berkeley: University of California Press, 2007.

———. *One Night on TV Is Worth Weeks at the Paramount: Popular Music on Early Television.* Durham, NC: Duke University Press, 2012.

Friedman, Ryan Jay. *Hollywood's African American Films: The Transition to Sound.* New Brunswick, NJ: Rutgers University Press, 2011.

Friedwald, Will. *Straighten Up and Fly Right: The Life and Music of Nat King Cole.* New York: Oxford University Press, 2020.

Fusfeld, Daniel Roland, and Timothy Mason Bates. *The Political Economy of the Urban Ghetto.* Carbondale: Southern Illinois University Press, 1984.

Gabbard, Krin. *Jammin' at the Margins: Jazz and the American Cinema.* Chicago: University of Chicago Press, 1996.

Gates, Henry Louis, Jr. *Stony the Road: Reconstruction, White Supremacy, and the Rise of Jim Crow.* New York: Penguin, 2019.

Gibson, Campbell, and Kay Jung. "Historical Census Statistics on Population Totals by Race, 1790 to 1990, and by Hispanic Origin, 1790 to 1990, for Large Cities and Other Urban Places in the United States." US Census Bureau Population Division Working Paper No. 76, Washington, DC, February 2005. https://www.census.gov/library/working-papers/2005/demo/POP-twps0076.html.

Giddins, Gary. "The Mirror of Swing." In *Faces in the Crowd: Musicians, Writers, Actors and Filmmakers,* 117–125. New York: Oxford University Press, 1992.

Goodwin, Doris Kearns. *No Ordinary Time: Franklin and Eleanor Roosevelt: The Home Front in World War II.* New York: Simon & Schuster, 1994.

Grant, Barry Keith. *Film Genre Reader III.* Austin: University of Texas Press, 2003.

Green, Adam. *Selling the Race: Culture, Community, and Black Chicago, 1940–1955.* Chicago: University of Chicago Press, 2007.

Gregory, James N. *The Southern Diaspora: How the Great Migrations of Black and White Southerners Transformed America.* Chapel Hill: University of North Carolina Press, 2005.

Hall, Jacquelyn Dowd. "The Long Civil Rights Movement and the Political Uses of the Past." *Journal of American History* 91, no. 4 (March 2005): 1233–1263.

Hall, Stuart. "What Is This 'Black' in Black Popular Culture?" In *Black Popular Culture*, edited by Gina Dent, 21–33. Seattle: Seattle Bay, 1992.

———. "The Whites of Their Eyes: Racist Ideologies and the Media." In *Silver Linings: Some Strategies for the Eighties*, edited by George Bridges and Rosalind Brunt, 28–52. London: Lawrence and Wishart, 1981.

Harpster, Jack. *King of the Slots: William "Si" Redd*. Santa Barbara, CA: Praeger, 2010.

Hegarty, Marilyn E. *Victory Girls, Khaki-Wackies, and Patriotutes: The Regulation of Female Sexuality during World War II*. New York: New York University Press, 2008.

Herzog, Amy. "Discordant Visions: The Peculiar Musical Images of the Soundies Jukebox Film." *American Music* 22, no. 1 (Spring 2004): 27–39.

———. *Dreams of Difference, Songs of the Same: The Musical Moment in Film*. Minneapolis: University of Minnesota Press, 2010.

———. "Fetish Machines: Peep-Shows, Co-Optation, and Technological Adaptation." In *Adaptation Theories*, edited by Jillian Saint Jacques, 47–89. Maastricht: Jan van Eyck Academie, 2011.

———. "Illustrating Music: The Impossible Embodiments of the Jukebox Film." In *Medium Cool: Music Videos from Soundies to Cellphones*, edited by Roger Beebe and Jason Middleton, 30–58. Durham: North Carolina University Press, 2007.

Hewitt, Roger. "Black through White: Hoagy Carmichael and the Cultural Reproduction of Racism." *Popular Music* 3:33–50. Cambridge, UK: Cambridge University Press, 1983.

Historical Statistics of the United States Colonial Times to 1957: A Statistical Abstract Supplement. Washington, DC: United States Bureau of the Census, 1960. https://www.census.gov/library/publications/1960/compendia /hist_stats_colonial-1957.html.

Hughes, Stefan. *Catchers of the Light: The Forgotten Lives of the Men and Women Who First Photographed the Heavens*. London: ArtdeCiel Publishing, 2012.

Humes, Edward. "How the GI Bill Shunted Blacks into Vocational Training." *Journal of Blacks in Higher Education* 53 (Autumn 2006): 92–104.

Hyatt, Wesley. *A Critical History of Television's* The Red Skelton Show, *1951–1971*. Jefferson, NC: McFarland, 2004.

James, Rawn, Jr. *The Double V: How Wars, Protest, and Harry Truman Desegregated America's Military*. New York: Bloomsbury, 2013.

Jefferson, Margo. *Negroland: A Memoir*. New York: Pantheon, 2015.

Jones, John Bush. *The Songs That Fought the War: Popular Music and the Home Front, 1939–1945*. Waltham, MA: Brandeis University Press, 2006.

Kakoudaki, Despina. "Pinup: The American Secret Weapon in World War II." In *Porn Studies*, edited by Linda Williams, 335–369. Durham, NC: Duke University Press, 2004.

Katznelson, Ira. *Fear Itself: The New Deal and the Origins of Our Time.* New York: Liveright Publishing, 2013.

———. *When Affirmative Action Was White: An Untold History of Racial Inequality in Twentieth-Century America.* New York: W. W. Norton, 2005.

Kelley, Andrea J. "'A Revolution in the Atmosphere': The Dynamics of Site and Screen in 1940s Soundies." *Cinema Journal* 54, no. 2 (Winter 2015): 72–93.

———. *Soundies Jukebox Films and the Shift to Small-Screen Culture.* New Brunswick, NJ: Rutgers University Press, 2018.

Kemp, Larry. *Early Jazz Trumpet Legends.* Pittsburgh, PA: RoseDog Books, 2016.

Kendi, Ibram X. *Stamped from the Beginning: The Definitive History of Racist Ideas in America.* New York: Nation Books, 2016.

Knight, Arthur. *Disintegrating the Musical: Black Performance and American Musical Film.* Durham, NC: Duke University Press, 2002.

———. "Star Dances: African-American Constructions of Stardom, 1925–1960." In *Classic Hollywood, Classic Whiteness,* edited by Daniel Bernardi, 386–414. Minneapolis: University of Minnesota Press, 2001.

Koppes, Clayton R. "Regulating the Screen: The Office of War Information and the Production Code Administration." In *Boom and Bust: American Cinema in the 1940s,* edited by Thomas Schatz, 262–281. Berkeley: University of California Press, 1999.

Koppes, Clayton R., and Gregory D. Black. "Blacks, Loyalty, and Motion-Picture Propaganda in World War II." *Journal of American History* 73, no. 2 (September 1986): 383–406.

———. "What to Show the World: The Office of War Information and Hollywood, 1942–1945." *Journal of American History* 64, no. 1 (June 1977): 87–105.

Koszarski, Richard. *Hollywood on the Hudson: Film and Television in New York from Griffith to Sarnoff.* Brunswick, NJ: Rutgers University Press, 2008.

Lasser, Michael. *America's Songs II: Songs from the 1890s to the Post-War Years.* New York: Routledge, 2013.

Lauterbach, Preston. *The Chitlin' Circuit and the Road to Rock 'n' Roll.* New York: W. W. Norton, 2011.

Lee, Ulysses. *The Employment of Negro Troops.* United States Army in World War II, Special Studies. Washington, DC: Center of Military History United States Army, 2000. http://www.history.army.mil/books/wwii/11-4/index.htm.

Leonard, Kevin Allen. "'In the Interest of All Races': African Americans and Interracial Cooperation in Los Angeles during and after World War II." In *Seeking El Dorado: African Americans in California,* edited by Lawrence B. de Graaf, Kevin Mulroy, and Quintard Taylor, 309–342. Seattle: University of Washington Press, 2015.

Lingeman, Richard R. *Don't You Know There's a War On? The American Home Front, 1941–1945.* New York: G. P. Putnam's Sons, 1970.

Lipsitz, George. *Time Passages: Collective Memory and American Popular Culture.* Minneapolis: University of Minnesota Press, 2001.

"L.O.L. Productions, Inc., Plaintiff-Respondent, against Soundies Distributing Corporation of America, Inc., Defendant-Appellant." New York State Supreme Court Trial Term Part XVI, 1944. Included in the 1945 records of the New York Supreme Court Appellate Division—First Department, digitized under public domain fair use by Google Books. Witness testimonies begin on page 72. https://books.google.com/books?id=d_Eb-tbjfeIC&pg=RA1-PA71&lpg=RA1-PA71&dq=LOL+Productions+Supreme+Court+Trial+Term+Part+XVI+1944&source=bl&ots=rIO5adp_K9&sig=ACfU3U3ircyVgSy66DsQxkSMaQgH4UdNIQ&hl=en&sa=X&ved=2ahUKEwi6z46jpNXoAhWzgnIEHasJB30Q6AEwAHoECAwQKA#v=onepage&q=LOL%20Productions%20Supreme%20Court%20Trial%20Term%20Part%20XVI%201944&f=false.

Lott, Eric. "Double V, Double Time: Bebop's Politics of Style." *Callaloo* 36 (Summer 1988): 597–605.

———. *Love and Theft: Blackface Minstrelsy and the American Working Class.* New York: Oxford University Press, 1993.

Lukow, Gregory. "The Archaeology of Music Video: Soundies, Snader Telescriptions, and Scopitones." National Video Festival program book. Los Angeles: American Film Institute, 1986.

Lusane, Clarence. *Hitler's Black Victims: The Historical Experiences of European Blacks, Africans and African Americans in the Nazi Era.* New York: Routledge, 2002.

MacAdams, Lewis. *Birth of the Cool: Beat, Bebop, and the American Avant-Garde.* New York: Free Press, 2001.

MacGillivray, Scott, and Ted Okuda. *The Soundies Book: A Revised and Expanded Guide.* New York: iUniverse, 2007.

Madinger, John. *Money Laundering: A Guide for Criminal Investigators.* Boca Raton, FL: CRC Press, 2012.

Malcomson, Scott L. *One Drop of Blood: The American Misadventure of Race.* New York: Farrar, Straus, Giroux, 2000.

Massood, Paula J. *Black City Cinema: African American Urban Experiences in Film.* Philadelphia: Temple University Press, 2003.

———. *Making a Promised Land: Harlem in 20th-Century Photography and Film.* New Brunswick, NJ: Rutgers University Press, 2013.

McCarthy, Anna. *Ambient Television: Visual Culture and Public Space.* Durham, NC: Duke University Press, 2001.

———. "'The Front Row Is Reserved for Scotch Drinkers': Early Television's Tavern Audience." *Cinema Journal* 34, no. 4 (Summer, 1995): 31–49.

McGee, Kristin. *Some Liked It Hot: Jazz Women in Film and Television, 1928–1959.* Middletown, CT: Wesleyan University Press, 2009.

McWilliams, Carey M. *Southern California Country: An Island on the Land*. New York: Duell, Sloan and Pearce, 1946.

Miller, Monica L. *Slaves to Fashion: Black Dandyism and the Styling of Black Diasporic Identity*. Durham, NC: Duke University Press, 2009.

Miller, Richard E. *The Messman Chronicles: African Americans in the U.S. Navy, 1932–1943*. Annapolis, MD: Naval Institute Press, 2003.

Mills Novelty Company. "Soundies Panoram." Sales booklet for prospective Panoram operators. Chicago: Mills Novelty, 1940.

Mishel, Lawrence, Josh Bivens, Elise Gould, and Heidi Shierholz. *The State of Working America*. 12th ed. Ithaca, NY: Cornell University Press, 2012.

Moon, Spencer. *Reel Black Talk: A Sourcebook of 50 American Filmmakers*. Westport, CT: Greenwood, 1997.

Moore, Shirley Ann Wilson. *To Place Our Deeds: The African American Community in Richmond, California, 1910–1963*. Berkeley: University of California Press, 2001.

Murray, Florence, ed. *The Negro Handbook, 1946–1947*. New York: A. A. Wyn, 1947. https://archive.org/stream/in.ernet.dli.2015.6221/2015.6221 .The-Negro-Handbook_djvu.txt.

Nalty, Bernard C. *Strength for the Fight: A History of Black Americans in the Military*. New York: Free Press, 1986.

O'Day, Anita, and George Eells. *High Times, Hard Times*. New York: Limelight Editions, 2004.

Otfinoski, Steven. "Alexander, William." In *African Americans in the Visual Arts*. Rev. ed. New York: Infobase Publishing, Facts on File Library of American History, 2011.

Peiss, Kathy. *Zoot Suit: The Enigmatic Career of an Extreme Style*. Philadelphia: University of Pennsylvania Press, 2011.

Petty, Miriam J. *Stealing the Show: African American Performers and Audiences in 1930s Hollywood*. Berkeley: University of California Press, 2016.

Rajchman, John. "Thinking with Shiraga." In *Kazuo Shiraga*, 269–274. Exhibition catalog. New York: Dominique Lévy Gallery and Axel Vervoordt Gallery, 2015.

Ramsey, Guthrie P., Jr. *Race Music: Black Cultures from Bebop to Hip-Hop*. Berkeley: University of California Press, 2004.

Reed, Bill. "Over Here . . . Over There: Valaida Snow." In *Hot from Harlem: Twelve African American Entertainers, 1890–1960*, 64–69. Jefferson, NC: McFarland, 2010.

Reid, Mark A. *Black Lenses, Black Voices: African American Film Now*. Lanham, MD: Rowman & Littlefield, 2005.

Roberts, Brian. *Blackface Nation: Race, Reform, and Identity in American Popular Music, 1812–1925*. Chicago: University of Chicago Press, 2017.

Rose, Kenneth. *Myth and the Greatest Generation: A Social History of Americans in World War II*. New York: Routledge, 2008.

Sampson, Henry T. *Blacks in Blackface: A Sourcebook on Early Black Musical Shows*, Vol. 1. 2nd ed. Lanham, MD: Scarecrow, 2014.

Savage, Barbara Dianne. *Broadcasting Freedom: Radio, War, and the Politics of Race 1938–1948*. Chapel Hill: University of North Carolina Press, 1999.

Schatz, Thomas. *Boom and Bust: American Cinema in the 1940s*. Berkeley: University of California Press, 1999.

Scott, Ellen C. "Black Movement Impolitic: Soundies, Regulation, and Black Pleasure." *African American Review* 49, no. 3 (Fall 2016): 205–226.

———. "Race and the Struggle for Cinematic Meaning: Film Production, Censorship, and African American Reception, 1940–1960." PhD diss., University of Michigan, 2007. https://deepblue.lib.umich.edu/handle/2027.42 /57696.

Seagrave, Kerry. *Jukeboxes: An American Social History*. Jefferson, NC: McFarland, 2002.

Seibert, Brian. *What the Eye Hears: A History of Tap Dancing*. New York: Farrar, Straus and Giroux, 2015.

Sickels, Robert. *The 1940s*. Santa Barbara, CA: Greenwood, 2004.

Singer Barry. *Black and Blue: The Life and Lyrics of Andy Razaf*. New York: Schirmer Books, 1992.

Sismondo, Christine. *America Walks into a Bar: A Spirited History of Taverns and Saloons, Speakeasies and Grog Shops*. New York: Oxford University Press, 2011.

Sitkoff, Harvard. "Racial Militancy and Interracial Violence in the Second World War." *Journal of American History* 58, no. 3 (December 1971): 661–681.

Sklaroff, Lauren Rebecca. *Black Culture and the New Deal: The Quest for Civil Rights in the Roosevelt Era*. Chapel Hill: University of North Carolina Press, 2009.

Soundies Parade of Hits. Catalogs. 1st and 2nd eds. Chicago: Soundies Distributing Corporation of America, 1942 and 1945.

Squires, Catherine R. *African Americans and the Media*. Cambridge, UK: Polity, 2009.

Statistical Abstract of the United States 1968. Washington, DC: US Department of Commerce. https://books.google.com/books?id=xZNCAQAAMAAJ &pg=PA461&dq=car+financing+1940&hl=en&sa=X&ved= 0ahUKEwjljYHS9snjAhWiSt8KHQ3nCTIQ6AEIPTAE#v=onepage&q=car %20financing%201940&f=false.

Stentiford, Barry M. *Tuskegee Airmen*. Santa Barbara, CA: Greenwood, 2012.

Stewart, Jacqueline Najuma. *Migrating to the Movies: Cinema and Black Urban Modernity*. Berkeley: University of California Press, 2005.

Stratemann, Klaus. *Duke Ellington Day by Day and Film by Film*. Copenhagen: Jazz Media, 1992.

Thompson, Robert Farris. "An Aesthetic of the Cool." *African Arts* 7, no. 1 (Autumn 1973): 41–43, 64–67, 89–91.

Toll, Robert C. "Social Commentary in Late-Nineteenth-Century White Minstrelsy." In *Inside the Minstrel Mask: Readings in Nineteenth-Century Blackface Minstrelsy*, edited by Annemarie Bean, James V. Hatch, and Brooks McNamara, 86–109. Middletown, CT: Wesleyan University Press, 1996.

Tolson, Melvin B. *"Gone with the Wind* Is More Dangerous Than *Birth of a Nation."* In *Caviar and Cabbage: Selected Columns by Melvin B. Tolson from the* Washington Tribune, *1937–1944*, edited by Robert M. Farnsworth, 215. Columbia: University of Missouri Press, 1982.

Trenka, Susie. *Jumping the Color Line: Vernacular Jazz Dance in American Film, 1929–1945*. New Barnet, UK: John Libbey, 2021.

Tucker, Sherrie. *Swing Shift: "All-Girl" Bands of the 1940s*. Durham, NC: Duke University Press, 2000.

Wald, Gayle F. *Shout, Sister, Shout! The Untold Story of Rock-and-Roll Trailblazer Sister Rosetta Tharpe*. Boston: Beacon, 2007.

Washburn, Patrick S. *The African American Newspaper: Voice of Freedom*. Evanston, IL: Northwestern University Press, 2006.

West, Cornel. "On Afro-American Music: From Bebop to Rap." In *The Cornel West Reader*, 474–484. New York: Basic Civitas Books, 1999.

Willis, Deborah. *Posing Beauty: African American Images from the 1890s to the Present*. New York: W. W. Norton, 2009.

Wynn, Neil A. *The African American Experience during World War II*. Lanham, MD: Rowman & Littlefield, 2010.

Yanow, Scott. *Jazz on Film: The Complete Story of the Musicians and Music Onscreen*. San Francisco: Backbeat Books, 2004.

———. *Swing*. San Francisco: Miller Freeman Books, 2000.

Young, Kevin. *The Grey Album: On the Blackness of Blackness*. New York: Graywolf, 2012.

INDEX

Cooke, Charles L., 67, 80

cool: as quality of urbane city dwellers, 101, 103–4; as quality of war-themed Soundies, 86, 88, 90

Cooper, Ralph, 23, 24

Coslow, Sam, 49, 51, 52, 148, 325, 347n4, 350n41; career after Soundies, 213; career background of, 50; in Chicago, 55–56; Dandridge performances prized by, 161; on Dandridge "jungle" Soundies, 51, 141, 148, 154; Ellington Soundies and, 177, 178; polished production values of, 57; on popularity of Dandridge, 151, 170; as song writer, 50, 52

Count Basie and His Orchestra, 165

country-western music, 190

Counts and the Countess, The (Smith, Faire, and Wilder), 51, 188

Covered Wagon Rolled Right Along, The (Barry/Waller-Murray, 1941), 110

Cow Cow Boogie (Coslow-Berne, 1942), 5, 23–24, 161–63, *163*, 171, 217, 363n17, 363n21

Crash Dive (film, 1943), 22

Crawford, Llewelyn ("Lou Crawford," "Lou Ellen"), 58, 60, 101

Crawford, Traverse, 103

Crease, Robert P., 365n15

creative autonomy, 44

Cripps, Thomas, 348n19, 349n28

Cron, Roz, 202, 369n22

Crosby, Bing, 20, 123, 126, 155, 157, 203, 341–42n6, 359n7, 369n26

Crouch, William Forest, 14, 16, 25, 53, 57, 182–83, 186, 207, 325, 347n4; Berne and, 51, 148; career after Soundies, 212; cheesecake shots and, 58, 141, 143–44; court testimony of, 12–13, 34, 35, 36, 41, 44, 49; fact-finding tours of, 35, 59; Filmcraft Productions, 56; interest in Black-cast film production, 58, 59; as key figure in Soundies Corporation lineup, 55; lack of Hollywood background, 56–57; L.O.L. output analyzed by, 38–40; M films produced by, 67; number of Soundies produced/directed by, 57–58; shift from management to production, 56, 63; with

Tuxedo Junction cast/crew, 217; war-related Soundies and, 77, 80, 81, 90; WFC Productions company of, 56

Crowther, Bosley, 168

Cuban Episode (Coslow-Berne, 1942), 101

Dalfiume, Richard M., 76, 79

Dallas Bartley and His Orchestra, 189

Dan Burley's Original Handbook of Harlem Jive (Burley, 1944), 357n32

dance, 95, 101, 114, 115, 140, 147, 162, 175, 194, 195; jitterbug dancing, 97, 98, 99, 100, 101, 123–25, *126*, 141, 146, 153, 176, 182, 193, 360n14; Lindy hop, 92, 98, 110, 146, 357nn22–23; tap dancing, 110, 155, 166, 195. *See also* Whitey's Lindy Hoppers

Dance Your Old Age Away (Crouch-Crouch, 1944), 110

Dandridge, Dorothy, 42, 75, 137, 173, 182, 200, 217; in *Blackbird Fantasy*, 160; in *Carmen Jones*, 152, 167–71; in *Congo Clambake*, 51, 154; in *Cow Cow Boogie*, 5, 23–24, 161–63, *163*, 171, 363n21; in *Easy Street*, 103, 135, 156, 166; as first Black performer to star in Soundies, 151; in Hollywood movies, 152, 165–66; Hollywood "specialty numbers" of, 154–55, 165, 168; in *Jungle Jig*, 51, 143, 154, 155; "jungle" Soundies of, 141, 148, 154; in *Lazybones*, 156, 194; in *Paper Doll*, 51, 148, 164, *165*; as pinup figure, 142, 167; as pivotal figure in depictions of Black women, 150, 171; in race films, 151; in *Swing for Your Supper*, 19, 51, 141, 152–56, *153*, 170, 171; thwarted career of, 168, 170; in *Yes, Indeed!* 43, 103, 119, 155–56; in *A Zoot Suit*, 157, *158–59*, 159–60, 167, 171

Dandridge, Vivian, 75, 151

Dandridge Sisters, 151, 166, 361nn2–3, 363n19

Daniels, Billy, 347n52

Dark Manhattan (film, 1937), 23

Darktown Revue, The (film, 1931), 119, 359n4

Darktown Strutters' Ball, The (Barry/Waller-Murray, 1941), 117, 131, *132*, 174

Davis, Amon, 119

Davis, Charley, 348n22

Holland, Clinton, 103
Hollywood, 4, 6, 13, 16, 78, 139; depictions of
Black people, 5, 20, 92; federal censorship
and, 43; film language, 11, 17, 45, 46, 78,
128, 129, 133, 139, 165; "fourth wall" of
classical cinema, 45, 109, 165; minstrel-
style productions, 20; musicals, 46; "myth
of the southern box office" and, 68; racism
in movies, 16, 21, 29, 90, 361n18; RCM
Productions in, 9; resistance to Soundies, 9;
Soundies used to promote films, 339n21;
southern censorship and political influence,
21, 68; "specialty numbers," 154–55, 165,
168, 207; stereotypes and, 15, 156, 176,
192, 199; studio production system, 10;
turn away from Black-cast films, 22
Hollywood Pictures, 211
homosexuality/homoeroticism, 196, 203,
369n25
Honey Chile (Adams-Crouch, 1945), 138
Honeymooners, The (TV show), 212
Honeysuckle Rose (Waller-Murray, 1941), 133
Hooray for Love (film, 1935), 356n15
Horance, John Shadrack, 122, 190
Horne, Lena, 24, 129, 142, 167, 169, 200
Horne, Marilyn, 169
"Hot Cha," 29, 114–15, 344n11
Hot Chocolate ("Cottontail") (Coslow-
Berne, 1941), 92, 98, 99–100, 101, 177,
178, 365n15
Hot Chocolates (Broadway revue, 1929),
348n20
Hot Frogs (cartoon animation, 1942),
349n40, 362n9
Hot Mikado (Broadway show, 1939), 77,
352n17
House on 52nd Street (Crouch-Crouch,
1946), 190
Howard, Bob, 46, 89, 207–8, 209, 215, 355n62
Howard, Camille, 186, 187
Humes, Helen, 367n38
Hutton, Betty, 140

I Ain't Gonna Open That Door (short film,
1947), 212
I Can't Give You Anything But Love
(Crouch-Crouch, 1944), 113

I Don't Want to Walk without You (Barry/
Waller-Owen Murphy, 1942), 195
I Dreamt I Dwelt in Harlem (Barry-Snody,
1941), 116–17, *118*
If You Can't Smile and Say Yes (Crouch-
Crouch, 1944), 88, 354n53
If You Only Knew (Hersh-Gould, 1946), 188
If You Treat Me to a Hug (Crouch-Crouch,
1943), 81, 131, 140
I Got It Bad and That Ain't Good (Coslow-
Berne, 1942), 95, 177, 347n7, 357n25
I Gotta Go to Camp to See My Man
(Crouch-Crouch, 1943), 77–78, 82, 90
I Like It 'Cause I Love It (Crouch-Crouch,
1944), 186
I'll Be Glad When You're Dead You Rascal You
(Betty Boop cartoon, 1932), 362n7
I'll Be Glad When You're Dead You Rascal You
(Coslow-Berne, 1942), 73–74, 74, 77, 84
I'm a Good, Good Woman (Crouch-Crouch,
1944), 135, 186
I'm a Shy Guy (Crouch-Crouch, 1946), 209
I'm Tired (Crouch-Crouch, 1944), 140
International Sweethearts of Rhythm, 61, 62,
189, 201–2, 203, 349n37, 368n13; in *Jump
Children*, 202; in *She's Crazy with the
Heat*, 201, 202; in *That Man of Mine*, 202
In the Navy (film, 1941), 109
Introducing Dorothy Dandridge (made-for-TV
biopic, 1999), 152
Irene (film, 1940), 361n3
Island in the Sun (film, 1957), 170
Is You Is or Is You Ain't My Baby (Hersh-
Berne, 1944), 138, 187
It's Me, Oh Lord (Hersh-Berne, 1945), 122
I've Got a Little List (Coslow/Moulton-
Moulton, 1942), 75, 77, 84, 90, 91. See also
Mikado, The
I've Got to Be a Rug Cutter (Hersh-Berne,
1945), 188
I Want a Big Fat Mama (Barry-Primi, 1941),
136, 173, 174, 182
I Want a Little Doggie (Crouch-Crouch,
1945), 89, 200, 203
I Want a Man (Alexander-Sandiford, 1946), 202
I Was Here When You Left Me (Crouch-
Crouch, 1945), 141